AFFLUENCE AND POVERTY
IN THE MIDDLE EAST

The Middle East is a region where affluence and poverty exist side by side and where the conspicuous display of wealth by governments and rich individuals contrasts sharply with widespread deprivation.

Affluence and Poverty in the Middle East explores the causes and consequences of the persistent poverty and extreme inequality that have characterized the region. Using extensive empirical evidence, **M. Riad El-Ghonemy** helps us to understand the impact of co-existing affluence and poverty. In the first part of the book, he investigates the common cultural and economic factors that have brought about such an extreme polarization of living standards. He focuses particularly on historical origins, religion, economic foundations, military spending, educational policy and corruption, using a number of case studies to illustrate how each factor has affected different countries in the region. The second part consists of country studies that examine how particular governments and NGOs have responded to vast inequalities in the distribution of wealth, income and opportunities.

Dr El-Ghonemy brings his considerable knowledge and experience of the Middle East to this study. His exploration of the past, present and future of wealth distribution and poverty in the region highlights the prospects and challenges that the Middle East faces in the twenty-first century, including the use of peace dividends for alleviating poverty.

M. Riad El-Ghonemy is Senior Research Associate at the University of Oxford, Fellow of the American University in Cairo and Emeritus Professor, Ein-Shams University, Cairo, Egypt. He is the author of several books, including *The Political Economy of Rural Poverty* (1990).

AFFLUENCE AND POVERTY IN THE MIDDLE EAST

M. Riad El-Ghonemy

London and New York

First published 1998
by Routledge
11 New Fetter Lane, London EC4P 4EE

Simultaneously published in the USA and Canada
by Routledge
29 West 35th Street, New York, NY 10001

Typeset in Baskerville by
J&L Composition Ltd, Filey, North Yorkshire
Printed and bound in Great Britain by
Redwood Books, Trowbridge, Wiltshire

British Library Cataloguing in Publication Data
A catalogue record for this book is available
from the British Library

Library of Congress Cataloguing in Publication Data
El-Ghonemy, Mohamad Riad.
Affluence and poverty in the Middle East/M. Riad El-Ghonemy.
First published: London: Routledge, 1998.
Includes bibliographical references and indexes.
1. Poverty – Middle East. 2. Middle East economic conditions.
3. Income distribution – Middle East.
4. Land reform – Middle East.
I. Title
HC415.15.Z9P624
339.2'0956 – dc21 97–27681

ISBN 0-415-10032-1 (hbk)
ISBN 0-415-10033-X (pbk)

To Queen Elizabeth House, University of Oxford
and the Department of Economics,
American University in Cairo,
which provided the intellectual atmosphere
I was privileged to enjoy

CONTENTS

CONTENTS

CONTENTS

FIGURES AND TABLES

Figures

Tables

xi

PREFACE

The urge to write a book on this subject came to me fifty years ago, when I was spending my school summer vacation in my village, Gabaris, in the Delta of Egypt. The entire village land was owned by ex-King Farouk's cousin, who lived in a luxurious villa in Switzerland. Most of the villagers were poor tenants and landless hired workers, living in increasingly appalling conditions of poverty, exploited by the landlord's agent. During the flood season many of them were taken by the police force to work, without wage payment, on strengthening the Nile dikes.

For a long time, as a trained agricultural economist, I have been concerned with the problems of land tenure and rural poverty in developing countries. Through my research work and policy-making assistance to governments, I have realized that poverty problems in agriculture cannot be separated from the structural forces operating in the national economy, and that the chain of rural and urban poverty is indivisible. This expanded perception became clearer in 1986–9, when I was invited to give seminars at the Universities of Glasgow, Cambridge, Bath, Cornell, Arizona (Tucson), North Carolina (Raleigh) and the Institute of Development Studies at the University of Sussex. My understanding of development issues has been reinforced during my research work at Queen Elizabeth House of the University of Oxford and during the writing of my earlier book, *The Political Economy of Rural Poverty* (1990). In 1993 I gave two seminars on the economics of the Middle East to the graduate students of economics at the American University in Cairo and the School of International Management, Glendale, Arizona. The students' probing questions helped me to examine the reference of conventional economics to the analysis of affluence and poverty, and to explore the links between rising religious militancy, deepening economic recession and growing discontent with the social dimension of the structural adjustment programme.

This book is written against a background of the author's forty years of personal and professional experience in the Middle East and his first-hand knowledge of its development problems. It is based on many years of country studies that began in the late 1950s when I was working with the UN Food and Agriculture Organization (FAO). During the decade 1970–80, I had the opportunity to combine teaching at the University of Einshams in Cairo with conducting field studies on different aspects of rural development in all the countries of the Middle East except Israel and Mauritania. The findings of the studies were presented and discussed at regional seminars and conferences held during this period and attended by specialists and ministers, respectively. They were published in my *Economic Growth, Income Distribution and Rural Poverty in the Middle East* (1984) and *The Dynamics of Rural Poverty* (1986).

The writing of this book sprang from a number of concerns. The first is for the fearful implications, for serious instability and social unrest, of the increasing apathy and irresponsibility on the part of several governments with regard to worsening inequalities in the distribution of wealth, income and opportunities for progress that are manifested in the persistence of poverty, malnutrition, and high unemployment. This fear of instability is strengthened by the prevailing limitation of political freedom and popular participation, at a time when economic liberalization is being pursued by speedy economic reforms and when the vigorous revival of Islamic extremism is spreading as an expression of discontent with lack of governmental accountability, corruption and economic hardships.

My second concern is that during my university seminars I have seen that students interested in the study of the multiple sources and consequences of vast inequalities of personal wealth and job opportunities seem to be frustrated by the restrictions imposed by the conventional apparatus of economics. The difficulty lies in the focus of this narrow approach on resource-use efficiency, within strict assumptions that make the results of analysis depend on which are most relevant to the situation studied. Moreover, this approach distances itself from such realities as cultural norms, inheritance arrangements, history and politics.

Third, in their current structural adjustment policies, governments, as well as donor countries and international financing agencies, are giving prominence to efficiency in resource allocation and monetary/fiscal reforms needed to repay foreign debts, without due consideration for their adverse distributive consequences. My critical assessment of these reforms neither disregards the countries' needs for them, nor undermines the World Bank's recent attention to the resulting burden on the poor. My concern is with two related questions. One is the exclusion both of governments' redistributive role in redressing market failure, and of the necessity of military spending cuts (as part of budget deficit reduction) to be targeted for the poor. The other is that all indications point to the fact that the extent of poverty, hunger, illiteracy and income inequality is greater in the mid-1990s than it was in 1980, before economic reforms.

Finally, it is important to define the intended audience. The book is written for a wide readership. Its content concerns policymakers, development analysts and practitioners, as well as students of development economics, sociology, international relations and other branches of social science who are interested in development problems. The topic is also of interest to the non-specialist reader of Middle Eastern affairs; the region is interesting in itself for its history, its culture and the existing contradictions of a concentration of wealth and extravagance in consumption co-existing with the persistence of hunger and poverty.

ACKNOWLEDGEMENTS

I am indebted to each of the following scholars who has read, in type-script, one or more of the chapters of this book and has been generous enough to offer valuable comments: Gouda Abdel-Khaleq, Galal Amin, Adel Beshai, Magdi Mowafi, Frances Stewart, Godfrey Tyler and Mourad Wahba. I was saved from errors in the interpretation of the religious foundations of present inheritance rules by Abdel-Mageed Dekhale, Saad Hamza, Hussain Hamid, Rabbi Julian Jacobs and Sheikh Mohamad Mubarak. At Routledge, I am grateful to Gordon Smith and Patrick Proctor who have been patient with my frequent delays and helpful in the course of preparing the manuscript, to the anonymous referees/reviewers who have been very encouraging and to Judith Willson, the copy editor, who introduced several improvements to the original typescript. I am indebted to Gill Short, not only for giving up her leisure time to edit most of the manuscript but also for her interest in the subject matter. Roger Grosvenor was also very helpful in improving the linguistic style of the early version of the first three chapters and Simon Dradri assisted in the compilation of data and preparation of the tables for Chapter 10.

The appearance of this book resulted from several sources of help. Material was provided by Sabry and Azza Aglan, Abdul-Latif Huneidy and my brother Ahmad (Egypt); Abdul-Rahman Musaigher (Bahrain and UAE); Jawad al-Anani and Ahmad al-Hazen (Jordan); Lea Ashdut, B. Bourstein, Dan Yaron and J. Yahav (Israel); Gulay Aslantep and Banu Akkuzu (Turkey); Ibrahim Amouri (Tunisia); Martin Ravallion and Gauran Datt (the World Bank); and Nikos Alexandratos, Samir Miladi, Colleen McGowan-Maroni and N. Naiken (FAO). I acknowledge with thanks the provision of useful information on the economy of, and education in, the Arab states by UN/ESCWA and UNESCO regional offices in Amman, Jordan. Likewise, this work could not have been completed without the administrative support provided with understanding by Julia Knight and Penny Rogers of Queen Elizabeth House, of Oxford University, and Sonia Victor of the Department of Economics of the American University in Cairo.

Needless to say, none of the above professors, scholars, officials and institutions has any responsibility for the contents of this book, for which I am solely responsible.

The complex subject of this study has required much searching for material in libraries. I am grateful to the generous assistance of several librarians in Cairo and Oxford where the bulk of the book was written during 1993–6. In particular, I mention with gratitude the kind assistance of Sheila Allcock, Bob Townsend, Gill Short and Dawn Young of the Queen Elizabeth House library, Diane Ring, the librarian of the Middle East Centre of St Antony's College, Philip Sheen of the Institute of Economics and Statistics library, the several helpful staff of the Radcliffe Camera and PPE Reading Room of the Bodleian Library, all of Oxford University. At the American University in Cairo, Aida Nosseir and Shahira El-Sawy and their team at the circulation unit were extremely helpful. My deep thanks go to Jane Gaul for her efficiency in word-processing the entire manuscript, and to my sons Anwar and Hamdi for the layout of the numerous tables and figures. Lastly, my wife Marianne has patiently read the barely legible drafts and corrected the linguistic errors. She and my daughter Samira have put up with my long absences abroad and solitary work at night. Their deep understanding of my preoccupation has helped me during all the stages of this book's preparation. To all these kind people, I am most grateful.

Riad El-Ghonemy
Queen Elizabeth House,
University of Oxford
December 1996

ACRONYMS AND ABBREVIATIONS

AFSED	Arab Fund for Social and Economic Development (Kuwait)
AID	Agency for International Development
CAPMAS	Central Agency for Public Mobilization and Statistics (Cairo)
CPI	Consumer Price Index or retail price index, referred to as cost of living index
EIU	Economist Intelligence Unit
EPCV	*Enquête Permanent sur les Conditions de Vie des Ménages*
ESCWA	United Nations Economic and Social Commission for West Asia (Amman)
EU	European Union or European Community (Brussels)
FAO	Food and Agriculture Organization of the United Nations (Rome)
FIS	Islamic Salvation Front (Algeria)
FLN	National Liberation Front (Algeria)
GCC	Gulf Cooperation Council
GDP	Gross domestic product or national income
GNP	Gross national product, referred to as national income
ha	Hectare = 2.4 acres = 2.28 feddans
HES	Household Expenditure Survey
HDI	Human Development Index
IBRD	International Bank for Reconstruction and Development (World Bank, Washington, DC)
ID	Iraqi dinars
IFAD	International Fund for Agricultural Development (Rome)
IFPRI	International Food Policy Research Institute
IISS	International Institute for Strategic Studies (London)
ILO	International Labour Organization (Geneva)
IMF	International Monetary Fund (Washington, DC)

ACRONYMS AND ABBREVIATIONS

INEAP	Institut National des Études et d'Analyses pour la Planification (Algeria)
INP	Institute of National Planning (Cairo)
INS	Institut National de la Statistique (Tunis)
JD	Jordanian dinar
E£	Egyptian pound
P£	Palestinian pound
LL	Lebanese lire
MFC	Mechanized Farming Corporation (Sudan)
MNC	Multinational corporation
NGO	Non-governmental organization
NIF	National Islamic Front (Sudan)
NII	National Insurance Institute (Israel)
NIS	New Israeli shekel
ODA	Overseas Development Administration (UK)
OECD	Organization for Economic Cooperation and Development (Paris)
ONS	Office National de la Statistique (Mauritania)
OPEC	Organization of Petroleum Exporting Countries (Vienna)
PDS	Popular Development Schemes
PPP	Purchasing Power Parity
RNEA	FAO Regional Office for the Near East
SDR	Special Drawing Rights
SERISS	Sudan Emergency and Recovery Information and Surveillance System
SFD	Social Fund for Development (Egypt)
SIPRI	Stockholm International Peace Research Institute
S£	Sudanese pound
SR	Saudi riyal
TL	Turkish lira
UAE	United Arab Emirates
UGTT	Union Général des Travailleurs Tunisiens (General Confederation of Tunisian Trade Unions)
UM	Mauritanian ouguiya
UNCTAD	United Nations Conference on Trade and Development
UNDP	United Nations Development Programme
UNESCO	United Nations Educational, Scientific and Cultural Organization (Paris)
UNESOB	United Nations Economic and Social Bureau
UNFPA	United Nations Fund for Population Activities (New York)
UNICEF	United Nations International Children's Emergency Fund (New York)

UNRWA	United Nations Relief and Works Agency for Palestinian Refugees
USAID	United States Agency for International Development (Washington, DC)
VAT	Value Added Tax
WCARRD	World Conference on Agrarian Reform and Rural Development
WEP	World Employment Programme
WHO	World Health Organization (Geneva)

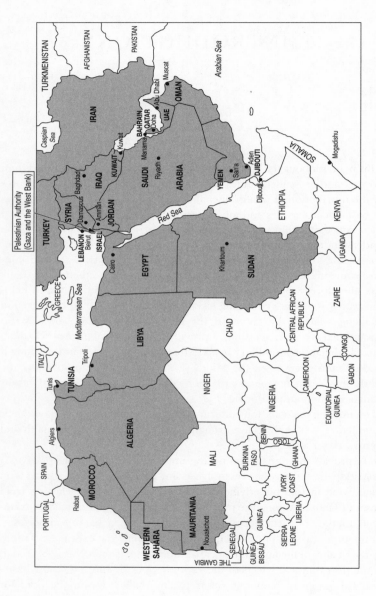

The countries of the Middle East as defined in this book

INTRODUCTION

This book is about the cumulative causes and consequences of persistent poverty and gross inequalities. It is concerned with the essential features of the distribution of wealth, income and opportunities, including access to basic social services and job opportunities. The focus is not on formal theorizing, modelling or a technical style of analysis. Rather, it is on understanding – in ordinary parlance – the form, origins and impact of co-existing affluence and deprivation, and what governments and non-governmental organizations (NGOs) are doing about them. The book has, therefore, a broad scope. Based on empirical investigation, it helps the reader to understand some lessons of the past and the prospects and challenges facing the region at the turn of the century. Towards this comprehensive understanding, it provides an analytical framework, making each chapter a building block. Moreover, the book's aim of filling a gap in knowledge about the Middle East has a positive motivation; the study may lead, not necessarily immediately, to some practical results enhancing human well-being. This task of building knowledge is by way of identifying the common cultural and economic factors which – in their interaction over time – have brought about such extremes in wealth and deprivation.

To provide this understanding, the emphasis in analysing the behaviour of Middle Eastern economies and assessing policies and programmes is on identifying factors underlying successful experience and learning from cases of failure. Among the many development issues and policies examined, four are of particular concern. The first is the debatable importance of the dramatic rise in oil revenues in determining the existing variations in the quality of life and human capabilities among countries. The second is the distributional effects of the 1980s debt crisis and the World Bank- and IMF-induced economic reforms. The third is the implications for stability and sustained human development of rising Islamic extremism as a way of articulating dissatisfaction with the increasing inequalities, rising

1

unemployment, corruption and poverty that co-exist with ostentatious consumption. The fourth is the likely effects on living standards of expected cuts in military expenditure once an acceptable Middle East peace agreement is established.

I cannot claim that this endeavour is the first on the subject. Some aspects of inequalities and poverty can be found in the existing material on the Middle East that is examined in the course of my discussion and cited in the bibliography. Yet, my view is that none has conceptually and empirically concentrated on the determinants and consequences of affluence and poverty in a broad analytical perspective. Closely related studies are those by Galal Amin (1974), and by Richards and Waterbury (1990). The former, though dated, covers nine Arab countries, and provides valuable material on the situation in the 1960s, and the latter offers an insight into the dynamics of imbalance and class formation.

The timing of the preparation of this study was opportune. We are still witnessing the impact of both the 1991 Gulf War and the structural adjustment programmes. We also anticipate beneficial peace dividends from the conclusion of a peace agreement between Israel and the Arab countries. This presents policymakers with the great challenges of raising the quality of life and promoting the Palestinians' economic security. Importantly, as the 1990s draw to a close and the twenty-first century approaches, in considering the prospects for human well-being we are able to learn lessons from the past successes and failures both of the market mechanism and of government policies.

For the purpose of this study, the region is defined to include all Arab countries as well as Israel, Iran and Turkey. Perhaps it is the first time an Arab author has included Israel with the Arab countries in a regional study.

Plan of the book

The book consists of two principal parts. Part 1 begins with the fundamental concepts and questions, and a regional perspective on related evidence (Chapter 1); followed by a consideration of the historical origins of the distribution of property rights, wealth and personal earning power (Chapter 2) and the religious foundations of justice and wealth distribution (Chapter 3). Further, Chapter 3 offers a possible explanation of existing conflicts between Islamic extremists and governments, on the one hand, and existing economic hardships, affluence and poverty, on the other. Chapters 4 and 5 examine the effects of wide variations, both in natural resources and in the policies pursued on increasing inequalities and the variations in economic performance of rich and poor countries.

Chapters 6, 7 and 8 discuss the salient structural features of public and private/personal consumption, with a focus on investment in human capital and the adverse effects on education and health of excessive military spending. Corruption as a form of embezzlement of public funds and illegal enrichment is the subject of Chapter 7, and the characteristics of poverty based on the results of case studies are specified in Chapter 8. The purpose of Chapters 2–8 is to understand the roots of variations among countries and classes within individual countries. These chapters take a broad view of the possible sources: historical, social, political and economic.

Part 2 examines the response of governments and NGOs to vast inequalities in the distribution of wealth, income and opportunities as characterized in Part 1. Based on case studies and my first-hand knowledge of the situation in the region, Chapter 9 makes an assessment of the principal redistributive policy instruments and programmes intended to mitigate social insecurity and poverty. An attempt is made in this chapter to identify informal sources of secondary income and the role of NGOs in income transfers. Chapter 10 examines the distributional effects of the economic reforms (stabilization and structural adjustment programmes) supported and monitored by the World Bank and the IMF in eight countries, with the emphasis on the gainers and losers among income classes. An inter-country comparison of economic and social effects is conducted.

The last chapter presents the prospects and challenges facing the region at the turn of the century. It estimates the extent of deprivation in the year 2000, compared to that in 1980. Further, it explores how the countries would cope with the adverse effects of economic reforms and the prospects for matching economic liberalization with the popular participation in parliamentary democracy that may reduce inequalities and bring about social stability. This chapter also examines the potential welfare gains, once a genuine peace is established. The emphasis is on the diversion of the savings from anticipated cuts in defence spending to enhance the capabilities of the poor. Only time will tell whether potential developments discussed in this chapter are a real possibility or a mirage in the Arabian desert.

Each chapter ends with a summary and a suggested reading list.

The approach

In a study such as this about the sources and consequences of affluence and deprivation, economics of production and distribution cannot be isolated from politics, history and social organization. Foremost among

3

the components of social organization are bureaucracy, property rights, laws and rules, religion and customary beliefs, people's value systems, tribal power and the class structure. These non-economic and non-quantitative components influence the functioning of the market, public and private savings and investments, economic growth and the distribution of income.

The discipline of political economy as a branch of social science enables us to study the empiricism of the totality of these components within each country's overall social system. It is also relevant to the ensuing debate on the welfare effects of the currently shrinking interventionist role of government, relative to the free play of the market. Through case studies of individual countries and inter-country comparisons, this approach allows the reader to understand the various dimensions of the development problems within a broad international context, by addressing questions such as the following.

1   Why and how do the determinants of inequality and poverty in country A differ in scale and composition from those in country B? If they do not, are similarities due to common elements of concentration or dispersion of wealth within and among families? Are they due to inheritance arrangements, marriage between members of the same income class? Do kinship and patronage relationships and nepotism influence the variations in wealth accumulation? In the whole economy, are the differences in levels of living due more to natural resource endowments (for example, oil wealth, water resources and productive land), than to the government provision of investment in human capital (health, nutrition and education)? Or are they located in such historical forces as colonial rule, discriminating against certain socioeconomic groups?

2   How relevant are the principles of conventional economics to an understanding of the sources of inequality of personal income distribution if they habitually ignore prevailing arrangements for inheritance, corruption and nepotism, as well as the vested interests of the military élite and the biased role of bureaucracy in wealth accumulation? Does people's worth depend only on what they produce and earn? Or, does it depend more on what they do not earn and are given?

3   What is the real meaning of well-being? Can affluence and poverty be characterized only in terms of possession of material wealth and total and per head average income? Does the living standard of a society depend less on per head income and more on human capabilities, resulting from policies that maintain a complementarity between investment in physical capital and in human capital? If so, is it likely that we find measurements of living standard in a rich country surpassed by those in a poorer country? Why, then, do governments and many economists still

treat total output growth as the principal objective and achievement of development?

4 What is the meaning of social imbalance in affluent and poor nations? Do governments' own policies create the imbalance? Do high illiteracy and malnutrition rates exist in rich and poor countries alike, and why? How is it possible that, in some countries, the juxtaposition of obesity and hunger persists, and why? What are the countries' own policies that bring about social imbalance and unbalanced development?

5 In their adoption of the World Bank- and IMF-supported adjustment programmes, have governments succeeded in reducing severe macro-economic imbalances while deprivation has increased and income distribution worsened? Who are the losers and gainers from these programmes?

6 What are the development and human costs of militarization? What are the possibilities of a peace dividend for the elimination of most deprivations by using cuts in military spending for primary education and health care? Do governments realize that the economics of military spending and its social-opportunity cost are development issues too important to be left to their own military élite in coalition with arms traders?

However, raising these questions without an explanation is misleading. First, I am aware of the importance of economic growth (total and per head real income) in raising living standards. Economic growth enables governments to sustain the provision of subsidized social services and income transfers to low-income groups, and to invest in employment expansion. But economic growth is meaningful only if studied in its social context, the understanding of which requires multi-dimensional, rather than purely economic measurements. For example, such measurements include the shares of the richest and poorest classes in the total income, changes in the composition of consumption, poverty levels, life expectancy, illiteracy, nutritional status and obesity measurement and mortality rates among children under 5.

I view economic growth and equity as two interdependent complements of a skilfully oriented anti-poverty strategy. Such a strategy has a balanced combination of a deliberate state policy and local community participation, instead of borrowing a standard path for development that may be alien to the society's tradition and value system. I also believe that while the Middle Eastern countries are busy privatizing their economies, the private sector can only provide health care and education to the well-to-do, not to the poor, who cannot afford payments. For the well-being of the poor, the market mechanism is not an alternative to the state, particularly for combating persistent illiteracy, widespread unemployment and preventing starvation and famine. However, while external factors are important, it is hard to deny that the real causes of these human sufferings lie more in governments' own policy failures than in market failures. It is also important to acknowledge that public concern over poverty and vast differences in wealth between rich and poor are not confined solely to governments. NGOs also have a positive part to play, particularly in the important role of family support, in working with tribal organizations and in the mandatory transfer of secondary income to the poor (for example, *zakat* in Islam).[1]

The questions raised and development issues presented are complex and their examination in the following chapters is predictably more complicated than one might think. The complexity is not merely in the identification and interpretation of *causal* factors of gross inequalities and poverty. It is also in the diversity of views on fundamental concepts and measurements, as we shall find in the next chapter. Furthermore, moral principles and beliefs exist with regard to what is right, what is wrong and what is desirable, or should be desirable, within the overall social system of a country. These are norms established in a country's constitution and development goals and in the moral standards of each religion. Furthermore, to think of the state or the people as a homogeneous entity is a distortion of realities. The social fabric of a nation is divided into institutions, occupational groups, and asset-owning, assetless and destitute classes. Therefore, we need to specify whose well-being and interests we are concerned about, who gains, who loses, and by how much, from dominant market forces, national policy instruments and locality-specific projects.

Lastly, my approach confronts several technical difficulties. For example, it is difficult to distinguish between the direct and indirect effects of a redistributive policy that brings about simultaneous income or consumption changes. It is also hard to deny that many terms used are ambiguous, with no meaning on which all users agree (for example, affluence, poverty, living standard, well-being, accessible opportunities, social stratification, deprivation, destitution, exploitation, fairness, and social welfare). These have connections with ethics and morality that cannot be disregarded, and they are analytically difficult. All the same, in spite of such problems, such terms must be used, although attempts will be made to clarify their meanings first.[2]

Some economists, particularly the followers of the neo-classical discipline that we call 'conventional economics', distance themselves from many of these concepts, on the grounds that they are mostly expressions of personal value judgements. The controversy over their usage has reached extreme degrees. Whereas some contemporary economists consider their usage an essential expression of development problems (Abdel-Khaleq (1982), G. Amin (1974), Atkinson (1975), Galbraith (1973), Issawi (1982), Robinson (1979), Roemer (1982), Sayigh (1990), Sen (1981), Singer (1992), Stewart (1993, 1995), Stiglitz (1989) and Streeten (1981), to mention just a few), others assert that their usage is inappropriate and even immoral (e.g., Bauer (1982) and Hayek (1978)). The former argue that the individual's wealth or income level is determined not by any individual or government but only by the market mechanism and, therefore, the outcomes should not be described as equitable or exploitative. What the person gets is what he or she deserves from interacting with the market.

In short, with all its limitations, my approach provides some perspective on the vast inequality problem and a broad diagnosis of poverty as a structural phenomenon. It also provides some lessons from the past to enhance present development efforts and to reduce the likelihood of making mistakes in future.

Part I

THE ROOTS

1

BASIC CONCEPTS AND
REALITIES

This chapter sets the conceptual framework for the discussion through-out the book, and presents a regional summary of empirical evidence on the characteristics of inequality and poverty. The first of these two main sections clarifies the meaning of the primary concepts that will be frequently used. The second presents a quantitative summary of the realities.

Some key concepts

Before proceeding with the main subject of this study, the key terms are discussed. These are linked to each other, and their order of presentation does not imply relative importance. They are: inequality, affluence, poverty, food security, justice, exploitation and opportunity choice.

Inequality

The co-existence of affluence and poverty in a society is simply one expression of flagrant inequality in the distribution of wealth, income and opportunities for employment. By wealth is meant exchangeable physical and financial assets, as well as personal skills, including education and the ability to bear risk and to establish business connections that can generate income. How all these elements act and react upon one another is the chief question to which this study addresses itself.

The concept of inequality of personal income distribution during a given period of time is frequently used instead of personal consumption/expenditure. This preference is due to practical considerations: income is easily understood, and the data are available. Yet there is no consensus on the meaning of income among the users of the term, whether with regard to its source (primary, from assets owned, such as land and secondary, such as subsidy and *zakat*); population unit (individual, family, household);

11

value (current, real or purchasing power); or the period for comparisons (week, month, year). Atkinson (1975: 34) argues for the inclusion of allowances or fringe benefits enjoyed by virtue of official status, such as paid holidays, a free house, car and driver or, in the case of top executives, a country home and servants. In judging inequality, individual income distribution is more unequal than household income, which is a pool of individual incomes. Also, the specification of expenditure is essential for understanding the consumption components (food, education, health, clothes, transport, leisure or luxury expenditure, etc.).

We turn now to some principles of income distribution and welfare economics most relevant to this inquiry. They are the least developed principles in economic science. Since the seminal work of Kuznets (1955, 1966) on the relationship between inequality and the rates of economic growth, analysis of the sources of income inequality has not advanced in a significant way. At present, to the best of my knowledge, there is no coherent, formal theory of income distribution that is free of restrictive assumptions and would empirically explain all relationships in the process of wealth accumulation and the distribution of income over time.[1] Likewise, the conventional theories of consumption, welfare economics and utility, in which income distribution is central, are essentially normative propositions based on certain constants for the sake of easy analysis.[2] Even the two plausible contributions (computable general equilibrium models and social accounting matrices) are inadequate for dealing with the dynamic features of *personal* income distribution. They are chiefly an extension of the conventional production-function analysis, and are based on several assumptions, and on splitting total income (GNP or GDP) into *functional* shares of labour and capital among institutions (households, government, enterprises). In practical terms, the results depend on which assumptions are used and which are most applicable to the situation studied.

Whereas the production-function and the general equilibrium systems of analysis have been developed since the work of the classical economists, notably Ricardo, they are more concerned with efficiency in resource allocation (relative to income earned from owned factors of production) than with personal distribution of income or consumption,[3] related to the integrated structure of the following areas of concern to us here:

1   the effects of colonial rule and the mechanisms of inheritance and class differentiation;
2   wealth accumulation by virtue of status in society, nepotism, corrupt practices and inter-family marriage;

3   the changing demand for different products caused by rapid urba-
     nization (or modernization); globalization and advertising.

We have, therefore, to understand the influence of social and
political institutions on the economic factors that determine inequality
between and within the different income groups. Such institutions
include political colonialism (Chapter 2); the legislative framework of
production and trade; kinship relations; bribery; client–patron relations in wealth accumulation (Chapter 7); the politics of physical and
human capital investment (Chapters 5, 6 and 9) and the religious
principles that determine property inheritance and borrowing (Chapter 3). They also include class stratification, that is, the sociological
expression of how the population is arranged in a class hierarchy. The
basis of this stratification may be grouped into subjective and objective criteria derived from human attitudes and the cultural values of
the community. Subjective criteria include the patterned psycho-social
behaviour in inter-class relationships (self-affiliation, dress, the behaviour of the poor working class towards rich and powerful bureaucrats, the social distance kept by the rich, etc.). Objective criteria, on
the other hand, refer to income and consumption levels, ownership of
material assets, occupation and land tenure status.

The quantification of inequality faces data limitations. The very rich
and the very poor are usually excluded from surveys on household
income/expenditure. Those who are included do not always give correct
information. In many cases, these surveys are not carried out regularly
and their results are not always comparable, making it difficult to judge
inter-temporal changes in a given country (Chapter 8). Furthermore,
data collected by the tax authorities on sources and levels of income are
usually considered secret information. Apart from the ability of rich
people to evade taxes, particularly on income earned abroad or
transferred to overseas tax-free accounts, we face another particular
problem. A substantial number of households in the informal sector,
which play an important role in the economies of the Middle East,
tend to be excluded from direct taxation and many household family
consumption surveys.

Ownership of land is a principal source of prestige and wealth distribution in the Middle East. However, in many census results, female
landowners are neither separately identified nor counted as farmers. At
least in Arab societies, economically active women in agriculture are
underenumerated because their husbands, who provide the information,
do not classify their wives and daughters as farmers, no matter how much
they are involved in farming and animal husbandry. But these and other

limitations of quantitative information should not deter or defer the investigation until better data become available. In some instances, we may learn about inequality (and also affluence and poverty) from qualitative information and descriptive material, while the reader is reminded, when necessary, to treat some of the data with caution.

Affluence and poverty

As noted above, the phrase 'affluence and poverty' is a special formative expression that holds together all the elements of flagrant inequalities. The word 'affluence' is often used as synonymous, or virtually so, with abundant wealth, property, flow of money and extreme riches or opulence. It is a descriptive form of a combination of a *high level* (quantity) of wealth owned and the *pattern* of goods and services consumed relative to *wants*, in a particular time period. The question of the 'how' of affluence, of the sources and ways in which wealth is accumulated, is crucial. The founders of economics reckoned that opulence meant the possession of wealth in terms of commodities: hence the important standards of gross and per head national income or domestic product. In turn, it has been believed that high growth and greater opulence tends to eliminate poverty over time, although for how long is socially questionable (Chapters 5, 8 and 10). Equally, the single measure of income is not necessarily indicative of the lifestyle that an individual or a society leads. Health, nutritional standards and literacy are of fundamental concern. This suggested bundle of the formative elements of affluence can be applied to a group of individuals or families who share features of wealth ownership and visible consumption behaviour, termed a 'social class'. Depending upon the emphasis in the chosen criteria for stratification, the class may be given several adjectives: economic, social and even genealogical.[4]

The notion of needs to be satisfied requires clarification. First, a distinction has to be made between basic or indispensable needs that must be satisfied, and unnecessary (luxury or superfluous) goods and services that are of low urgency (Chapters 6 and 8). This distinction is arbitrary and subject to controversy. But such basic things as the minimum quantity and quality of food required for a minimum level of healthy life, elementary health care, primary education, shelter, fuel and safe drinking water are, I think, indisputable necessities for human survival. What may be disputable is whether these necessities for private consumption are an end in themselves, or a means of functioning effectively in life.[5] With regard to government expenditure, the provision of the population's necessities can be judged in comparison with such items of unnecessary spending as excessive bureaucracy and military establishments (Chapters 6 and 11). Second, what is necessary in a certain community is superfluous in other cases, because of variation in culture and climate. Examples are woollen clothes and the heating of houses in a cold climate or living in a brick house in urban areas rather than a tent, which is indispensable for both rich and poor bedouin in tribal rural areas.

Third, it is important to distinguish between the consumer's right to spend his or her money according to the chosen lifestyle (consumer sovereignty), and the public concern with regard to conspicuous consumption that creates social tension and rouses the poor. There are social constraints that condition the behaviour of a rich person. This argument does not imply that all rich people are extravagant and only concerned with their own personal well-being, or that they disregard moral rules and social constraints. In fact, there are some members of the rich class who help the poor, donating towards the construction of schools and hospitals and who feel ashamed about prevailing hunger and poverty in their society.

What has been said so far leads to the difficult question of measurement, and the controversy over relative and absolute affluence and poverty. Relativity in measurement (for example, the average income/expenditure of the poor being below one-third or one-quarter of the national average) misses the crucial characteristics of personal well-being, that is, the status of nutrition, health and education. Relativity is also manifested in seeing affluence as a visible type of consumption associated with high levels of income and wealth ownership such as a luxurious dwelling, cars, spending holidays abroad, lavish birthday parties, etc. Thus, affluence specification depends on the researcher's own judgement in the selection of actual consumption items and the criteria used for defining extremes in lifestyle.

In short, while it is controversial and difficult to establish an affluence line above which people are classified affluent in a certain society at a given point in time, it is widely accepted that a nutritionally based poverty line should be established for defining absolute poverty and estimating who are the poor and how many they are. Because of variations among individuals' age, physiological characteristics and activities, it is preferable to establish a band or a narrow range of income-based calories required for a minimum level of active healthy life, i.e. a lower level below which a person suffers from undernourishment or destitution and an upper limit which ensures an adequate nutrition level for a satisfactory state of health (Lipton, 1983, 1988 and 1995 and Stewart, 1995: Diagram 1.1). Because of wide differences in household size and for inter-country comparison, the World Bank

(Ravallion *et al.*, 1991; and *World Development Report*, 1992) has established a range of internationally comparable poverty lines per person at constant 1985 international dollars. This measurement enables us to estimate who are the poor and what is the possible magnitude of the numbers of the poor and poorest or destitute at the lower and upper poverty lines.

Among the several methods of poverty estimation, the head-count ratio (i.e. the proportion of the population falling below the poverty line) is widely understandable, particularly by policymakers. Despite its statistical shortcomings, this method is used in this study. In my review and assessment of actual countries' experience, the reader is warned, where necessary, of the methodological and conceptual problems that exist in establishing poverty lines. In those situations where no reliable poverty line has been established, we can use such indicators of the standard of living as life expectancy at birth, nutritional level, mortality rates of children under 5 and illiteracy rates, especially among mothers. Real wage rates and the United Nations Human Development Index[6] are equally useful and used.

Food insecurity and poverty: a vicious circle

The core of a person's poverty is undernutrition linked to ill health and both are inseparably tied to a low level of real income. Together, they determine the person's ability to do desired things in life. Thanks to the collective contribution of a number of nutritionists, statisticians and physicians, a wide range of minimum food-intake standards has been established for different individuals' requirements by age and activities. In Arabic, staple cereals are termed *aish*, meaning 'survival'. Thus, ensuring access to food acquisition by the poor should be of public concern in order to prevent starvation and to break the vicious circle: low food-intake leads to low physical activity and productivity, which in turn leads to low income, low purchasing power and low food-intake (M. R. El-Ghonemy, 1995: 19).

Being a normative concept, food security may be generally applied as the counter-meaning to food insecurity. Domestic food production which keeps pace with a country's population growth leads to food self-sufficiency and food security in that country. Recently, both IFAD (1992) and FAO (1992 and 1993) established two composite food security indices as an indication of a country's situation with regard to food availability.[7] They combine estimates of food production instability, productivity and self-sufficiency ratios and the distribution of average daily calorie supply per person. All are national estimates. But the mere *presence* of food in the country, or in the local market, does not automatically mean that it is accessible to and actually eaten by the poor. Thus, the food-insecure person who is unable to eat the minimum amount of daily calories and proteins is absolutely poor. Therefore, an estimation of the incidence of undernourishment or hunger among the population is essential for a meaningful monitoring of progress made in poverty alleviation. Though the identification of the threat of food insecurity is a matter of judgement, we can list possible sources relevant to the Middle East:

1   uncertainty of water resources for food production in terms of rainfall, prolonged drought, and floods affecting areas where people on low incomes live;
2   crop failure;
3   the household's low economic capacity (when meagre assets are owned and a low wage earned) to acquire the necessary amount of food;
4   instability of food aid due to changes in political relations between donor and recipient countries;
5   sudden rise in grain price caused by a coalition among traders and falling supply;
6   civil unrest or war.

In rural societies, my proposition is that a legally secured access to productive land is a household life asset and an insurance against the risk of undernourishment and absolute poverty. This is to be realized by way of a combination of intensive family labour use to raise productivity, increasing self-produced food, and adequate pricing of crops. For the landless and net buyers of food among low-income groups (especially the poorest), the provision of subsidies on certain items is a popular way to ensure food security, i.e. reducing the consumer price without reducing the producer price. But not all food buyers are in need of subsidies, and no government can possibly know who are the truly needy, except through nutrition and household expenditure surveys. Thus, instead of the wasteful and politically favoured universal coverage, food subsidies should be targeted to the needy or to certain localities where the poor are concentrated. Case studies will enable us to judge whether governments tackle the root causes of food insecurity and undernutrition, or deal only with the eventual consequences of severe hunger (and famine in the case of Sudan). This assessment also enables us to understand the vested interests of bureaucracy and traders, and the role of NGOs in the alleviation of food insecurity.

Justice and exploitation

In every society, justice (or fairness) and exploitation are of personal and public concern. Both concepts are also among the moral principles which distinguish between right and wrong. Whereas laws define and protect rights of property enforced by the legal system, religious principles make people conscious of what is permitted, and what is prohibited. Nevertheless, perfection does not exist in the real world: the law with its loopholes tends to be violated, and the religious principles (having different interpretations) are not always observed. Both violations are manifested in fraudulent transactions, embezzlement of public funds, exploitation of low-income groups, the lending of money at unfair rates of interest (*riba* or usury), charging tenants unfair rent or evicting them without compensation, the exercise of monopoly power for selfish purposes, and so forth. Violations and practised injustice also include the grabbing of tribal and public lands by colonial powers, influential politicians, corruption and other means of unethical income transfers. It appears that fairness and justice are synonyms, and that one of the meanings of exploitation is unfairness and utilization of opportunities for one's own advantage (Le Grand, 1991: 8). But in John Rawls's contractual theory of justice (1972), injustice and inequalities would be justified only if they benefited the least advantaged members of society.

A brief clarification of the meaning of exploitation, as viewed in economics and in Islamic principles (as an example of the power of morality contained in other religions, too) may help the reader to understand the arguments presented in the rest of the book. In academic debate, the controversy over the meaning of exploitation was initiated by Karl Marx's conception of transaction associated with private ownership and exchange of the means of production in a capitalist economy. Having his eye on the factory system in England, he equated rich landlords with factory owners, and explained the mode of market power relations in the exchange of resources, which could be viewed as exploitation. In his intellectual construction, and based on his compiled data from Irish and English agriculture during the period 1851–71, Marx made it necessary to divide society into an exploiting and an exploited class, as a consequence of the capitalist mode of production. He identified the owners of land and capital as the exploiters, and the wage-earners (labourers) as the exploited living in 'increasing misery'.[8]

An alternative academic meaning of exploitation comes from two American scholars, Robert Nozick (1974) and John Roemer (1982). Each places a different emphasis in his system of analysis. Nozick argues that the exploited do not possess the scarce entrepreneurial abilities and skills to innovate and to bear market risks. For Roemer, exploitation takes the form of limited freedom of choice and inequalities due to relationships of dominance by a privileged few. Another suggested criterion of exploitation is the inequality of opportunities manifested in an uneven access to means of production, because of imperfect functioning of the competitive market and the vast inequality of wealth between the rich and poor. All these examples of academic contributions to the meaning of exploitation are formed by individual scholars with diverse backgrounds, and within each author's unique system of analysis.

In the moral force of Islam, the religion of an overwhelming majority of the population in the Middle East, while there is a consensus on the prohibition of usury (*riba*) as the cardinal sin, there are diverse interpretations of transactions with regard to exploitation. For example, are commercial banks, charging pre-fixed interest on loans, exploiters? Different interpretations exist. Whereas some Islamic jurists have considered sharing profits and loss with financing institutions permissible, others strongly argue that charging any interest payment above the principal borrowed is usury (*riba*), and should be abolished. Hence, the call for the replacement of interest-rate payment by an innovative instititional arrangement (the Islamic Bank) for sharing benefits and loss.[9]

The above discussion on the interpretations of exploitation by philosophers, economists and Islamic jurists suggests the continuing ambiguity of the term and its equation with unjust transfer of income from a poorer to a richer person. Also, the conflicts and confrontation between governments and religious extremists are increasing steadily, with alarming consequences (Chapter 3).

Opportunity choice

Deprivation and the human feelings of submission, shame and fear are rooted in having no or limited choice. They are also connected with inequality of opportunity for access to necessities (food, health care and primary education) and jobs. It seems that insecure workers' fears grow with increasing affluence in a capitalist economy that does not provide equal job opportunities and protection from losing jobs.[10] Mass unemployment in order to maintain efficiency and achieve greater affluence, especially during periods of economic adjustment, can plunge the unemployed and their children into poverty and vulnerability to undernutrition, particularly in urban areas (Chapter 10). Hence, the sense of hopelessness can be socially dangerous.

Thanks to Commons (1934), the double meaning of opportunity choice is clarified by a distinction between accessible and inaccessible opportunity. The distinction, though it appears obvious, is concealed at present in the discussion on the provision of access to good quality education, health services and food subsidies. In a real world of scarcity, economists have habitually *assumed* accessibility and equality of opportunities. Hence, choices for action guided by personal abilities have to be made between alternatives, one at the expense of others, that is, the opportunity cost or the substitution cost. Logically speaking, I think, the choice is made between alternatives that are actually available, and it is absurd to choose an inaccessible opportunity. For example, faced with low earnings and credit rationing, a poor tenant has no choice between the inaccessible goal of owning a piece of land to command the food he eats and the worse alternative of being a hired worker dependent for his or her livelihood upon the seasonality of employment in agriculture and on traders for the acquisition of food. To continue as a poor tenant is the choice of a lesser evil.

There are several factors beyond the control of the disadvantaged sections of the population which inhibit the achievement of equality of opportunity. They include initial poor endowment (for instance, non-existent inheritance of material wealth), and discrimination in education according to race, sex, family background and income class (Chapters 2 and 8). These constraints also include stopping the education of bright children so that they can support their poor parents through child labour, and geographical location (living in backward, remote areas with no basic social services, for example). Hence the need to examine whether or not the recent shift away from economic and social protection towards a greater reliance on market mechanism has further narrowed poor people's opportunity choice (Chapters 8 and 10). We may also ask whether economic insecurity is an integral element of the dominant market and profit-making private sector.

The realities: a regional summary of evidence

The extent of absolute poverty, illiteracy, undernutrition and inequality in the Middle East is staggering. Despite data limitations, I have compiled some primary estimates in summary Tables 1.1 and 1.2 to help give the reader a bird's-eye view of the realities.

Widening income gap

During 1960–91, income inequalities between countries markedly increased, owing to a few countries' windfall gains from a single commodity, oil, whose price rocketed from less than US$2.0 per barrel in the 1960s to US$30–4 in 1980/1. The sudden affluence has widened the income gap between the seven oil-rich Arab states and Israel, on the one hand, and the middle- and low-income countries, on the other.[11] Of the region's total population of 337 million in 1991/2 the share of the rich states was about 9 per cent, while their share in the total income of the region was 39 per cent. These are in sharp contrast with the shares of the group of four low-income countries (Egypt, Sudan, Yemen and Mauritania) which were 28 and 7 per cent, respectively (see Table 1.1). The marked increase in income inequality over a short time is illustrated by the changes in average annual income per person in Egypt relative to that in Saudi Arabia between 1940 and 1991: Egypt's was double that of Saudi Arabia in 1940, plunging down to only 5 per cent of the Saudis' in 1980 and 7 per cent in 1991 (Chapter 4).

Yet, sudden affluence in oil-rich Arab states alone does not bring about rapid human development achievements. Of the total nineteen countries for which comparable data are available, the richest four (the UAE, Kuwait, Israel and Saudi Arabia) are not always the top four in reducing illiteracy and the mortality rate of children under 5, with Saudi Arabia being the worst performer among the richest group and its achievements ranked below such middle-income countries as Turkey, Jordan and Tunisia (Chapter 6).

Inequality of personal consumption or income among households has also increased in terms of the shares of the richest and poorest classes in total income or expenditure. This worsened inequality is revealed by household surveys conducted in seven adjusting countries before and after economic reforms during the 1980s and 1990s (Chapters 8 and 10).

Increasing undernourishment

Despite the dazzling evidence of opulence, tens of millions of poor people in the Middle East are unable regularly to obtain even the minimum amount of food required to maintain body weight and allow an active, healthy life. This deprivation results in ill health, slow mental growth, and a feeling of shame. In every country of the region, some form of involuntary hunger or malnutrition exists.[12] The extent and severity differ across countries according to the measurement used. In 1992, the two international organizations which specialize in the subject,

Table 1.1 A summary of selected socioeconomic indicators of the Middle East, 1991–2

Total population, including 1.7 million Palestinians in the Gaza Strip and the West Bank	
1991	337 million
2000	426 million
	(projected)
Total income (1991 GNP)	US$747 billion

Average annual growth in per person income

1970–80	1980–90	1991
3.1%	−2.5%	−4.6%

Share of income groups (excluding Palestinians) in total population and total income (1991)

Rich group (8 countries)	
Share in total population	9.3%
Share in total income	38.7%
Weighted average income per person	US$9,271
Middle-income group (8 countries)	
Share in total population	62.4%
Share in total income	53.8%
Weighted average income per person	US$1,915
Low-income group (4 countries)	
Share in total population	28.1%
Share in total income	7.5%
Weighted average income per person	US$597
Ratio of average income of the rich group to low-income group	15.5

Adult illiteracy rate (excluding Israel and occupied territories)

Total	45%
Female	57%
Total number	80 million
Male	32 million
Female	48 milion

Mortality rate among children under 5 (1993)	70 per 1,000
Number of undernourished children under 5	4 million

People living in absolute poverty

Total number	96 million
Percentage of total population	29.0–33.1%

Sources: UN *Statistical Yearbook* 1992 and 1993 (United Nations, 1960–93), *World Development Report* 1992 and 1993 (World Bank, 1978–96) and Tables 4.2 and 11.2 in the present book. Shares are taken from Table 4.2. Mortality and nutrition rates for children: *The State of the World's Children* 1995 (UNICEF, 1984–96). Growth rates of GNP per person: *World Development Report* 1992 (World Bank, 1978–96), Table 1.2. Undernourishment: Table 11.1 and note 13.

Notes

Figures are rounded. For the year 2000 estimate of population, see Chapter 11, note 2. Total income is GNP per person multiplied by total population. The rich group consists of (in descending order by GNP per person, 1991): UAE, Kuwait, Qatar, Saudi Arabia, Bahrain, Oman, Libya and Israel. The middle-income group is: Iraq, Iran, Algeria, Turkey, Tunisia, Syria, Jordan and Morocco. The low-income group is: Egypt, Sudan, Yemen and Mauritania. See Chaper 4, p. 58 for my cut-off income levels for this classification.

FAO and WHO, estimated that the number of people in the Middle East whose daily food consumption was too little to meet even the minimum calorie needs had increased from nearly 24 million in 1980 to 31 million, average 1988–90.[13] During the same period the average daily food supply (not *actual* consumption) of an adult increased from K/calorie 2,810 in 1980 to 2,920 in 1990, suggesting that the deterioration is not simply a production problem.[14] Instead, it is in the domain of the grossly unequal distribution of personal income/consumption suggested by Table 1.2, i.e. the shares of population quintiles (the richest and poorest 20 per cent) in total consumption, except in Israel where it is in total income. Accordingly, inequality is highest in Mauritania, followed by Jordan; while it is very low in Israel and moderate in the rest.

Worsening undernourishment in the Middle East between 1980 and 1990 contrasts with a notable decrease by 18 per cent in East and South Asia, where world poverty is concentrated. What is more alarming is the worsening of nutrition among children under the age of 5 in terms of weight for age and weight for height. They suffer from stunted growth, mental abilities and body weight, the worst consequence of which is dying before their first birthday. The 1992 FAO/WHO study cited above reveals a significant increase: from 1.8 million in 1975 to 2.7 million in 1990. Since then the number of undernourished children must have been swollen, both by the increasing misery in southern Sudan owing to the civil war and by the Iraqi catastrophe following the 1991 Gulf War. I estimate the latter alone at 1.1 million (Chapter 6). In the richest countries of the region (the Gulf states) undernutrition of children also prevails in terms of anaemia, which co-exists with high incidence of obesity and other affluence-related diseases caused by excessive food consumption (diabetes, heart disease, stroke, dental caries and some types of cancer).[15] These diseases are found to be positively correlated with affluence, that is, the higher the personal income, the higher is the incidence of diabetes and obesity (Chapter 8).

The current emphasis on the supply side of food rather than on the effective demand for food is reflected in the estimates of IFAD's Food Security Index[16] for twelve countries given in Table 1.2. The data show that half the countries of the Middle East for which data are available are in the category of low food security (those whose index is below 0.8). They comprise one affluent country, Oman, one middle-income, Jordan, and three poor countries, Sudan, Yemen and Mauritania, and all suffer from year-to-year fluctuation in rainfed cereal production.[17] Another poor country, Egypt, is classified by this Index as a highly food-secured nation (over 1.0). This is attributable mostly to Egypt being a large recipient of food aid and to its extensive area of irrigated food crops

Table 1.2 Inequality of consumption distribution, undernutrition and food security in eleven countries, 1987–93

Country[a]	Year	Inequality of distribution Consumption share of households/ year		Ratio of highest to lowest	Undernutrition in children under 5 as % of total age group, c. 1991	Food Security Index, 1988[b]
		Lowest 20%	Highest 20%			
		1		2	3	4
Oman	1992/3[b]	n.a.	n.a.	n.a.	n.a.	0.423
Israel	1988	7.6	39.8	5.2	n.a.	n.a.
Algeria		6.9	46.5	6.7	9	1.191
Turkey	1990	n.a.	n.a.	n.a.	10	0.837
Tunisia	1992	5.9	46.3	7.0	6	0.996
Jordan	1990/1	6.5	50.1	7.7	6	0.751
Morocco	1991	6.6	46.3	7.0	9	1.010
Egypt		7.3	44.0	6.0	9	1.310
Sudan		n.a.	n.a.	n.a.	20	0.780
Yemen	1987/8	n.a.	n.a.	n.a.	30	0.792
Mauritania		3.5	46.3	13.2	48	0.692

Sources: Column 1, *World Development Report* 1994: Indicators (World Bank, 1978–96), except Israel: Achdut (1993) and Egypt, Chapter 10, pp. 184–213. Column 3, *The State of the World's Children* 1995 and 1996: Table 2 (UNICEF, 1984–96). Column 4 (IFAD, 1992: Table 1, Appendixes).

Notes

n.a. = not available.

a Countries are listed in descending order of GNP per person, 1991.

b See definition of Food Security Index in note 7 of this chapter.

c Income and not consumption expenditure.

Column 2 is calculated as the ratio of the highest 20 per cent to the lowest 20 per cent in column 1.

and, therefore, its very low degree of food production instability; only 4 per cent compared to 97 per cent in Jordan.

Two alarming trends are related to the worsening food supply. The first is the increasing scarcity of water in the Middle East. With only 13 per cent of the average water supply per person that is available in the rest of the world, the region has the lowest availability of water per person in the world. Moreover, 53 per cent of the region's population live in areas with less than the region's average of about 1,071 cubic metres per person. This average is expected to halve by the year 2025. The second alarming reality is the very limited cultivable area; the present and potential land representing only 11 per cent of the region's vast area of 1.5 billion hectares. Considering the Middle East's increasing dependency on food imports, including food aid, these alarming downward trends would mostly harm the low-income groups and poorest households who are net buyers of food and who are the most vulnerable to food insecurity risks (Chapter 4).

Persistent poverty

Remarkable progress has been made towards counting the poor and estimating the severity of their deprivation. Several countries have established national, rural and urban poverty lines below which people are defined as living in poverty. Though useful for anti-poverty policy and monitoring progress in its alleviation, these country-specific measurements are not comparable. As noted earlier, the World Bank has established internationally comparable poverty lines based on available household consumption surveys. The estimates for the Middle East show that the numbers of the absolutely poor, such as chronically undernourished people, are increasing by all poverty measurements.[18] Those people who failed to realize the US$31 per month poverty line were estimated at 73 million in 1990; an increase between 1985 and 1990 at an annual rate of 4 per cent, which is higher than the average rate of population growth. This suggests that the increase in poverty is not solely due to population growth, but to highly unequal and deteriorating purchasing power. In proportionate terms, the numbers of poor relative to the total population of the World Bank's narrowly defined Middle East region, which excludes Israel, Mauritania and Sudan, has increased from 30.6 per cent in 1985 to 33.1 per cent in 1990.[19] The proportion would have been higher had the two poorest countries of the region (Mauritania and Sudan) been included. Using available data on the average real consumption per person and poverty estimates, we can add roughly

20 million people to the World Bank's estimate of 73 million for 1990 (18 million in Sudan, 1.5 million in Mauritania and half a million in Israel).[20] Country-specific estimates of poverty and our review of the experience of eight middle- and low-income countries that accepted the standard economic reform package from the World Bank and the IMF show that unemployment, poverty and inequality of income distribution increased in most of them. Only Tunisia managed to reduce poverty and income inequality (Chapter 10).

Increasing inequality of opportunity for progress: rising illiteracy and unemployment

The underlying proposition in this study is that, like other assets, education determines life-time earning abilities and skills in the workforce, and expands opportunities for progress, while illiteracy disables people. Moreover, in the process of poverty generation, illiteracy is both a cause and a result of poverty.

According to the UNESCO's standardized definition of illiteracy, in 1992 nearly 80 million adults were illiterate (unable to read and write) in the Middle East. In eleven countries, the rate exceeded the 1992 average of 35 per cent in all developing countries, and in five Middle Eastern countries, including four oil-rich countries, it exceeded 50 per cent. Illiteracy is consistently and significantly higher among girls and women, the regional average being 57 per cent of all adult females, compared to only 17 per cent in Latin America. Likewise, our selected health indicator shows that 65 childen per 1,000 live births die in the Middle East before reaching the age of 5, compared to 47 in Latin America and 56 in East Asia.

An important factor behind this state of deprivation of fundamental capabilities is the striking social imbalance in the allocation of public resources in both rich and poor countries, i.e. the neglect of education and health relative to governments' annual foreign debt service payments and expenditure on militarization and the police force (beyond minimum security needs and territorial integrity). In most of the countries undergoing the economic and structural adjustment programmes of the World Bank and IMF, debt service payments exceed the combined allocation for health, education and social security (Chapters 10 and 11). Using the IMF-established criteria (IMF, 1990), and given each country's primary characteristics during 1975–86, the analysis suggests that (a) in 60 per cent of the Middle Eastern countries studied, allocations to health and education are highly inadequate (Chapter 6); and (b) the military spending index is excessive, reaching more than double that of all developing countries. A striking manifestation of this imbalance is the region's total military spending of US$720 billion between 1980 and 1992, compared to US$450 billion spent on health and education. I have estimated (Chapter 11) that by saving a very small proportion (0.2 per cent) of the 1994 regional *annual* military spending of US$50 billion an amount of US$800 million could be used for eradicating the large scale of adult illiteracy (80 million people). I have also estimated that a tiny fraction, only 6 per cent of total interest charges actually paid on total foreign debts in a single year, 1992, could create jobs for all the 9 million unemployed persons in four adjusting countries that have the largest number of unemployed adults, many of whom are the victims of implemented structural adjustment programmes (Chapter 11). The unemployment problem has been compounded by the failure of the private sector to meet investment expectations, to offset the negative effects of cuts in public investment, and to create alternative jobs.

Summary

This chapter has attempted to clarify the fundamental development issues to which this book is addressed, by presenting a number of primary and inter-related concepts to guide the discussion and a regional summary of empirical evidence. It has argued against some narrow analytical reasonings connected with affluence and poverty. I have underlined the importance of such non-economic and non-quantitative factors as moral principles, historical forces and the institutional arrangements that influence and interact with economic factors within a cohesive social system. Emphasis has been placed on the need to trace how wide differences in wealth and income among individuals and families were created in the first place. We have a long way to go in the rest of the book before we can judge how this approach can contribute to an understanding of the staggering realities that have been sketched here.

Suggested readings

Ahmad *et al.* (1991) *Social Security in Developing Countries.*
Atkinson (1978) *The Economics of Inequality.*
Baranzini (1991) *A Theory of Wealth Distribution and Accumulation.*
Bigsten (1983) *Income Distribution and Development*, particularly Chapter 4, 'The Measurement of Inequality and Poverty'.
El-Ghonemy (1990b) *The Political Economy of Rural Poverty.*

Galbraith (1973) *The Affluent Society.*
Haslett (1994) *Capitalism with Morality.*
Meade (1994) *Efficiency, Equality and the Ownership of Property.*
Paukert (1973) 'Income Distribution at Different Levels of Development: A Survey of Evidence'.
Roemer (1982) *A General Theory of Exploitation and Class.*
Sahota (1978) 'Theories of Personal Income Distribution: A Survey'.

Additional readings can be found in notes and in the Bibliography.

2

HISTORICAL ORIGINS

This chapter outlines the historical factors that, in my opinion, have influenced the prevailing distribution of wealth and levels of living. Together with the next five chapters, it helps the reader to understand the root causes of variations in income structure and poverty between and within countries.

Following an introductory outline of the forms of colonial rule, the discussion consists of three main sections. The first identifies the origin of affluent lifestyles in the region. The second traces briefly the historical origins of the current distribution of property rights and wealth, emphasizing the relevant colonial practices in wealth-holding and the introduction of a Western economic system and secular legal framework. The third explores the roots and consequences of educational discrimination by different income groups and in turn the differentials in earning abilities and social status.

Types and objectives of colonial rule

Before we examine the effects of lengthy colonial rule on the distribution of wealth, a few words on the underlying forms of colonial rule may be helpful to the reader who is not acquainted with the history of the Middle East.

Of the present Middle Eastern countries, only Turkey, Iran and part of Saudi Arabia were not subjected to colonial rule. The Ottoman Empire dominated the region for some 400 years from the sixteenth century. After it lost control, the British, French and Italians became the masters in the region in the nineteenth and twentieth centuries, until the countries gained independence.[1] The territories of what are now known as Syria, Lebanon, Jordan (former Transjordan), Kuwait, Bahrain, Qatar, the United Arab Emirates and Yemen were carved out of pre-existing administrative entities into new states by the colonial powers. Israel and the Palestinian territory were created in 1948 out of British Mandatory Palestine, after a long and bitter civil war. Egypt, which was conquered by France in 1798 and Britain in 1882, was named a protectorate in 1914. That ended in 1922, making the country nominally independent until the departure of the British troops in 1954. The present Mauritania, formerly known as the Arab Shinqit Emirates, was annexed to Senegal by France in 1901, and in 1946 sliced out of French West Africa.

Thus, the Middle East was ruled by Europeans and Ottoman Turks under various names: (a) as provinces of the Ottoman Empire; (b) as direct colonies in the case of Algeria, Tunisia, Libya and South Yemen (Aden); (c) as mandates and protectorates in the case of pre-existing Israel and Palestine,[2] Syria, Lebanon, Egypt, Jordan, Iraq, Morocco and the Gulf oil-based sheikhdoms; (d) as a pacification in Mauritania; (e) as a condominium in Sudan; and (f) under the terms of a British-imposed treaty in Trucial Oman. This variety of colonial arrangements for rule had different aims. Apart from the shared object of extending European power into the region and protecting their military interests in the Mediterranean and the Red Sea, each colonial power had its own purpose. The aims of the longest-ruling colonial power, the Islamic state of the Ottoman Empire, were religious and fiscal; the protection of Islam, and the extraction of exorbitant tax and rent from Arab provinces. The latter was realized through assigned agents (*deys*, janissaries, *makhzan* tribes and influential families) in exchange for the granting of vast areas of land and the exercise of absolute local power. Britain, France and Italy tended to secure the supply of food and raw materials for their own home countries, and to expand markets for their industrial products and businessmen's contracts, and to provide employment for their citizens. In addition, France and Italy intended to settle the poor sections of their own populations on the most fertile land in North Africa.

To achieve their economic objectives, Britain, France and Italy pursued a common policy of imposing their capitalist system, consumption pattern and secular legal framework upon the long established indigenous social order. Invariably, the colonial mechanism was a centralized bureaucracy in alliance with wealthy merchants, large land-owners and tribal sheikhs (chiefs), and linked the economies of occupied countries to their own. To realize the linkage, the European powers monopolized foreign trade as well as the supply and management of public utilities. They also tied local currencies and foreign trade earnings to their central banking systems.

The origins of affluent lifestyles

Capital cities and ports, from which power emanates, were westernized to give comfort to, and serve the needs of, foreign residents, the troops, wealthy merchants, and the native élites. With the westernization of major urban centres, a wide gulf was created between them and the villages in which the vast majority of the population lived in appallingly backward conditions. Such conditions of dual culture and extreme levels of living were often viewed by the colonial administration as if they were natural.

Local ethnic minorities (mostly Greeks and Armenians), together with native wealthy Jewish businessmen, lived where the Turks, British and French had their luxurious residential quarters in cities.[3] They considered themselves socially superior to ordinary Arab people. Obsessed with the way of life of the Western colonial powers, native wealthy families and politicians spoke their languages in local social circles. Proficiency in English and French, not in Arabic, was (and still is) associated with affluence and aristocracy. Members of this class went further in the emulation of their imperialist masters by joining their exclusive clubs (e.g., the Alweya in Iraq, the Gezira Golf Club and the Mohammed Ali Club in Egypt) in anticipation of being hand-picked for cabinet and senior official posts. Some men even wore dark woollen suits, dinner jackets and starched white collars in the warm climate of the Middle East. Likewise, native wealthy families and politicians imitated the Western consumption pattern and style of residence.

The European influence on indigenous culture was so powerful that even societies that were not ruled by foreign powers (Turkey and Iran) emulated the West European way of life. During the 1920s their leaders, Mustafa Kemal Ataturk and Mustafa Reza Shah respectively, replaced the native dress of turbans and flowing robes with Western styles. In 1924, Ataturk's abolition of Islamic schools was followed by his prohibition of the wearing of the native headcover, the fez, which was to be replaced by a European-style hat. He went further in his rejection of the Turkish cultural identity, replacing the Islamic Hijra calendar by the Christian (Gregorian) calendar on 1 January 1925. He also abolished the Islamic Shari'ah laws and put in their place the Swiss civic code and the Italian penal code. Moreover, Ataturk abolished the use of Arabic script, introducing in its place the Latin script in law no. 1353 of 1928. Later, in 1935, the Islamic weekly holiday on Friday was replaced by Sunday.

Wealth concentration

How wealth concentration in the largest economic sector in the economy, agriculture, and in its principal form of wealth, land, was created during the long period of colonial rule, requires an explanation. Under colonial rule, the most fertile land situated in the high-rainfall areas of Morocco, Algeria, Tunisia, Libya and Palestine was purchased or rented, or in some cases seized from tribal groups and natives, for the settlement of French, Italians and immigrant Jews, respectively. Within the sphere of the European capitalist system, technology and entrepreneurial skills were combined with local cheap labour and fertile land for developing the newly created settlements into a modern farming sector. Within that sector, the cultivation of grapevines for winemaking was promoted, against Islamic principles which prohibit drinking alcohol, and the growing of the highly profitable hashish and opium in a few countries was tolerated.

Unlike the French and Italians in North Africa, the British did not colonize lands in Egypt, Iraq and Sudan for settling poor farmers from Britain. Instead, their interest was in the promotion of markets for British trade and manufactured goods and in employment opportunities for professionals. They also invested in land development and constructed dams under granted contracts. Hence the technological base of inequality, through irrigation and the rapid rise in the profitability of land. Another British action that affected profit making and income distribution was the prohibition of the slave trade and slave labour, which was still practised despite being proscribed by Islam.

Polarization originated by way of the concentration of wealth and income in a few hands within increasingly market-oriented transactions. The result was rising indebtedness, the formation of large estates with absentee landlords and the emergence of a poor peasantry and landless wage-workers. The process of polarization was put in motion through modernization. The old-established and economically egalitarian system of tribal communal landholding (*mushaa'* and *dirah*) was broken up into individual holdings for usufruct rights and private property (*khas*) in settled agriculture. This shift shook the basis of the indigenous system of social security. It laid the foundation for the emergence of a powerful class of moneylenders and real estate bankers, using land title as collateral against mortgage. Out of the accumulated landed property, the conquerors granted land to influential family heads, senior officials, and religious leaders in exchange for their political support. By virtue of their official and social status, the new class of landlords were able to accumulate more land, either free of charge or at low prices, with tax concessions. Progressively, the pre-colonial moral and social orders were almost destroyed.

The polarization of colonized societies: an illustration from Iraq and Algeria

Iraq became a British mandate at the end of the First World War, soon after the long rule of the Ottoman Empire (1535–1915) had come to an end. By then the rights of land use granted by the Sultan in Istanbul to tribal sheikhs, city merchants and the Kurdish *aghas* (village heads in Northern Iraq) had been mostly converted into individual ownership (*tapu*). This initial distribution of wealth was confirmed by the Ottoman Land Code of 1858, which legislated for the individualization of communal landholding. Huge private properties of a few notables were legally established over the heads of the millions of peasants (fellaheen) who were denied access to the land which they and their ancestors had tilled for centuries. By way of enacting the 1931 *istihlak* (taxation) and Land Settlement laws, the British recorded the balance of unregistered land as state property (*miri sirf*).

The result was an excessive concentration of wealth. While about 70 per cent of the Iraqi farming population possessed 3 per cent of the cultivated area (with an average of five acres each) just five large landlords possessed nearly 4 per cent of the total land with an average property area of 60,000 acres (24,300 hectares) each. The rest (93 per cent of the total area of farm land) was held by *sirkals* (heads of clans), chiefs of smaller tribes and city traders, who together controlled nearly one-third of the cultivable area.[4] It needs no great effort of the imagination to judge the blighting effects of this semi-feudal system upon the masses of small cultivators and nomads. On the British policy, Issawi (1982: 147) remarks: 'The British did not attempt to alter the system for fear of antagonizing the landlords and tribal chiefs, on whose support they were dependent.' These lucky, wealthy families were the principal beneficiaries of the large-scale irrigation works constructed later by the British around the two major rivers, the Tigris and the Euphrates.

The excessive injustice in the pre-independence distribution of Iraqi wealth was less severe, though, than that imposed by the French and Italians in North Africa, about which I have written extensively (M. R. El-Ghonemy, 1967 and 1993). It may be useful to illustrate briefly the French colonial policy in Algeria, which was a deliberate destruction of the country's national identity and indigenous social system. The method was to make the entire economy, the legal system and administration function as a province of metropolitan France, after the collapse of the Ottoman regime. The flow of nearly 700,000 French emigrants was a rapid and practical solution to the rising unemployment and social unrest in France which peaked in the 1850s. A massive wave of dispossession and confiscation of Algeria's tribal lands dislocated tens of thousands of the farming and nomadic population, who were pushed to the low-rainfall south and the less fertile land.

In addition, most of the land owned by the people of the Kabyle region was sequestrated. Forced indemnity payments of 37 million francs to the French authorities were also extracted as a punishment for the Kabyle inhabitants' revolt against the French regime in 1871 (Abun-Nasr, 1971) as a desperate expression of the misery that had followed the 1866 and 1870 famines. Moreover, the traditional system of holding lands under trust for charitable and private purposes (i.e. the Islamic institution of *waqf* or *habous*) was abolished, and lands were purchased and put at the disposal of French and other European settlers. This colonial policy resulted in the virtual destruction of the two traditional institutions of Algeria – the *waqf* and the land-based tribal power.

By the 1950s, the French population in Algeria totalled nearly one million, many of them poor. The settlers, numbering about 23,000 families, owned some 2.8 million hectares (6.9 million acres) of the most productive and well-situated land of Algeria (*tell*), representing over one-third of the total cultivated land. There was a high degree of wealth concentration measured in terms of average land distribution: 400 hectares per colonial settler compared to only 8–10 hectares per native landholder. Moreover, there was a great variation in land productivity and incomes, considering that the land of Algerian Muslims was on the less fertile slopes of mountains and in areas receiving low rainfall. Furthermore, French migrants made profits from land mortgages, lucrative trade, construction contracts and from monopolizing private businesses, such as bars, restaurants, hotels and transport.[5]

Gross inequality of income distribution was closely associated with a dualism in production structure, i.e. the co-existence of the modern French and the traditional Muslim sectors, with a wide gulf in between. Productivity of the French-held lands, which grew vines, citrus fruits, sugar cane, beetroot, tobacco, vegetables and cereals, was nearly nine times that of Muslim-held lands. The imbalance was large indeed. Although the French settlers (*colons*) and their families represented about 5 per cent of the total population, their income share was 60 per cent of total gross agricultural income and 52 per cent of net profit from agriculture (Griffin, 1976: 26–8). Ruedy (1992: 123) reported that between 65 per cent and 75 per cent of the Algerian rural population were living in poverty.

Colonial policy and famines

In North Africa, including Sudan, the bias of the colonial administration towards developing the European-settled sector and modernizing capital cities had disadvantaged the traditional sector and its millions of nomads and their livestock. Subjected to prolonged droughts, the nomads and small farmers suffered from hunger and even disastrous famine. During this century, the few documented famines are indicative of colonial mismanagememt. For example, the 1939 famine in the Equatoria province of Sudan was viewed by its British Governor in Juba as a natural punishment of the poor farmers for not obeying his orders 'issued in their real interests'. The Governor's instructions were to grow cotton instead of the staple food, sorghum, in order to have sufficient cash to pay poll tax, and to buy grain when needed. The Governor considered relief aid unwise, because 'the fellaheen had refused or failed to take necessary steps to protect themselves against famine'.[6]

Another example is from Morocco, during French rule (1912–55). The 1945 prolonged drought in the south depleted cereal reserves (cereals occupied 80 per cent of the total arable land). A disastrous famine killed most of the nomads' livestock and an unspecified number of the poor fellaheen in rainfed areas starved. Yields of wheat and barley fell from an average 500 and 670 kilogrammes per hectare in the preceding years to 170 and 120 kilogrammes, respectively. The distressed fellaheen and nomads sold their lands and livestock to merchants at very low prices and fled to the cities. The French administration's response, too late and bureaucratic, was to issue a law prohibiting the sale or mortgaging of lands below 7 hectares in rainfed areas.[7]

This discussion of the historical origins of unjust distribution of wealth should not be interpreted to mean that the colonial powers did only damaging things. On balance, they modernized the pre-capitalist economies, and linked the economies to the world market. In some countries, they even initiated agro-industry and introduced the European capitalist system of banking and foreign trade. They constructed irrigation works and ports and developed hotel, telephone, telegraph and postal services. The colonial powers introduced also the European concept of democracy, which most countries (especially the oil-rich) have rejected, despite fostering the Western economic system.

Class stratification

Political colonialism polarized the social organization of most Middle Eastern countries. The concentration of wealth in a few foreign and privileged native hands, together with the introduction of an affluent Western lifestyle, had created two distinct classes. The very rich were made up of large landlords, wealthy merchants, tribal sheikhs, *sirkals* and Kurdish *aghas* (village heads) in Iraq, cotton *pashas* in Egypt, sultans in South Yemen, cotton lords and irrigation-pump traders in Sudan, village heads (*mukhtars*) and collaborators with the colonial rulers (e.g. the *basha-gha* in Morocco). The wealthy élites also included the Azhar sheikhs, the rich Copts in Upper Egypt and the Maronites in Lebanon, the city merchants and the Jezira grainlords in Syria, and former *multazims* (tax collectors), the Ottoman élite (*zawat*), the family members of the ruling house and foreign landowners and bankers. At the present time, the descendants of these families still make up most of the rich class in these countries.[8]

At the other extreme of the social strata were the vast masses of poor landless workers, sharecroppers, nomads and city pedlars. Between the very rich and the poorest there was an amalgamation of several occupational groups that cannot be classified as a class with distinct properties that all its members possess. Rather, it was a single middle class of many classes: bureaucrats and members of the military establishment, the relatively few trained professionals, some Muslim learned men (*ulama*), the urban artisans and the private moneylenders, mostly Armenians, Greeks and Jews. The latter group of minorities served as capitalist intermediaries and assumed important responsibilities in the orientation of the pre-capitalist economies of the Middle East towards the private-property market.[9]

Political colonialism and educational discrimination

What has been presented above about the gross inequalities in *material* asset-holding seems to be associated with the colonial system of discriminated access to a principal *human* asset, education, by different income groups and races.

As a fundamental human asset, education determines the skills in the occupational structure of the workforce, expands opportunities for progress, and develops income-yielding abilities, while illiteracy disables people from one generation to the next. Empirical evidence has established a positive correlation between a person's level of education (number of years of schooling) and his or her level of lifetime earnings.[10] This is because educational spending pays off in the form of a higher lifetime income for an educated person than for the illiterate. It follows that, other things being equal, an education system biased towards higher-income

Table 2.1 Primary education, dropout and illiteracy rates in nine countries, 1940–5

Country	Estimated population (millions)	Children in primary schools		% of dropouts[b]	Estimated % adult illiteracy and year of estimate
		Number in millions[a]	%		
Algeria	5.4	0.1 M	9.0 M	n.a.	86 M (1944)
Egypt	18.0	1.4	47.4	40	84 (1937)
Iraq	4.5	0.7	20.0	90	n.a.
Lebanon	1.1	0.1	72.7	15	47 (1945)
Libya[c]	2.0	0.03	12.0	80	87 (1950)
Morocco[c]	8.5	0.27	45.0	50	86 (1940)
Palestine					
(Arabs)	1.3	0.1	51.6	45	n.a.
(Jews)	0.5	0.06	60.0	n.a.	6.3 (1948)
Syria	3.0	0.14	39.4	n.a.	n.a.
Transjordan	0.4	0.14	28.0	80	n.a.

Sources: Data for all countries (except Algeria, Libya and Morocco) are calculated from: Matthews and Akrawi (1949). Algeria: Ruedy (1992: Table 5.4 and p. 126). Libya: World Bank (1960) and UNESCO *Statistical Yearbook* 1963 (UNESCO, 1963–95). Morocco and Palestine (Jews): *Statistical Yearbook* 1963 and 1964 (UNESCO, 1963–95).

Notes
n.a. = not available.
M = Muslim Algerians.
a Children attending in relevant age groups, which vary from 6–11 to 6–13, and the percentage enrolled compared to all children in these age groups.
b Number of children not completing primary elementary education as a percentage of those who attended the first year.
c Estimates refer to 1950–2.

groups increases income inequalities. For society at large, greater access to education is, in a way, an investment in the future productive capacity of the population, leading to the realization of a greater national income.[11] Because of this significant contribution, education is a recurrent theme throughout this book. In this section, educational discrimination during colonial rule is examined, focusing on the ways in which educational policy and family background created inequality of opportunity among the children of different ethnic and income groups. By 'family background' is meant parents' educational level, wealthholding, income and political connections.

The scattered information available on illiteracy estimates and the primary education situation during the last decade or so of colonial rule in each country is pieced together and presented in Table 2.1. This helps us to understand the post-independence situation examined in Chapters 6, 8, 10 and 11. Though imperfect, the figures in Table 2.1 show that, except for the very low percentage of enrolment in Algeria (9) and the high in Lebanon (72.7), only 42 per cent of children of primary school age in the nine countries were on average enrolled during the period 1940–5. Lebanon and the Palestinian Arabs and Jews had the highest enrolment rates and the lowest percentage of children dropping out of primary schools. At the other extreme, Iraq, Jordan, Libya and Morocco were the worst. In the 1940s, the worst-off among Arab children were the Algerian Muslims. The table also suggests that of the six countries for which illiteracy estimates are available for the period 1937–50, four had an average of 86 per cent adult illiteracy rate. However, these estimates have to be treated with caution, because of the different definitions used in the 1940s. These were standardized by UNESCO, starting in 1958.

At the time of independence, adult illiteracy was indeed appallingly high in the occupied countries.[12] Around 1960, it ranged from 70 per cent in Syria and Tunisia, to 85 per cent in Algeria, Iraq and Libya. The lowest rates were in Kuwait (53 per cent), Lebanon (45 per cent) and the highest were in Sudan (90 per cent) and Mauritania (95 per cent). When Egypt became partially independent much earlier, in 1922, 85 per cent of the adult population were illiterate. In all these countries the illiteracy rate was much higher (and still is) among females, the low-income strata of society and in rural areas (where illiteracy was almost double that in cities). Illiteracy among adult females was invariably 35–40 per cent above the national average and almost universal (89–98 per cent) in Morocco, Saudi Arabia, Libya and Yemen. Another indication of this very low human quality around 1960 is the primary school enrolment rate. Here again, children in Mauritania and Sudan, particularly those of nomadic parents, were the most disadvantaged; the enrolment rate was only 5 per cent and 25 per cent, respectively. The percentage was much higher in Egypt (66) and in Syria and Jordan (78), while it was highest in Lebanon (90).

Without the traditional primary schooling (*kuttab* and *zawia*, institutions consisting of a single teacher and one class), illiteracy would have been higher at the time of independence. These native places of learning in villages and towns were established by Islamic institutions and individual enthusiasts to teach children (mostly boys) the Qur'an and an elementary knowledge of Arabic and arithmetic. These indigenous primary schools were disrupted by such colonial actions as the abolition of the *waqf* system of religious endowment. This starved them of funding and was met with strong indignation from the religious leaders. The frequent military conflicts associated with the colonial administration's assault on local rebellious tribes and independence movements also destroyed many schools and dislocated the pupils who had to move with their parents.

The education-based social system

In the literature on human capital investment, it is well established that: (a) preferences in the allocation of public resources for education, especially with regard to the quantity and quality of primary schooling, determine the degree of income inequality; (b) as wage employment expands, the contribution of educational status to the total inequality of opportunities is likely to increase; and (c) reliance on parents' ability to pay school fees tends to increase lifetime inequality between privileged children and the disadvantaged poor whose parents cannot afford private sector education. By 'quality' is meant the relative degree of excellence of school buildings, teachers' qualifications, curriculum, teaching materials, student–teacher ratio and the quality of library and sports facilities.

The European colonial powers had allocated to education public funds from tax revenues and from earnings from the colonies' accumulated foreign trade. Data on public expenditure during colonial rule are scanty and hard to obtain. However, all sources agree that public expenditure on civil education during the long Ottoman rule was negligible; hardly 1 per cent of total expenditure, on average. For example, Ruedy (1992: 126) reports that the French colonial authorities in Algeria allocated only 20 per cent of total public expenditure on education to the Muslims, who represented nearly 90 per cent of the total population. Moreover, Issawi (1982: 113–14) found that the British administration in Egypt allocated to education and health, combined, only 1.5 per cent of total government spending in 1891 and that the Italian colonizers 'did next to nothing for Muslim education'. At its independence (1951), Libya had just two men with university degrees, representing a ratio of one in a million inhabitants. Mauritania had only one, who, in November 1960, became the first president after independence (Gerteiny, 1981). Hourani reports that after forty-three years of French rule in Morocco, there were only nineteen Muslim doctors and fifteen engineers in the total population of 11 million people, although rather more lawyers (1991: 389). When Iraq gained independence in 1931, there were sixteen university graduates, but the enrolment rate in primary (including elementary) schools was a mere 8 per cent.

In order to understand the process of educational discrimination by religion, race and language consider, for example, the colonial policy of the British Mandate in Palestine. Two parallel systems of education were established. One was for the Jews – taught mainly in Hebrew and of a high standard – and the other, of lower quality, was for Arab children. The two were, and, in the Occupied Territories, still are, administered separately. In 1940, the ratio of students to teachers was 45:1 in the Arab schools and 24:1 in the Jewish schools. A fundamental source of this wide variation that disadvantaged the Arab children's education was the substantial financial support provided by Jewish non-governmental organizations from the USA and Europe. For example, it was reported that in 1930 this external source accounted for 41 per cent of the total educational budget of Jewish schools in Palestine. Of the balance, 10 per cent came from the colonial administration budget and 49 per cent was contributed by the Jewish community within Palestine. In terms of expenditure per student, an annual average of 21 Palestinian pounds (P£1 equalled US$4.0 in 1930) was spent for a Jewish student, compared to only P£6 for an Arab student, i.e., the former was 3.5 times that of the latter.[13] This striking duality in educational system created the roots of a stratified social system, racial hatred and a gross inequality in employment opportunities between the children of the Jews and the Arabs.

In general, the colonial rulers established schools for their own nationals which replicated the educational system and quality in the colonizers' home countries. There were also bi-cultural schools in which the language of the colonizer was almost exclusively dominant (such lycées and schools as Brummana, St Joseph, St Marc, Les Frères, Antura, Aleppo and Victoria Colleges, for example). All these types of schooling were ranked high in the educational quality hierarchy. This upper category of schools was accessible to the privileged children of rich natives who could afford the high fees, and who were politically friendly to the colonial administration. One cannot ignore or underestimate the contribution of these quasi-foreign and bi-cultural schools to intellectual life and development efforts both in individual countries and in the region. Nevertheless, in this social system their graduates were brought up possessing a sense of superiority over others, and were able to climb the educational ladder to the best universities in Britain and France. This advantage gave them a much higher lifetime earning power than other native students, thereby increasing inequality of opportunity. For the rest of the native children, there were government primary and secondary schools. They were established in large towns and were of much lower educational quality and social rank than the schools for the privileged. Their fees were much lower, yet still almost 10 times those of indigenous places of learning.

To illustrate how government primary schooling had created barriers, denying the children of low-income families equal access to education, I offer my personal experience. In my childhood in the early 1930s, I received a three-year education in the local *kuttub* and *madrassa ahleya* (a native pre-primary school). In these indigenous schools, annual fees were very low (about one pound sterling) and the wearing of native dress (*galabia* and *shibsheb*) was common. The educational system in primary and secondary schools was a basically British model, and remained unchanged after Egypt became partially independent in 1922. At the age of 8, I was enrolled in a government primary school. The mockery lay in the necessity to wear a Western-style woollen uniform, black shoes and fez, in addition to the payment of annual fees amounting to £12 sterling that my father could ill afford. (These were hard years of economic recession; average real income per person was E£38 and cotton prices fell sharply to their 1925–9 levels – one Egyptian pound equalled almost one pound sterling or US$4.13.)

These barriers denied my *ahleya* school-mate, Sayed el-Sa'dani, the opportunity to enter the Western-style formal system of education. His father (a building worker) objected to his son wearing shorts in public but, more importantly, he could not afford to pay the fees from his low earnings. Sayed, whose school marks were better than mine, was forced to join the child labour market as a daily-waged worker in a butcher's shop. When I finally graduated to secondary school, I had to make a daily round trip in the countryside of 50 kilometres by donkey and local train. However, I managed to complete university and postgraduate training. At the age of 30, I met Sayed after I had completed twenty-one years of education compared to his three years of elementary schooling. By then, he was a worker in the main slaughterhouse of Cairo. Sadly, he had become illiterate and my annual earnings were 8 times as much as his.

Before we conclude the discussion on educational policy during the long period of colonial rule, let us pause for a moment to draw from the preceding paragraphs some of the elements that generated inequalities of income and opportunity, in order to come to grips with our principal concern.

First, in sharp contrast to the ideological principles of West European powers about equality of opportunity and advancement of knowledge to all, the same powers practised the opposite in their colonies. They introduced educational discrimination by language, race, income and parental political connections. The irony is that Britain and France – having distinguished parliamentary democracies – preached these ideals in the League of Nations after the First World War, and in schools in the colonies, whose students realized from bitter experience the fallacy of what they were taught. The educational discrimination they practised had created lifetime earnings differentials between the vast uneducated mass who were doomed to poverty and the educated few.

Second, colonial educational policy was detrimental to developing the skilled labour force that was required for the economic activities in the colonized countries. Instead, the conquerors imported their own engineers, technicians, doctors, lawyers, accountants, senior civil servants, business managers and even the bulk of the school teachers. This foreign workforce was supplemented locally by a few trained natives and the enterprising ethnic minorities (Greeks, Armenians, Jews and, in some countries, the educated native Christians).

Third, the colonizers' bias against public spending on the education of the subject population had deprived the colonized countries and their economies of the potential social yield of education. By 'social yield' is meant the high earnings of the educated public, together with the potential earnings from goods and services that the illiterates would have produced if they had been educated and working, i.e. the lost contribution to national income during colonial rule.

Lastly, it would be wrong to imagine that educational discrimination in colonial times and its effects on the social structure have, since independence, been fully reversed. The inegalitarian education systems were deep-rooted and, and as we shall learn from Chapters 6 and 8, their extension into post-independence times is worrying, despite official intentions and the substantial progress that has been made. Invariably, although the countries' proclaimed policy objectives have placed emphasis on equal access to education, most of these ideals have proved to be at variance with reality.

Summary

In this chapter, we have explored the historical roots of the inequality of two fundamental assets, landholding and education, which is inherited from colonial rule. With regard to landholding, the major form of wealth and source of political power in pre-independence times, we have learned that colonial policy had fundamentally distorted the indigenous social order by the imposition of a Western legal framework, combined with a capitalist system. Consequently, rich and poor strata developed around landholding, with a wide gulf in between, together with Western patterns of culture, residence and consumption. Likewise, educational discrimination by ethnic group and family background reinforced this gross injustice. The roots of the inegalitarian systems were so deep that the descendants of the then rich and poor strata still, today, make up most of the rich, educated few and the deprived illiterate majority, respectively.

Suggested readings

For understanding the distributional impact of the colonial policies on the Middle East's social systems:

Amin (1966) *L'Economie du Maghreb.*

Hourani (1991) *A History of the Arab Peoples*, especially Chapter 17, 'European Empires and Dominant Elites (1860–1914)'.

Issawi (1982) *An Economic History of the Middle East and North Africa.*

Warriner (1948) *Land and Poverty in the Middle East.*

The relationship between inequality of income distribution and education is examined in:

Bhagwati (1973) 'Education, Class Structure and Income Equality'.

Blaug (1968) *Economics of Education.*

Knight and Sabot (1990) *Education, Productivity and Inequality.*

Tilak (1989) *Education and its Relation to Economic Growth, Poverty and Income Distribution: Past Evidence and Further Analysis.*

Additional readings can be found in notes and in the Bibliography.

3

RELIGIOUS FOUNDATIONS OF JUSTICE AND INHERITANCE

This chapter explains the primary religious doctrines which lay down the moral rules of justice, inheritance and caring for the poor, and the consequences of their violation. After making some general remarks, I identify the relevant norms and trace the moral foundations both of wealth accumulation through inheritance arrangements and of the transfer of personal income to the poor. This is followed by an explanation of the increasing confrontation between secular states and organized religious groups, with examples from Egypt and Iran.

The importance of religion

Middle Eastern society differs from others in terms of the nearness of its people and institutions to the places where three major world religions (Judaism, Christianity and Islam) originated and where the miraculous events relating to Moses, Jesus and Mohammed took place. This reality serves as a constant reminder of moral obligation. Islam, as the faith of an overwhelming majority of the region's population, constitutes the focus of discussion in much of this chapter. At this point in the discussion, the reader may ask why religion is examined within the political and economic context of affluence and poverty. The connection lies in understanding that cultural forces, especially religion, influence civil laws, policy formulation and the conduct of economic activities within social organization. Religion also provides the moral foundations for fairness in the distribution of property, income and opportunity.

There is a significant difference between the region's three major religions with regard to the source of holy revelation. Unlike the Christian belief in the gradual revelation of the Old and New Testaments, and Judaism's corpus of teachings that make up the Torah (moral law or *halakhah*),[1] Muslims believe that their religion was revealed in a single,

44

complete sacred text, the Qur'an or the Book of God, Allah, expressed in a single language, Arabic. It has been preserved unchanged since the time when it was revealed to the Prophet Mohammed in 114 chapters over nearly twenty-three years, fourteen centuries ago. Together with the Prophet's authenticated interpretations (sayings or Hadith) the Qur'an constitutes the source of fundamental Islamic principles. The word qur'an means 'reading' and 'teaching'. It lays down the Muslim's and Islamic society's religious duties, and states punishments for their violation.

Let us begin with a resumé of some of the distributional means that believers are obliged to practise. Divinely given orders have, for many centuries, obliged all faithful believers to transfer their property, on death, to eligible heirs and for charitable purposes in different ways and proportions. They have made many Muslims, irrespective of their economic position, exchange their savings for the mandatory payment of *zakat* and *sadaqah* (a voluntary donation) to the poor, and for pilgrimage to Mecca. Many people from the low-income strata of Muslim society willingly bear the expense of travelling long distances to shrines to seek blessings and to give offerings to their sheikhs. In this way, and out of their meagre savings, poor families pay talismanic persons and heads of religious orders (*turuq*).[2] The latter make fortunes whose major source is the poor, who are made to believe in these people's mediation as a channel for God's blessings and grace, in spite of Islam's prohibition of mediation. From this expenditure, the poor derive the spiritually uplifting satisfaction of converting income into utility with a value that cannot be rationally measured.

Ideal moral standards: the immorality of deprivation

Value judgements as to what is morally right and what is a violation of standards are based on principles laid down in the holy books of the three religions, to which believers should conform. In this section, I outline the Islamic principles that are relevant to the study, as understood by an educated Muslim with little knowledge of Islamic jurisprudence.

1   Allah (God) guides every Muslim, through the Qur'an, to follow a straight path (*al-sirat al-mostaqeem*) for which each individual, without mediation, is accountable to Him after death on the Day of Judgement. Islamic Shari'ah courts of law are for settling conflicts in human conduct, and to ensure the observance of the rules governing inheritance.

2   There is an obligation to give *zakat* (*zakat al-mal* and *zakat al-fitr*). These are alms given by the head of the household as a portion of earnings above a minimum level (*nisab*) specified in detail in the Qur'an.

This transfer of income is not an optional charity, given out of benevolence, but a mandatory payment for the benefit of the poor, orphans and needy; without it they would be worse off (Qur'an, *al-Baqara*: 270–3, and *al-Nissa*': 37–9).

3   The strict prohibition of usury (*riba*) in lending money. The Qur'an says, 'Those who live on usury shall rise up before Allah, like men whom Satan has made evil by his touch, for they claim that usury is like trade. But Allah permitted trading and prohibited usury' (Qur'an, *al-Baqara*: 275). In modern times, Western-style interest-bearing credit, which is viewed by some sections of Muslim society as a form of usury, is intended to be replaced with a partnership between the lender and the borrower, with the bank charging an administrative fee for transactions. Both parties share in the profit and loss (*musharakah*) of credit-financed projects. Apart from achieving social acceptability, this procedure is attractive to risk-averse borrowers and amounts to an amalgamation of profit and interest, risk-bearing and capital transaction.[3]

4   The institution of private property is protected and respected by Islam, provided that it does not violate the Islamic goals of justice and social welfare (*masaleh*), and that all parties concerned are treated equally by law. Ownership of other human beings (slavery) is alien to Islam. Property rights and legitimate earnings are to be used in the Muslim community without exploitation of the weak, orphans and needy, and without gambling, bribery, speculation and hoarding.

5   Extravagance (*israf*), indulgence in luxuries, and excessive wealth accumulation (*takathor*) are admonished. This is clearly stated in the Qur'an (*al-Imran*: 14 and *al-Forqan*: 67). In the Prophet's authenticated Hadith as recorded by al-Bokhari and Abu-Muslem, the desire to show off richness in terms of ostentatious behaviour and the acquisition of gold, silver and silk are condemned, while moderation of consumption and humble attitudes are considered an important aspect of the faith (*al-iman*). These are enjoined in the Qur'an (*al-Layl*: 8–11).

6   Family welfare is based on the institution of marriage and the principle of eliminating sources of harm. Accordingly, family planning or birth control is permissible and it originates in the two-year period of breastfeeding prescribed in the Qur'an (*al-Baqara*: 233). Other methods, termed *al-azl* or *coitus interruptus*, are subject to different explanations by jurists.[4]

7   Whatever social system exists, it must be rooted in consultation with the community (*mushawarah*). On this point, the divine command in the Qur'an is: 'And consult them in their affairs' (*al-Omran*: 159); 'And they conduct their affairs by mutual consultation', 'The unjust persons suffer and have severe punishment' (*al-Shura*: 38 and 42).

The ideal moral standards outlined above have to be understood in the context of the fundamental Islamic belief that God has endowed people differently, but that each individual is accountable to Allah on the Day of Judgement. To express it in economic terms, the time horizon of the Muslim's demand schedule and pattern of consumption is extended to include benefits and satisfaction (utility) to be rewarded after death, that is, certain aspects of unnecessary pleasure are forgone in the Muslim's lifetime.[5] In a worldly system of governance, what is essential is the upholding of the body of Islamic principles (Shari'ah), and guarding against what is considered deliberate and socially unjust wrongdoing. Within this broad concept, the notion of moderation and maintaining a balance in daily life is fundamental.

Inheritance foundations

God-given inheritance rules determine the distribution of wealth from one generation to the next. Whereas inheritance guarantees the continuity of wealth-holding within a family, in economic terms it makes possible the acquisition of assets, without hard work or dexterity. This inherited wealth is an important means of becoming rich without having to earn the fruits of one's own efforts and abilities.

Christian and Jewish rules

In Christianity, inheritance rules differ widely from those of Judaism and Islam. The Christian tradition reveals a great deal of diversity. It ranges from passing the property undivided to a single heir (usually the first-born child or the surviving spouse, an arrangement known as right of primogeniture), to allowing at least one-third of the property for the surviving spouse or for charitable purposes. In the Coptic branch of Christianity in Egypt, inheritance rules are close to those followed in Islam. In the Protestant tradition, inheritance expressed in a written will permits placing the property after the owner's death at the disposal of whomsoever the owner pleases and on whatever terms, thus perpetuating inequality in wealth ownership. In a sense, this practice violates the Western capitalist ideal of 'to each according to his or her productivity': this has led an American philosopher to call for the abolition of inheritance.[6]

Judaism, on the other hand, generally defines the distribution of property among the legitimate heirs according to specified shares. I say 'generally' because there is flexibility in Judaism between writing or not writing a will (*katub*); passing the entire property to a single heir; deciding on the distribution of property of an intestate person by means of the rabbinical courts or giving freedom of testament that can disinherit one or more eligible heirs. In setting out the order of precedence of the heirs, the Torah rules that the eldest son inherits double the share of others. However, a father can make a will whereby he empowers one or more of his inheritors to acquire his whole estate, thereby denying the others their share. Justice in inheritance is provided by the early rabbis' rulings that brothers were obliged to provide fully for the needs of their sisters, even if they were thereby reduced to poverty themselves.[7] Should a person wish not to follow this divine mandate, he or she can provide the means of support as a gift. In Israel, however, Jewish people maintain a high level of observance, especially within the Orthodox and Conservative section of the population.

Islamic inheritance rules

Rules of inheritance in Islam are mandatory, laid down in precise terms in *Surat al-Nissa'*: 11–13 and *al-Baqara*: 241 of the Qur'an. Subsequently, the rules were explained for practical application by the Prophet in Hadith. Only the subdivision of indebted property and the shares of non-primary inheritors were differently interpreted by jurists (Abu-Zahra, 1963: 25). Known in Arabic as *mirath*, the principles of inheritance guarantee the rights of legitimate inheritors, particularly minors, and also of creditors. The principles also give the estate owner the option to allocate, after death, up to a maximum of one-third of his or her private property for charitable purposes (*wassiya*), but not to legitimate inheritors (*la wassiya li wareeth*).[8] The balance constitutes the compulsory inheritance (*furud al-tarikah*) to be subdivided in clearly stipulated shares among entitled heirs, after funeral expenses and any debts owed to creditors have been met.

The first and fundamental principle is the mandatory subdivision of the inherited estate into shares, *nasseeb*, i.e. one-half, one-fourth, etc., whereby the male's share is double that of a female heir. The second is *takharroj*, by which an heir may withdraw in favour of one or all of the remaining inheritors. Once the heirs have been identified and their shares applied by an authorized judge, the physical splitting of inherited land is not mandatory. It can be retained and managed by one of the heirs who is trusted as a single production unit. Thus, while these inheritance arrangements can preserve the productiveness of property, its size distribution from one generation to the next is determined by population growth and family size. Also, the property owner's longevity is an important factor: the longer he or she lives, the slower the process of splitting up the property among heirs and the longer the cycle in the transfer of property rights.

Conflicts and confrontation: an explanation

Conflicts between secular states and organized religious groups demanding change have increased in frequency and intensity. In development studies, confrontations are viewed as serious challenges to existing regimes; deterrents to foreign investment and destabilizers of a country's economic activities. Recently, the religious debate has become a part of the current debate on the adverse distributive effects of current economic reforms (for example, devaluation and the removal of food subsidies, leading to rising prices and living costs that harm the unprotected poor). As we learn from historical experience, when significant events occur, new theoretical perspectives arise. In the realm of Islam, jurists (*ulama*) and theologians have joined economists in rethinking the virtues of the countries' experiences in following capitalist or socialist approaches in relation to Islamic principles of justice and total welfare (*falah, masaleh*). By using analytical reasoning, this intellectual exercise has given birth to the new field of Islamic economics as a branch of development economics.[9] Further, two extremely complex issues have emerged. One concerns the specification of the guardian of the faith and who has the legitimate authority to administer, and interpret the fundamental rules of the faith. The other is whether or not religion and politics are separable.

The most forceful expression of discontent with the morality of policy and the political system has come from the Islamic militants. They call for equal participation in the political system, and they question the legitimacy of governments' decisions to ban their participation (except in Turkey, Sudan, Jordan and Lebanon). In some societies, they claim that the return to the historical roots of the Islamic state with a strict application of Islamic principles and laws is the only solution to problems of injustice and to widespread corruption. They are disappointed to see governments tolerating such sins as the drinking of alcohol, gambling, bribery, excessive monopoly profits, illegal enrichment, trade in gold and silver, usury, morally offensive advertisements on television and so on. Islamic militants are particularly against bringing mosques and the chief centres of Islamic learning such as al-Azhar in Egypt, Zaytuna in Tunisia, Tlemcen in Algeria, Fez in Morocco and al-Najaf in Iraq under tight government control. Also, while militant Islamic movements seem to be agreeable to technological advance and economic liberalization, they object to exploitation of low-income groups and to monopoly powers. Lastly, their writings and public speeches suggest that they are alarmed about social systems that make morally good people suffer undeservedly while some wicked people undeservedly prosper and gain political advantages.[10]

The connection between conflicts and economic hardship: the case of Egypt and Iran

My proposition is that the combination of Islamic reassertion or reawakening and outbreaks of social unrest is associated both with worsening economic conditions and with anxiety about decaying moral standards as observed in Egypt, Iran and Turkey. The deterioration is manifested in increasing inequalities and poverty, rising unemployment and living costs, as well as widespread corruption. The proposition does not imply a definite causal relationship. Rather, it is a simple explanation of a perception about a real social problem that arouses curiosity. Let us briefly examine this possible connection in Egypt and Iran.

Egypt has, during this century, pursued a secular path and has had the longest experience of the call for Islamic renewal. The first organized movement was the Muslim Brothers (Jama'at al-Ikhwan al-Muslimun). It was initiated by a school teacher, Hasan al-Banna, at the end of the 1920s. As the world depression dragged on and Egypt's economic crisis deepened, the movement expanded in the 1930s and 1940s. During these two decades, falling total and per head real income (the average annual growth of national income per head was around a negative 0.2 per cent) combined with a grinding poverty which I estimated in the late 1940s to affect 56.1 per cent of the rural population. In a capitalist economy with minimal government intervention, unemployment and underemployment was high (except during the Second World War), wealth ownership was concentrated in a few hands, and the rates of illiteracy, malnutrition and infant mortality were appallingly high.[11]

For their part, the Muslim Brothers movement claimed that the country's socioeconomic problems were rooted in the decaying moral standards and gross inequalities within Western materialism, manifested in the evils of gambling, usury, sexual scandals and free access to alcohol. In their opinion, the solution was a return to the roots of Islam for a just society. This organized movement was suppressed after the murders of the Cairo Chief of Police and the Prime Minister, Nokrashy Pasha, leading to the assassination of al-Banna himself by the government intelligence service in 1949. This was not the end of the movement. To the contrary, it was the start of a new phase in which the Muslim Brothers branched out in Egypt under different names, and spread across other Arab states such as Jordan, Syria, Lebanon, Saudi Arabia and Sudan.

The following two decades were a period of both a steady welfare-oriented economic growth and a development strategy that favoured the poor, including radical land reforms, heavy food subsidies and substantial housing rent reductions. With a steady annual growth in GDP of 6 per cent coupled with low inflation, real wages went up, income distribution improved, and the poverty level declined in 1965 to half its level in 1950 (M. R. El-Ghonemy, 1990b: Table 6.11). In the 1980s and the early 1990s the economy quickly deteriorated. As described in Chapter 10, economic reform has resulted in a sharp rise in prices, increasing unemployment and poverty, and a deterioration in the purchasing power of low-income groups, especially in urban areas. In the mean time, many businessmen and public sector managers suddenly became very rich, and bribery and corruption became normal practice (see Chapter 7).

Against this background, Islamic militants have intensified their violent protests and mounted their confrontations. Between 1990 and 1995 these resulted in the loss of many innocent lives, the murder of several police officers, the execution of many Islamic militants and, in 1993/4, the collapse of tourism, one of the important pillars supporting the Egyptian economy.[12] In expounding their dissatisfaction, activists found ready listeners among destitutes and the unemployed youth. Violence erupted in the economically disadvantaged rural provinces of Fayoum, Qena, Sohag, Assiut and the suburban slums of Cairo, whose illiteracy and poverty levels are the highest in the country.

As they had in Egypt in the 1930s and 1940s, politico-economic conditions in Iran deteriorated in the 1970s when religiously based uprisings peaked, resulting in the fall of the Shah's secular regime and its replacement by an Islamic state. Despite its considerable affluence arising from oil exports (representing 55 per cent of GDP in 1977–9) the regime's mismanagement of the economy and misuse of resources resulted in economic deterioration and a high concentration of wealth in a few hands, especially absentee landlords, rich city merchants and the foreign business community (see Chapters 5 and 9). In 1971–6, people in absolute poverty were estimated at 50–4 per cent of the total population. Inflation rocketed from almost zero in the 1960s to an average annual rate of 24 per cent in the 1970s, swiftly raising the cost of living. During my visits to Tehran in 1972 and 1976, I saw – amid unprecedented affluence – thousands of destitute shanty dwellers around the Parisien-style city of Tehran, whose population was increasing at an annual rate of 6 times that of rural areas.

In addition to the mismanagement of the economy and widespread injustice, religious leaders were angered by an excessive westernization of education and the judicial system that weakened the application of Muslim laws and the authority of the clergy. Among the worst problems was the abolition of the old Islamic *waqf* system which had financially supported the religious institutions. Consequently, the entire Islamic clergy system was in financial crisis. Worse still were the widespread corruption among the bureaucrats and executives of the public sector of the economy and the cruel harassment and oppressive actions by the military and the Shah's intelligence service (SAVAK), supported by the US Central Intelligence Agency (CIA). Among the Shah's imprisoned opponents was Ayatollah Khomeini himself, who was later forced to leave the country in exile.

Influenced by the Islamic militants among the clergy, the anger of the Iranian people reached its climax in the sacred month of Muharram (December) 1978. Almost 2 million people demonstrated peacefully in Tehran but were fired on by a military helicopter. The masses called for the imposition of Shari'ah and the rules of Islamic justice, and the return of Khomeini to lead the Islamic Republic of Iran.[13]

Summary

Three issues have emerged from this discussion of the role of religion in the distribution of wealth and in social stability. The first is that inheritance arrangements tend to continue the concentration of wealth within rich families and between individuals by heredity. Yet these arrangements are ignored by conventional economics but appreciated by anthropologists and sociologists. Second, the moral obligation to religious doctrines entails income transfers to the poor. However, the strong and unconditional belief in mystical events, particularly among low-income groups, has led to the widely practised custom of making offerings and the enrichment of religious brokers.

Lastly, but of critical importance to social and economic stability, my simplified account of the historical experience of Egypt and Iran suggests that in the absence of parliamentary democracy there is the likelihood of: (a) the intensity of the violent reassertion of Islam being closely associated with widespread corruption, rising unemployment and the increasing hardships of daily life; and (b) zealots tending to find ready listeners among the exploited, unemployed youth and the destitute.

Suggested readings

On inheritance in principle and practice in Islam:
Abu-Zahra (1963) *Ahkam al-Tarikah wal Mawareeth* (Laws of inheritance).

For understanding inheritance in Judaism:
Scheftel (1947) *The Jewish Law of Family and Inheritance.*

For Western views of religious resurgence:
Sivan and Friedman (1990) *Religious Radicalism and Politics in the Middle East*.
Wright (1992) 'Islam, Democracy and the West'.
The Economist, 'The Fundamental Fear' and 'Islam and the West', 6 August 1994.

For understanding the interaction between worsening economic conditions and
   the upsurge in popular support of the Islamist movement in Turkey:
Sayari (1996) 'Party Systems and Economic Reforms: The Turkish Case'.

Additional readings can be found in notes and in the Bibliography.

4

ECONOMIC FOUNDATIONS

The natural resource base

In the preceding two chapters, I characterized the common historical and cultural roots of present inequalities in the distribution of wealth and income. In this chapter, we begin our exploration of economic determinants with an assessment of inter-country variations in natural resource endowments: oil, cultivable land and water, leaving variations in human resource capabilities to Chapter 6. The first section highlights the problems arising from the increasing shortage of these natural resources under growing population pressure. In the second section, we investigate the impact of the sudden oil-based affluence. The third section focuses on the welfare effects of the increasing scarcity of cultivable land and of water. The concern here is over the increasing risks of environmental deterioration and food insecurity in poorer countries which lack the economic capacity to invest in both land development and water conservation.

Throughout this examination of the quantitative economic aspects of the vast differences between rich and poor countries, the frequent use of average income (GNP) per person does not suggest that this measurement is the same thing as development. As was emphasized in the Introduction and Chapter 1, it is but one important aspect of the process of development because it does not tell us how national income and growth benefits are actually distributed among income classes within a given society. Nor does it explain why differences in the quality of life among countries do not necessarily depend on vast differences in income levels resulting from the dramatic surge in oil revenues.

Abundance and scarcity

In the development experience of the Middle East, two natural endowments have contributed to the sudden changes both in levels of income and in food security. One is a single commodity, oil, whose price fluctuation is largely influenced by the uncertain world market. The other is the availability of cultivable land and of water, both surface and ground-water. Given the arid nature of most of the region's land, the capacity to invest in water conservation and irrigation expansion for greater food production is a crucial factor. In the case of such exhaustible resources as oil and groundwater, the degree of scarcity depends on their insufficiency to satisfy the growing population needs of the locality in question at a particular time. It depends also on government policies and public awareness, so that the rate of extraction for current use does not compromise the needs of future generations. Like most groundwater aquifers, the existing stock of oil as an exhaustible natural resource and the rates of its extraction are critical in terms of long-term development. These concerns over the increasing scarcity of oil and water are important for a number of reasons.

First, the Middle East possesses just under half (between 45 and 48 per cent) of the estimated world oil reserves, nearly 80 per cent of which are concentrated in the Gulf states.

Second, the estimated oil extraction time remaining is relatively short in Algeria and Libya (25–30 years from 1994) but much longer in Saudi Arabia, Kuwait and Iraq (60, 150 and 135 years from 1994, respectively).[1]

Third, oil wealth is concentrated in a few countries. Saudi Arabia holds almost one-fifth of the region's total reserves, and produces about 12 per cent of the world's total.[2] Likewise, Algeria possesses the fourth largest gas reservoir in the world, and produces annually 27 per cent of the total production of the region (based on the average for 1989–91).

Fourth, as the region is in the arid and semi-arid climatic zones of the world, nearly 53 per cent of its total population live in areas with less than the acceptable minimum level of 1,000 cubic metres of water per person.[3] What is more alarming is that availability of water per person in 1995 was only one-third of its 1960 level and if present rates of use continue, the average is expected to halve by the year 2025. Such an increasingly diminishing supply, combined with the rising competition for water use between agriculture, industry, drinking and other domestic purposes, necessitates country and collective regional actions for rational water use and the conservation of existing agricultural land, not only to feed the growing population but also to prevent further desertification and famines. Alas, like the downward trend in water availability, all indications suggest increasing land degradation and desertification by way of waterlogging, salination, topsoil loss, deforestation and overgrazing. Poor countries (Sudan and Mauritania) and the poorest rural households are most affected by the worsening situation. This downward trend gives cause for concern, given the increasing dependency of the Middle East on food imports (including food aid) and given that the poor are the most vulnerable to food insecurity risks, as will be documented later.[4]

Oil windfalls: from poverty to sudden affluence

Around 1940, Libya and Saudi Arabia were among the poorest of the underdeveloped countries. Within a tribal organization, more than half their population were nomadic or semi-nomadic bedouin. Their economies were chiefly dependent on grazing, camel raising, growing cereals when rainfall permitted, fishing, and exporting sheep, hides and dates. In addition, Saudi Arabia relied upon pilgrimage revenues, roughly estimated at US$20 per person.[5] To illustrate how poor Libya was, its government was unable to initiate the first development programme without external donations. Not so long ago, between 1954 and 1958, grants from the USA, the UK, France, Egypt and Turkey, together with the United Nations' assistance, represented nearly half the government's total revenue.[6] To illustrate further the sudden oil-based affluence, Egypt and Lebanon in the 1930s and 1940s were much advanced relative to Saudi Arabia and Libya in terms of income per person, educational level, health services, physical and institutional infrastructure, advanced industrialization and strong linkages with world trade. In 1939/40, income per person in Egypt was estimated at US$60 compared to approximately US$30 in Saudi Arabia, US$25–35 in Kuwait (1945) and roughly US$40 in Libya.[7] Among all Arab countries, Lebanon was at the top, with its income per person at US$140 in 1949.

Unprecedented pace of affluence

Unprecedented windfall gains followed the discovery of petroleum by foreign companies and their investment in its extraction and export in Saudi Arabia (1944–50), and in Libya (1959–62). Accordingly, the average annual income of a Saudi rocketed in a short period of only five years, reaching a level in 1962 that was 40 times higher than in 1957, and had risen a further fourteenfold by 1970. The most dramatic jump was between 1979 and 1981 when oil revenue almost doubled, reaching US$113.3 billion and income (GNP) per person increased 75 per cent in only two years. In Libya, the jump was even greater.[8] To the best of my knowledge, human history has not previously experienced such a scale of affluence gained in such a very short period of time. For instance, in less than twenty-five years, Libya had reached an average annual income of US$7,170 per person in 1985, a level of GNP per person that had taken the currently rich industrialized countries 220 years (1750–1970) to attain.[9] With such sudden, rapid affluence the lucky governments of the oil-rich states were so overwhelmed by the flow of plentiful oil revenues that nearly three-quarters of their countries' natural gas wealth (a by-product of crude petroleum) was wasted. In their careful study, Issawi and Yeganeh (1962: Table 4) estimated the extent and effects of this foolish extravagance.

Table 4.1 shows how between 1960 and 1991 oil markedly increased inter-country inequalities in income, stock of international capital reserves and, in turn, opportunities for progress. Countries are ranked by the 1991 GNP per person, which would not fundamentally change if we were to use the new estimates of GDP based on purchasing power parity (PPP) in international dollars for 1990. This change, made by the UN Statistical Office, indicates how much of each country's currency is required to buy the same amount of goods and services in the domestic market as one dollar would buy in the USA. According to these new estimates, the ranking order of the Middle East countries would result in Egypt's higher ranking above Morocco, the classification of Jordan above Syria and Tunisia and of Turkey above Algeria and Iran.[10] Whichever income concept is used, Sudan, Yemen and Mauritania remain the poorest countries. The unanticipated jumps in wealth and income originate in the pace of the oil price boom, which was in sharp contrast to the sluggish trade in such non-oil minerals as phosphates in Morocco and Jordan, which are among the world's five largest producers of this commodity.

Considering the low cost of oil production per barrel in the Middle East, the price boom of the 1970s has brought a sudden high economic rent (profit) to a few governments and particular ruling families. Stauffer (1987: 30) estimated this windfall gain at nearly 80 per cent of the price of each barrel. Perhaps no other exportable primary commodity produced in the region (e.g. cotton, sugar, tobacco and phosphates) has included in its price so high an element of profit. Furthermore, oil windfall gain has accrued with little productive effort on the part of society. Internationally, a significant indication of the emerging power of oil-money were the loans of US$10 billion granted in 1981 by Saudi Arabia to the IMF and US$800 million to the World Bank when commercial creditors in the Western countries were so weakened by recession that developing countries had almost no access to international borrowing. Instead of directly helping needy countries, the Saudi loan enabled the IMF to respond to their acute needs.

Against a background of deprivation and foreign command over their oil industry, the now oil-rich governments and the ruling families received either the full economic rent or a contract rent resulting from

Table 4.1 National income, gold and other international reserves per person, in US dollars, 1960–91

Income group	Average annual income (GNP) per person, US$				Per person gross international reserve including gold		
	1960	*1970*	*1980*	*1991*	*1958–62 average*	*1980–5 average*	*1991*
High							
United Arab Emirates	—	n.a.	26,850	20,140	n.a.	10,889	3,736.0[c]
Kuwait	—	9,210	19,830	16,180[b]	200	2,411	
Qatar	—	6,040	26,080	14,770	n.a.	1,288	
Saudi Arabia	336	3,100	11,160	7,820	53	3,662	863.5
Bahrain	n.a.	n.a.	5,560	7,130	n.a.	3,309	
Oman	550	2,490	4,380	6,120	—	1,191	1,103.1
Libya	990	3,530[a]	8,640	5,310	58	3,364	—
Israel	930	2,050	4,500	11,950	133	1,027	1,311.8
Weighted average		3,585	10,785	9,271			
Middle							
Iraq	228	850	3,020	3,508[b]	33	n.a.	—
Iran	200	870	2,160	2,170	11	n.a.	—
Algeria	540	780	1,870	1,980	n.a.	294	134.6
Turkey	240	440	1,470	1,780	7	60	115.5
Tunisia	210	340	1,310	1,500	16	85	105.6
Syria	240	390	1,420	1,050	29	403	286.6
Jordan	189	390	1,420	1,050	29	403	286.6
Morocco	190	300	900	1,030	n.a.	28	130.3
Weighted average		593	1,735	1,915			
Low							
Egypt	100	170	580	610	10	35	115.4
Sudan	140	160	410	610	13	1	0.3
Yemen	100	110	430	510	n.a.	155	38.0
Mauritania	100	210	440	510	n.a.	74	36.0
Weighted average		161	511	597			

Sources: GNP per person: 1960 and 1970: World Bank (1988) and UN *Statistical Yearbook* 1960 (United Nations 1960–95), except (a) which refers to 1973 and is taken from *World Tables* 1976, 1980 and 1991 (World Bank, 1976–95). 1980 and 1990 are taken from *World Development Report* 1982 and 1993: Indicators (World Bank 1978–96), except (b) which refers to 1989 and is taken from *Human Development Report* 1992 (UNDP, 1991–6): Table 2 and technical note, Table 2.1; (c) refers to 1992. Gross international reserves per person are calculated from UN *Statistical Yearbook*: section on finance (United Nations, 1960–95) and from *World Development Report* 1984, 1987 and 1993 (World Bank, 1978–96).

Notes
n.a. = not available
Countries are classified and ranked in descending order by GNP per person, 1991. Lebanon is not included because of incomplete data. See definition of GNP and international reserves in *World Development Report* 1991: technical notes; Table 1, Basic Indicators and Table 18, repectively (World Bank, 1978–96). Averages are weighted by population.

the nationalization of the oil industry which was begun in the Middle East in 1953 by Mohammed Mosaddeq, the then Prime Minister of Iran. Accordingly, payments by oil companies to governments greatly increased between 1950 and 1975: by 1,700 times in Libya; by 658 times in Kuwait and by 240 times in Saudi Arabia.[11] Typically, they have become rentier states.[12] A manifestation of their sudden affluence is the sharp rise in gold holdings and in vast reserves of foreign exchange. By keeping a large stock of wealth in the industrialized countries of the West in the form of gold and financial assets (e.g. bond issues and shares), the rulers of these rich countries have denied their people and economies the opportunities for developing the unutilized potential that otherwise could have increased productivity in non-oil sectors.

According to the IMF data presented in Table 4.1, Saudi Arabia's gross international reserve, including *official* gold holdings, jumped by 133 times between the average for 1958–62 and the average for 1980–5. The average reserves *per person* (including gold) in Saudi Arabia rose sharply between these two periods by a factor of nearly 70, with the UAE being the highest in the Middle East. Iran also tended to favour holding its international reserves in gold whose quantity (weight in ounces) was greater than in both Kuwait and Saudi Arabia. Likewise, Libya, which was classified by the United Nations in 1950 as a poor, underdeveloped country, had in 1980 the highest value of international reserves per person in the Middle East, US$4,969 (including gold). This is an extremely high level of affluence, compared to that of Israel (US$1,084) and the rich industrial countries, for example US$753 in the USA and US$566 in the UK in the same year.[13] As we shall see in Chapters 5, 6 and 8, these criteria for ranking are misleading. Oil-rich Arab states in the top category of Tables 4.1 and 4.2 are developing countries, with a high degree of economic dependence on external forces outside their own control. They are also characterized by under-developed institutions and infrastructures, as well as by an extensive social and economic imbalance. Yet, the GNP of the six rich Arab states combined was equivalent to only 7 per cent of the USA's GNP and was nearly one-third of that of the UK in 1980, when oil revenues peaked.

Table 4.2 shows the extent of income inequality between rich and poor countries. In absolute terms, the total income (GNP) of a single country, Saudi Arabia, was US$120,428 million in 1991, which exceeded the total income of seven countries, Egypt, Jordan, Mauritania, Morocco, Syria, Tunisia and Yemen, whose population numbered 145 million, representing 43 per cent of the region's total population at that time. The table shows also that while the income gap between the richest and poorest nations widened between 1960 and 1980, it narrowed

Table 4.2 Income inequality between countries, 1970, 1980 and 1991

Income group	1970 Population millions	%	Total income US$ million	%	1980 Population millions	%	Total income US$ million	%	1991 Population millions	%	Total income US$ million	%
High												
United Arab Emirates	—	—	n.a.	—	1.0	0.4	26,850	5.2	1.6	0.4	32,224	4.3
Kuwait	0.75	0.4	6,889	5.9	1.4	0.6	27,762	5.4	2.0	0.6	32,360	4.3
Qatar	0.11	0.1	664	0.6	0.2	0.1	5,216	1.0	0.5	0.1	7,385	1.0
Saudi Arabia	5.70	3.1	17,670	15.1	9.0	3.7	101,340	19.6	15.4	4.6	120,428	16.1
Bahrain	—	—	n.a.	—	0.4	0.2	2,224	0.4	0.5	0.1	3,565	0.5
Oman	0.65	0.4	1,560	1.3	0.9	0.4	8,442	1.6	1.6	0.4	9,782	1.3
Libya	1.90	1.1	6,707	5.7	3.0	1.1	25,920	5.0	4.7	1.4	24,957	3.4
Israel	2.90	1.6	5,945	5.1	3.9	1.6	15,795	3.1	4.9	1.5	58,555	7.8
Subtotal	12.11	6.7	31,435	33.8	19.8	8.1	213,549	41.3	31.2	9.3	289,266	38.7
Weighted average			3,585				10,785				9,271	
Middle												
Iraq	9.4	5.2	7,990	6.8	13.1	5.4	39,562	7.6	18.9	5.6	66,301	8.9
Iran	28.4	15.6	24,708	21.2	38.8	16.0	83,808	16.2	57.7	17.2	125,209	16.8
Algeria	13.7	7.5	10,686	9.2	18.9	7.7	35,343	6.9	25.7	7.7	50,886	6.8
Turkey	35.3	19.4	15,532	13.2	44.9	18.5	66,003	12.8	57.3	17.1	101,994	13.6
Tunisia	5.1	2.8	1,734	1.4	6.4	2.6	8,384	1.6	8.2	2.4	12,300	1.6
Syria	6.3	3.5	2,457	2.1	9.0	3.7	12,060	2.3	12.5	3.7	14,500	1.9
Jordan	2.2	1.2	858	0.7	3.2	1.3	4,544	0.9	3.7	1.1	3,990	0.5
Morocco	14.9	8.2	4,470	3.8	20.2	8.3	18,180	3.5	25.7	7.7	26,471	3.6
Subtotal	115.3	63.2	68,435	58.6	154.5	63.5	267,884	51.9	209.7	62.6	401,651	53.8
Weighted average			593				1,735				1,915	

Low

Egypt	33.0	18.0	5,610	4.8	39.8	16.4	23,084	4.5	53.6	16.0	32,696	4.4
Sudan	13.9	7.6	2,224	1.9	18.7	7.7	7,667	1.5	25.8	7.7	15,738	2.1
Yemen	6.8	3.7	7.48	0.6	8.9	3.6	3,827	0.7	12.5	3.7	6,500	0.9
Mauritania	1.2	0.7	25.2	0.2	1.5	0.6	660	0.1	2.0	0.6	1,020	0.1
Subtotal	54.9	30.1	8,834	7.6	68.9	28.3	35,238	6.8	93.9	28.1	56,054	7.5
Weighted average			161				511				597	
Total*	182.31	100.0	116,704	100.0	243.2	100.0	516,671	100.0	334.8	100.0	746,971	100.0
Weighted average			640				2,124				2,231	

Sources: UN *Statistical Yearbook* 1971 (United Nations, 1960–95), *World Development Report* 1982 and 1993 (World Bank, 1978–96) for data on population size and GNP per capita, 1980 and 1991.

Notes

* Total income is GNP per capita multiplied by total population. Percentages may not add up to 100 because of rounding. Averages are weighted by population.

slightly in 1991 following the oil slump of 1981–6. Mismanagement of oil windfalls in the rich countries during the boom (1974–80) and the good growth performance of the region's poorer countries (see Chapter 5) were both contributing factors in this. Another way of judging the extent of inequality among countries is by taking the index number of the richest countries as 100. In this way, we find the index of the poorest countries falling sharply from 16 in 1960 to 1.7 in 1970. It fell further to 1.5 in 1980, but improved slightly, to 2.4 in 1991. For example, in 1980 a person in the UAE or Qatar had, on average, an annual income that was 63 times greater than that of a person in Sudan or Yemen.

This general picture of oil-based income inequality among countries is also depicted in the changes in the shares of each of the three income groups both in the region's total income and in its total population in 1970, 1980 and 1991 (the results for the last year were summarized earlier, in Figure 1.1). The year 1960 is not included in Table 4.2 because of incomplete data. The table shows that between 1970 and 1980, the rich countries' combined share of the region's total *population* rose slightly from 6.7 per cent to 8.1 per cent, but that their share in total *income* was 5 times greater in each of these two reference years, increasing from 33.8 per cent to 41.3 per cent. The eight countries in this group of rich countries are all small in terms of their domestic market and population size.

At the other extreme, the group of low-income countries comprise a little less than one-third of the total population of the region, but saw their share in the total income fall from the already low 7.6 per cent in 1970 to 6.8 per cent in 1980. Although it improved slightly in 1991, it remained below its 1970 share. Within this group, the skewed nature of the distribution of shares is the reverse of that in the group of rich countries (i.e. the share of population of each country ranges from 4 to 6 times greater than their regional share in the total income). The situation is less unequal in the intermediate income group, because it includes three oil-based economies (Iraq, Iran and Algeria), and two large countries (Iran and Turkey) whose population accounts for over one-third of the region's total.

Sharing oil windfalls: financial aid and workers' remittances

For various motives, rich Arab states have transferred substantial sums of oil money to poorer countries directly through untied financial aid and indirectly by way of migrant workers' remittances. Between 1973 and 1990 nearly US$50 billion were unconditionally provided for poorer Arab states and Turkey, mostly in the form of bilateral and concessional assistance (almost grants).[14] In addition, I estimate that an amount of US$88 billion was transferred by migrant workers to their Arab home countries during the same period. In terms of its proportion to national income (GNP), financial aid from rich Arab states has, since the sharp rise in oil prices of 1973, exceeded the UN target of 0.7 per cent and the average of rich industrialized donors (0.3 per cent). It was high at 5.9 per cent in 1973/4 and fell steadily to 1.8 per cent in 1990 and 0.8 per cent in 1991. Saudi Arabia is the largest donor by far; its share in total Arab financial aid jumped from 51 per cent in 1973–9 to 75 per cent in the 1980s. In terms of aid per head of the population of donor countries, Qatar and the UAE surpassed Saudi Arabia.

One would expect that this sizeable transfer of oil money from rich Arab donors would have effectively contributed to human development and poverty alleviation in recipient poorer countries if it had been directed to activities that diminish poverty directly. Alas, non-developmental considerations, especially military spending, have been so dominant that financial aid can hardly be classified as 'development' assistance. In retrospect, this was a missed opportunity for the recipient countries' emancipation of their people from deprivation. To appreciate this point, consider the fact that the Arab aid of US$50 billion was more than three times the sum of US$14 billion given in the US Marshall Plan in 1947–52 for Western Europe's speedy recovery from the devastation, hunger and poverty caused by the Second World War. It seems that both Arab donors and recipient countries lacked the sort of vision and development-oriented leadership of such statesmen as Harry Truman, George Marshall and Dean Acheson of the donor country (the USA) and Clement Attlee, Ernest Bevin, Charles de Gaulle and Conrad Adenauer of the recipient European countries.

The reality is that most of the financial aid after the military defeat of Egypt, Jordan and Syria in their 1967 war with Israel has been mandated by the heads of Arab states in their summit meetings, and the exact size and timing of disbursement are usually kept secret from the public. Unlike the financial assistance from rich industrial countries, no system of surveillance exists between Arab donors and recipients, which is strange considering that these heads of state call themselves *asheqa'* (brothers), and refer to their countries as *shaqiqah* (sister). One possible explanation is the almost complete absence of democratic machinery for accountability and for monitoring the allocation and the effects of disbursed bilateral financial aid, in both donor and recipient countries. Nor do donors seem to be interested in crushing destitution, unemployment and flagrant inequalities. I personally experienced this apathy when I was responsible for a fund amounting to US$21 million as a grant from

Saudi Arabia and Kuwait for assisting poorer countries.[15] Over five years, the representatives of donors did not trouble themselves to learn how the money was used, to visit recipient countries, or to undertake the tasks of surveillance and targeting aid to benefit the poor directly. Instead, they opted for actions to improve soil salinity, animal health and horticulture production, all of which benefited larger farmers.

With the prominence of military and political considerations, aid fluctuated sharply. I believe that almost half the multi-billion dollars of aid disbursed to poorer countries have ended up in rich industrialized economies via the world armament market. I give two examples of the political basis of the sharp swing in Arab financial aid. The first is a special aid fund of US$2 billion which was established by the Gulf Organization for Development in Egypt. Suddenly, this institution was dissolved and the aid cancelled after Egypt's Camp David Agreement with Israel in 1978. Moreover, the Arab heads of state punished Egypt at their summit conference in Baghdad (November 1978) by discontinuing its receipt of other forms of Arab aid. Likewise, Arab donors banned aid to Jordan, Mauritania, Sudan and Yemen because of their political support of Iraq in its conflict with Kuwait in 1990/1. The second example is the reported Saudi contribution of US$25.7 billion to Iraq[16] for the purchase of arms during that country's long war with Iran (1981–9), owing to fear of Iran's military threat.

Perhaps workers' remitted earnings from oil-rich states to their home countries have more beneficial effects than financial aid. Since the start of the oil boom in 1973, labour migration across boundaries and remittances have constituted an important source of both household and national incomes, which will be examined in case studies presented in Chapters 8, 9 and 10. Despite data limitations, available estimates of remitted earnings' share in the national incomes of labour-sending countries during the 1980s varies considerably: from a peak of one-third in Yemen and one-quarter in Jordan (mostly Palestinian migrants) to one-tenth in Egypt, and only 4 per cent in Turkey.[17]

This brief account of past experience in using oil windfalls for helping poorer countries suggests that the flow of both financial aid and migrant workers' remittances is substantial but highly unpredictable. According to a study carried out by the IMF (1991a: 30–5 and Appendix Table 49) the combined flow of official financial aid and workers' remittances from Arab donors during the period 1973–89 was as high as 123 per cent of total capital investment in Yemen and 114 per cent in Jordan. The percentage was at lower levels in Mauritania (54 per cent), Egypt (53 per cent) and Sudan (48 per cent). (The economies of Jordan, Mauritania, Sudan and Yemen must have suffered greatly since the 1991 Gulf

War owing to the banning of both financial aid and migrant workers.) The limited impact of financial aid on development is revealed by the results of the IMF study: where the military component was high (as in the case of Egypt and Syria) the variation in annual financial aid flows was not positively correlated with changes in annual growth rates of GNP and total investment. In fact, the relationship was *negative* in ten out of fifteen years (1974–88), that is, the variation in aid flows did not influence rates of economic growth and total investment where the military component was high. This contrasts sharply with Morocco and Tunisia, whose financial aid was not defence- but development-oriented and where the impact was positive over most of the period.

Economic capacity to develop land and water resources

In a region where three-quarters of total land area is arid and whose population is growing at a high rate (3.1 weighted average), one would not expect degradation in land and water resources. The reality is that there is increasing risk of food insecurity arising from declining availability of cultivable land and water per person. The prolonged droughts of the 1980s, leading to famine that killed thousands of poor farmers and herders and their livestock in rainfed areas of Sudan and Mauritania, are viewed here in terms of weak financial capacity. This disadvantage prevented these countries' many pastoralists and poor farmers from benefiting from existing advanced technology in land development. These two poorest countries possess nearly 80 per cent of the total potentially cultivable area in the Middle East: 67 million hectares in Sudan and around 2 million hectares in Mauritania (see Table 4.3). Nor could the policymakers benefit from the forecasting of climatic fluctuation, with a small margin of error, by sophisticated remote sensing and simple statistical techniques. An illustration from Sudan clarifies this connection. The low rainfall of 1981–2 in Sudan, followed by the severe drought of 1984–5 that caused crop failure in rainfed areas and brought about famine, did not come as a surprise. From his analysis of rainfall records over a period of thirty years (1951–80) and remote sensing information, Abdulla (1986), a Sudanese authority on the subject, asserts that the severity of drought was forecast at 85 per cent probability by extrapolating the trend of past rainfall data.[18]

Table 4.3 Cultivable land, its ratio per person and potential expansion in eighteen Middle Eastern countries, 1965–91

Countries in alphabetical order	Cultivable land			Irrigated land			Land/Person Ratio		Potential	
	Total cultivable area (million ha) 1990	As a % of total area of the country	Annual growth % 1965–90	As a % of cultivable area (average 1988–90)	Annual growth % 1970–80	1981–9	1969–71	1989–91	Area (million ha)	As a % of currently cultivable land
Algeria	10.7	3.0	0.5	5	0.6	4.6	4.9	5.4	2.6	24.0
Egypt	2.6	2.5	-0.6	98	-1.5	0.6	0.6	0.4	0.08	3.0
Iran	12.0	8.6	-0.4	39	-0.5	1.9	4.4	3.5	0.34	0.3
Iraq	8.2	12.0	0.5	47	1.7	4.7	4.5	5.2	3.41	41.6
Israel	0.44	21.0	0.2	45	0.8	2.5	3.8	5.7	—	—
Jordan	0.4	3.5	0.9	15	0.8	5.5	13.4	13.9	1.19	49.5
Lebanon	0.5	20.3	-0.3	29	—	—	2.5	4.1	0.21	42.0
Libya	2.4	1.0	0.3	11	0.8	5.5	13.4	13.9	1.19	49.5
Mauritania	1.1	1.0	-1.6	1	3.2	1.0	2.8	2.6	1.99	55.3
Morocco	11.8	19.4	0.9	14	2.8	0.4	3.1	3.1	1.60	13.5
Oman	0.06	0.1	2.6	85	—	—	0.3	0.3	0.04	66.7
Saudi Arabia	1.0	0.5	1.9	36	0.6	1.2	1.4	1.5	0.07	7.2
Sudan	81.9	5.2	0.5	15	0.8	0.7	3.2	2.6	66.98	81.7
Syria	5.4	26.6	-0.5	12	1.8	2.4	7.5	7.4	0.32	5.8
Tunisia	2.8	19.5	0.3	6	5.6	7.6	8.0	7.4	0.48	16.9
Turkey	30.2	32.3	0.2	8	1.4	0.7	2.4	2.3	6.42	21.2
UAE	0.02	0.3	7.2	13	—	—	—	—	—	—
Yemen	0.9	2.6	0.2	19	—	—	1.2	1.0	0.07	8.3
Total	172.42								85.91	

Sources: FAO (1993a: Table A5). Growth rates of land are taken from *World Development Report* 1994: Table A6 (World Bank 1978–96). Annual growth of irrigated land is from FAO Statistics Division. Land/person ratio is calculated from data in *Country Tables* 1985 and 1993 (FAO, 1985–93). Data for Oman are taken from Oman, Ministry of Information (1993: 105).

The region's acute water scarcity

Using water supply data for the period 1970–87 and population data for 1990, the estimates of the World Resources Institute are alarming indeed. The Middle East has the lowest availability of water and its water scarcity is the most acute in the world. Its annual water availability of 1,071 cubic metres per person is only 12.9 per cent of the world's average and less than one-third of that of Asia. It is a mere 5 per cent of Latin America's average. The largest single water-consuming sector in the Middle East is agriculture (89 per cent) followed by domestic use (6 per cent) and industry (5 per cent).[19]

These averages are, however, misleading. They conceal vast differences between the many countries which are highly dependent on unpredictable rainfall, and the few countries which have secure water, available all year round from the perennial flow of rivers (e.g. the Nile and the Euphrates). Another source is the groundwater aquifers combined with costly desalinated seawater at an average of US$1.0–1.5 per cubic metre. Examples of the latter situation are the oil-rich states of the Arabian Peninsula and some areas in Israel. Saudi Arabia is the largest investor in the production of desalinated seawater, which increased fiftyfold between 1975 and 1985. Thus, rich countries with a dry climate and desert land, such as Israel, Saudi Arabia and Libya, can afford the application of costly technology to attain high water availability for expanding the irrigated land area.

Libya is expected to meet this objective after the completion of the multi-billion dollar 'great man-made river'. Started in 1983, its first two phases, costing about US$8–10 billion (some US$20 billion if infrastructure works are included), provide for extracting or pumping water from deep layers of the aquifer in the coastal areas and the Kufra–Sarir Basin and from the Marzuq Basin reservoir, distributing it in huge pipelines 4,000 kilometres long. The third, fourth and fifth stages are to increase the capacity of the work completed in the first two phases. The total cost will reach approximately US$25 billion. By the year 2000, it is expected to irrigate nearly half a million hectares between Benghazi and Sert in the eastern region.[20] Considering the weakness in entrepreneurship and organization and the shortage of the Libyan farming population, it remains to be seen whether the colossal physical capital investment and the rapid depletion of the scarce groundwater for this scheme will be a miraculous achievement of President Moamar al-Qaddafi or a mirage in the Libyan desert by the year 2000.

Oil-rich countries are also able to spend lavishly in order to produce wheat and vegetables, irrespective of the very high costs of production and the low yield. These advantages of affluence may be illustrated by available studies of crop production in Libya during the oil boom (1974–80). The results suggest that the cost of production of 1 tonne of wheat in the large schemes of Jefara and the Kufra with a low yield of 0.7 tonnes per hectare was 10–15 times greater than the world average. Likewise, in Qatar and Kuwait the cost of production of 1 kilogramme of cucumbers, peppers or tomatoes using the sophisticated technologies of hydroponics and drip irrigation was roughly 20 times higher than the price paid after their importation from South Yemen, Egypt or Jordan.

With affluence everywhere in Libya and in the Gulf countries, economic considerations of comparative advantage and returns on investment in land and water development seem to be of no concern, compared to the temptation of gaining tangible prestigious benefits. This is in sharp contrast to the starvation and loss of life among Sudan's and Mauritania's poor people and their livestock noted earlier, in the two countries which possess the largest potentially cultivable area in the Middle East. Such affluent behaviour also contrasts greatly with the reliance of poorer countries on foreign capital, falling into heavy debt in order to conserve scarce water resources (as was the case, for example, with Egypt's High Dam, Turkey's Ataturk Dam and Syria's Euphrates Dam). In fact, the 1956 war between Egypt and Israel, supported by France and Great Britain, originated in President Nasser's nationalization of the Suez Canal to finance the High Dam, built for US$1.2 billion with the Soviet Union's aid. This and many other water-related disputes are warnings of future conflicts between countries which share the waters of a single basin and whose secure access to water is under threat.[21]

Increasing scarcity of cultivable land

Historically, the majority of the people of the Middle East have viewed land as the most secure way of holding wealth and gaining social and political advantages. Irrespective of their occupations, urban and rural people alike perpetually strive to own a piece of the scarce agricultural land, subject to financial capacity, or to expand their existing land assets. This high amenity value has intensified the demand for owning or leasing land, particularly in irrigated areas where productivity gains are high. The desire to possess farm land was manifested during the 1970s and the 1980s by migrants from Egypt, Jordan, Sudan and Yemen (mostly migrant professionals working in oil-rich countries) who used most of their remittances to purchase land at inflated prices.

What is of great concern is the fact that the area of present and potential land suitable for crop production is only 11 per cent of the region's vast area of 1.53 billion hectares (the area of the Middle East as defined in this study). According to the FAO and UNESCO's joint studies, most of the land suitable for crop production is already in use.[22] The area of potential land for future expansion by way of irrigation and/or intensification of the use of the existing area of rainfed land is also limited. It is estimated to be nearly 86 million hectares or half the present cultivable area and only 5 per cent of the region's total area. The rest consists of vast expanses of desert soils, rocky slopes, salt marshes, shifting sands, lakes, buildings and mountains. As shown in Table 4.3, most of the potential land with suitable soil fertility and moisture retention capacity is in Sudan (66.9 million hectares), followed by Turkey (6.4 million hectares), Iraq (3.41 million hectares), Mauritania (2 million hectares), and Libya (1.2 million hectares). The table does not include Bahrain, Kuwait and Qatar whose agricultural land area is tiny (between 1 and 2 thousand hectares each).

Table 4.3 also provides annual rates of expansion of both total cultivable land and irrigated land, as well as the change in the ratio of average land area per person working in agriculture. The choice of this ratio is meaningful for employment and productivity. My calculation shows a declining ratio in the large populated countries (Egypt, Iran and Turkey) between the two periods of 1969–71 and 1989–91, and an increasing ratio in the richer countries (Libya, Iraq, Israel, Algeria, Saudi Arabia and the UAE), as well as Jordan. These countries, together with Tunisia, were also able to maintain a steady expansion in irrigation between 1970 and 1989.

Irrigation is expensive: who benefits?

Past experience suggests that rich families with political power are able to benefit disproportionately more from irrigation schemes than are poor farmers. Available estimates also indicate that whereas irrigation is expensive everywhere, it is more costly in the Middle East because of its arid climate and its soil texture, which dries quickly under the heat of the long summer. Estimates of the costs of new irrigation schemes per hectare at 1985 prices show that the average capital cost was US$4,196 in the Middle East, compared to US$2,366 in the Far East and US$2,420 in Latin America.[23]

In implementing its irrigated development schemes, a government's spending level per hectare and per family settler is indicative of its degree of affluence. In the 1970s the government of Libya spent an average of US$210,500 per family and US$10,500 per hectare in five partially irrigated land settlement schemes. This lavish spending contrasts sharply with Egypt's average (over the same period) of US$2,500 per hectare in

North Tahreer province, west of the Delta, and with US$3,500 spent in the Euphrates region of Syria.[24] A Libyan economist, El-Wifati (1978), attributed the high cost in his country to the use of expensive building materials and irrigation equipment, and to the contracting out of surveys – and part of the implementation – to international firms charging very high fees, whose work was not monitored by government departments because they lacked qualified staff. With such extravagance, productivity of land in these schemes was extremely low: the average yield of wheat was merely 0.6 tonnes per hectare in Libya compared to 3.2 tonnes in Egypt and 1.5 tonnes in Syria during the same period.

Subsidizing rich farmers

In many government irrigation schemes, most of the beneficiaries are not landless agricultural workers or poor farmers. Mainly they are land-owners, land speculators among the urban élite, influential civil servants and former members of the armed forces. Whether the newly irrigated land was desert or under rainfed agriculture, the benefits from subsidized irrigation water follow the size distribution of land. The results of the agricultural censuses of 1970 and 1980 conducted in many countries of the Middle East show that inequality of land distribution is higher in irrigated lands than in rainfed areas and subsidized water charges benefit larger landowners more than small farmers (see M. R. El-Ghonemy: 1990a and 1993). This grossly unequal access to scarce land and water resources is documented by two studies conducted in Morocco (Daden, 1978) and Jordan (FAO, 1987: 6). The Moroccan study shows that in the Gharb region, rich farmers (those owning 50 hectares or more) who possessed only half of 1 per cent of the total land area captured about 45 per cent of total subsidies, including water charges which were 70 per cent below the irrigation maintenance costs. In Jordan, water charges paid by rich farmers were 90 per cent below the actual cost of operation and maintenance of the irrigation system in the Jordan Valley.

The biased role of bureaucracy: empirical evidence

The appropriation of land in new irrigation schemes by the erstwhile bureaucratic establishment in Egypt illustrates the decreasing access of the poor to government-reclaimed lands. Baer (1962: 189) reported that civil servants were able to exchange their pension entitlements at a low price for ownership of land and to compete with poor farmers through the auctioning of reclaimed lands. I have elsewhere (M. R. El-Ghonemy, 1990b: 159–60) documented that between 1935 and 1949 large landowners (owning over 50 hectares each) purchased 90.7 per cent of the total area reclaimed and sold by the government, agricultural college graduates purchased 7.6 per cent, while only 1.7 per cent was sold to poor tenants (*mudamin*). This biased policy occurred at a time when wage-dependent landless households were estimated at 3 million families or 40–60 per cent of all agricultural households, depending on the definition used. This pattern has persisted. A study conducted in 1980 on the actual beneficiaries of new irrigation projects using the High Dam's water ascertained that 54 per cent of reclaimed public land was owned and managed by giant state farms, 2 per cent by multinationals (joint ventures such as the Pepsi-Cola Corporation), 35 per cent by small farmers and the rest (9 per cent) by college graduates. Interestingly, the study found that yields were higher in small family farms than in larger farms and those of university graduate settlers.[25]

The vested interests in irrigation and the biased role of bureaucracy towards those who have wealth and political power is manifested in licensing without monitoring groundwater pumping and in tolerating the degradation of land. From field studies in Egypt, Libya, Oman, Saudi Arabia and Syria, there is evidence of government officials who turn a blind eye to the violation of existing laws and regulations by influential larger landholders (e.g. in well-spacing, drilling depth and in exceeding the permitted rates of groundwater extraction).[26] The results of this practice in the Nejd lands of the southern region of Oman and Egypt's Dakhla and Kharga oases are documented in H. El-Ghonemy (1992: 137–43). These violations resulted in lowering the water table in neighbouring small farmers' wells and even making their wells run dry. In Egypt's New Valley province, the unregulated flow of groundwater in the artesian wells of Kharga and Dakhla resulted in the lowering of the water table, causing the wells of numerous small farmers to cease to produce water. In Dakhla, only seven years after their costly installation, water ceased to flow from 300 shallow wells constructed by scarce public funds.

Abandonment of expensively reclaimed public land is due also to taking the land out of agriculture for urbanization, in spite of legal prohibition. For example, the construction boom in Egypt consumed nearly 640,000 feddans of highly fertile, advantageously situated and intensively cropped land between 1955 and 1977, and 250,000 feddans between 1978 and 1990. The loss of this asset, created over many centuries from the Nile water silt, occurred although the nearby desert land that represents 95 per cent of Egypt's total land area could have been used for construction instead. A more alarming method of taking fertile land out of cultivation is the illegal practice of contractual arrangements for the removal of 2–3 metres of Egypt's rich topsoil, at an annual rate ranging from 30,000 to 50,000 feddans, for making bricks (Biswas, 1991 and M. R. El-Ghonemy, 1993). Such a profitable trade by the influential, wealthy urban constructors has occurred despite several existing laws that prohibit this practice but which suffer both from legal loopholes and ineffective enforcement by easily corrupted bureaucrats (see Chapter 7). This tendency to take scarce productive land out of agriculture for urban purposes in Egypt can easily be found in most countries of the Middle East.[27]

Summary

Unprecedented oil windfall gains have suddenly made a few countries very affluent rentier states. A substantial portion of the easily accumulated oil revenues has been deposited abroad, mostly in the USA and Western Europe, thus denying the masses the opportunities for developing unutilized potential that could have increased productivity in the non-oil sectors of the economy. In the mean time, these oil-rich states have transferred substantial sums of oil money to poorer countries through financial aid and, more importantly, migrant workers' remittances. Political and military considerations have a commanding influence over the volume, usage and frequency of income transfers. However, the impact of direct financial aid on the development of the recipient countries is minimal, there being a negative relationship between aid, on the one hand, and gross domestic investment and GDP growth rates, on the other, in most cases where the military component of aid is high.

In the long-term perspective of an arid region, degradation of water and land resources must be stopped and the rates of extraction of oil and groundwater have to be planned carefully to meet the growing needs of the present generation without compromising those of future generations. This is because the Middle East has the smallest amount of water available per person in the world, and irrigation of its land is the most costly in the developing world. Moreover, such institutional factors as the lobbying strength of large landowners, the misuse of water rights and the biased role of bureaucracy have resulted in rich farmers and urban contractors capturing the benefits of the sizeable public investment in irrigation disproportionately more than the majority of poor farmers, to the disadvantage of the millions of nomadic people and small cultivators in rainfed areas. Readers are left to reach their own conclusions about the relevance of my arguments to the continuing debate on development and environment, the impact of affluence and a biased bureaucracy on widening income gaps and resource conservation and, particularly to such concerns as the ways in which a repetition of the disasters of desertification and human suffering of the last three decades may be avoided in the next century.

Suggested readings

On oil and natural gas in the region:
Issawi (1982) *An Economic History of the Middle East and North Africa*, Chapter X, 'Petroleum: Transformation or Explosion?'.
Issawi and Yeganeh (1962) *The Economics of Middle Eastern Oil*.

On land and water resources for crop production:
Biswas (1994) *International Waters of the Middle East: From Euphrates–Tigris to the Nile*.
The Cambridge Atlas of the Middle East (1987).
Dregne (1983) *Desertification of Arid Lands*.
M. R. El-Ghonemy (1993) *Land, Food and Rural Development in North Africa*.
Thomas and Middleton (1994) *Desertification: Exploding the Myth*: the case of Sudan is presented on p. 60–3.
Warriner (1948) *Land and Poverty in the Middle East*.

On potential land and water availability:
FAO (1993a) *Agriculture Towards 2010*.
World Bank (1995) *From Scarcity to Security: Averting a Water Crisis in the Middle East and North Africa*.

Additional readings can be found in notes and in the Bibliography.

5

UNBALANCED
DEVELOPMENT

This chapter is intended to synthesize the sources of inequality examined so far, within a framework of structural and institutional elements interacting throughout the development process within the whole economy, at both regional and sectoral levels. In this way the structural characteristics of two forms of unbalanced development can be identified. First, a case study of a poor country, Sudan, explains how its state-led development process has created and perpetuated inequality between traditional and modern sectors. Then follows an exploration of what has happened in three oil-rich countries (Algeria, Iran and Libya) during and after the oil boom period (1974–80). In both cases the employment and income effects of the movement of working people and public investment between the low and high earnings sectors will be examined. Throughout the chapter I shall address the central question of who benefits, and by how much, from the misallocation of resources.

The term 'unbalanced development', though interpreted in different ways, is viewed here as the interaction of structural elements such as investment, urbanization, employment, the production process and trade. (Social imbalance of public and personal consumption behaviour is examined in Chapters 6 and 8, respectively). These elements operate within a closely interlinked institutional framework of property rights, legal rules, the state's ideology and government bureaucracy. Like the terms 'inequality', 'underdevelopment' and 'underemployment', the term 'unbalanced development' is relative, describing the characteristics of the prevailing form that the development process takes during a certain period of time. In a sense, it is a departure from the notion of balanced, proportionate relationships (for example balancing food supply and population size or balancing manufacturing growth and agricultural growth).

Inequality and poverty in a dual economy: the case of Sudan

The development process of Sudan is typically dual across the economy's sectors, subsectors, regions and subregions. The Perspective Plan (1977–95) aimed at the realization of an annual growth rate of 8.5 per cent in real terms, with agriculture growing faster than the rest of the economy in order to reduce inequalities, and achieve a balanced development. The realities are in sharp contrast. The economy stagnated over the three decades between 1960 and 1990. Average annual growth of GNP per person was a negative 0.2 per cent and agricultural GDP annual growth was between a negative 5 per cent and 0.6 per cent during most of the 1980s. This poor agricultural performance has held back national economic growth, owing to the high direct contribution of agricultural output to national economic growth (agriculture was responsible for nearly 36 per cent of total economic growth in the 1980s).

What is more, Sudan has failed to feed its own people from domestic production, in spite of being rich in land and water resources. During the 1980s nearly 40 per cent of Sudan's food consumption was imported and was mostly given as grants, amounting to an annual average of 400,000 tonnes.[1] The persistent neglect of the vast southern region with all its unrealized potential has contributed to food insecurity and economic instability. Also, income inequalities between regions and households have increased, as is shown by the results of household sample surveys of 1967/8 and 1978/9 and the nutrition survey (SERISS) conducted in 1986/7. All are incomplete surveys because they exclude the seven provinces of the southern region which have suffered from the long civil war. Estimates of absolute poverty suggest that its incidence is massive, ranging between 70 and 85 per cent.[2]

The nature and outcomes of a dual labour market in urban areas

Over the three decades between 1960 and 1990, the economy not only remained overwhelmingly agricultural, but the imbalance between the sectors of the economy worsened. The share of manufacturing in total output and employment continued to be minimal; between 4 and 7 per cent of total income and only 5 per cent of the total workforce, compared to an average of 75 per cent working in agriculture. One single primary commodity for export, cotton, has remained the backbone of the Sudanese economy.

In the non-agricultural (urban) sector, the development process has generated a two-subsector framework of investment, credit systems, employment conditions and wage differentials. The structure and operation of the urban labour market is divided into a better-off formal, organized and unionized subsector, on the one hand, and the informal or casual and unskilled workers' subsector, where poverty is concentrated, on the other. The latter has expanded because of the easy entry of impoverished rural migrants (petty street traders, garbage collectors, private guards, car-washers, shoeshine boys, construction workers, laundrywomen and domestic servants, and so on).

Results of labour surveys suggest rising income inequality resulting from the different sets of rules which govern the payment system. A statutory minimum wage linked to the cost of living index has been periodically revised and enforced in the government and public sectors, as well as in large private manufacturing firms. However, it has not been enforced in the numerous small family firms employing fewer than ten workers, or for insecure and legally unprotected workers in the swelling informal sector, particularly in the rapidly expanding construction business.[3]

The gulf between the two urban subsectors increased with the rapid rates of migration of the poor from rural to urban areas owing to: (a) floods, frequent droughts and famine; (b) the long civil war, uprooting many people and destroying the economic base of their lives; (c) loss of access to land and work caused by the rapid introduction of labour-saving technology in the modern sector and increasing encroachment of mechanized farms onto grazing areas (see the section below); (d) high wages in the urban formal sector; and (e) excessive land fragmentation into economically unviable units.

These five factors explain the high urban population growth of 1960–92 – an annual rate of 5.4 per cent, compared to 4.3 per cent for all developing countries and 4.5 per cent for the Middle East. Together with structural adjustment programmes, they explain also the 14 per cent rise in unemployment in the formal sector between 1983 and 1985. These contributory factors are identified in a sample survey of urban workers conducted in 1982 by a team of Sudanese and ILO experts. The results of the survey show that 61 per cent of the sampled households in the three large urban centres (Greater Khartoum, Port Sudan and Kenana) had an annual income below S£500 which was set as the poverty line (S£1 equalled US$0.76 in 1982).[4]

The poverty process in a dual agrarian structure

The present form of extreme imbalance within and between agriculture and other sectors of the economy is certainly not new. It can be traced back to investment and production patterns established during the British colonial administration (1889–1956). Since independence, national policies and state institutions have perpetuated and accentuated the division of the agrarian structure into two distinct sectors: the wealthy technology-based modern sector comprising large-scale irrigated schemes and mechanized rainfed farms, on the one hand, and the traditional sector where the mass of small farmers and pastoral nomads live and where recurrent famines have taken place, on the other.

With abundant labour and hand tools in the traditional sector, millet and sorghum are grown when rainfall permits. Gum (*arabica*) and live-stock are the primary products. In sharp contrast, the modern sector is capitalist, receiving most of the public investment and institutional credit, and producing tradables: cotton, sugar cane, beans and sorghum. During the 1970s, average public investment per working person in this sector was estimated at almost 40 times as much as investment in the traditional sector.[5] The linkages between the two sectors are largely the poor landless workers and the rich traders and money lenders. Employment linkage is seasonal and weak because of rainfall instability and the dominance of self-employed family labour in several irrigated schemes.

This striking dual structure is rooted in the establishment around 1910 of the Gezira scheme for irrigated cotton production. The modern sector was started south-east of Khartoum with capital provided by wealthy American and British businessmen in an area of 10,000 feddans (4,200 hectares) of fertile land granted by the British colonial administration. This grant was made profitable by the construction of Sennar Dam from public money. Encouraged by its profitability, the Khartoum central administration expanded the Gezira scheme very rapidly, reaching half a million feddans at the time of independence in 1956. The modern sector expanded further in two other forms. One was the Blue Nile pump irrigation scheme, whose area increased dramatically to become 32 times larger in 1956 to enable the production of cotton and sesame for export. The other was the tractor-based mechanization of rainfed lands in the Gadaref region for the production of sorghum, sesame and groundnuts (see Figure 5.1, map of Sudan). Importers of foreign irrigation pumps and tractors, together with a few big cotton growers, accumulated substantial profits at the expense of the disadvantaged nomadic population. Simpson (1987: 274–5) says: 'Some of these early pioneers had 20 units (600 feddans each), and had encroached on undemarcated land, including the corridors left for the passage of nomads and their animals.'

Since independence, this form of unbalanced development has become continual. Both the Gezira and pump schemes have been substantially enlarged in terms of the size of public investment and of the irrigated area. Likewise, the mechanized rainfed scheme has been extended immensely by state institutions into the lands traditionally held by tribes for grazing and growing cereals (when rainfall permits), mostly in Kasala and the southern districts of Kordofan and Darfur provinces. Consequently, an entire socio-ecological system has been disrupted. Rapid expansion of mechanized cultivation of dryland has proved to have three detrimental effects: (a) it has reduced the areas available for livestock production; (b) it has increased desertification, particularly through wind erosion; and importantly (c) it has displaced pastoral nomads and small subsistence farmers to areas with lower rainfall. Some have become hired workers in the modern sector and others have migrated to towns.

Government affluent behaviour: creation of vast inequalities

During my field study on Sudan's rural development strategy in 1972 and 1977, my interviews revealed that the majority of the enterprising rich in the mechanized rainfed farms were former government officials and members of the armed forces, urban merchants, private professionals (lawyers, teachers, accountants and medical doctors) and rich traders who were involved in joint ventures with multinational corporations. They had little, if any, experience in agriculture. Nor had they the experience and knowledge of management of capital-intensive farming business (the average size of holdings was 3,000 feddans).

I found hypocrisy and contradiction in the policy of the then Numeiri administration, which proclaimed itself to be socialist, caring for the poor and enlisting their participation in development. Between 1970 and 1980 the government's budget deficit was nearly 5 per cent of national income, Sudan had a balance of payments deficit of about US$430 million and a total foreign debt amounting to nearly US$3 billion. Yet the government behaved as if it were wealthy rather than the government of a country three-quarters of whose population were living in absolute poverty. State-owned land in units of 600–800 hectares was handed out to the lucky leaseholders of mechanized farms for a renewable period of twenty-five years. In most cases, the land had already been cleared of trees and bushes by public funds (costing on average S£10 per

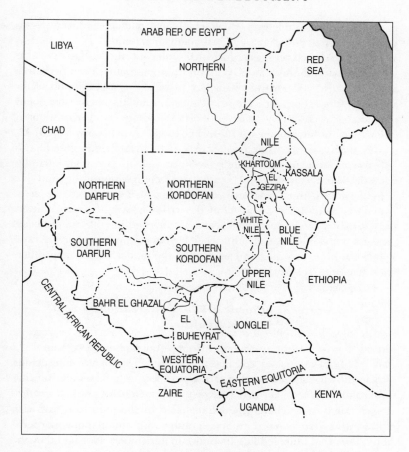

Figure 5.1 The Democratic Republic of the Sudan: regions and provinces
Source: IFAD, 1988

feddan) and the essential infrastructural facilities were in place. The landholders also had preferential access to subsidized credit from the government-owned Agricultural Credit Bank (e.g. about S£7,000 of subsidized credit to purchase a tractor, imported using scarce foreign exchange borrowed from abroad).

One would have expected the government of a debt-burdened poor country to eliminate all subsidies to such wealthy people, and to levy full charges for the means of production and costs of land clearance. Instead, I learned that the government agency (the Mechanized Farming Corporation) charged these wealthy people a very low rental value of only S£1 per feddan (half an American dollar at the parallel commercial rate in 1977). This low nominal value remained unchanged, despite rising inflation (16 per cent annually in 1970–80, jumping to 46 per cent in 1985–90), and the increased profit of producers from the high price of sorghum purchased by Saudi Arabia. Other examples of the Sudanese administration's extravagant behaviour were the generous concessions granted to the giant multinationals involved in the supply of tractors and their spare parts, in large-scale production of sorghum seeds, irrigated sugar cane and in fattening of sheep and cattle. Abdel-Karim (1988: 42) reports that a single corporation, Lonrho, was given the absolute monopoly power to import all capital goods, as well as to cultivate 82,000 acres (33,198 hectares) of sugar cane, and to manufacture sugar.

In the mean time, gross inequality of asset-ownership was created. State-owned fertile land was allotted to individual cultivators (permanent tenants) in units of 17 hectares each in the Gezira scheme, reduced to 6 hectares in the neighbouring Managil scheme, and reduced further to 4 hectares in irrigation-pump schemes in the Blue Nile province. As we have already noted, for the huge mechanized rainfed scheme the size of demarcated units (with subsidized credit for the purchase of a tractor) is 600–700 hectares. Whether through the corruption or the generosity of government, field studies show that wealthy absentee landholders managed to acquire from the government several demarcated units of 3,000 hectares and even 14,000 hectares each (ILO, 1984: 27). In contrast, a few of those pastoral households displaced by the scheme who were able to protest publicly were pacified by the allotment of 15 hectares each on average. Even so, it was found (El-Hassan, 1988: 165–73) that the land allotted in Southern Kordofan was of low quality, uncleared of trees and bushes, and situated in rocky hills. Also, these disadvantaged families were unable to borrow from the Agricultural Credit Bank, which had been originally established in 1956 to support small farmers. Instead, they had to borrow from local merchants, resulting in an extensive chronic indebtedness affecting three-quarters of the total households in Delami village and over one-third in Fayo village.

Available studies agree that poor peasants (fellaheen) in the traditional rainfed sector have no access to credit from banks, which concentrate on meeting the credit needs of large-scale farmers in mechanized dry-farming schemes.[6] They are deprived of opportunities for progress. They have no access to improved seeds, fertilizers, veterinary services for their livestock or jute sacks for marketing their small amount of surplus products. Hence the fellaheen's heavy reliance on the traditional system of linking credit with the sale of crops, an arrangement known as *sheil*. Their needs for cash credit are met by merciless merchants at interest rates of between 100 and 150 per cent. Alternatively, and in order to avoid charging interest payment in a conservative Muslim society, the shrewd *sheil* traders purchase crops at a price much lower than the market level, requiring the peasants to pledge their animals as collateral. A Sudanese economist, Ali (1986: 343), estimated that this transaction amounted to a payment of disguised interest at a rate ranging from 60 to 280 per cent. Thus, despite the polemics of Islamic fundamentalists in the central government, the prohibited usury (*riba*) is still practised. A comparison between the conditions of these poor peasants and the destitute masses in the southern region with those of the rich landholders in mechanized farms and the wealthy cotton-growers in the Gezira scheme provides a convincing demonstration of how government-created dualism leads to vast inequality of opportunity and persistent poverty.

Oil-based unbalanced development: Algeria, Iran and Libya

We now explore another form of unbalanced development, created by mismanagement of oil-based economies during and after the oil-boom period (1974–80). In this examination we study policy makers' responses both to the large oil windfall gains realized over the 1970s and to the subsequent slump during the post-1980 period.

Have these three oil-rich countries and their powerful central governments failed to seize the opportunity to diversify and balance the economy, and to improve the distribution of income? Which parts of the economy and which income classes have benefited most and which have been neglected and suffered severely? Do these countries' experiences show the undesirable symptoms of what has become known since the 1970s as the 'Dutch disease',[7] that is, the weakening of the agricultural and manufacturing-industry sectors associated with appreciation in the exchange rate and the resulting movement of resources to fast-growing sectors (e.g. construction) that can neither produce tradable commodities nor substitute for the loss of oil revenues during the slump period? From my assessment, readers may judge for themselves whether I have been ungrateful for the sudden affluence in describing the effects of oil windfalls as a disease or a social curse.

The three countries differ greatly in size of population, the size of their pre-oil-boom industrial bases and in the extent of their affluence. The 1994 population of Iran was 62 million, Algeria 27 million and Libya 5.2 million. Iran had a larger manufacturing base than Algeria and Libya, and has a large labour supply. On the other hand, Libya is capital-surplus and labour-scarce. Moreover, Iran witnessed economic and political instability during the second half of the 1970s, leading to the collapse of the Shah's regime, which was then followed by its long war with Iraq in the 1980s. Yet the three countries share common characteristics: dependence on oil and gas exports; state-controlled economies and centralized political power; and their populations are overwhelmingly rural. It would be interesting to find out whether and how the countries differ in their growth and equity outcomes, and whether or not their oil-based affluence has enabled their economies to perform better than such lower income countries as Egypt, Morocco, Syria, Tunisia, and Turkey.

Economic growth: an ill-conceived strategy

In broad terms, the declared objectives in the three countries' successive national development plans emphasize three common aims: the diversification of the economy away from its dependency on oil; the attainment of greater equalities; and the realization of food self-sufficiency. Nevertheless, empirical evidence suggests contrasting realities.

1   There was a deceleration in economic growth, compared to the pre-boom period. Libya and Iran fared worse: a sharp fall in national income (GDP) growth rate from 24.8 per cent per year before the oil boom (1960–70) to a negative 6.1 per cent during the subsequent slump period (1981–6) in Libya, and from 13 per cent to 3.4 per cent in Iran during the same period. For the three countries, economic growth was worse in terms of GNP per person, a negative 0.2 per cent per year, the weighted average of the three countries during the long period 1965–90 (see Table 5.1).

Table 5.1 Economic growth in Egypt, Morocco, Syria, Tunisia and Turkey compared to Algeria, Iran and Libya, 1965–90

| | *Average annual growth rate (%)* | | | | | |
	Egypt	Morocco	Syria	Tunisia	Turkey	Average for Algeria, Iran, Libya
GDP 1970–80	7.4	5.6	10.0	4.5	5.9	3.9
GDP 1980–8	5.7*	4.2	1.6	3.4	5.3	0.3
GNP per person 1965–90	4.1	2.3	2.9	3.2	2.6	−0.2

Sources: *World Development Report*, 1982, 1990 and 1992: Development Indicators (*World Bank*, 1978–96).

Notes
Average rates in the last column are weighted and calculated by the author.
*   See note 10 of this chapter.

2   There was premature contraction of the two non-oil sectors, agriculture and manufacturing, which employed most of the workforce and produced tradable goods and on whose growth long-term development depends. Both sectors lost their pre-boom position in the economy as the fast-growing non-oil-productive sectors. Instead, they have become the most backward sectors in the economy. The worst misallocation of resources during the oil boom was in Iran and Libya, where the combined shares of the two sectors in total public investment were 30–40 per cent less than those of construction and government administration, which are less productive, and do not produce tradables.[8]

3   The neglect of agriculture, particularly its food crops subsector, led to the countries' increasing dependence on food imports, especially wheat, to feed their own people. Between the pre-boom period (1969–71) and after (1988–90), the ratio of dependency doubled in Algeria, tripled in Iran and rose by 14 per cent in Libya.[9]

With its small population, Libya's falling growth rate of income per person is striking. This may have been caused by the population more than doubling (from 2 million to 4.5 million between 1965 and 1990) and the sharp fall in oil revenues in the 1980s, when oil and gas export revenues tumbled from the equivalent of US$23 billion in 1980 to only US$5 billion in 1986–7. In addition, the Libyan economy was severely weakened by the imposition of trade sanctions by the US government, together with the withdrawal of American oil companies from Libya, and by the excessive military expenditure required for the two-year Libyan war against Chad.

What is of developmental interest is that the economic growth of Algeria, Iran and Libya (also Saudi Arabia) was considerably outperformed by such lower-income economies as Egypt, Morocco, Syria, Tunisia and Turkey (see Table 5.1). Although both groups of countries have suffered from the world economic recessions in 1974–5 and 1981–3, rising real interest rates and the debt crisis in the 1980s, the economies of the group of five countries grew faster than those of the group of the three oil-rich economies during the same period.[10] Moreover, most of the slow economic growth in Algeria, Iran and Libya represents an increased production of a single primary commodity, petroleum, while it is an outcome of less unbalanced sectoral investment and growth in the other group of five countries. For instance, in Tunisia there is a very low deviation between growth rates of agriculture (4.2 per cent), manufacturing (6.0 per cent), and the average of total income, GDP (4.1 per cent) during the period 1980–5. Its relatively high and sustained growth rate of income per person over a quarter of a century (1965–90) is a result of this well-conceived development strategy, combined with an estimated low fertility rate of 3.6 in 1990 (compared to 6.7 in Libya, 5.1 in Algeria, 6.5 in Syria and 6.2 in Iran).[11] I shall have occasion in Chapters 6 and 10 to say more on these relationships.

Missed opportunity

Another aspect of resource mismanagement is that Algeria, Iran and Libya have failed to meet their common development goals, outlined earlier. In fact, they were more dependent both on food imports and on oil and gas export revenues in 1990/1 than before the oil boom. To understand this missed opportunity, we shall concentrate on the situation in Algeria and Iran, whose data are more detailed.

Despite Algeria's increasing emphasis on manufacturing industry and reducing dependency on oil in its five national plans during the period 1967–89, its share in total income (GDP) decreased from 15 per cent in 1970 to 10 per cent in 1991. The share of manufacturing goods in total exports declined from 7 to 2 per cent, while the share of petroleum increased from 73 to 97 per cent during the same period (*World Development Report* 1993 (World Bank, 1978–96)). In the meantime, the government nationalized almost all the industrial and financial sectors and assumed the major role in total capital accumulation, investment and credit supply. Through a series of *Plans Quinquennials*, most of the investments went to capital-intensive heavy industry (petroleum, iron and steel). Yet the annual growth rate of the giant public sector's industry dropped significantly, from 7.6 per cent before the boom in 1965–70 to a negative 1.1 per cent in 1981–8. Furthermore, available estimates suggest that labour productivity (output per worker) in this sector decreased substantially by an average 3.8 per cent yearly over the period 1967–84, worsening the distribution of income.[12]

In broad terms, a similar trend existed in Iran. From the start of the oil boom, not only did the importance of labour-intensive manufacturing in the Iranian economy diminish, but the greatest decline was in the manufacture of goods that are dependent on domestic resources and are consumed by low-income groups, for example cotton textiles, footwear, cheap furniture and sugar. In contrast, the production of heavily protected luxury goods, including television sets and the assembly of luxury cars, increased. Whereas the production of cotton textiles (which were greatly in demand) fell by one-quarter, the number of domestically manufactured private cars increased fourfold. In the mean time, the number of workers in the labour-intensive textile industry fell by one-third, while the factories were working at only 61 per cent of their productive capacity during this period of unprecedented affluence (1974–9).[13]

In sum, the three oil-rich countries have pursued ill-conceived policies in using the windfall gains from oil and gas revenues. The poor performance of these affluent economies and similar others has been of concern to several scholars from the region who regarded such sudden affluence as a source of destruction of the fundamental fabric of their societies. Two Arab economists offer some explanation for the lack of public concern about the adverse effects of the oil windfalls. Galal Amin (1974) views the effects in terms of a modernization of poverty. After examining the economic growth of Kuwait, Saudi Arabia, Iraq and Libya during the period 1961–70, he says (p. 14) that the failure to face their weaknesses has been covered up by the increase in oil revenues, which enriched many influential families. Yusif Sayigh (1990: xi) views this situation in terms of a deep crisis of short-sightedness in overproduction, depletion of oil resources and a lack of development-oriented leadership. He attributes the lack of concern in the region to the influence of those for whom the oil boom has opened the doors to financial opulence, in many instances on an astronomical scale.[14]

Effects on income distribution

The discussion turns now to examine how the type of unbalanced development analysed in the preceding section affects the distribution of income through two channels. The first is employment and the changing wage rates associated with the movement of labour from the declining to the booming sectors of the economy. The second channel is the windfall profits accruing to a few businessmen contracted by governments to undertake public works in the rapidly expanding construction sector.

Employment and wages

The experiences of Algeria, Iran and Libya suggest a steady rise in real wage income until around 1981, particularly in Libya, owing to its shortages in both skills and labour supply.[15] Under Algeria's socialist regime, nearly three-quarters of all employees were in the giant public sector, where rises in the statutory minimum wage rates and fringe benefits exceeded inflation rates until 1980. In the mean time, the overall average productivity (output per worker) dropped in 1981 across all sectors of the Algerian economy to half its level in 1969, i.e. before the oil boom.[16] One explanation is over-staffing in a command economy in which most economic activities are in the hands of government. It seems that the Algerian government preferred to sacrifice considerations of efficiency to a guaranteed expansion in jobs and increasing nominal earnings for the workforce, as a socialist means of spreading the benefits from the oil windfall. Be that as it may, Algeria's employment policy and land reforms (Chapter 9) contributed to improving living standards between 1968 and 1981. This improvement could not be sustained after the collapse of oil prices and in the face of an increasing foreign debt burden and a deteriorating economy (see Chapter 10). In fact, average per person income, in real terms, fell from US$2,230 in 1982 to US$1,840 in 1992, and the cost of living index doubled.

In contrast, Libya's employment policy after the downswing in oil revenues has had income effects that are more favourable than in Algeria. By keeping inflation below 1 per cent, capital-surplus Libya has been able to continue its generous policy on housing, social security, wage rates and salaries. This egalitarian approach has been made possible by its small population relative to the country's unprecedented affluence and the tiny size of the workforce. These peculiarities have given the labour market specific characteristics. Between 10 and 15 per cent of the workforce are foreigners, engaged in agriculture and construction as cheap labour from Egypt, Tunisia, Sudan, South Korea, the Philippines, Turkey and Palestine. Cheap foreign labour and interest-free loans from government-owned banks must have substantially increased the luxurious incomes of building contractors and landowners. The initial effect of government wage policy was the rapid migration of skilled labour from rural to urban centres. This rapid movement led the already small agricultural workforce to fall sharply by more than one-third between 1962 and 1980, which in turn led to the premature rise in part-time farming. By the late 1970s, it was estimated that 45 per cent of all landholders were part-timers, earning most of their income from unproductive but highly paid jobs in government and public enterprises.[17]

Construction profits

In Iran, between 1973 and 1981, the profits of building contractors and traders in manufactured building materials rocketed. A few rich families, including the Pahlavis (the royal family) managed to control the cement market, the manufacturing of which was protected and its price subsidized by 50 per cent. A black market was created whereby cement was sold at 5 times its official price.[18] The substantial windfall profits created by the urban construction boom have widened the income gap between rural and urban areas and between households within the cities. Three researchers analysed the results of the Iranian household surveys of 1971 and 1976 and agreed that the numbers of urban rich increased nearly fourfold between 1972 and 1976, and that most of the urban poor in 1976 were unskilled, illiterate, rural migrants working in construction and petty jobs in the informal sector.[19] The reader may recall from Chapter 3 that social unrest and violent confrontations with the Shah's regime occurred in cities during this period.

In Libya, too, construction profitability surpassed that of any other business and employment expanded by one-fifth over the initial period of the oil boom (1974–7). Construction and public works absorbed 27 per cent of total oil revenues and nearly 40 per cent of total public investment in the multi-million-pound land-settlement schemes. When oil windfalls increased, the government patronized a few businessmen who made fortunes from the construction boom.[20] On this point, Allan says: 'Substantial sums found their way into "kickbacks" and in other ways "stuck to the fingers" of those handling development funds' (1981: 131–2).

Summary

This chapter has examined the elements of two forms of unbalanced development, their economic growth and distributional outcomes; one in a poor economy, Sudan, and the other in three oil-rich countries, Algeria, Iran and Libya. It was concerned to understand the nature of inequality and the poverty process through a consideration of how government misallocation of oil windfalls has influenced the distribution of income in the three oil-based economies, both among the different sectors of the economy and between social classes. It is hoped that the reader has gained an insight into the realities of 'unbalanced development' from the discussion of the situation in specific countries.

The Sudanese story suggests how the state-led dualistic development process has primarily generated a two-sector framework, both in the urban labour market and in the structure of the vast agrarian sector. Yet there was profligate behaviour by government in its allocation of public funds, which have been steered towards the non-poor in the privileged modern sector. Likewise, the examination of the development performance of three oil-rich countries during and after the oil boom shows how state mismanagement of the large oil windfalls of 1974–80 has weakened the two non-oil-productive sectors (agriculture and manufacturing) in favour of construction, a rapidly expanding but less productive sector. Their development strategies have failed to diversify their economies or reduce inequalities and dependency on food imports. The oil-rich countries' growth and equity failure seems to have been hidden behind the veil of an intentional public unawareness and government handouts of oil money to many influential institutions and a few privileged individuals.

Suggested readings

On the meaning of unbalanced development:

Bhalla (1992) *Uneven Development in the Third World: A Study of China and India.*

Chenery (1979) *Structural Change and Development Policy*, especially the section on 'Balanced Development' in Chapter 1.

Chenery and Syrquin (1975) *Patterns of Development.*

Lipton (1977) *Why Poor People Stay Poor: Urban Bias in World Development*, especially Chapters 1, 2 and 3 viewing unbalanced development in terms of urban–rural bias instead of industrial–agricultural imbalance.

Stewart (1983) *Work, Income and Inequality*, especially her discussion of inequality in the distribution of income resulting from different payment systems in different sectors of the economy, presented in Chapters 1 and 12.

Streeten (1983) 'Development Dichotomies' examines different types of dualism in development.

For a perception of the results of unbalanced development in the Middle East:

G. Amin (1974) *The Modernization of Poverty: A Study of the Political Economy of Growth in Nine Arab Countries 1945–1970.*

Jazayeri (1988) *Economic Adjustment in Oil-Based Economies* discusses Iran.

Sayigh (1990) *Elusive Development: From Dependence to Self-Reliance in the Arab Region.*

On unbalanced development and the symptoms of the 'Dutch disease' in oil-based economies:

Corden (1984) 'Booming Sector and Dutch Disease Economics: Survey and Consolidation'.

Gelb and associates (1988) *Oil Windfalls: Blessing or Curse.* See the country study of Algeria in Chapter 10.

Several indicators of economic conditions in the Middle Eastern countries are clearly presented in:

Wilson (1995) *Economic Development in the Middle East.* See Chapter 4 for an excellent discussion on population growth and urbanization.

Additional readings can be found in notes and in the Bibliography.

6

SOCIAL IMBALANCE IN PUBLIC EXPENDITURE
Health, education and defence

The discussion now shifts from unbalanced development outcomes
brought about by government misallocation of physical capital investment to human capital, that is, the analysis of causes and results of
inadequate investment in people, the most valuable asset in a civil
society. My guiding proposition is that regardless of affluence levels,
the process of development requires a trained, healthy and adequately
nourished workforce. We need to keep in mind that both public and
private consumption/expenditure and the complementarities between
investment in physical capital and investment in human capital coalesce
in the realization of the principal objective of development: raising the
standard of living in order to eradicate hunger and poverty. Besides
being a provider of social services, including government administration
and defence, the state's economic role ranges from being a direct producer and regulator of the economy to being a distributor of income.
This chapter concentrates on the first role, namely the provision of
resources for health (including sanitation) and primary education, and
examines their order of priority relative to military spending.

The resource-allocation base

The issues of unbalanced development and social imbalance highlight
the importance of understanding how governments do or do not enable
poor people to acquire and expand their own fundamental capabilities:
literacy, longer life, adequate nutritional standard, freedom to seize
opportunities for remunerative employment, and so forth. As we
approach the year 2000, why do 70 children per 1,000 live births die
in the Middle East before reaching the age of 5, compared to 47 in Latin
America and 56 in East Asia? Why does the region still have about
80 million adults unable to read and write, while its governments spend
yearly about US$50 billion on military weapons?

No ordinary person can alone acquire basic human capabilities without public action for the provision of primary health, sanitation and education services. These are fundamental rights and must neither be left to the goodwill of government officials nor be class-biased. The poor are absolutely dependent on public services, not because they prefer government paternalism but simply because they cannot afford to acquire fundamental capabilities from the private sector.

Nevertheless, resources available to governments in the short run are not infinite. They cannot satisfy the needs of all sections of the population, or give equal consideration to everyone's well-being. There is a need to set increasingly stringent priorities in public spending, giving more consideration to the education and health of poor people and backward areas than to the rich and advanced localities. Therefore, in government budgeting as in private consumption, maintaining a balance between the necessary and the luxury components of expenditure is just as important as maintaining a balance between the sectors of the economy (discussed in Chapter 5). Failure to maintain an appropriate balance between the different demands for expenditure is likely to spread social tension and can result in social disorder. In fact, the co-existence of affluence and absolute poverty in the same society at the same time is a strong indication of social imbalance.

These issues of the origins and consequences of social imbalance are now more widely recognized through international forums and the adoption of universal but ambiguous plans of action. In March 1995 the haunting fear of the consequences of past policy failures was apparent in the statements made in Copenhagen at the Social Development Summit conference by governments and scholars, including those from the Middle Eastern countries. Several commitments made earlier in other international conferences have remained largely rhetorical.[1] Past experience has taught us that redressing social imbalance is not only the responsibility of governments, but also of those NGOs that represent the interests of the poor.

The term 'social imbalance' has a more ambiguous connotation than does 'unbalanced development' and is more difficult to analyse because of its several constituents and elements. My task is modest and practical. I view social imbalance as a process creating and perpetuating poverty and inequality of opportunity for social progress. Given each country's socioeconomic characteristics, I judge imbalance by the proportionate deviation of the actual from certain norms, that is, what is expected.

Because of its complexity, no single measurement could ever capture the range of social imbalance outcomes. One way is to judge them in terms of the mortality rates of children under age 5, undernourishment measures and illiteracy rates. Under-5 mortality represents an end result of a wide variety of factors, such as parent's income, mother's educational and nutritional status, access to sanitation, safe water and health services. The UN human development index (HDI) is also used here.[2] Though this is an arbitrary set of measurements, we can indirectly judge the contents of a country's development strategy and its priorities in resource allocation between necessary and luxury expenditure items. It is hoped that the use of these indicators will enable governments in both rich and poorer countries to identify those weaknesses and gaps in their statistics that are particularly needed to judge the scale of social imbalance, and to monitor progress made. One of these data weaknesses lies in the calculation of national income, in which investment in people is misrecorded as consumption and that aggregate (national) consumption is then obtained as a residual (GDP minus investment and net exports).

In this evaluative judgement, and aside from public investment in economic activities, the components of public expenditure are broken down into those that may be considered socially productive or non-productive. Socially productive or essential expenditures include health, education, sanitation and nutrition, which are viewed as non-consumptive human-capital formation (creating a skilled workforce and a literate and healthy population with a long life-expectancy). On the other hand, non-productive public consumption includes unnecessary military spending (beyond minimum security needs) and expenditure on excessive government administration beyond the needs for efficient delivery of essential public services and beyond the provision of internal security for citizens. This second category of public consumption also includes wasteful government expenditure on intelligence services, secret police and other forms of militarization provided for the protection of autocratic or undemocratic regimes and for the suppression of opposition. These non-productive activities compete for the use of limited resources, both domestic and foreign, including aid, and may lead to the sacrifice of resources urgently needed for the well-being of low-income groups, particularly the destitute.[3]

These concerns suggest the division of this chapter into three main sections. The first identifies the countries' priorities in public expenditure over the last three decades, and discusses their welfare implications. The second section makes an assessment of the outcomes. Against what one expects from information on country-specific characteristics, the adequacy or inadequacy of government allocations for human development purposes is assessed, using the comparable time-series data provided by the IMF,[4] supplemented by available information on government budgets. The third main section of the chapter concentrates on a case study of social imbalance in Iraq during the long period 1950–95. In this section, the role of militarism in public consumption is examined and the catastrophic outcomes are assessed.

Distorted priorities

The share of each country's public consumption in national income reflects its own government's preferences and the role of the state in development. The share differs by the extent to which a clear distinction is made between public and private consumption, especially in the several Gulf states in which the separation between the jurisdiction of a single family and government has been difficult. In examining these differences between countries, we need to answer the question of whether affluence alone brings about rapid achievement in human development.

Figures 6.1 and 6.2 and Table 6.1 show diverging trends in expansion of public consumption during the period 1960–90 according to different countries' affluence levels. The data show also that, with the exception of Kuwait, wealthy nations with their small populations were able to maintain higher proportions of their sizeable national incomes for public consumption in the 1970s and the 1980s than most of the poorer countries. Although there is a considerable controversy surrounding the relationship between public consumption expenditure and economic growth (GDP), one would expect that in the short run, say ten years, the annual rate of expansion of the former should not exceed that of the latter, in order to permit national savings and investment expansion. Countries' experiences show that in 1980–91, Israel, Syria, Tunisia, Turkey, Iran and Egypt succeeded in this respect.[5] While the proportion of total public consumption expenditure to national income presented in Table 6.1 is useful in inter-country comparison it is more important in a study of the variations in human well-being caused by affluence level to investigate how rich and poor nations have used their resources to enhance the capabilities of their people in general, and to reduce deprivation in particular. Table 6.2 helps us to understand the differnt countries' varying priorities in our three areas of public concern (health, education and defence), expressed in terms of percentages of both total expenditure and national income (GNP).

Affluence and priority concerns

The set of data given in Table 6.2 suggests two broad features of priority concerns. First, in most countries of the region, governments have progressively devoted more resources to education than to health. Second,

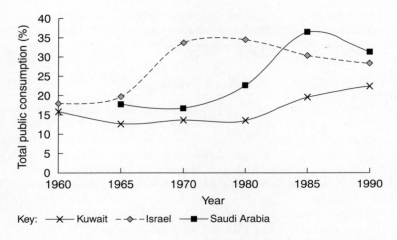

Figure 6.1 Public consumption as a percentage of national income (GDP) in three countries with an annual average national income per person in 1991 over US$5,000

Source: See Table 6.1.

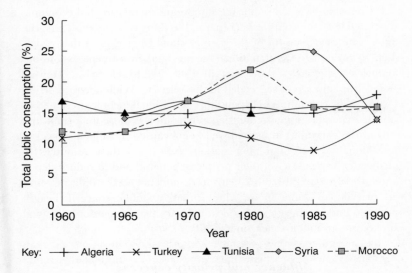

Figure 6.2 Public consumption as a percentage of national income (GDP) in five countries with an annual average national income per person in 1991 of US$1,000–5,000

Source: See Table 6.1.

Table 6.1 Public consumption and domestic investment as a percentage of national income (GDP) in seventeen countries, 1960–91

Countries	Total public consumption (%)						Gross domestic investment (%)			
	1960	1965	1970	1980	1985	1990	1960	1970	1980	1991
Over US$5,000										
UAE	n.a.	n.a.	13	10	17	19	n.a.	n.a.	28	22
Kuwait[a]	16	13	14	14	20	23	n.a.	12	17	19
Israel	18	20	34	35	31	29	26	27	22	23
Saudi Arabia[a]	n.a.	18	17	23	37	32	n.a.	16	26	21
Oman[b]	n.a.	n.a.	13	24	n.a.	32	n.a.	14	22	17
Libya	n.a.	14	18	23	24	n.a.	43	17	32	n.a.
US$1,000–5,000										
Iraq	18	20	21	n.a.	29	30	20	16	33	26
Iran	10	13	16	n.a.	n.a.	11	17	19	n.a.	20
Algeria	15	15	15	16[c]	15	18	42	36	37	28
Turkey	11	12	13	11	9	14	18	23	27	20
Tunisia	17	15	17	15	16	16	27	20	28	26
Syria	n.a.	14	17	22	25	14	n.a.	14	25	10
Jordan	28	34	n.a.	30	24	24	n.a.	n.a.	21	32
Morocco	12	12	17	22	16	16	10	18	21	22
Under US$1,000										
Egypt	17	19	25	19	17	14	13	20	31	23
Sudan	8	12	n.a.	12	11	14	9	14	12	n.a.
Mauritania	n.a.	19	n.a.	39	15	10	n.a.	22	n.a.	16

Sources: World Bank files and UN *Statistical Yearbook*. Iraq and Egypt 1985 and 1990 are calculated from ESCWA (1994b).

Notes
n.a. = not available.
Insufficient data are available for Bahrain, Lebanon, Qatar and Yemen.
Countries are presented in descending order of their average annual income per person in 1991 as given in Table 4.1 of this book.
a Data are for 1989, not 1990 and 1991, because of the Gulf War.
b Data for public consumption refer to 1991, not 1990.
c Data are for 1983.
The World Bank defines public consumption as general government consumption comprising all current expenditure and capital expenditure, including government administration and defence.

in budgeting public funds since 1960, most governments have consistently given military spending higher priority than education and health combined. These two striking manifestations of social imbalance require closer examination both at regional and country levels.

Militarization in the Middle East has been a prominent characteristic, in terms of its share of total imports, of public expenditure and of national income, compared to the shares of health and education.

Thus, in the name of the narrow meaning of 'security', governments of rich and poor countries alike tend to devote more foreign exchange and domestic resources to military purposes than to human security against illness, disease, malnutrition and illiteracy, which are still pervasive. Of the thirteen countries for which data are available, ten countries' imports of arms as a percentage of total imports exceeded the 3.1 per cent average of developing countries as a whole, reaching the high level of 48 per cent in Iraq, 29 per cent in Syria and 15 per cent in Yemen.[6]

The supremacy of military spending over health and education has reached an overwhelming scale. In a region where nearly 80 million adults are illiterate, and in which ten countries have infant mortality rates above the average of 50 per 1,000, governments in 1986–91 spent an annual average of US$52 billion on defence, compared to US$26 billion on education and US$10 billion on health.[7] This means that military spending was 1.4 times that of expenditure on health and education combined and 5 times larger than expenditure on health. To further illustrate this point, in 1990 Saudi Arabia spent about US$200,000 per person on its armed forces. This average is higher than the USA (US$130,000) and is 12 times the public spending on education per person, although nearly 40 per cent of Saudi men and 60 per cent of women are illiterate. I roughly estimate that in 1981–90 a total amount of US$171 billion was transferred from Saudi Arabia to the arms manufacturers in the USA and Europe through intermediaries (the annual average is US$17.1 billion, according to the Stockholm International Peace Research Institute).

With regard to the distribution of total public expenditure, Table 6.2 shows three rich countries (Oman, Saudi Arabia and United Arab Emirates) spending nearly half of that total on defence, and Israel spending 40 per cent in 1960 and 1980. Likewise, other countries in lower-income categories allocated to military purposes, on average, very high portions of public funds: Syria 37.0 per cent and Yemen 33.2 per cent during the same period. It should be noted that Israel, like Egypt, is not only a big arms importer but also a manufacturer and exporter of weapons. While it is debatable whether rich countries can afford to devote a high proportion of their huge national incomes to defence, it cannot be justified on human development grounds. This is particularly true in such poor nations as Yemen, where there is no obvious external threat to security and territorial integrity. For example, the government of Yemen, which is among the world's poorest countries, spent more on military establishments in 1980 and 1991 than on its people's education and health. In 1991 Yemen spent about US$11,600 per person on the privileged armed forces, compared to a meagre US$5 for health services per inhabitant.

Table 6.2 Shares of health, education and military spending in national income and total government expenditure in eighteen countries, 1960–91

Countries[a]	Health, education and military spending as a percentage of:																		Ratio of military spending to health and education combined		
	Total public expenditure									National income (GNP)											
	Health			Education			Military			Health			Education			Military					
	1972	1980	1991	1972	1980	1991	1960	1980	1991	1960	1980	1991	1960	1980	1991	1960	1980	1991	1960	1980	1991
Over US$5,000																					
UAE	4.5	7.5	6.7	16.0	11.3	14.2	24.5	47.5	44.0	n.a.	0.8	1.9	n.a.	1.1	2.9	n.a.	6.2	8.3	n.a.	310	173
Kuwait[b]	5.5	4.9	7.4	15.0	9.0	14.0	8.4	12.2	25.4	n.a.	0.5	2.9	n.a.	1.0	3.4	n.a.	2.9	6.5	n.a	193	123
Israel[b]	3.5	3.6	3.7	9.0	9.9	10.0	39.0	39.8	25.4	1.0	2.8	2.1	2.4	3.4	3.9	6.9	25.0	13.0	203	403	217
Saudi Arabia	n.a.	n.a.	n.a.	n.a.	n.a.	17.8	n.a.	50.0	43.0	0.6	3.6	3.1	3.2	5.0	6.2	5.7	16.6	14.0	150	193	151
Oman	5.9	2.9	5.4	3.7	4.8	11.4	39.3	51.2	35.4	n.a.	0.7	2.1	n.a.	1.2	3.5	n.a.	13.0	16.4	n.a.	684	293
Libya	n.a.	8.0	n.a.	n.a.	18.0	n.a.	n.a.	n.a.	n.a.	1.3	1.4	3.0	2.8	3.8	8.0	1.2	8.1	7.8	24	156	65
US$1,000–5,000																					
Iraq[b]	n.a.	n.a.	n.a.	n.a.	n.a.	n.a.	n.a.	n.a.	n.a.	1.0	n.a.	0.8	5.8	5.0	4.6	8.7	29.7	16.0	128	550	271
Iran[b]	3.6	6.4	7.9	10.4	21.3	22.4	24.1	15.9	10.3	0.8	3.0	1.5	2.4	5.2	4.1	4.5	20.1	2.1	141	245	38
Algeria	n.a.	n.a.	n.a.	n.a.	n.a.	n.a.	n.a.	n.a.	n.a.	1.2	1.2	5.4	5.0	4.9	9.1	2.1	2.0	1.6	31	43	15
Turkey	3.3	3.6	3.0	18.2	14.2	17.6	15.4	15.2	10.4	0.8	2.0	1.5	2.6	2.8	2.5	5.2	3.8	6.0	159	79	111
Tunisia	7.4	6.5	6.3	30.5	15.5	17.5	4.9	11.1	5.6	1.6	2.5	3.3	3.3	5.6	6.1	2.2	3.9	2.9	45	48	31
Syria	1.4	0.8	1.9	11.0	5.5	7.4	37.0	47.7	31.5	0.4	0.5	0.4	2.1	6.8	4.1	7.9	17.3	16.8	316	243	373
Jordan	n.a.	3.7	5.0	n.a.	7.3	14.0	n.a.	25.5	27.0	0.6	1.7	1.8	3.0	6.3	5.9	16.5	13.1	10.6	464	164	138
Morocco	3.0	3.4	3.0	19.2	17.2	18.0	12.3	17.9	13.0	1.0	1.1	0.9	3.1	7.0	5.5	2.0	6.1	4.6	49	76	72

Under US$1,000

Egypt	n.a.	2.4	2.8	n.a.	8.0	13.4	24.1	11.4	12.7	0.6	0.5	1.0	4.1	9.0	6.1	5.5	3.0	4.0	117	32	52
Sudan	5.4	1.4	n.a.	9.3	9.6	n.a.	24.0	12.9	n.a.	1.0	0.3	0.2	1.9	2.6	4.0	1.5	2.8	4.0	51	96	95
Yemen	3.6	n.a.	n.a.	4.0	n.a.	n.a.	32.6	33.2	n.a.	n.a.	2.1	1.5	n.a.	8.2	5.8	n.a.	15.0	14.4	n.a.	146	197
Mauritania	n.a.	n.a.	4.0	0.5	n.a.	n.a.	n.a.	n.a.	n.a.	0.5	1.2	2.0	2.1	4.1	4.7	4.1	9.9	4.1	n.a.	187	61

Sources: *World Development Report* 1983, 1984, 1993: Indicators (World Bank, 1978–96). *Human Development Report* 1994: Human Development Indicators, Table 21 (UNDP, 1991–6). *World Military and Social Expenditure* 1993: Table 11 (Sivard 1983, 1985, 1993). Wulf (1991). UNDP and Word Bank (1992). Libya, health and education spending as a percentage of total government expenditure for 1980 is estimated from data in EIU (1991).

Notes

n.a. = not available.

Insufficient data are available for Bahrain, Lebanon and Qatar.

a Countries in descending order of their average annual income per person, 1991, given in Table 4.1 of this book. Data for 1991 refer to 1990 or 1991.

b Data refer to 1982 and 1989, not 1980 and 1991. Iraq's data on military spending (1980) refer to average 1980–5.

This indication of a highly unbalanced allocation of public money in both the richest and poorest countries of the region is in contrast with that of Tunisia, a middle-income country whose average income per person in 1991 was only one-tenth that of Saudi Arabia. After independence in 1962, Tunisia allocated in the early 1970s the highest percentage of total public expenditure in the region to education (30.5 per cent) and health (7.4 per cent) and the least to defence (4.9 per cent). This order of priority has, since then, been consistently sustained, both in terms of shares in total public spending and in national income (see Table 6.2 and Chapter 10). One wonders whether the millions of people in countries with high military expenditure who are sick and illiterate or the parents who have lost their children before they reached the age of 5, feel secure because of their governments' lavish military spending. Or do they nevertheless feel insecure after what happened during the 1991 Gulf War, when the oil-rich, ultra-military-spending states were saved only by foreign forces from the devastating consequences of the Iraqi invasion?

Outcomes and estimates of imbalance

Many development observers would agree that since the 1960s there has been substantial progress in improving the quality of life in the Middle East. Would they also agree that there has been a high social loss incurred by lowering the priority in public spending from health and education in favour of the military establishment, despite the region's population having more than doubled over the last thirty years?

While the differences in levels of public spending are helpful for inter-country comparisons, we should acknowledge other important determinants. One is the efficient and unbiased management of public institutions such as hospitals, clinics and schools. Another factor is the variations in effective access of the poor to health clinics, primary health care, medicine, safe drinking water and primary education. A third factor is the different share of philanthropic institutions and profit-oriented private services in the total health and education services in each country at a given time. I shall have occasion in Chapter 10 to discuss the present tendency among the World Bank, the IMF and foreign donors to pressurize governments into enhancing the private sector's involvement in the provision of education and health services at market fees that are unaffordable by the poor.

Pervasive illiteracy

Why does illiteracy remain pervasive in most Middle Eastern countries? One explanation given in Chapter 2 is that it is the result of a deeply rooted policy of educational discrimination pursued during colonial rule. But Table 6.3 shows that illiteracy is also high in an uncolonized and oil-rich country, Iran, even higher in 1991 than the weighted average of 35

Table 6.3 Some education indicators and real income per person in eighteen Middle Eastern countries, 1990/1

Countries ranked in descending order of GNP per person (1991)	International $	Adult illiteracy age 15 and over and ranking		Primary education estimated dropout rates	Average years of schooling	
		Total %	Female %	%	Male	Female
Kuwait	16,150 (1989)	27 (4)	33	10	6	4.7
Israel	11,950	10 (1)	9	n.a.	11	9.0
Saudi Arabia	7,820	38 (9)	52	10	6.0	1.5
Oman	6,120	55 (14)	n.a.	9	1.0	0.3
Bahrain	7,130	33 (5)	31	3	3.9	3.2
Libya	5,310 (1989)	36 (7)	n.a.	n.a.	5.5	1.3
Iran	2,170	46 (11)	57	11	5.5	1.3
Algeria	1,980	43 (10)	55	12	4.4	0.3
Turkey	1,780	19 (2)	29	4	4.7	2.3
Palestine (Occupied Territories)	1,700	40	n.a.	n.a.	n.a.	n.a.
Tunisia	1,500	35 (6)	44	20	3.0	1.2
Syria	1,160	36 (7)	49	12	5.2	3.1
Jordan	1,050	20 (3)	30	16	6.0	4.0
Morocco	1,030	51 (12)	66	37	4.1	1.5
Egypt	610	52 (13)	66	5	4.0	1.6
Yemen	520	62 (15)	74	26	1.3	0.2
Mauritania	510	66 (16)	79	32	0.5	0.1
Sudan	a	66 (16)	79	32	0.5	0.1
Weighted average[b] Middle East excluding Israel		45	57	16	3.6	1.7
All developing countries		35	46	31	4.6	2.7

Sources: *World Development Report* 1991, 1993 (World Bank, 1978–96) and *Human Development Report* 1993 (UNDP 1991–6). Oman's total illiteracy is taken from IFAD (1990: 45). Data on Palestine (Occupied Territories) are from World Bank (1993a: vol. 1, Box 2.4). The estimates of per person GNP and illiteracy refer to 1991 for the Occupied Territories.

Notes
n.a. = not available.
No available data on GNP per person for Iraq, Lebanon and Qatar.
a GNP per person in Sudan is not included in the sources cited above. It ranges from US$550 to US$600.
b Weighted by size of population. Dropout rates are calculated from UNESCO data on enrolment in first grade and completion of primary education.

per cent for all developing countries. Illiteracy is still high despite countries' post-independence development plans that have always emphasized equality of educational opportunity and the provision of free, compulsory public primary schooling. At the 1990 UNESCO conference governments committed themselves to eradicate illiteracy by the year 2000. Yet there are still nearly 80 million illiterate adults, representing one-quarter of the total population of the Middle East.[8] Table 6.3 also shows that only four countries have managed to reduce illiteracy rates below 35 per cent. It gives the average rate in all developing countries and shows that illiteracy in eleven countries exceeds that average, while in five of them it exceeds 50 per cent. Furthermore, it is striking that these include oil-rich states (Saudi Arabia, Libya, Iran and Oman).

One would have expected that the greater the country's affluence, the lower would be its illiteracy rates, because rich countries have sufficient resources to ensure literacy for everybody. Empirical evidence suggests that the causal connection is not straightforward. Is this complex connection a combination of the quality of primary education with government spending priorities between primary and post-secondary education levels? The unbalanced priorities in public spending within the educational system are manifested in the fact that in the Middle East between 1965 and 1990 enrolment in primary schools increased by only 29 per cent, while it rose sharply by 400 per cent in universities and other higher education institutions. Country data also show a connection between the inferior quality of public primary education and the dropout rates among children of low-income and illiterate parents with large numbers of children. The mother's educational level is an influential factor: both dropout and mortality rates are high among children of illiterate mothers.[9] These factors that disadvantage the poor – even if education is free – are reflected in the data given in Table 6.4. The data suggest an inverse relation between rates of illiteracy and average years of schooling, particularly those of adult females. The ten countries with high adult female illiteracy (over 40 per cent) have the lowest number of schooling years (between 0.1 and 1.6 years).

This alarming situation of low quality public primary education and high dropout rates has been studied by UNESCO in fifteen Arab states. The results show that in nine countries, nearly one-fifth of the children enrolled in the first grade between 1981 and 1984 left school before reaching the sixth grade.[10] In most cases, classes were overcrowded, teachers were poorly paid and their absenteeism was frequent as they searched for supplementary earnings. One dimension of inequality of educational opportunity is revealed by enrolment in private pre-primary (for children aged 3–5 or 4–6) and primary schools, whose tuition fees

SOCIAL IMBALANCE IN PUBLIC EXPENDITURE

Table 6.4 Selected indicators of quality of life in nineteen countries by their income levels, 1960–92

Countries and their income rank[a]	Deaths of children under 5 (per 1,000 live births and rank)		Average annual rate of reduction of mortality (% and rank)	Life expectancy at birth (years and rank)	Adult illiteracy (% and rank)	Human Development Index and rank
	1960	1991	1960–91	1991	1991	1992
1 UAE	239	29 (4)	8.1 (3)	71 (3)	45 (11)	0.771 (4)
2 Kuwait	128	17 (2)	7.8 (4)	75 (2)	27 (4)	0.809 (2)
3 Israel[b]	39	12 (1)	4.6 (12)	76 (1)	5 (1)	0.900 (1)
4 Saudi Arabia	292	43 (6)	7.4 (5)	69 (4)	38 (8)	0.742 (5)
5 Bahrain	208	18 (3)	9.3 (1)	69 (4)	33 (5)	0.791 (3)
6 Oman	378	42 (5)	8.4 (2)	69 (4)	65 (16)	0.654 (11)
7 Libya	269	108 (15)	3.6 (13)	63 (8)	36 (7)	0.703 (8)
8 Iraq	171	80 (13)	3.3 (16)	65 (7)	40 (9)	0.614 (13)
9 Iran	233	62 (12)	5.2 (10)	65 (7)	46 (12)	0.672 (10)
10 Algeria	243	61 (11)	5.4 (8)	66 (6)	43 (10)	0.553 (14)
11 Turkey	216	89 (14)	3.5 (14)	71 (3)	19 (2)	0.739 (6)
12 Tunisia	254	58 (9)	5.7 (7)	67 (5)	35 (6)	0.690 (9)
13 Syria	217	47 (8)	5.9 (6)	67 (5)	36 (7)	0.727 (7)
14 Jordan	180	46 (7)	5.3 (9)	69 (4)	20 (3)	0.628 (12)
15 Morocco	216	89 (14)	3.4 (15)	63 (8)	51 (13)	0.549 (16)
16 Egypt	260	60 (10)	5.0 (11)	61 (9)	52 (14)	0.551 (15)
17 Sudan	292	169 (16)	2.2 (18)	51 (11)	66 (17)	0.276 (18)
18 Yemen	378	182 (17)	2.8 (17)	52 (10)	62 (15)	0.323 (17)
19 Mauritania	321	209 (18)	1.7 (19)	47 (12)	66 (17)	0.254 (19)
Regional average	238	79	5	65	40	0.637

Sources: *The State of the World's Children* 1993 (UNICEF, 1993–6), *Human Development Report* 1994 (UNDP 1991–6) and Table 6.3.

Notes

Figures in parentheses refer to the ranking order. Countries with the same value of indicators are ranked the same.

There are no available data on the indicators for Lebanon and Qatar during this period.

a Countries are ranked by average income per person in 1991, given in Table 4.1 of this book.

b See p. 102 for an explanation of Israel's low rank in under 5 mortality reduction.

are prohibitive for poor parents, but whose quality of education is superior to that of the government-subsidized public schools where tuition is free. Between 1970 and 1990 expansion in enrolment in private schools, both pre-primary and primary, was rapid, and the rate of growth accelerated after economic reforms.[11]

These key features of deterioration in primary public schools demonstrate a great deal of wasted resources and a substantial loss of potential talent, particularly among bright poor children in rural areas and in city slums, where government primary schools are of poor quality. By denying these schools essential current and capital expenditure, the system is failing too many poor children, many of whom can barely read and write by the age of 11 or 12. They tend to remain at the bottom of the income hierarchy.

Poorer countries but better performers in human development

Table 6.4 shows that the top four countries, ranked by income, namely the United Arab Emirates, Kuwait, Israel and Saudi Arabia, are not always the top four in health, education and in the index of human development (HDI). But of this rich group, only Kuwait and Israel, whose populations are small, were also at the top in life expectancy and HDI and in reducing the absolute level of child mortality in 1991. Considering that its first hospital was only built in 1949 and that it started the period under review (1960–91) with a higher number of deaths per 1,000 live births than Israel (128 in Kuwait compared to 39 in Israel) total percentage reduction in Kuwait was higher than in Israel. From this initial vast difference, the annual rate of reduction in child mortality in Kuwait has been faster than that of Israel, namely a reduction of 7.8 per cent and 4.6 per cent, respectively. The worst performer in the richest group is Saudi Arabia: it ranks eighth in adult illiteracy, sixth in child mortality and fifth in HDI.

Among the bottom four countries in terms of income ranking (Egypt, Sudan, Yemen and Mauritania) there is also a divergence. The poorest three are also the worst performers in mortality levels, life expectancy and HDI. However, heavily populated Egypt differs; the ranking of all its human development indicators is superior to its income rank of 16. In terms of these indicators, Egypt is better than such richer countries as Oman (for illiteracy) and Libya (for mortality reduction). Likewise, among the intermediate-income group, the level of life expectancy in Jordan is the same as that in the three rich countries (Saudi Arabia, Bahrain and Oman). Turkey's public spending on health and education combined was higher than its military spending in 1980 and 1990, bringing about the third-best level of life expectancy, the second-best in reducing illiteracy and an advanced rank of HDI compared to its eleventh rank in income. Thus, if there is anything to be learned from these countries' experience it is that affluence alone does not bring about rapid achievement. Nor can government spending alone explain all the variations in people's health and education. What matters most in translating affluence into a healthy, literate and longer life is the efficiency in, and class-unbiased management of, services as well as consistency in public spending priorities in each country's development plan and budget.

The right-hand column of Table 6.1 shows that while gross investment rates fell in 1991/2 almost everywhere, due largely to world recession and low rates of savings while maintaining high rates of consumption, several middle-income countries that are good performers in human development had in 1970 and 1980 investment rates higher than those of several rich countries (Kuwait, Saudi Arabia and Oman). In a sense, these countries' experience has not fully complied with the conventional wisdom in economics, which is that poorer countries' high public expenditure on social development (investment in people) is at the expense of national savings and investments that are necessary to generate faster economic growth.

Estimating social imbalance

We now have an idea of Middle Eastern countries' varying priorities in the allocation of public resources to health and education, compared to defence and the consequences thereof. In this section the IMF estimates of the extent of the adequacy or inadequacy of these allocations are used. These were calculated by comparing the actual expenditure share of each expenditure area in national income during 1975–86 with its expected share, given each country's socioeconomic characteristics. This kind of estimation implies a judgement of both policies and priority shifts. Nevertheless, and despite being controversial and tentative, the IMF's inter-country comparison method is used below.[12] It differs from an evaluation of a specific human development programme with regard to the beneficiaries among income classes.[13]

The calculated ratio of actual to expected levels multiplied by 100 produces an index for inter-country comparison; above 100 means the country is spending too much and below 100 indicates lower spending than one would expect.[14] The expected (or predicted) level is estimated by way of the IMF's sophisticated statistical techniques employing values of several factors assumed to influence both the levels of allocations and the shifts between health, education and defence between 1975 and 1986. These factors are summarized as follows:

1   the country's level of development in terms of average income per person, the scale of urbanization, and size of the foreign debt;
2   population size, growth rate and age structure;
3   social factors such as infant mortality, population per 1,000 physicians, access to safe drinking water and the enrolment ratio of children in primary schools;

4   the country's sources of total revenue, official reserve and budget-
     ary deficits.

These factors are quantifiable, interconnected and, in some cases, overlapping. Moreover, because of incomplete data on the required statistical
indicators, only fourteen countries out of the total eighteen presented in
Tables 6.2 and 6.3 are covered by the IMF study. Algeria, Iraq, Iran,
Libya and Saudi Arabia are excluded. The results show a striking neglect
of the two human priority areas, health and education. Of the Middle
Eastern countries studied, 60 per cent have indicators far below 100,
which means that their government allocations to health and education
are highly inadequate, according to their socioeconomic characteristics.
These countries comprise rich Oman and two poor countries, Sudan and
Mauritania. Alarmingly, the average index for health in the Middle East
– where a large number of oil-rich countries are concentrated – is much
lower than the average of all developing countries during the same
period (1978–86), which was at 89 compared to their 102. At the
regional level, the average index of Middle Eastern government expenditure on education is slightly above that of all developing countries, 105
compared to 102. Probably this slight advantage is due to the influence
of the good education indicators of Israel and Turkey on the regional
average index.

With regard to military spending, the regional index rose sharply from
100 in 1975–7 to 223 in 1978–80, standing at more than double the
military spending index of all developing countries. On average, nearly
80 per cent of the Middle Eastern countries recorded an excessive
military spending, and the index is over 100 during the longer period
1975–86. These include two rich countries, the UAE and Kuwait, and
two poor countries, Yemen and Egypt. These dismaying statistics point
to the conclusion that many of the poorer countries spent on defence
almost 200 per cent more than the expected level and between 30 and 70
per cent less on health than would have been predicted from their own
socioeconomic characteristics.

We now move from this general comparison to an examination of a
specific situation of social imbalance and its welfare impact: the experience of Iraq during the long period from 1950 to 1994.

Militarism and social imbalance: the case of Iraq

By militarism is meant the form of state management that has three
specific features: large-scale military expenditure, rapid bureaucratic
expansion, and an authoritarian system of decision making.[15] After

destroying the power of their potential challengers, a small group of military officers mobilize resources for military purposes simultaneously with rapid modernization and human development efforts.

Iraq is endowed with large reserves of oil, natural gas, sulphur and phosphates. It also has abundant cultivable land and water resources, and is not over-populated. Yet in 1958, Iraq was poor and underdeveloped. Despite the rapid increase in its oil and gas revenues, from 5 per cent of national income in 1950 to 28 per cent in 1958, the benefits of economic growth and government expenditure were disproportionately captured by a few semi-feudal tribal chiefs and their estate managers (*sirkals*), rich city merchants and foreign businessmen. The 1947 and 1957 population censuses showed high adult illiteracy (90 and 85 per cent respectively). Life expectancy at birth was very low at only 44 years, and around 1958 the national average of infant deaths was as high as 140 per 1,000 live births and about 350 per 1,000 in rural areas. In 1956, Fenelon, the government's Director of Statistics, estimated the national income for 1950–6, indicating that, in real terms, the average annual income per person was 30 Iraqi dinars (ID) rising with the oil contribution to 51 ID (about US$96 and US$163 respectively).[16] Despite the small population of 6 million, land- and water-rich Iraq could not sustain itself; the daily calorie supply per person was only between 77 and 83 per cent of requirements.[17]

The oil boom: from poverty to affluence, 1958–80

Militarism in Iraq dates from Brigadier Abdul-Karim Qassim's bloody *coup d'état* in July 1958. It overthrew the monarchy, murdered the senior male members of the royal family together with leading politicians, introduced a series of radical land reforms in 1958 and 1972, and confiscated, without compensation, all properties of former senior officials. The military regime also nationalized foreign-owned companies, including the two giant oil companies, bringing the oil revenues, 40 per cent of national income, under the grip of the military regime. In terms of the Gini index (see Appendix 8.1), these redistributive measures rapidly reduced the vast inequality in wealth and income distribution: landholding from 0.902 in 1958 to 0.394 in 1982 and personal income distribution from 0.630 in 1972 to a greater degree of equality in 1979 at 0.220.[18]

This abrupt institutional transformation towards 'Arab socialism' was fierce indeed. During that period, I witnessed the brutality of the military rulers as they dragged the mutilated bodies of the King, the Crown Prince and the Prime Minister through the streets and left them hanging to rot in Baghdad's main square. I witnessed also the introduction of egalitarian policy measures in which I was a participant in an advisory capacity. Uncertainty and political instability were manifested in three *coups d'état* and eighteen cabinet changes during the 1960s; each espoused a different ideological base for state control over the economy.

Under these circumstances, development planning lost its meaning and momentum. For example, the bulletins of the Central Bank of Iraq indicate that in 1959–65 only half the planned public investments were actually implemented, after a long time lag. A telling example is given by Jalal (1972: 78–9). He reports that in 1958 a state-owned industrial project costing 6.7 million ID (US$21.4 million) was prepared by, and its contract awarded to, an American firm. After construction had started, the military *coup* of the same year cancelled the contract and the military rulers decided to include it in the Iraqi–Soviet cooperation programme concluded in 1959. While construction was in progress, the new military leaders of the 1964 *coup* withdrew the project, arranged for a new study, and in January 1965 the original American firm was awarded the contract for exactly the same project that had been designed in 1958, but at an additional 12 per cent of its original costings. This example shows the loss to the economy of seven years' output, employment earnings and the increased drain of public funds.

These events may be familiar to readers from countries whose governments were brought about by the force of military action. The Iraqi military heads of state (Qassem, the two Aref brothers, al-Bakr and Saddam Hussein) have accorded priority to such visible and rapid achievements as the construction of giant factories, the redistribution of landed property and public housing, extravagant urbanization and the purchase of sophisticated weapons that can be exhibited in military parades as a symbol of power. At the heart of exercising their state power is rapid expansion of the armed forces, primarily to guarantee the security of the regime, and to protect the privileged positions of the military élite (their special advantages in pay and fringe benefits, for example). Likewise, militarism has been manifested in the control over the economy via a large-scale and centrally managed public sector, in which the new class of the military élite hold senior positions.

Although the period 1960–80 was comparatively peaceful and relatively free of hostility around the Iraqi borders, even without obvious external threat military build-up soared.[19] During this period, the share of military expenditure in national income more than trebled, and the purchase value of arms imports was one-quarter of total imports, reaching US$4.3 billion in 1981. This swollen military spending amounted to an average expenditure per person more than double the average spent on education and health. To give an idea of the order of magnitude of Iraq's military expenditure, it almost equalled the 1980 national income of Jordan and Yemen (YAR) combined. This scale of military build-up was made possible by the sharp rise in government revenues from oil and gas.[20] In 1970–80 income per person increased annually by 5.3 per cent, despite the rapid annual average population growth of 3.5 per cent. This unprecedented oil-based affluence made Iraq a major donor, whose aid reached US$0.9 billion in 1980, representing about 3 per cent of national income, a share that was over 4 times that established by the UN and exceeded by far those of rich industrialized countries.

Social imbalance originates in the first development plan, for 1955–9, prepared by the Development Board (Majlis al-Imar).[21] The Board, whose function was the allocation of oil revenues, devoted less than one-third of what it spent on the military and police to education and health.[22] By 1981, allocations to defence were 5 times as much as those to education. In terms of public expenditure per member of the armed forces relative to expenditure on education per person, the ratio was appalling indeed, 370 per cent higher.[23]

Deepening militarism: wastefulness and hunger, 1981–95

Following the sudden affluence during the 1960s and 1970s, militarism deepened in the 1980s when the eight-year war with Iran was followed by the invasion of Kuwait in August 1990, both with disastrous outcomes. From its apex in 1979–80, the economy's downward trend began immediately after the start of the war with Iran in August 1980. The oil sector collapsed with the destruction of the export infrastructure, which reduced oil exports (and revenues) by nearly two-thirds. Nevertheless, with military spending supreme in the use of foreign exchange, Iraq's purchase of arms increased between 1980 and 1983 by about 3 times, from 12 to 34 per cent of the value of total imports, in addition to the reported financial support provided by Saudi Arabia and Kuwait, amounting to roughly US$25 billion.[24] While the war dragged on tediously, Iraq's bill for military expenditure rocketed, its international reserves were eroded, foreign debts mounted and the country's position as a major donor in the Middle East reverted to that of aid receiver.

According to the IISS and SIPRI, the size of the armed forces trebled between 1980 and 1984, reaching 1 million persons in 1988 (a fivefold increase between 1980 and 1988). In the mean time, production of food was disrupted, particularly wheat and rice, of which Iraq used to be an exporter. Data from the UN/ESCWA 1983–92 *Statistical Abstract*

(ESCWA 1994b) show that industrial and agricultural production indices were in 1990 40 and 35 per cent below the 1983 levels respectively.[25] With this scale of deterioration in production, combined with increasing inflation, almost 10 times that of the 1970s, there was a dramatic rise in the consumer prices index. But the worst was still to come.

Less than two years after the end of the Iran–Iraq war, a disastrous chain of events commenced in August 1990 when Iraqi military rulers decided to invade Kuwait. Massive destruction of the existing productive infrastructure took place in January and February 1991 when the USA and allied forces launched an intensive bombing raid on Iraq's vital installations. The destruction included most of the drinking water facilities, sewage pumps, modernized public utilities, electricity power stations, railways, bridges, ports, the recently completed advanced telecommunications system and the international expressway. The completed section of the latter alone absorbed about US$6 billion from the public purse in 1987. In addition, the imposition of an international system of trade embargoes and several forms of sanctions, together with the freezing of Iraqi foreign assets, inflicted huge losses upon the economy and the Iraqi people.

Existing estimates of the effects of the two wars suggest that whereas wasteful military expenditure and lost production, including the loss of oil revenues, can be easily estimated, it is difficult to assess the human costs of war in terms of death and the negative effects on low-income groups in terms of nutrition, health and their children's education and health care. For example, assuming the continuation of military spending at the pre-Iran–Iraq war annual level of US$15 billion, we can estimate that US$150 billion was wasted between 1980 and 1991. Oil revenues lost during the Iran–Iraq war were estimated at US$180 billion, to which we should add some US$75 billion for oil export earnings loss over the five years of 1991–5 (an average annual amount of US$15 billion).[26] The sum of this roughly calculated loss amounts to nearly US$420 billion. Such a colossal amount does not include the cost of the non-military constructions that were destroyed and the wasted productivity (opportunity cost) of the 1 million military conscripts, i.e. the output which would have been produced if they had remained in their productive civilian activities.

The human costs of militarism

Deaths

Robert McNamara (1991), the former President of the World Bank, estimated the number of Iraqi people killed during the Iran–Iraq war at 660,000. An Iraqi scholar, Alnasrawi (1994: 79–86), gives us a very wide range in the estimated numbers of additional human lives that were lost during the forty-three-day Gulf War that followed Iraq's invasion of Kuwait. He says, 'estimates indicate that anywhere between 50,000 and 120,000 Iraqi soldiers were killed . . . and between 5,000 and 15,000 civilians', in addition to about 50,000 civilians killed in the post-war internal uprisings. Alnasrawi also cites another estimate of deaths made by the United States Census Bureau, 'as of the end of 1991, 86,194 men, 39,612 women and 32,612 children had died at the hands of the American-led coalition forces and during the domestic rebellions that followed' (p. 95).

Hunger and destitution

The resulting conditions of poverty and hunger have been assessed through field studies conducted by different international researchers.[27] The focus of research was on food supply, distribution and prices. Though limited in scope and duration, the studies agree on a number of effects:

1   the deterioration of food supply and the quality of cereals consumed, making UN food assistance vital;
2   the high incidence of undernutrition, especially among women and among children below the age of 5 (rising from 9 per cent in 1991 to 35 per cent of children surveyed, by weight and age in 1993);
3   reduction in deaths among children under 5 slowed down substantially in 1980–94 to one-quarter its annual rate in 1960–80;
4   food rations targeted to the most vulnerable sections of the population were effectively distributed, but provided only about one-half of the 1990 calorie level;
5   the presence of pre-famine indicators in terms of:

    a   very high food prices rising at the monthly rate of nearly 15–20 per cent;
    b   depletion of personal assets through an involuntary sale;
    c   the rapid increase in the numbers of the destitute. The numbers of the poorest doubled between 1989 and 1994, reaching roughly 6 million, and included orphans, the elderly, female heads of households (widows) and those physically handicapped as a result of war.

Poverty and the collapse of purchasing power

As one would expect, living costs rose sharply and poverty among low-income Iraqis gradually increased between the years of affluence (1973–80) and the years of misery (1990–5). According to the household-budget surveys carried out in 1972 and 1976, annual income per head (GNP) at constant 1975 prices was 154 ID and 389 ID respectively, equivalent to US$493 and US$1,245 (1 ID equalled US$3.2). With steadily increasing prosperity, that average rose in real terms at 1975 prices to US$1,674 in 1980 (M. R. El-Ghonemy, 1990b: 222–4). It started to fall as a consequence of the Iran–Iraq war, down to US$1,075 in 1985 and declined further to US$780 in 1990. The collapse was particularly severe between August 1990 and August 1991, when real monthly earnings declined rapidly and the food price index increased by 1,500 to 2,000 per cent in that year. For example, the percentage increase in the price of wheat flour was 4,531; 133 per cent for meat (lamb). Even the price of dates increased by 239 per cent in one year.[28] The FAO mission (FAO and WFP, 1993: Table 3) reported a severely continuing erosion of wages and salaries: the minimum monthly wage established by the Ministry of Planning at 54 ID (US$170) in January 1986 plunged after the Gulf War to 174 ID (US$2.5) in August 1993 (US$1 was about 70 ID in 1993).

One year on, earnings deteriorated further (Ward and Rimmer, 1994: Table 1). As the market rate of exchange was US$1 to 75 ID, average annual income per person was 10,920 ID, equivalent to US$145. This was a catastrophic collapse of purchasing power, especially for those families who had lost their productive assets. Poorest were the families displaced by both wars, estimated by the study to account for 45 per cent of the total numbers of the poor and 12 per cent of all women surveyed. A further deterioration was reported by UNICEF: child mortality was 3–4 times higher in just one year. Dreze and Gazdar (1992: 938) concluded that 'a majority of householders in Iraq now earn real income below the Indian "poverty line" in terms of calorie purchasing power. In that sense, the incidence of poverty in Iraq today is greater than in India.'

Summary

After defining the meaning of social imbalance and its measurement problems, the chapter has examined different countries' experiences. It was concerned with variations in people's acquisition of fundamental capabilities, that is, literacy, longer life, adequate nutritional standards, and so forth. My analysis has shown that the governments of two-thirds of the Middle Eastern countries, rich and poor, have consistently given military spending higher priority than education and health. In fact, the share of arms in total imports has exceeded that of all developing countries in ten countries, and reached nearly half the value of total imports in five countries of the Middle East.

Examination of the relationship between the countries' income ranking and government spending on health and education reveals that affluence alone does not bring about rapid achievement of human capabilities. Likewise, the discussion suggests that several poorer countries were able to achieve levels of health and education better than many oil-rich countries and, at the same time, they realized higher rates of national investment and economic growth.

The discussion of militarization-related social imbalance was then extended to concentrate on the development experience of oil-rich Iraq during the long period 1950–95. Our brief review of the Iraqi experience during the 1960s and 1970s suggests a rapid realization of equitable distribution of wealth. In the mean time, oil revenues were lavishly used for already swollen military spending, which in 1980 reached 29 per cent of Iraq's national income (GNP). Following the oil boom, militarism deepened social imbalance and the economy's dramatic downward trend began immediately after the start of the eight-year war with Iran in August 1980, worsening following Iraq's invasion of Kuwait. As a result, affluent Iraq was transformed in 1991–5 into a poor society; there was widespread undernourishment and the numbers of the destitute doubled.

Suggested readings

On principles of public spending for human capital formation:
See the suggested readings for Chapter 1 of the present book.
Griffin and McKinley (1994) *Implementing a Human Development Strategy.*
Sahota (1978) 'Theories of Personal Income Distribution: A Survey'.
Streeten *et al.* (1981) *First Things First: Meeting Basic Needs in Developing Countries.*
UNDP (1991–6) *Human Development Report* 1991.
World Bank (1978–96) *World Development Report* 1993: 'Investing in Health'.

On the analysis of military expenditure:
Papers by Robert McNamara, Saadat Degar and Somnath Sen in *Proceedings of the Annual World Bank Conference on Development Economics*: World Bank, Washington DC, 1991.

Additional readings can be found in notes and in the Bibliography.

7

CORRUPTION:

The embezzlement of public funds

Though it is as real, visible and extensive as the vast area of the Middle Eastern desert, corruption, especially its role in increasing inequality of wealth distribution, has not received adequate attention in the region's development studies. It is a complex subject, and remains analytically difficult and unrecognized not only by the ruling political élite, but also by conventional economists. Furthermore, there is little agreement as to what a corrupt practice is and whether corruption is inevitable in dealings involving government officials. Corruption and public expenditure are linked by government officials' attitudes towards public funds: hence this chapter is a continuation of the discussion in Chapter 6.

The causes and forms of corruption are best understood through an empirical knowledge of people's and institutions' relevant behaviour. After explaining the analytical arguments, this chapter presents illustrations of embezzlement in two distinct settings: rich and tribally organized Saudi Arabia and low-income Egypt. Egypt has an extensive bureaucracy and excessive, vaguely worded laws that are riddled with loopholes, encouraging a corrupt person to take advantage of their defects and overlapping objectives. However, these countries share two features: the belief in a private-property-market economy and a system of governance that is basically authoritarian, with very little accountability to people through their own representatives.

Conflicting views and analytical problems

Corruption, which is synonymous with bribery, fraud and embezzlement in ordinary parlance, is defined in this study as the illegitimate transfer of public money and property rights for private gain.[1] It is an abuse of power and privilege, as well as an unlawful and immoral channel for rapid enrichment and wealth accumulation. Recently, its spread in most of the Middle Eastern countries, combined with repression, has been

behind violent confrontations between Islamic militants and governments (Chapter 3). Corruption has been also behind several *coups d'état*
in the Middle East and the deposition of the Emir of Qatar in 1995.

Yet, in the analytic system of conventional economics, corruption-like
inheritance arrangements and nepotism in wealth accumulation are
habitually ignored in the theory of income distribution that provides
the apparatus for understanding the sources of income and wealth
accumulation. In this tradition, emphasis is placed on the efficient allocation of scarce resources in the formal sector of productive activities,
and not on the actual institutional means of wealth distribution and
accumulation that run parallel with formal activities. At best, the complex causes of corruption are oversimplified through the employment of
the narrow concepts of rent-seeking in trade licensing and lobbying for
advantageous gains. In this way, corruption is viewed as a reward for the
scarce entrepreneurship and skills of civil servants and private businessmen. It should be noted that in most cases, until the introduction of
economic reforms around the mid-1980s, government agencies monopolized the supply of most scarce goods and services (sugar, cement,
insurance services and import licences, for example). Western-style corruption interprets bribery or commission payments as justifiable actions
that pay off in higher profits, preferential advantages and speedy transactions, without regard to their consequences, i.e. the misfortune of those
who are made 'worse off', to use the terminology of the Pareto principle
of economics. Take, for example, a public school building, poorly constructed by a corrupt contractor in coalition with corrupt civil servants,
which collapses, killing the school children and teachers. Could any
amount of money be adequate for compensating these victims for
their shortened life expectancy?[2]

Also overlooked are corruption-related arrangements that increase the
costs of doing business and induce smuggling and the transfer of income
from one pocket to another. These arrangements are widespread where
the public sector is large, laws and regulations are excessive and bureaucracy is cumbersome. In addition, the prevalence of illegal enrichment
tends to increase uncertainty about the protection of property rights and
create mistrust in a government's capacity to enforce laws. Hence the
necessity for investors and ordinary citizens to pay the heavy charges for
the services of an intermediary, which, in turn, increases the costs of
transactions.

Other social scientists, especially some development economists,
sociologists and political scientists have been realistic in their studies of
corruption as a development problem. Studies of the upsurge in corrupt
practices in industrialized countries (for example, Belgium, Great

Britain, Italy, Japan and Russia) have also changed the widely held belief that corruption is basically a feature of underdevelopment that is entrenched in the Third World. In the mean time, aid-giving agencies and donor governments have increasingly come to believe that effective outcomes of development assistance require 'good', corruption-free government with a high standard of integrity.

Lastly, it seems that the alliance of mutual benefits between corrupt – but enterprising – government employees and businessmen tends to resist the adoption of economic reforms. They fear losing their special powers and trade privileges, which are likely to diminish within a competitive market economy. Moreover, they tend to take advantage of government weakness resulting from the breakdown of the public sector and the enforcement of austerity measures (budget cuts, for example). Furthermore, inequality is likely to result from the sudden enrichment of certain groups of employees who are strategically positioned to accumulate huge gains from the sale of public economic enterprises, and who take advantage of their official power.

I therefore believe that a study of corruption is relevant to this inquiry into the determinants of inequality and poverty in the Middle East, a region in which:

1   average public expenditure was about 20 to 25 per cent of the countries' national income in 1960–90 (compared to an average of 13 per cent in other developing regions);
2   the press and public media are mostly under the control of the government, and are unable to check the abuse of power and privilege by heads of governments and senior officials;
3   there are few parliamentary democracies and many over-centralized decision-making structures whose systems of public control, accountability and transparency are generally weak, if not absent;
4   the judicial system is not completely independent of other state institutions. In some countries, where the head of state is the supreme head of the judicial system, it is politically oriented;
5   the prevalence of traditional hospitality in the social setting leads to the usage of such terms as 'gifts' and 'gratuities' instead of the morally offensive terms 'corruption' and 'bribery';
6   there is some evidence that ordinary citizens and foreign business people in some countries may have to bribe public employees in order to secure transactions, ranging from contracts for construction and manufacturing or export–import licences, to the issue of driving licences or certificates of tax payment.

Ironically, the region's numerous *coups d'état* have been justified by military rulers as radical measures to wipe out corruption, which remains today as pervasive as ever. In sum, this study of corruption may help to explain how certain cases of wealth accumulation were created in the first place.

Channels for embezzlement: evidence

Institutional arrangements for illegal enrichment may be grouped into two main overlapping channels, through which a rapid transfer of public funds and property occurs.

Ambiguity of rules governing property rights and the award of contracts

We typify this situation in Saudi Arabia. As its name suggests, this wealthy country is ruled by the descendants of King Abdul Aziz ibn al-Saud (reigned 1932–53). Since its creation out of the former Ottoman Empire between 1926 and 1932, its national emblem – the sword and the palm – has symbolized the supremacy of the ruling family's power over the country's fortunes.[3] This characteristic has made it difficult to distinguish between the personal and official jurisdictions of the royal family over the possession and dispensing of public wealth.[4] This is especially true of oil revenues, which increased by 15 times in just seven years (1973–80), the royalties of which were, until the early 1960s, considered to be the royal family's property.

As the financial wealth from petroleum grew, so too did the power of the members of the ruling family and their business associates. The people also looked for a share in this windfall wealth or *risq* (blessed fortune from Allah). As in other oil-rich Gulf sheikhdoms, the policy-makers and senior officials have often been members of the ruling family. This situation is further complicated by the increasing expectations of the Saudi people and the international Muslim community that high moral standards should be practised by the officials of state institutions and their associates in business conduct. This is particularly expected because of the role of the Saudi state as the guardian of the most holy Islamic shrines, with the king as their servant.

One of the sources of manipulation of public wealth for personal gain is the vague definition of 'economic development activity' for any private business action that is carried out according to the royal decrees governing the awarding of contracts for foreign capital investment and the formation of companies and joint ventures in which the sponsorship rights of the Saudi partners are exercised. This extensive legal framework requires a Saudi partner, at least for the provision of land, the ownership of which is prohibited for foreigners. In addition, the ambiguous Contracts Law and Tenders Regulations of 1977 make it obligatory for any non-Saudi to find a Saudi sponsor prior to undertaking private business, including the bidding for tenders on the construction of public works and the supply of goods.[5] Of critical importance among contracted public works have been the multi-billion-dollar international airports, the two Olympic-size sports cities, the extensive asphalted roads and main highways, the construction of two enormous harbours at Dammam and Jeddah and the six-billion-dollar project for installing a new telecommunications system.

Another ambiguous term is 'project'. Nearly 70 per cent of the total public expenditure was in project form as outlined in the first four development plans designed between 1975 and 1990. On average, US$15–25 billion was provided for projects to be implemented annually over this period by way of contracts awarded by high-ranking decision makers. Whereas development plans and published annual budgets exclude military spending and payments to members of the royal family, available outlines of some budgets show the category 'others' among government expenditure, representing 35–48 per cent of the total in the 1970s and 39 per cent in 1990–5.[6] This large share includes allocations for the royal household, internal security and monthly stipends for individual tribal chiefs. However, princely payment from public funds varies widely, depending on the degree of direct lineage from the founder of the dynasty, King Abdul Aziz ibn al Saud. Public funds may also have been used for such purposes as bribing the foreign media to prevent publication of news hostile to the royal family. An example of the latter was the payment in 1978–80 of nearly US$500 million from public funds to prevent Arab states and the Western media from showing the film *Death of a Princess*.[7]

Personal gains from public property are officially termed 'consultant services', or they are in the form of commissions of fees to agents that are hidden in the inflated values of contracts. Assuming that the 1977 established rate of 5 per cent commission is adhered to, an average of US$400 million is received for the servicing or the approval of any of these large-scale schemes of US$6–7 billion each. The case of the establishment of a new telephone system is telling. An important contract-fixer was allegedly paid a personal commission in 1978 of US$500 million by the Dutch company Philips and the two American companies Western Electric and International Telephone and Telegraph (ITT) in connection with the US$4.5-billion contracts for the new telephone system.[8]

Another example of enrichment through awarding contracts is arms deals. I noted in Chapter 6 that Saudi Arabia ranks top among military spenders (43 per cent of total public expenditure, or nearly US$12 billion in 1989, rising to an average of US$17 billion a year in 1990–4, compared to an average of US$1 billion in 1975–8).[9] Given the increasing unemployment and balance of payments deficit in the arms manufacturing countries of the West, the keen Saudi desire to acquire sophisticated weapons swiftly has multiple benefits: job gains in the exporting countries, enormous profits for the manufacturers and high commissions and agents' fees received by those who are involved in the negotiations for multi-billion-dollar arms deals. Perhaps the largest arms deals have been those agreed with the US companies Lockheed, McDonnell Douglas, Raytheon and Northrop, and with the UK multinational companies British Aerospace, Westland and Rolls-Royce.[10] Take, for example, the British arms deals known as al-Yamamah I (about US$10 billion in 1985) and Yamamah II (around US$40 billion over ten years from 1988). These arms deals led to investigations by the British parliament and press in which Mark Thatcher, the son of the former Prime Minister, was reported to have received a personal slice of US$20 million of the US$500 million already realized in commissions by several Saudi agents at the early stage of this deal.[11]

Patronage arrangements within a parallel state

Intitutional arrangements for corrupt practices by the low-salaried public establishments mainly take the form of patronage relationships between unequals in terms of connections, status and power. This form of bureaucratic corruption is widely practised within a parallel state structure in which the political and economic powers of the leading figures provide informal protection for the participants in rapid embezzlement of state funds and property.[12] By 'parallel state' is meant the existence of informal networks of influential protectors and benefactors who control sections of state institutions and the informal market for the purpose of rapid enrichment and personal political gains, so increasing the costs of doing business. To exercise public-office-based powers for personal gain, a predatory bureaucrat's strategy is simple but shrewd: the formation of disguised alliance and patronage arrangements with officials in high office, powerful businessmen and multinational corporations' representatives who have important connections. Kinship relationships have priority in these clandestine and self-serving formations.

As suggested at the start of this chapter, Egypt provides a good example of these two channels (hardship-based bureaucratic corruption and the functioning of a parallel state structure). Let us begin with a characterization of the former. Bureaucratic corruption and fraud has, since the mid-1970s, become rampant, to the extent that it is no longer viewed as shameful. Instead, it is considered by many Egyptians and foreigners as a self-serving process necessary in dealing with government and public enterprise affairs.[13] On investigating the subject in 1994, I was shocked to find out that if the rules and regulations were strictly enforced, the majority of public officials would be in prison. Corrupt practices are often described as if they were a natural phenomenon. However, they are rapidly weakening the foundations of trust between the people and government.

The main cause of pervasive bureaucratic corruption is the inadequate level of salaries in government and public enterprises. The system of vigilance is increasingly deteriorating and salary purchasing-power is being eroded by the removal of subsidies and the rapid rise in living-costs. In real terms, the average salary level of government employees in 1991–3 was one-third of its 1973 level. We should note that since the sweeping nationalization and sequestration of major firms during the period 1956–62, government and public enterprises have been the largest single employer. The public sector's share in employment in 1992 was nearly one-third of the total workforce, and accounted for half the non-agricultural employment. The share would be even greater if we added the members of the armed forces, police, and government employees in the bureaucratically run and over-staffed cooperatives that are officially included in the 'services' category of the workforce. However, the share of civil employees and workers' salaries and wages in total government current expenditure only rose from 22 per cent in 1979 to 28.9 per cent in 1993.[14] With surging inflation, the deterioration in government employees' purchasing power left most public employees more vulnerable to accepting bribes and looking for second jobs (moon-lighting).

The misery of a large section of government employees, particularly the petty clerks in urban areas, was revealed by the results of the 1981/2 household survey, showing that about 30 per cent of the urban poor were employees of government and public enterprises (World Bank, 1991: 48). Many employees have taken advantage of the power and authority attached to their public positions, entrusted to them by numerous laws that are vaguely worded and riddled with loopholes. Critical among these powers exercised for personal gains are:

1   control over public enterprises' production and distribution of

essential goods in the context of scarcity and government control, especially food items, public housing and cement;[15]

2   the issuing of permits or licences for imports and exports as well as certificates for the purchase or lease of state-owned lands and buildings;

3   originating and awarding construction contracts for public works;[16]

4   assessment and collection of direct taxes and customs duties;

5   determining which of the four government-administered rates of exchange – which prevailed in the 1970s and 1980s before the IMF-induced price liberalization in 1991/2 – should be granted for different transactions.[17]

Now let us see how patronage relationships function within the parallel state. Following the post-1952 'revolutionary' and authoritarian regime, successive governments have set up numerous gigantic vigilance institutions. Clearly, a corrupt person and his patron take advantage of these institutions' overlapping and ambiguous functions.[18] Furthermore, the judicial system has, since 1980, been weakened by the setting up of a parallel structure, in which a controversial strange new Law of Vice or shame (Qanoun al-Aib) was introduced. For its enforcement, a complex legal machinery headed by al-Mud'ai al-Ishtiraki (the Socialist Prosecutor) was established to indict any person charged with ambiguous political or ethical acts, including corruption. The defendant is sued and brought to trial before a specifically set up court, Mahkamat al-Qeyam (the Court of Public Morality and Values). As one would expect from this dual judicial structure, government measures to curb corruption have proved ineffective. In fact, several academics and journalists maintain that corruption is rampant, and growing, particularly among high officials, managers of public enterprises and members of parliament.[19] A few examples based on extensive reading of parliamentary records, confidential reports, published work and newspapers are presented here.

With the adoption of the late President Sadat's 'Open Door' policy (i.e. partial economic liberalization) in 1974 the web of elements of the parallel state has flourished under the leadership of the construction tycoon, Sadat's friend Othman Ahmad Othman. Starting in the 1940s as a low-income engineer, in the 1970s Othman became the second most powerful man in Egypt after President Sadat. By the mid-1980s, his assets in the Arab Contractors Company were estimated at E£1,500 million, gained primarily from exercising its monopoly power in the construction of public works.[20] Othman became Deputy Prime Minister for Housing and Construction and an influential member of parliament. His son married Sadat's daughter. In addition, he was put in charge of the government's popular development and food security schemes (PDS hereafter). To finance these schemes, a special bank (Bank al-Tanmeya) was established with public funds.

Under the energetic leadership of Othman, the functions of the parallel state were expanded further by the entry of a new class of corrupt businessmen who wanted to share some of their protector's privileges in order to skim public resources. They included the Alexandrian member of parliament, cigarette smuggler and drug dealer Rashad Othman (not a relative of Othman A. Othman) and a few powerful food importers and foreign currency black-market profiteers. Also prominent was Ismat Sadat (brother of the President) who managed within a few years to jump from being a lorry driver to a multi-millionaire in 1982. His unearned fortune was estimated at E£150 million accumulated from hashish deals, unlawful possession of state-owned land, and from trading in huge quantities of the Ministry of Supply's subsidized consumer goods.[21]

The enlarged scale of unlawful wealth sucked away from public resources by these individuals was revealed during their trials in 1982– 4 (after the assassination of President Sadat in October 1981). The trials revealed alarming information. Several members of parliament and senior officials were named and accused of embezzlement and receipt of bribes. For example, it was made public that in alliance with another Alexandrian building contractor and member of parliament, Tala'at Mustafa, Rashad illegally acquired private property rights to 150 acres of state-owned land in al-Amereya, a district of Alexandria. This extensive area of urban land was allocated by the government for a housing scheme for 3,192 poor families who were homeless, or living in cemeteries. To the best of my knowledge, the privatized rights in state property continue, and the housing scheme for the poor has never been implemented.[22]

Of particular public concern was the embezzlement of PDS funds for personal purposes and for the dumping of imported food that was past its sell-by date (meat and dried milk for children) on the Egyptian market, reported in the semi-official newspaper *al-Ahram* (12 February 1993, p. 15). This corrupt practice led to the collapse of PDS and the loss of hundreds of millions of Egyptian pounds from public money. The public was outraged to learn from official investigations that customs and health officers were bribed to certify that the shipment of imported meat was lawful and not harmful to health. This gross outrage was revealed when the senior officials of Alexandria harbour reported that they had learned of this scandal only when many rats had been suddenly found dead where the imported meat was stored. Several human deaths and cases of children's illness were reported and large sums of public money and scarce foreign exchange were wasted. The embezzlement of public funds, putting public health at risk and children's lives in danger, has continued. In December 1994 the Minister of Supply and Trade, Dr Ahmad Guwaily, announced in parliament that as many as 45,000 cases of fraud had been reported in that year, including one involving dried milk for children's consumption. He also announced that since the existing law on fraud dated back to 1941, providing a maximum penalty of E£100 (equivalent to market exchange rate of US$29 or £19 sterling in 1994), he was preparing a new law. This was issued in late 1995.

The scope of parallel state functions extended to include several strategic areas:

1 making extensive exemptions of tax and customs duty in favour of private clients (which reached E£5.2 billion in 1991/92 or 4 per cent of national income);[23]
2 awarding contracts for public works to relatives and unqualified people, leading to the loss of life from the collapse of recently built schools, hospitals and low-income housing schemes during the 1992 earthquake;
3 using public funds to enable groups of senior officials, police officers and members of parliament to perform the holy pilgrimage at no personal cost. (I personally witnessed this while I was in Saudi Arabia in May 1994.)[24]

The trials on criminal charges of the suspected killers of another leading patron, the former president of the parliament, Rifat al-Mahgoub and of the financial magnates the al-Rayan brothers and Ashraf al-Sa'd on charges of corruption uncovered multiple practices of illegal, quick enrichment of participants in the parallel state.[25] Many of these practices were made known in a parliamentary debate called for in May 1994 by the then leader of the opposition, Mr Khaled Mohyi el-Din. He accused the staff of the Socialist Prosecutor themselves of corruption, of abusing their authority and of charging service fees for the total amount of funds and assets in their trust. The fees amounted to E£75 million, for which the Prosecutor's office failed to provide an account to parliament.

Summary

In this chapter, an attempt has been made to examine an often neglected source of both accumulation of wealth and inequality in the distribution of personal income. It has focused on two main channels through which embezzlement of public funds and property for illegitimate personal enrichment takes place. In the first section, controversies surrounding the concept of corruption and related analytical procedures were discussed. In the second section, corrupt practices were illustrated in two contrasting situations: rich Saudi Arabia and poor Egypt.

The primary concern in this chapter has been to understand the procedures for rapid enrichment from embezzlement, hoping that their identification will help in the formulation of anti-corruption measures to eliminate the evil of this drain on public funds. Lastly, and for the interest of students of a range of social science and development studies, our discussion and the empirical evidence challenge the legitimacy of a proposition habitually made in the analytical system of conventional economics, that corruption and kinship relationships, like inheritance arrangements, are unimportant sources to be discarded in an analysis of the determinants of the distribution and accumulation of personal income and wealth.

Suggested readings

On the definition of corruption and its causes:
Doig (1995) 'Good Government and Sustainable Anti-Corruption Strategies'.
Gellner and Waterbury (1977) *Patrons and Clients in Mediterranean Societies*.
Heidenheimer (1978) *Political Corruption: Readings in Comparative Analysis*.
Myrdal (1968) *Asian Drama*, Chapter 20.
Springborg (1979) 'Patrimonialism and Policy Making in Egypt'.
United Nations Department of Technical Cooperation for Development (1989) *Corruption in Government*.
Van Roy (1970) 'On the Theory of Corruption'.

On the analysis of corrupt practices in economic terms:
Ades and di Tella (1995) 'Competition and Corruption', for understanding the application of the economic analytical system to the subject of corruption.
Krueger (1974) 'The Political Economy of a Rent-Seeking Society', for the concept of rent-seeking.
North (1990) *Institutions, Institutional Change and Economic Performance*, especially Chapters 4 and 8 for understanding increased costs of doing business 'Transaction Costs'.

On the analysis of country experiences:
Gellner and Waterbury (1977) *Patrons and Clients in Mediterranean Societies*, for Mediterranean countries, with case studies of Egypt, Jordan and Lebanon.
Gould and Amaro-Reyes (1983) *The Effects of Corruption on Administrative Performance: Illustrations from Developing Countries*, for examples from Asia, Africa, Latin America and Lebanon.

Myrdal (1968) *Asian Drama*, for South East Asia.

Sadowski (1991) *Political Vegetables? Businessmen and Bureaucracy in the Development of Egyptian Agriculture*, on corrupt practices in the Egyptian agricultural sector.

On the meaning of good government and the control of corruption by NGOs:

Clayton (1994) *Governance, Democracy and Conditionality: What Role for NGOs?*, especially pp. 20–3.

Edward and Hulme (1995) *Non-Governmental Organizations: Performance and Accountability*, particularly pp. 3–13.

Additional readings can be found in notes and in the Bibliography.

8

INEQUALITY IN PRIVATE
CONSUMPTION

The discussion on the roots of inequalities turns now from public spending and its links with corruption opportunities to the private expenditure of individuals and families. The focus is on consumption patterns with regard to necessities and luxuries and the scale of poverty and inequality among social classes. From the results of available surveys, those people whose actual consumption is absolutely insufficient to meet their essentials are identified. The characteristics of ostentatious consumption by the rich are also identified, and the question of whether obesity and the diet-related diseases of affluence co-exist in the same society with deprivations and undernourishment is considered. What are the main differences in consumption items between different income classes? What are the principal factors behind these differences? What is the general trend in consumption composition with regard to shifts between traditional and foreign-branded products? What is the role of advertising in these shifts and the effects these changes have on poor consumers?

The chapter begins by identifying the broad features of private consumption in the region. I argue that, contrary to conventional economics, preference for items purchased does not originate *solely* in the individual's income level and freedom of choice, independent of the producer's or manufacturer's influence.[1] I show instead that it is significantly influenced by producers through globalized, aggressive advertising and by emulation across income categories and from rich to poorer countries. The last two sections present country case studies, exploring the features of poverty and consumption inequalities. Defining the categories of the poor by occupation and the severity of economic misery helps to know who the poor are and how many of them there are.

Regional features of consumption

A Western visitor to the Middle East tends to observe profound contradictions in private consumption. Notable are the apparent number of private cars seen side by side with donkey-driven carts, skyscrapers not far from crowded slums, sophisticated supermarkets functioning side by side with an army of petty peddlers. Another striking phenomenon is the number of advertisements for Western-manufactured consumer goods, exceeding even their density in Western societies. The visitor may also be puzzled by a conspicuously high proportion of obesity among adults. Many people seem to eat most of the time and speak of the number of loaves of bread and amount of meat consumed as a status symbol. Most of the cities are crowded with imitative bits of Western consumption features, which I call 'the hamburger culture'.

I use the World Bank data on changes in national accounts (the structure of demand) which are available for eleven Middle East countries and a comparable set of data on the structure of household consumption expenditure in eight countries. The latter comprise the share of expenditure on each of food, housing (excluding house purchase), medical care, education, transport and durable consumer goods (furniture and appliances such as sewing machines, refrigerators and washing machines). In what follows, I present two salient features suggested by these data, despite their limitations.[2]

The dominance of food spending by rich and poor

The data tell us that the average share of food in the total consumption expenditure of a family is consistently higher than that in countries of other regions belonging to the same income categories. At the Middle East aggregate level, the average share is 40 per cent, compared to 32 per cent in other developing regions. The average family expenditure on food items is 60 per cent in poor Mauritania and much lower in rich Israel at 21 per cent, but still higher than in such countries of similar income level as Hong Kong (12 per cent) and Singapore (19 per cent).[3] The dominance of food consumption is in contrast to the low shares of expenditure on housing and household durable goods, and the very inadequate share of expenditure on medical care and education combined. Both necessities are at only 8 per cent in poorer countries (Egypt and Sudan), a share that is much lower than in other African low-income countries (for example Kenya, 13 per cent and Zambia, 22 per cent).

Rapid expansion in private car ownership and resulting health risks

On average, transport expenditure (including the purchase of cars) is between 2 and 4 per cent of total family spending in the low-income

Table 8.1 Index number of private cars, their density and ratio to public buses in nine countries, 1970–93

Country by income group	Number of cars in 1,000s 1970	Index (1970 = 100) 1980	1983–5	1992	Density ratio 1992/3	Ratio of private cars to public buses 1992/3
High income						
Kuwait	112	356	464	518	106	170
Bahrain	9	456*	733	1,211	55	29
Saudi Arabia	65	235*	2,855	3,588	81	50
Oman	1	800*	10,100	17,330	35	27
Israel	151	275	407	611	70	165
Middle income						
Iraq	67	254*	587	1,000	27	20
Turkey	137	411	718	1,468	34	27
Jordan	15	380*	873	1,167	43	38
Low income						
Egypt	130	335	588	778	34	90

Sources: ESCWA (1994b). Egypt: *Statistical Yearbook* 1994: Table 4–19 (Egypt, CAPMAS, 1981–95). Israel: *Statistical Abstract of Israel* 1970 and 1993 (Israel, Central Bureau of Statistics, 1970–93). Kuwait: *Annual Statistical Abstract* 1990: Table 184 (Kuwait, Ministry of Planning, 1990–3). Turkey: *Statistical Yearbook for Turkey* 1994: Table 280 (Turkey, State Insititute of Statistics, 1991–6).

Notes
* refers to 1978, not 1980.
Index number expresses the absolute number of private cars in each year related to the number in the base year (1970) multiplied by 100.
Density ratio refers to the number of private cars in use per 1 kilometre of paved roads.
Ratio of private cars to public buses refers to the number of private cars per public bus, excluding buses for personal use.

countries (Sudan and Egypt respectively), rising to 5–8 per cent in the middle-income group (Iran, Turkey, Tunisia and Morocco) and rising further to 9 per cent in oil-rich Bahrain and 10 per cent in high-income Israel, which is close to the rich industrialized countries' average of 13 per cent. Other data on the number and density ratio of private cars (luxury items) are available for nine countries: see Table 8.1.

First, the data suggest a faster rise in the number of private cars than in the essential transport service of public buses during the period 1970–92. However, the aggregate numbers of private cars conceal differences in size and value. For example, in Egypt, based on data obtained from CAPMAS, the number of imported small cars of four cylinders each (1000cc) more than doubled in just six years between 1987 and 1993. On the other hand, the number of luxury cars (mostly Mercedes imported for private use) with an engine capacity over 1000cc (of six and eight cylinders) increased from 1,351 to 11,673 cars in the same period, a rise of 860 per cent. Contrary to expectations about public welfare in poor Egypt, the increase in the number of public buses was negligible: a ratio of 1 bus to 110 private cars in 1991–3. Also, the production of bicycles fell by 45 per cent in 1987–93.[4] This disappointing form of conspicuous affluence does not reflect a real prosperity. In fact, the Egyptian economy deteriorated from an annual growth of 6.7 per cent in 1985 to just 1 per cent in 1990 and real income per person declined from US$760 in 1986 to US$640 in 1992. Thus, the car boom reflects an income concentration in a few hands, combined with widespread corruption in the collection of customs duty on cars and in the importation procedures.

Second, the high number of cars relative to paved roads across countries has led to affluence-related health risks from pollution and road accidents. According to the World Health Organization (1992) high density of car use increases the emission of carbon dioxide and lead, causing about 3–5 per cent of total deaths in urban areas worldwide. Between 1965 and 1990, these fatal emissions have increased in the Middle East faster than in South Asia and Latin America (by 510 per cent, 427 per cent and 260 per cent respectively). Similarly, the quantity of carbon dioxide and lead emissions per person in the Middle East exceeds by far the averages in the other two regions.[5] The health risks include chronic bronchitis, which contributes to heart diseases and heart attacks as well as strokes. But the deplorable human costs are also seen in the increasing numbers both of seriously injured people and of those killed in car accidents in rich and poor countries alike. For example, in rich Israel the number of injured persons tripled and the number of deaths doubled between 1970 and 1992. In poorer Morocco, the number of deaths in car accidents increased by 112 per cent, from 1,580 to 3,350 persons during the same period.

Changing consumption patterns

There have been significant changes in private consumption. The major factors influencing these changes include: oil windfalls; the rapid expansion in population and urbanization; the strong links between increasing globalized production systems fostered by multinational corporations, international advertising agencies and the mass media in marketing foreign-branded consumer goods; and the long period of colonial rule, which has left a deep-seated preference for Western styles of housing, food, drink and clothes.

There is sufficient evidence of a shift away from traditional products which meet the taste and demand of large sections of the population, particularly the poor, towards modern, expensive items consumed in affluent societies and designed according to Western tastes, using Western raw materials and a labour–capital relationship. These products include baby food, bread, soap and synthetic detergents, household appliances and footwear. For example, the traditional soap consumed by low-income groups, produced with local raw materials on a small scale and with intensive labour has given way to large-scale and capital-intensive American or European brands of soap and synthetic detergents.[6] While rich and middle-income consumers can afford the purchase of complementary equipment (washing machines and dishwashers), low-income and poor consumers cannot, especially in villages without electricity and piped safe water. The same fate has overtaken the purchase of locally produced bicycles, which have been quickly replaced by the foreign brands preferred by better-off consumers.[7]

Likewise, there has been a gradual displacement of traditional varieties of such foods as cheap and nutritious bread, dairy products, cooking oil, fruits, sweets and native soft drinks. Nutritionists have consistently established the higher nutritional values of the displaced native food items compared with most of the new items consumed. Examples of displaced items are date bread (*khubz al tamr*), millet or sorghum and wholegrain wheat, hard goat's milk cheese, dates and barshoumi figs.[8] Traditional sheep, camel and goat meat and dairy products are rapidly giving way to beef, frozen chicken and imported dairy products, especially powdered milk and processed cheese. Another obvious shift is in soft drinks. Such traditional drinks as sour milk, mint drink, *irksous*, mint tea, *karkadeh* and almond milk have been rapidly displaced by American carbonated drinks (Coca-Cola, Seven-Up, Pepsi-Cola, and so on). This is in addition to the early introduction of alcoholic drinks (especially beer and wine) by the British, French and Italians during their long colonial rule.

The invasion of hamburger culture

What and how we eat is part of our culture. With rapid urbanization, the migrant rural poor, school children of poor parents and small-scale business workers have relied on cheap street foods, available at the time and place required. A wide range of tasty ethnic foods at low cost are enjoyed by millions of low-income and poor consumers who cannot afford alternative sources. The extensive sale of popular, traditional goods provides jobs for a large section of the unskilled workforce, particularly women. However, and despite its socioeconomic benefits, this native food sector has been denied the necessary facilities and capital to develop its employment potential on a sound basis that meets food safety, hygiene, and sanitation requirements. A study by the Nutrition Division of the FAO (1990: 6) concluded that 'it is believed that many poor and low-income families would be worse off if there were no street food vendors to serve fast, inexpensive foods . . . nutrition documentation does show that freshly cooked traditional meals have quite satisfactory nutrient content'.

The beginning of the end of this popular, pro-poor food service has been marked by the invasion of Middle Eastern cities by the Western-based fast-food firms. Designed for affluent consumers, backed by aggressive advertising, and supported by government policies, Anglo-American brands of fast foods such as McDonald's, Burger King and Pizza Hut have become a status symbol. Like the sale of cups and saucers, the sale of these ready-to-eat foods conditions the purchase of their complements: American soft drinks, coleslaw or potato chips.

This new food culture is not an isolated phenomenon. It is an integral part of a wider tendency for the standardization and homogeneity of consumption patterns across Middle Eastern countries. From Manama and Dubai in the south to Istanbul and Beirut in the north, in Rabat, Tunis, Amman and Cairo, this homogeneity is manifested mostly in the fashion for eating hamburgers, drinking Coca-Cola, wearing Levi jeans, smoking Marlboro cigarettes, and using Palmolive soap. These integrated elements of a transferred culture and the costs involved are beyond the means of the millions of poor and undernourished people. Some consumers also question the conformity of the preparation of beef and chicken to Islamic rules. The widespread use of these symbols of modernity and affluence has made the millions of deprived people more envious of those who are able to satisfy these created and non-urgent wants.

The survival of many old-established native drinks and popular foods such as *falafel, shawerma, foul medames, sugok* and *bessisa*, and their vendors' earnings, are seriously threatened by the mighty monopoly power of the giant multinational firms (McDonald's, Coca-Cola, Pepsi-Cola and Nestlé/Nescafé) whose market shares in total multinational sales rank them among the world's top five corporations. They are so powerful that their volume of annual sales and branded value exceeds the entire national income of several countries of the Middle East.[9]

The powerful role of advertising

Advertising is a powerful influence in shaping private consumption patterns. Through its dominance of the mass media, advertising by multinational agencies in native languages and local dialects plays an

increasingly important role in cultural homogeneity, dollarization and
the standardization of consumer goods across the Middle East. Because
of widespread illiteracy in most countries of the region, advertisers prefer
television and radio to the printed media. Available estimates show the
share of the former to be nearly 60 per cent in total advertising expenditure, compared to 20–30 per cent on average in Western Europe. The
following data on television and radio commercial advertising revenue in
Egypt and Turkey are an example of its increasing importance.[10]

	1989/90	1992/3	Percentage increase
Egypt (E£, million)	35.8	94.9	164.6
Turkey (TL, million)	569,526.0	707,873.0 (1991/2)	24.3

Table 8.2 Advertising expenditure in ten Middle Eastern countries compared to
five selected industrial and middle-income countries, 1979–90

Country	Advertising expenditure per person in US$		Advertising expenditure as a % of national income (GNP)	
	1978	1990	1978	1990
UAE	n.a.	43	n.a.	0.3
Kuwait	17.7	57	0.1	0.9
Israel	16.7	127	0.4	1.2
Saudi Arabia	9.6	10	0.2	0.2
Bahrain	41.0	22	0.7	0.4
Oman	n.a.	8	n.a.	1.9
Turkey	6.3	8	0.6	0.5
Jordan	2.5	3	0.5	0.2
Morocco	n.a.	1	n.a.	0.1
Egypt	1.5	2	0.4	0.3
France	47	228	0.7	1.2
Germany	48	225	0.7	0.9
United Kingdom	40	275	1.0	1.7
Mexico	7	32	0.4	1.0
South Korea	5	65	0.7	1.2

Sources: 1978 data are from United Nations Centre on Transnational Corporations (1979:
Table 1–4). For 1990, Mooij (1994: Tables 2.2, 6.3 and 6.4). For Egypt, Kuwait, Jordan and
Morocco, the data refer to 1989 and are taken from Zenith Media Worldwide (1990: 73).
Data for Turkey (1990) were obtained by the author from the Secretary General, Turkish
Radio and Television Corporation (TRT), Ankara. Total expenditure was estimated for
Turkey (1990) on the basis that television and radio's share was 50 per cent of total.

Notes
n.a. = not available.
Countries of the Middle East are listed in descending order of per capita income, 1991.

Table 8.2 shows the extent of advertising importance in terms of total expenditure per person and the percentage share in national income in 1978 and 1990 for ten Middle Eastern countries for which data are available. For the purpose of comparison, I have included in the table France, Germany and the UK, whose income level is close to the rich Middle Eastern countries, and two middle-income developing countries (Mexico and South Korea) which belong to the same upper-income category as many countries of the Middle East. The data suggest that the richer countries, Kuwait and Israel, have the fastest growth in advertising expenditure's share of national income and the highest per person level in 1990. They are joined by Oman, whose percentage of 1.9 is the highest in the sample of fifteen countries, both inside and outside the Middle East.

The few pieces of information available suggest that the marketing of foreign-branded items consumed in the Middle East is highly concentrated in a few multinational producers and global advertising agencies situated in the USA, Japan, Switzerland and the three European countries listed in Table 8.2. The influence of such monopoly powers on private consumption patterns is particularly important in certain items of foreign origin (for example cosmetics, soap and detergents, cigarettes, soft drinks, household electric appliances and commercial baby foods). A significant contributor to this globalization is the electronic revolution in the communication and information media, especially television. Through cable and satellite dishes, American and European-based advertising reaches tens of millions of households directly, through channels such as NBC, CNN, Sky, Astra, ITN and MBC[11] which are outside the control of national governments. Lucky consumers who can afford these advanced communication media tend to trust their advertisements simply because they come from rich Western countries. Ordinary consumers in the Middle East believe these countries' advertising agencies and do not realize that many may exploit poorer countries, especially with regard to health effects (advertisements stress 'buy. . ., it is what you really need and is the best for you').

Despite the fact that Western countries are increasing restrictions on smoking for health reasons, we find that their own multinational producers and advertisers operating in the Middle East are aggressively marketing cigarettes to potential consumers, particularly the young. Evidence from different countries shows a rise in tobacco consumption between 1975 and 1990 and that consumption per person has almost doubled in several countries. While disregarding the obvious hazards of lung cancer, bronchitis and heart disease, these advertisers are successful in creating an image of relaxation and glamour in the minds of low-income consumers and of manhood and bravery in the minds of the young (Marlboro man, for example).[12] Moreover, they are not discouraged by governments that greatly profit from the advertising fees charged by state-owned television and radio. They profit also from outdoor sales taxes and from outdoor tobacco advertisements. The brunt of tobacco-related disorders, including lung cancer deaths, is mostly borne by the poor, whose consumption of tobacco is much higher than that of the rich, according to my analysis of the results of some countries' family-budget surveys (see pp. 134–5).

Of special concern are the health risks of the rapid expansion in consumption of commercial baby foods produced and advertised by multinationals. The urgent call for the protection of babies from these risks peaked in the early 1980s, and corrective measures were arranged jointly by WHO and UNICEF.[13] Yet nutritionists' anxiety has continued about the resulting health risks to infants. Their field studies[14] show that fifty-five foreign brands of baby foods are heavily consumed in the Gulf oil-rich countries, as part of modernity in a rather backward environment. The findings also reveal that the old-established practices of giving sheep ghee to infants at birth for a period of three days to lubricate the intestines, followed by two-year breastfeeding according to the Qur'an's teachings, have rapidly diminished. This traditional practice has given way to the introduction of bottle-feeding as early as one month after birth among the high social class in urban areas.

Two possible explanations are offered for related health risks. One is that because of widespread illiteracy mothers cannot read the specifications of content and the instructions, particularly with regard to the date of expiry and the appropriate preparation of foreign-made powdered or condensed cow's milk (for example, the milk to water dilution ratio, the maximum temperature and duration of heating and the cleansing of bottles). The second is the use of unsafe water for diluting concentrated or powdered milk. An authority on the subject adds 'sadly, unfair food trade practices are widely prevalent in the Gulf . . . It is generally believed that the people are consuming processed food with unsafe additives', and 'bottle-fed children of illiterate mothers have the highest proportion of recurrent attacks of gastroenteritis [compared to children] of educated mothers' (Musaiger, 1987: 127–8 and 141).

Family consumption inequality: case studies

The discussion turns now from a regional to a country-specific perspective, examining the extent of poverty, and inequality in two groups of countries. The first is a group of three countries where there have been expenditure surveys: Israel, a high-income country with a unique social organization; Tunisia, a middle-income country; and Mauritania, the poorest in the region. In the second group (Bahrain, Kuwait and Saudi Arabia) some features of affluent consumption in the oil-rich states are presented.

Israel

We know from Chapter 4 that Israel is among the rich countries of the Middle East. Its high level of income/consumption per person is the outcome of a combination of sustained economic growth (4–6 per cent in 1960–92) and the good distributional performance of the Israeli economy, suggesting that the benefits from growth have been widely shared. As early as 1957, the poorest 20 per cent received 6.7 per cent of total personal income before tax. In 1993, this moderate share increased to nearly 8 per cent, compared to only 3.5 per cent in Mauritania and 5.9 per cent in Tunisia. Thanks to such distributive measures as progressive taxation and social benefits payments, the initial low degree of inequality has been sustained over four decades.[15]

Israel's Central Bureau of Statistics has carried out periodic Family Expenditure Surveys, and Annual Income Surveys. Although they do not include rural areas and the non-Jews of East Jerusalem, they do comprise nearly 90 per cent of the total number of households in the country. The results of these surveys are regularly adjusted by price index in order to make them comparable and to provide a sound basis for the assessment of policy impact on poverty and inequality. Furthermore, income, population unit and the poverty line definitions have remained virtually unchanged. The regular user of these data is the National Insurance Institute (NII) which estimates poverty and inequality, and monitors their trends.

In her careful analysis of these trends during the period 1979–91 at 1979 constant prices, Lea Achdut (1993) shows the very strong impact of high inflation (1979–June 1985) and unemployment (1980–91) on income distribution and poverty incidence. During the period 1979–93, there was an overall upward trend in inequality, despite year-to-year fluctuations. In terms of the Gini index (see Appendix 8.1), the degree of inequality – though moderate – increased slightly from 0.366 to 0.376 for the distribution of gross income and from 0.318 to 0.322 for net income. On examining the results of the last three Family Expenditure Surveys (1979/80, 1986/7 and 1992/3), we find that the variations in the shares of employment earnings and cash benefits from the social security programme have had significant effects. For example, rising inequality in 1993 was due primarily to 81 per cent of the total number of adults in the poorest tenth of families surveyed being unemployed. Inequality could have worsened if it had not been for the regularly adjusted government social security payments, as well as indexation of wages and social benefits. The role of the highly unionized labour force in protecting real wages from erosion and the special allowances paid to the increasing number of low-income immigrants to Israel as guaranteed income support have also been important.

With these generous social security payments, absolute poverty remains moderate at national level but high among certain sections of the population. Based on a poverty line fixed at the high cut-off level of half the median (average) net income per person in 1979/80, the Luxembourg Income Study estimated that 14.5 per cent of the Israeli population surveyed were living in absolute poverty, amounting to nearly half a million persons.[16] Poverty was higher, at 23.8 per cent, among the elderly (over 65 years) whose poverty level was worse, at 56.8 per cent, before social security payments. Yet, poverty has persisted, reaching 21 per cent in 1984, when inflation peaked at 450 per cent. Even at 1979 constant prices, the studies carried out by the NII show that the poverty level had risen from 14.5 per cent in 1979 to 17 per cent in 1988–91 because of rapidly increasing unemployment associated with economic recession.

The Israeli poor are concentrated in certain demographic sections of the population, mostly among the elderly and large families of four persons and over. Another significant feature of poverty by age is that inequality of consumption distribution measured in terms of the Gini index is greater within the group of the elderly of 75 years and above than within other age groups.[17] The very rich and very poor co-exist in this 75-plus age group. Many at this age continue to work and accumulate wealth, including high property and capital incomes. The results of the two recent Family Expenditure Surveys (1986/7 and 1992/3)[18] reveal that over this six-year period, the consumption gap between the rich and poor widened; the real value of a person's consumption in the top rank increased from 6.5 to 8 times as much as that of a poor person in the bottom rank (the lowest 10 per cent).

The misfortune of the poor was manifested in housing. The burden of the sharp rise of 260 per cent in rent and housing material prices was much heavier on the poor, whose expenditure on housing was proportionately almost double that of the rich. Moreover, the results of the two Family Expenditure Surveys suggest that what a rich person spends in one month on luxury items of sports and travel abroad is almost equivalent to an entire poor family's average consumption expenditure on the two essentials, food and housing, combined. Sadly, the only superiority in consumption the poor have over the rich is in spending on alcohol and smoking, in proportionate terms.[19] Out of their meagre earnings and social security benefits, the poorest of the poor spend on these two health risks proportionately 3 times as much as do the rich.

Tunisia

Since 1966, the central statistics agency, the Institut National de la Statistique (INS, hereafter) has conducted household surveys, as well as periodic food consumption and nutrition surveys. The results of these surveys show that, at constant 1990 prices, the average consumption per person rose annually by 4 per cent between 1975 and 1985, but its growth slowed down to 1 per cent during the period of economic difficulties (1985–90).[20] During the entire period (1975–90) there was a slight reduction in inequality of consumption shares among income classes due to a deliberate policy of protecting the poor during economic hardship years (see Chapter 10). The fall in inequality is manifested in a decline in the share of the rich class (consumption of 1,200 dinars and more per person per year) in total consumption expenditure from 33 per cent in 1980 to 31 per cent in 1990, while the share of the poorest (less than 150 dinars per person) increased from 1.9 per cent to 2.3 per cent. In the mean time, the consumption shares of the middle class have increased.

However, these indications of improvement at the national level in 1975–90 conceal wide variations among social classes and between districts. Whereas the average consumption level of a person in an urban area has remained virtually double that of a person in a rural area, disparity has increased more *within* urban than rural areas. Inequality has also increased between the top decile and the poorest classes; the difference in their average consumption levels increased from a factor of 7 in 1980 to a factor of 13.4 in 1990. The net gainers in this process of inter-class consumption shifts have been the high-level professionals, top managers in commerce and industry and big landowners producing meat and cash crops. Inter-class disparity is reflected in expenditure shares on essentials, as opposed to luxury items. The results of the 1990 survey show that a rich individual spent on his or her private cars, foreign drinks and sports an amount equivalent to nearly 4 times what the poorest spent on food and housing combined.[21] These essentials absorb 85 per cent of the poor person's total expenditure. There is also an excessive consumption of meat by the rich, who spent 15 times as much on it as the poor. As in Israel, the share of smoking in total expenditure of a poor person was almost double that of the rich (4 per cent and 2.5 per cent respectively) in 1990.

Table 8.3 Incidence of poverty in Tunisia, 1975–90

	1975	*1980*	*1985*	*1990*
Rural %	18	14.2	7.0	5.7
Urban %	26	11.8	8.4	7.3
National %	22	12.9	7.7	6.7
Total number (1,000s)	1,223	823	554	544

Sources: Tunisia, Ministry of Planning and Regional Development (1993: 36–9) and the results of previous surveys published by Institut National de la Statistique, Tunis.

With regard to poverty and undernourishment trends, the number of people living in absolute poverty,[22] as a percentage of the total population, has substantially decreased from 75 per cent in 1957 (one year after independence) to 43 per cent in 1968. Starting with the 1975 household survey, the INS has made separate poverty estimates for localities, given in Table 8.3. The estimates show an impressive downward trend in poverty. Yet the core of the estimates, the poverty line, has been subject to criticism. During my work with the INS in 1982 on the formulation of Tunisian socioeconomic indicators of rural development[23] (based on the results of the 1980 Family Expenditure Survey), it was found that food and non-food components of the 1980 poverty line were unspecified and that the poverty line in rural areas was arbitrarily fixed at half the value of the urban poverty line, 60 and 120 dinars respectively. The problem was in the use of a uniform consumer price index for costing rural and urban items consumed. Another source of bias was the assumption that all calories come solely from cereals, while the 1980 Family Expenditure Survey data indicate that only about 55 per cent do so. These important methodological issues were carefully examined and specified, by a team of ILO experts in 1988. They found that the nutrition base of the poverty line estimate was too low, leading to a lower poverty line.[24] According to their own calculation of actual quantities consumed and prices paid, the ILO team estimated the rural poverty level for 1985 at 31 per cent instead of the government's 7 per cent. However, the revised estimates for 1980 and 1985 indicate a significant reduction in poverty in this period.

The downward trend of poverty is confirmed by the results of Tunisia's 1990 nutrition survey, and is supported by the World Bank's poverty estimates for several developing countries, including Tunisia, at different levels of minimum real consumption per person.[25] At an arbitrary cut-off point of a quarter of the average real consumption per person in 1985 and 1990, poverty levels of 11 and 7 per cent respectively were estimated for Tunisia. Though higher than those of the government (the INS) they nevertheless point to a reduction. Studies on the nutrition situation also show a significant decline in undernourishment, particularly in rural areas. Between 1980 and 1990, the number of *mal nourris* (those failing to meet 80 per cent of daily minimum calorie requirements) fell from 12.4 to 8.2 per cent of the total population.[26] The highest proportion of the undernourished was among the lowest income group in 1990. They suffer from a deficit of 16 per cent in their daily calorie consumption and about 40 per cent in calcium and iron requirements. At the other extreme, the 1990/91 food-consumption data by income class show the rich having an excess above the standard for all nutrition elements: of 19 per cent in calories, of 112 per cent in protein, of 33 per cent in calcium and of 14 per cent in iron.[27] The most welcome nutritional improvement is among children under the age of 5: the proportion of children whose weight for age is below 80 per cent of the standard has significantly decreased, from 18 per cent in 1975–80 to only 6 per cent in 1991.

Several factors have contributed to the reduction of poverty and inequality. Apart from sustained economic growth at a handsome rate within well-balanced development efforts, certain policy instruments have had a direct influence. They include:

1 the post-independence redistribution of wealth, especially the size-able area of fertile land recovered from the French colonists and redistributed among the fellaheen;
2 the early initiation of family planning in 1963 and women's parti-cipation in the formal labour market;
3 the promotion of rural-to-urban and international migration to Algeria, Libya and France, which in 1970–80 increased labour productivity of those who remained in agriculture fourfold, the highest increase in North Africa,[28] and remarkably increased the remittance receipts from less than US$1 million in 1963 to US$0.6 billion in 1990;
4 the top priority accorded to the disadvantaged areas in regional development investment, defined in the *Carte des Priorités Régionales*;[29]
5 the provision of income transfers to low-income groups through subsidies, social security benefits and school meals.

Mauritania

This is the poorest and most food-insecure country in the Middle East. Nearly half its population live in absolute poverty and 58 per cent of its total food requirement is imported. In contrast to Tunisia's sustained progress, Mauritania experienced a steady fall in annual income per person over 1965–92, and the real consumption per person is only one-third of that of Tunisia. Hence, Mauritania is among UNICEF's sixteen worst nations of the world, with the highest infant and under-5 mortality rates in 1995. This state of poverty and hunger originated in those very foundations of inequality and poverty suggested in Chapters 3–6: long colonial rule; political instability; systematic discrimination in education by sex, ethnic group and income class; high vulnerability to frequent long droughts and food-production instability resulting from a very weak financial capacity to develop what is potentially the second-largest productive area of land in the Middle East (after Sudan); unbalanced economic and human development; and the heavy reliance on donors for alleviating food insecurity and financing development programmes. For example, in 1980–90, average annual development aid was US$180 million, or nearly one-quarter of the national income (GNP), US$95 per person.

The results of a range of surveys seem to agree that poverty and hunger are pervasive.[30] There are wide variations in earnings between districts and socioeconomic groups and between and within the two main production systems, iron ore mining and farming, caused by differences in the sources of irrigation, land tenure arrangements and the size of land and livestock holdings. There are also differences between the regularity of earnings in the small and stable formal sector and the irregular flow of earnings in the large informal sector, especially as regards nomadic people's activities. In addition to education, these sources of inequalities are reflected in the results of the 1990 ONS survey of a sample of 1,600 sedentary households, published as *Enquête Permanent sur les Conditions de Vie des Ménages (EPCV)*. The results show that inequality within rural areas is higher than in urban areas, and is responsible for 63.5 per cent of inequality at the national level. Had the nomadic people been included in the *EPCV* surveys, this percentage would have been higher. Amadou Mangane (1984: 13) estimated the nomads to be roughly 25 per cent of the total population, falling to 15 per cent after the 1980s drought-induced exodus that increased the population of the capital city, Nouakchott, by almost 50 per cent.

Because of the positive correlation between education status and income inequality, illiteracy is highest among the poorest fifth of the population: in urban areas the rate is 50 per cent for males, 63 per cent for females; in rural areas it is 73 and 85 per cent respectively. At the other extreme, the richest group (the top 20 per cent) are fortunate: only one-fifth of rich males are illiterate in urban areas and one-third in rural areas. Inequality in educational opportunity is also manifested in a wide variation in access to schooling. Only 5.7 per cent of the poor have access to secondary education in rural areas. Systematic educational discrimination by sex is staggering everywhere, among rich and poor females alike. A mere 15 per cent of urban and 5 per cent of rural poor girls in the age group 12–17 years attend secondary schools.[31]

When we examine the pattern of food consumption expenditure among income classes, we find vast differences, particularly in meat consumption.[32] As in Israel and Tunisia, of the total expenditure on meat (including camel meat) in 1990, 45 per cent was from the richest households (the top 20 per cent), while that of the poorest 20 per cent of households was only 0.3 per cent. This is indeed an over-consumption by the rich in contrast to a deprivation among the poor, who suffer from diseases of protein deficiency and chronic undernutrition (actual cereal expenditure being below 80 per cent of the average minimum require-ments). Yet this large poor stratum received only 14 per cent of total food aid in 1990. According to the results of the 1990 *EPCV,* the rich in the fertile plains of the Senegal river captured 40 per cent of total food aid. What is dismaying indeed is that the relatively few rich residents of the capital city, Nouakchott, received 16 per cent; a higher share than that of the rural poor masses.

Who are the poor and how many are there? Using the results of the *EPCV* of 1990 and following the World Bank's procedure, the national statistical office (ONS) established two poverty lines: a lower line at 24,400 ouguiya (UM) per person per year and a higher line at 32,800 UM. The number of people in absolute poverty as a percentage of total population was estimated at 44.7 per cent and 56.6 per cent, respectively. Poverty among the sedentary rural population is overwhelming, between 69 and 74 per cent. Most of the poor in rural areas are the illiterate landless, wage-dependent workers and sharecroppers. In urban centres the poor are mostly casual unskilled workers in the informal sector, the majority of whom were rural poor who involuntarily migrated to urban areas during the prolonged droughts of the 1970s and 1980s. On the other hand, the rich are mostly senior officials of government and public enterprises, self-employed businessmen, nobles and former warriors in the tribal system and the religious leaders among the Moors.

McKay, Houeibib and Coulombe (1992 and 1993) ranked quality and level of education at the top of the determinants of poverty. Others are family size (the larger the number of dependents and elderly, the poorer the family) and unemployment and the degree of earning instability, particularly in the vast non-irrigated areas (*dieri*). Children under the age of 5 are the most vulnerable to hunger and poverty during years of prolonged drought such as the periods 1973–4 and 1982–4 in Mauritania. The results of eighteen nutrition surveys with a wide range of sample size show that in the drought year of 1983 21.5 per cent of children surveyed suffered from acute undernutrition (measured by weight for height or wasting, defined as a high deviation from the average weight for height of healthy children).[33] During the good-rainfall year of 1988, this percentage fell sharply to only 4.3 per cent. However, the rate of under-5 mortality in 1994 was the highest in the Middle East, 199 per 1,000 live births compared to the region's average of 65.

The coexistence of affluent consumption and malnutrition in the Gulf countries

In these richest countries of the Middle East, my focus is on food consumption and diet-related diseases by income class, with illustrations from Kuwait, Bahrain and Saudi Arabia. The question addressed is: do obesity and affluence-related diseases such as diabetes, heart disease (cardiovascular combined with hypertension), dental caries and some types of cancer coexist with nutrition deprivation?[34] What are the characteristics of affluence-related diseases and nutrition deprivation?

Available studies and casual observations suggest that overconsumption of food is common in these oil-rich countries. Examples are the excessive consumption of meat combined with high quantities of rice, fat, salty and spicy food and sweets, and the frequent eating of sizeable snacks between meals. This broad pattern of affluent food consumption has nutrition and health consequences that are difficult to quantify, for three reasons. First, the actual food intake per individual is difficult to measure, because families often eat together from a big tray or from the same plate. Second, because of illiteracy and lack of nutrition education, such diseases as diabetes and dental caries are not considered by ordinary citizens as illness. Third, deaths occurring at home are not always registered, especially in rural areas, because a death certificate is not always officially required for burial. Hence, causes of death are under-reported.

Available studies show that obesity and diabetes are widespread, particularly among women. Nutritional status studies agree that heart disease is also prevalent in different forms (stroke, hypertension and cardiovascular diseases) among the nationals of these wealthy countries, owing to the high frequency of regular fatty meals and the lifestyle, which often consists of an inactive, sedentary life, dependency on chauffeur-driven cars, having permanent household maids and servants, watching television over long periods, and so forth. We may add a cultural factor in men's preference for obese women as marriage partners and society's high regard for obese men. In contrast to this manifestation of extravagant food consumption, anaemia is widespread, especially among children, reaching 38 per cent in Oman, 45 per cent in the United Arab Emirates, the richest Gulf country, and almost 50 per cent of all children below the age of 6 in Bahrain and Saudi Arabia.[35]

Kuwait

This second-richest country in the Middle East represents a grossly unequal consumption that exhibits a striking co-existence of obesity and undernutrition. In 1984–5 the daily consumption of fat per person (70 grams) was the highest in the Middle East and 40 per cent of Kuwaiti women, 24 per cent of men, 18 per cent of boys and 27 per cent of girls were obese. This ostentation contrasts sharply with undernourishment among one-fifth of the children whose weight for height was only 70–80 per cent of the Harvard standard. In 1990, according to UNICEF, rich Kuwait was in the same category of malnutrition as poorer Jordan, with 6 per cent of children under 5 underweight.

Affluence is associated with a chronic food wastage which peaks in feastings. My own experience may illustrate this point. The occasion was a wedding ceremony held by a wealthy family in the Kuwait Sheraton Hotel, where I was staying in the early 1970s. Expensive flowers were flown from the Netherlands together with a flower arranger. The following morning I saw the luxurious flowers thrown outside the hotel and large pieces of lamb and turkey were scavenged from two huge rubbish bins by a number of hungry boys, who seemed to belong to the Kuwaiti underclass. They were soon pushed away by a policeman who saw them being watched by me and photographed by foreign tourists. This polarization in consumption was quantified by the results of the household surveys conducted during the oil boom, and published in Kuwait's *Annual Statistical Abstract* 1990/1 (Kuwait, Ministry of Planning, 1990–3: 229–33). In 1973, monthly consumption spending per person in the top income class was 11 times that of the bottom class and expenditure on food alone was 3 times. By 1977, inequality increased substantially; monthly consumption was 14 times greater and spending on food was 5 times greater. The gap was even wider between the average consumption of Kuwaiti and non-Kuwaiti nationals.

Bahrain

Like the rest of the tiny Gulf sheikhdoms, Bahrain's wealth is primarily derived from oil. The size of its population was 510,000 in 1992, mostly urban (90 per cent) with nearly 30 per cent from Iran and South Asia. The country's real income per person of US$7,200 is a little less than that of Saudi Arabia. Bahrain is among the rich nations of the Middle East. By making the drinking of alcohol in public legal, Bahrain – and Dubai – the only Arab Gulf states that have adopted this policy – attract many visitors from neighbouring Arab countries, including over 1 million Saudi visitors to Bahrain in 1992. Imported drinks and tobacco represented one-quarter of the total value of food imports in 1992.[36] Yet there is persistent poverty. Based on the Ministry of Health's estimate of the daily minimum food requirement per person, and using the results of the 1983/4 household expenditure survey and its 1986 estimates, nearly 33 per cent of the total population were living in absolute poverty in 1984 and 24 per cent in 1986.[37]

The results of the 1983/4 survey and several nutrition studies show that affluence has had a negative impact on health of Bahraini people. Obesity is increasing, especially among uneducated adult women and schoolgirls, and is a high-risk factor for heart diseases and diabetes.[38] A sample survey distinguishing obese from non-obese schoolgirls by income class found that the grossly overfed girls consumed a large excess of calories, protein and fat. These excesses being costly, obese girls are from richer families than the non-obese. Nearly two-thirds of the total number of schoolgirls examined suffered from dental decay caused by affluent consumption habits, namely a high intake of such luxury items as chocolates, soft drinks, cakes and other high-sugar foods eaten between meals.

With this pattern of consumption and lifestyle, heart diseases have become the first cause of death in Bahrain, especially among rich businessmen and senior officials aged 50 years and above, among whom diet-related deaths increased by 50 per cent in 1977–86. Researchers attribute this increase to a high intake of saturated fatty acids, excessive dietary cholesterol, hypertension, heavy cigarette smoking, diabetes, drinking alcohol and a high intake of sodium in salty food. Nutritionists have found that this consumption pattern has been associated with a steadily decreasing consumption of traditional, healthy foods. Furthermore, some kinds of cancer (breast, colon and gastro-intestinal) have been found to be associated with high animal-fat intake. The daily consumption of animal fat per person increased by 78 per cent during the oil boom (1974–80). Sadly, these overweight people co-existed in an affluent society with anaemic and stunted Bahraini children, who receive less attention in food consumption than adults. They were suffering from hunger; 7 per cent of the schoolchildren surveyed in 1984 were stunted and as many as 41.4 per cent were suffering from wasting.

Saudi Arabia

Whereas the principal features of food consumption and the resulting health problems in Saudi Arabia are similar to those examined in Kuwait and Bahrain, the magnitude differs. This is due partly to the larger size of the Saudi population (17 million in 1992) and the wide variation in socioeconomic conditions between its vast geographical regions, as shown by the results of a series of nutrition surveys.[39] They show also that Saudi family size is quite large, seven on average, reaching twenty in the eastern regions where the oil industry and affluent families are concentrated. The results of a sample survey of 10,000 households conducted in June 1990 suggest that the connection between large family-size and malnutrition lies in high illiteracy rates among mothers according to their age (70 per cent in the age group of 30–40 years and the very high 91 per cent in the age group of 40–50 years). Among the factors influencing the large size of family, the results of the survey show that the average age of first marriage of women was 16 years and that the total fertility rate was 7.3, compared to the Middle East average of 5.7 and the average of 1.8 in the world's high-income countries in 1990.[40] Moreover, there are two important cultural factors prevailing in Saudi society: the belief that the number of children is 'up to God and a gift of God', and the practice of multiple marriage, that is, having up to four wives at the same time.

Despite the unprecedented affluence of the Saudi people, their food safety and nutrition status, like their high illiteracy, resemble those of many poor countries. It is striking to find a high incidence of anaemia (60 per cent among men and 56.7 per cent among women in 1990). But the worst finding is that nearly two-thirds of the surveyed children below 6 years of age suffered from acute anaemia and that in El-Qaseem region, 50.2 per cent of the population were malnourished, in terms of a high prevalence of iron deficiency.[41] Children's malnourishment indicators, combined with the prevalence of parasitic infections, are reflected in the 1994 rate of under-5 mortality, which was higher than in poorer countries (Jordan and Tunisia).[42]

Are obesity and diabetes positively correlated with personal income level? From a sample survey of 5,222 persons carried out in the western region, the results given in Table 8.4 support this positive relationship: the higher the income level, the more likely is the incidence of simultaneous suffering from diabetes and obesity. The data show that of the total richest persons examined, 73.3 per cent in the age group of 35–54 were both diabetic and obese. In the same age group, the percentage of low-income persons earning less than 3,000 rials per month was 45.5 per

Table 8.4 Obesity and diabetes by age and income class in the western region of Saudi Arabia, 1987

| | Diabetic and obese persons (%) | | |
| | Monthly income per person | | |
Age in years	Less than 3,000 SR	3,000–6,000 SR	Over 6,000 SR
15–34	20.0	37.5	70.0
35–54	45.5	54.5	73.3
55 and over	8.3	53.5	50.0

Source: Based on data given in Al-Shoshan (1992: 11–12 and Table 5).

Notes
SR = Saudi rial. US$1 = 3.75 SR.
Obesity is measured by the Body Mass Index (BMI) = weight in kilogrammes divided by square of the height in metres. A person is obese when BMI = 25 or more.

cent, lower than the rich category. The same positive relationship exists in the two other age groups.

Summary

This chapter has been concerned with some inter-related questions: what are the salient personal consumption patterns and the types of change in consumption items? How have these changes affected the locally produced traditional items consumed by the poor and low-income groups? This inquiry into consumption inequality has questioned the relevance of an important principle in conventional economics, namely that consumption is determined solely by the consumer's own sovereignty and free choice, without being influenced by producers through advertising and the multinationals' marketing power, or by the behaviour of other consumers or by cultural forces.

Country studies have enabled us to understand how poverty in affluent Israel differs in scale and in the composition of rich and poor from that of middle-income Tunisia and the poorest country, Mauritania. How have different methods in estimating poverty in Tunisia produced very different poverty levels? This chapter has highlighted the country-specific factors that have heavily influenced consumption inequality and poverty levels (educational discrimination, production and earnings systems and severe climatic changes in Mauritania, the Israeli demographic characteristics, free labour unions, the rapid flow of migrant Jews from abroad and high income/expenditure inequality among the elderly, for example). We have also been able to identify affluence-related food consumption problems and the resulting diseases in the rich Gulf countries.

INEQUALITY IN PRIVATE CONSUMPTION

Obesity and diabetes are found to be positively correlated with affluence, and diet-related coronary heart diseases have become the main cause of death in these countries. Moreover, ostentatious consumption in this group of affluent societies co-exists strikingly with prevalent anaemia and malnutrition, especially among children. Understanding consumer health conditions is necessary in the study of affluence and poverty.

The chapter has also examined the types and origin of change in products consumed. There has been a shift away from traditional items consumed by low-income groups and the poor towards modern high-income products with the characteristics of goods manufactured and consumed in rich Western societies. Their consumption in the Middle East is backed by aggressive advertising. Special attention has been paid to the advertising-based globalization of consumer products that are unaffordable by the poor, and whose effects on cultural values are increasingly questioned by the intelligentsia and religious militants.

Suggested readings

On private consumption and development:
James (1993) *Consumption and Development*, Chapters 1 and 2.
Robinson (1979) *Aspects of Development and Underdevelopment*, especially Chapters 1 and 2.

On the effects of technology on consumer products:
James (1993) *Consumption and Development*, Chapter 2, 'New Products'.
Zahlan and Magar (1986) *The Agricultural Sector of Sudan*.

On comparability of private consumption and poverty estimates across countries:
Fields (1980) *Poverty, Inequality and Development*, Chapter 2, pp. 21–32.
Ravallion *et al.* (1991) 'Quantifying Absolute Poverty in the Developing World' and (1994) 'Is Poverty Increasing in the Developing World?'.
Smeeding *et al.* (1990) *Poverty, Inequality and Income Distribution in Comparative Perspective* (The Luxembourg Income Study), especially Chapters 2 and 7.
van Ginneken and Park (1984) *Generating Internationally Comparable Income Distribution Estimates*, the chapters on Egypt, Iran and Sudan.
Other useful readings are listed at the end of Chapter 1.

On the role of advertising and multinationals in private consumption changes:
de Mooij (1994) *Advertising Worldwide*, especially Parts I and II.
Streeten (1981) *Development Perspectives*, Chapter 22, 'Trans-national Corporations and Basic Needs'.

Additional readings can be found in notes and in the Bibliography.

APPENDIX 8.1   MEASUREMENT OF PERSONAL CONSUMPTION INEQUALITY

The degree of inequality or concentration and its changes over time concern both policymakers and development analysts. In the text, I have used two simple but related measurements of the distribution of personal consumption expenditure or income. One is a crude measure of the proportion of the total expenditure corresponding to a certain percentile grouping of the total number of families or individuals surveyed (e.g. deciles of 10 per cent, 20 per cent, 30 per cent, and so on, or quintiles of 20 per cent, 40 per cent, and so on). For example, we may say that 60 per cent of the total people surveyed (households or individuals) possess or receive only 20 per cent of total income/expenditure, while 40 per cent have 80 per cent of the total. The other measurement used is the Gini index; a statistical summary of the degree of inequality. It ranges from a minimum of an absolute equality value of zero to a maximum value of absolute inequality of one. I have not used other complex measures of inequality among the poor (e.g. the Theil index or the Sen index).

Both measurements are calculated from a tabulation of data on the distribution of the two variables (consumption expenditure and numbers of households or individuals) classified by size class, starting with the lowest (e.g. less than US$100 followed by US$100–200, and so on). After that, the percentage relationships of these two variables are accumulated, ending with 100. The cumulative percentage relationships are then plotted into equal parts (deciles or quintiles), on a diagram, with the number of individuals or households on the horizontal axis and the expenditure or income on the vertical axis. The plotted percentage corresponding to each size of class produces a diagram known as the Lorenz curve of the distribution, which shows the cumulative consumption expenditure share corresponding to a specific decile (10 per cent or 20 per cent and so on) of total households or individuals. For the purpose of illustration, absolute equality is indicated in Appendix Figure 8.1 by the line 0A, which means that 10 per cent of the population have a

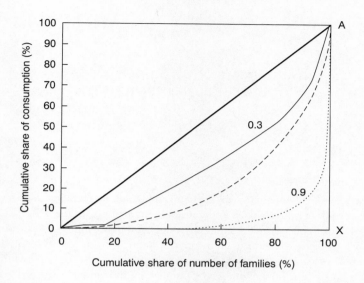

Appendix Figure 8.1 Shifts in Lorenz curves and corresponding values of the Gini
index of inequality in the distribution of families' consumption

Notes

———— 0.394

- - - - - - - - 0.566

. . . . 0.902

The diagonal is a line of perfect equality.

10 per cent of share in total household expenditure, 20 per cent have a
20 per cent share, and so on. It means also that the closer the curve to
this line, the less is the degree of inequality. The opposite is also true: the
further the curve is, the more unequal the distribution is.

The Gini index can be calculated from the Lorenz curve. The extent
of inequality is indicated by the area between the line of absolute
equality (0A) and the Lorenz curve as a proportion of the total area of
the triangle 0AX. From the data on shifts in the distribution presented by
three Lorenz curves in Appendix Figure 8.1, the Gini index of inequality
is decreasing from the highly unequal 0.9 to the moderate 0.3 and to the
hypothetical absolute equality zero (the line 0A).

Part II

POLICY CHOICE
Some countries' experiences

9

REDISTRIBUTION OF
WEALTH AND INCOME

An assessment

Tackling poverty and gross inequality at their roots, rather than treating their symptoms, requires more distribution of the tangible assets that generate direct primary income rather than a reliance on gaining secondary income support and on automatic benefit from economic growth. Nationalization of giant enterprises, the redistribution of rural wealth (land and capital), the expansion of education opportunities, and the support of low-income groups were the main distributive policies pursued by Middle Eastern governments at their initial stage of development. Education, an important asset that determines lifetime earning-power, has already been discussed in Chapters 2 and 6. Examples of programmes on taxation, subsidies, fixing minimum wages and the delivery of free social services have also been briefly presented in country studies; how economic reforms have affected them is examined in Chapter 10.

This chapter begins with a brief discussion of the principal elements that determine policy choice and who benefits. The second section examines the welfare aspects of nationalization. In the third section we assess two types of policies for the redistribution of wealth generating primary income: privately owned land and capital in Algeria, Iran and Egypt, and public land and oil money in Saudi Arabia. The fourth section examines income-transfers policy in Turkey and Jordan. The last section focuses on social security financed voluntarily by people's own organizations.

Policy choice: who benefits?

In the choice of policy content, say, redistribution of assets other than education, the procedure by which decisions are reached differs from country to country in many ways. One procedural system is parliamentary democracy, which is scarce in the region and the other is a totalitarian form of government, which is prevalent. Generally, nationalization, expropriation and redistribution of private property rights have been decided by small groups brought to power by force of *coups d'état* or liberation movements. The perceptible belief behind the policymakers' oligarchical procedure is that radical measures produce quick and tangible results that could not be realized by a parliamentary majority representing constituencies with diverse interests.

Whether by parliamentary majority or by oligarchy, arriving at a policy on redistribution of wealth and income is a result of compromises between ideal and realistic solutions to the problems of deprivation and vast inequalities in wealth and opportunity. Also, such a policy exhibits dissatisfaction with certain market failures, as deficiencies of capitalism and abuse of private-property rights. Reaching a compromise requires concessions with regard to setting time-bound targets for bringing about policy changes; and also to the scale of change, that is, the number and size of enterprises to be nationalized and the ceiling to be set on private landed property. Concessions are also required regarding who is to benefit from social security programmes and the minimum level of income that should be set for support. Such complex elements in policy making determine who will be the gainers and the expected losers, whether or not they are compensated, and how this will be done.

In most cases, policy objectives tend to be conveniently ambiguous. Preference is usually for such broad objectives as the speedy realization of justice, raising living standards, elimination of exploitation and feudalism (*iqta*), and so forth. In sum, the policy choice is a product of a combination of (a) the initial situation of poverty and income inequality; (b) the lobbying strength of interest groups and the configuration of the political power structure; (c) the will and commitment to poverty reduction; (d) the form of government (parliamentary majority or oligarchy); (e) the time period for the realization of policy objectives; and (f) the resources available for policy implementation, including the administrative capabilities and the technical skills of the civil servants.

Nationalization

During the 1950s and 1960s, most of the Middle Eastern economies witnessed an unprecedented wave of nationalization. It was intimately connected with politial independence and the rise of nationalist movements. Perhaps the most dramatic takeovers of foreign properties were that of the British-controlled oil industry of Iran in 1951 by the nationalist leader Mohammed Mossadeq; of the Paris-based Suez Canal Company in 1956 by the Egyptian leader Abdul Nasser; and of almost all French-owned estates in Algeria immediately after independence in July 1962. These events, together with the earlier nationalization of railways and mines in Turkey, led many other Middle Eastern countries to indulge in a sweeping takeover of foreign assets and major domestic enterprises.

Whether the motive is nationalistic, as an act of revenge against the old masters, or a socialist ideology, or an *ad hoc* response to a provocative international action, the focus of this study is on the welfare effects of nationalization in terms of:

1   breaking monopoly powers in private property rights and supply services, and abolishing related monopoly profits;
2   providing governments with more revenue for expansion of employment, health and education;
3   exercising public control of important productive enterprises and means of finance;
4   providing highly paid jobs to eminent supporters of the regime, a preference that increases inequality in employment opportunities.

With the exception of (1) these motives neither guarantee a greater equality nor shape public spending patterns in favour of the poorest sections of society. For example, the fiscal objectives of (2) could be achieved by heavy taxation of nationalized firms' profits, instead of the politically dramatic nationalization with its related problems of compensation payments and restriction of labour unions' rights.

Development experience suggests that the larger the extent of nationalized economic enterprises, the greater is government control of both job creation and earnings. The increasing number of employees in the public sector had, until the introduction of economic reforms around 1985, enjoyed a wide range of benefits: profit sharing, greater housing benefits, a higher statutory minimum wage, fewer working days and more guaranteed tenure of jobs than prior to nationalization. Along with the socialist policy pursued by several countries, the novel motive of 'Islamic immoral exploitation' was stressed by Iran to justify the sweeping nationalization that characterized Ayatollah Khomeini's development strategy between July 1979 and the end of 1982. During this period, most of the manufacturing sector was nationalized, and, as in Egypt, the confiscated assets of the royal family were put in a special fund to finance income-generating schemes for the poor.[1]

Land redistribution

The historical record of the Middle East suggests that the 1950s and 1960s were the 'fellaheen decades' when profound changes in property rights took place. To avoid ambiguity in understanding policy choice, a distinction is made between 'land reform' and 'agrarian reform' including land settlement. The former means the transfer of private property rights from big (mostly absentee) landowners to poor peasants and landless workers. It is a strong demonstration of political commitment to attack poverty directly, and to establish a more equitable social order. Agrarian reform, on the other hand, embraces a wider scope of institutional and technical changes associated with a greater access to land. For political purposes, the meaning of agrarian reform has been expanded to embrace one or more of the following: the distribution of public land for land settlement schemes, the registration of land titles, the consolidation of fragmented holdings and the purchase of land in the open market by way of public lending, the use of foreign aid, and so forth.

Nevertheless, there is a major difference between land reform and the distribution of public land for settlement or resettlement purposes. The difference is in the welfare and political philosophy. In land reform, a politically drastic action is taken to reduce landownership inequality and reform the power structure in the *existing* rural community. On the other hand, in settlement schemes, the land base is technically *created* through heavy investment and engineering work, including the construction of new houses and roads as well as the transportation of selected numbers of farmers and staff into the newly developed area. Thus, distribution of public land as an alternative to land reform leaves the concentration of landed property and the corresponding power structure unchanged, and may even strengthen them. Moreover, poverty and income inequality may not be significantly reduced in the national context. Similarly, in the case of the use of financial grants for land settlement, conflicting welfare outcomes result, as in the Jewish National Fund for the creation of immigration-based Jewish settlements on lands purchased or taken over from Palestinian Arabs.[2]

Land reform

Since most Middle Eastern economies were agrarian, the reform of the iniquitous institutions of land tenure and credit and of labour-use arrangements was a core policy. There is sense in this because pre-reform private-property rights in productive land represented political power and social security, and were the foundation of both income distribution

Table 9.1 Ratios of redistributed privately owned land and beneficiaries in eight countries, 1952–89

Country	Dates of land reform laws	Redistributed private land area as % of total arable land	Number of beneficiaries as % of total agricultural households
Algeria	1962, 1971	50	37
Egypt	1952, 1961	10	14
Iran	1962, 1967, 1989	34[a]	45 approx.
Iraq	1958, 1971	60	56
Morocco	1956, 1963, 1973	4	2
Syria	1958, 1963, 1980	10[b]	16
Tunisia	1956, 1957, 1964	57[c]	n.a.
Yemen (South)	1968, 1970	47	25

Sources: For Iraq and Egypt: M. R. El-Ghonemy (1990b); for Algeria, Morocco and Tunisia: M. R. El-Ghonemy (1993); for Yemen: M. R. El-Ghonemy in IFAD (1992); for Syria: Syria, Ministry of Agriculture and Agrarian Reform (1990: Table 6) (Arabic). For Iran, see pp.158–9.

Notes
n.a. = not available.
a   Includes the area reallocated by the Council of Determination in March 1989, which was occupied by peasants after the owners fled the country.
b   Refers to the land actually redistributed.
c   Includes the individualized *habous* or private *waqf* land, representing 29 per cent of total arable land.

and class stratification. Access to productive land has also been the major source of employment of the fellaheen's family-based labour and their control over the food they eat.

The magnitude of these changes is presented in Table 9.1, which is approximate and does not include the distribution of public lands. One reason for this presentation is the changing ideological preferences of the state, between retaining the expropriated land for direct management and its speedy redistribution. In Syria, for example, out of the total area of private land expropriated in 1958–62, amounting to 1.5 million hectares, an area of 621,355 hectares had, until 1990, been redistributed to peasants, the balance retained as state farms.[3]

Countries' experiences suggest that land reforms differ in aims, pace and scale of implementation, as do productivity and equity outcomes. For these reasons this chapter briefly reviews the experience of three selected countries with different historical and structural characteristics: Algeria, Iran and Egypt. We need to keep in mind the fact that as land reform is a sectoral reform, its production and distributional effects are not easily separable from the dynamic forces operating in the national economy. An example of these inseparable effects is apparent in Algeria and Iran; oil money has made it possible for their governments to develop reformed areas, and to pay full compensation to affected landowners.

Algeria: from colonial to socialist economy

Immediately after independence in July 1962, the Algerian leadership nationalized the French settlers' lands, totalling 2.8 million hectares (representing 37 per cent of total cultivable area). Backed by their government, the Algerians working on these farms resumed management of them as paid workers without breaking them up. By 1966, this sector had absorbed nearly 1 million workers (M. R. El-Ghonemy, 1968: 40–1). In addition, an area of some 100,000 hectares was confiscated from the *bachagha*, the rich Algerians who had collaborated with the French regime prior to independence. A network of government-controlled co-operatives was hurriedly established in both reformed areas, known later as the socialist sector.

The second phase, known as *la réforme révolutionnaire*, was initiated in 1971 by President Boumédienne and implemented during the oil boom. It was intended to abolish the sharecropping system, cancel small tenants' accumulated debts, and distribute about 700,000 hectares of state-owned lands among poor sharecroppers and landless workers. The state also expropriated 650,000 hectares of privately owned lands, exceeding an established ceiling of approximately 40–50 hectares (depending on land productivity), for distribution to nearly 60,000 beneficiaries, many of whom were poor tenants. The beneficiaries of these programmes received a unit of 10 to 15 hectares each. The criterion employed for determining the unit size was that it should provide the household with an annual income of 3,500 Algerian dinars in 1975 (3.9 dinars equalled US$1).[4]

The large scale of this programme was not matched by adequate public investment to enable the beneficiaries to attain the potential gains. As explained in Chapter 5, agriculture stagnated; productivity per working person in agriculture fell, and the country's dependency on food imports increased sharply. Land reform *per se* is not to blame for this failure, because raising output in a large reformed sector of nearly 3.4 million hectares requires more than, in the celebrated words of Arthur Young, 'the magic of property [that] turns sand into gold'. This magic could not work while agriculture was neglected and the motivation and production incentives of the beneficiaries weakened by tight government control.

Faced with the fellaheen's rising discontent about the bureaucrats' inefficient management of co-operatives and state farms, the government issued Law No. 9 in December 1987, providing for the individualization of collective farming, and the privatization of land and means of production, with optional membership in co-operatives. It also provided for the sale of most state farms to farmers, on favourable terms. By then, the income gap between the hitherto favoured socialist sector on the one hand, and the private and tribal sector on the other, had already widened. The results of INEAP's studies show that inequality of income distribution within agriculture was higher than between it and other sectors of the economy.[5]

Iran: a capitalist reform

The economic system under which land reform was initiated around 1960 in Iran differed substantially from that of Algeria. The economy was based on private property and when the reform programme was initiated, Iran's oil revenue (1955–60) was nearly 100 times that of Algeria.[6]

From the present author's first study of land tenure in Iran in 1955, it emerged that the social organization of its economy determined the distribution of benefits from oil and agriculture in favour of the privileged few, while denying the needs of the many.[7] With over two-thirds of the total population living in rural areas, the vast inequality in the distribution of wealth in Iran presented the extreme injustice of a quasi-feudal system. Wealth in rural Iran was based on the private ownership of entire villages and the landlords' control of the most scarce resource, groundwater channels (qanats). The royal family, together with large landlords and the Islamic establishment (the waqf endowments) possessed nearly 80 per cent of the total cultivable land, and its qanats. Rich landlords were absentee, living in Tehran, Isfahan or Europe, and their land was mainly cultivated by permanently indebted peasants. The average annual income of these peasants was estimated at US$50 per person, which amounted to less than one-quarter of the national figure and one-tenth of the price of a kilogramme of Iran's caviar, consumed by the rich in less than an hour. As a result, the distribution of national income by the mid-1950s was highly unequal: the share of the poorest 20 per cent of the total households was only 4 per cent, while that of the richest 5 per cent was 32 per cent.[8]

To grapple with injustice among the majority of the people, and without weakening capitalism and without antagonizing the landed aristocracy, the Shah decided to sell part of his private Crown land

and some state-owned land at 800–1500 rials per hectare. While most of the beneficiaries were peasants, some landlords, city merchants and military personnel were also land recipients. Yet the urge for a genuine redistributive reform continued.[9] The result was the land reform laws of 1960 and 1962, which limited ownership to a maximum of one village, with the balance purchased by the government for redistribution to the occupying tenants or sharecroppers. The area of a village ranged from 300 to 600 hectares. Later, the law of 1963 specified maximum land areas, ranging from 20 hectares in irrigated rice-growing areas to 150 hectares in rainfed wheat-growing areas.

I have always found it problematic to assess the redistributive effects of this puzzling, complicated programme. During my field visits in 1965, 1970 and 1972, it appeared that official statistics were exaggerated. Likewise, several heads of the departments concerned tended to discredit the achievements of their predecessors, and to give inflated figures differing from those of the Central Statistical Office.[10] But reliable sources agreed that the landless workers – estimated at one million in 1975 – were excluded from land reform and not all eligible tenants have benefited. Yet, without a violent upheaval (such as the *coups d'état* in Egypt, Iraq, Libya and Syria), nearly half the agricultural households have received title to units which they cultivated as tenants. In the mean time, the landlords have retained ownership of the most fertile land in Iran.[11]

Colonel Valian, a confidant of the Shah, brought from the army in 1963 to command the powerful Land Reform Organization and later Minister of Rural Affairs, arranged to pay a total of US$41 million from oil revenues (25 per cent of total compensation) immediately, in cash, to all affected landlords. The payment of the rest was guaranteed by the Central Bank. The beneficiaries, in turn, paid the government the purchase price by annual instalments, bearing no interest, but it was disguised in a high administrative cost of 10 per cent. The peasants' estimated gain was represented by the difference between the annual instalment and the share of the output (or annual rent) previously given to the landlord, plus expected increase in yields minus taxes. For example, my 1965 field study of twenty-nine household beneficiaries of land reform in Meshkin Abad village (45 kilometres west of Tehran) revealed that, with the two improved irrigation *qanats* and easy access to subsidized seeds and fertilizers, the new owners were able to grow annually two crops plus vegetables. From a unit of 7 hectares each beneficiary paid to the government an annual instalment of 5,300 rials plus 50 rials for a co-operative share, compared with an average of 13,000 rials, my calculated value of the crop share previously given to the landlord. Some families further increased their total earnings by weaving carpets.[12]

The rejoicing of the new owners at the rewards they reaped from operating their individual farms was short lived. In 1967, the Farm Corporations Law was issued, pooling all the lands of individual peasants to establish large-scale and heavily mechanized farms managed by government officials.[13] My visits to three farm corporations in 1970 and 1972 convinced me of the aggressive procedures which were followed, while ignoring the peasants' own preferences.[14]

After Ayatollah Khomeini's revolution in 1979, and based on different interpretations of the Islamic principles regarding property rights, conflicting views have emerged between the pro- and anti-land-reform factions. Some mullahs (religious leaders including ayatollahs) in the powerful Council of Guards and the Majlis (parliament) condemned land reform as a violation of private-property rights, and called for the return to their original owners of cultivated lands expropriated during the Shah's regime. Ironically, this faction in coalition with others was instrumental in the nationalization of manufacturing industry and major trading and banking enterprises, in 1979–82. Another faction took the opposing stand of continuing, with minor modification, the Shah's land policy, in order to promote social justice, considered to be the primary objective of the revolution. The conflicts between pro- and anti-land-reform factions within the Khomeini administration lasted a decade (1979–89), until Khomeini himself established the Determination Council to resolve, in March 1989, disputed land-tenure issues. The outcome was a redistribution of some 450,000 hectares of recovered land, privately owned by landlords who had fled the country, including the royal family, in addition to the distribution of 600,000 hectares of public land.[15]

Egypt: a partial reform

Egypt's historical record suggests that, aside from wielding absolute power in the supply of scarce Nile water for irrigation, the state has been the largest single landlord since Egypt's break from the Ottoman Empire in 1805. Subsequently, the state decides how much, by whom, and under what terms land should be held. With rising land profitability from growing cotton, wealthy Egyptians and Europeans accumulated more land and it became increasingly concentrated in a few hands.

The 1952 land reform was an outcome of the sharp swing in the political power structure that had been introduced in the same year by President Abdul Nasser's revolutionary government. It manifested a shift away from the policy-making apparatus dominated by landlords and protected by ex-King Farouk, towards an equity-oriented policy intended to benefit the poor fellaheen.[16] A series of laws issued between 1952 and 1961 redistributed 14 per cent of total cultivable land, including the confiscated estates of the royal family and the expropriated foreign-owned lands, against nominal compensation. Property rights in these lands were transferred to 346,000 ex-tenants who represented only one-tenth of total agricultural households. They received landownership in family farm units of 1 hectare each, on average. This partial reform left out two-thirds of total tenants and almost all landless wage-workers. However, the excluded tenants were protected, paying very reduced rent in real terms, and became virtually irremovable until the economic reforms of 1991–7.

Big farmers owning land above the size ceiling of 42 hectares were nominally compensated, but those renting out their land were hit hard by a sharp reduction in annual rental value in real terms. This reduction represented an outright transfer of real income from absentee landowners to tenants. In the mean time, shrewd absentee landowners decreased the area of rented land from 47 per cent in the early 1960s to 24 per cent in the 1980s.[17] Also, the regulations for the protection of tenants and enforcement of fixed rents were relaxed, finally coming to an end in 1994–7 under the strong lobbying of wealthy landowners and the wave of economic reforms.

With regard to the redistributive benefits to *new* owners, the government sold them the requisitioned land at less than half its market value, payable over forty years by annual instalments bearing a subsidized interest. They were also exempted, until 1987, from land tax. A sample survey of 611 household beneficiaries conducted by the author in 1973 (twenty years after the implementation of land reform) found that the new owners' average per person real gross income grew annually at 4.1 per cent.[18] Non-land assets (livestock) and non-agricultural income had increased substantially, compensating for the small size of the distributed units of land (2 acres on average). The survey indicated that cotton and rice yields were higher than the national average in the sampled areas. However, it cannot be asserted that productivity gains were universal in the redistributed areas. Nor can we ascribe the substantial improvement in the distribution of income and consumption in rural Egypt solely to this partial land reform. The degree of income inequality, measured in terms of the Gini index, was sharply reduced from a high 0.65 before land reform to 0.29 in 1965, but increased to 0.32 in 1991.[19] Rising inequality stems also from the pre-1992 heavy indirect taxation of producers, ranging from 22 to 84 per cent of gross income from traditional crops, grown mostly by smaller farmers.[20] Furthermore, there has been a shift in state policy away from according top priority to landless farmers in the distribution of newly reclaimed public lands (established in the late 1950s after the construction of the High Dam) towards their allocation to ex-members of the armed forces and university graduates and their sale to the highest bidders in open auction (see Chapter 4).

Welfare effects could have been greater if the scope of land reform had been wider (for example, setting a lower ceiling on private ownership than the existing 42 hectares). This maximum limit was fixed at a time when 95 per cent of total ownership units were below 2 hectares, and most of these were the minute size of one-quarter of a hectare. Perhaps the reformers wanted to minimize the damage to landlords in anticipation of their political and economic support. Certainly, landlords have continued to be influential in trade, local communities and in parliament, where they strongly advocated the liberalization of rent and crop prices, resulting in the virtual death of land reform in October 1997.

Public land distribution

Whereas Algeria, Egypt, Iran, Iraq, Libya, Syria and the former Republic of South Yemen combined the redistribution of privately owned land exceeding a maximum limit with that of public land, Saudi Arabia did not. Instead, it opted for the distribution of state-owned land.

Saudi Arabia

This oil-rich country is also endowed with a vast area of public land and despite being rainless, the country possesses plentiful groundwater. For the distribution of property and lease rights in land and water, the king grants directly, or through the Public Land Management Department, the rights of use (lease) or ownership to individuals and tribes (the bedouin).

In the early 1930s when the bedouin represented two-thirds of the population, King Abdul Aziz launched the public-land distribution programme (the *Hejrah*) in their favour. In exchange, they were obliged to sell their camels, sheep and goats and practise sedentary agriculture. Following the severe drought of 1960, the programme was expanded northward into Tabuk, al-Ula and Wadi Sarhan. In addition to receiving already developed land free of charge, each settler was paid 150 Saudi riyals monthly and guaranteed free access to pumped irrigation water. This was followed in 1965 by a technically better-designed scheme, in which a thousand bedouin households were settled in an area of 45,000 donums in Harad, Wadi Sahba.[21] Of nearly 170 million rials (US$39 million) that it cost to implement the scheme, two-thirds were absorbed in irrigation and drainage works. This sum of public funds does not include the market value of land and government expenditure on resource surveys, housing, and the construction of roads and public services. If all these items were added to irrigation and drainage costs, the total sum could easily double, reaching approximately US$78,000 per settled bedouin.

As was the case in the Libyan experience of land settlement, the Saudi government has concentrated on rapid technical change in production while overlooking the social questions of human development and the bedouin's participation in decision-making.[22] The unfavourable effects of this approach on nomadic culture are compounded by the rapid changes brought forth by the oil wealth, particularly among the tribes of Bani Khalid and Bani Hajeer in the eastern districts. Furthermore, the realization of income and productivity potentials has been constrained by prolonged uncertainty over property rights and the subjecting of the bedouin, for the first time, to the excessive bureaucratic procedures of several government agencies with uncoordinated functions. These obstacles were reduced in 1972 when settlers were granted property rights, and administrative responsibilities were consolidated in a single government department.

The sober reality is that this policy has contributed to increasing inequality and to inefficiency in production. Almost half the land and subsidy recipients were already wealthy men; merchants, government employees, influential tribal sheikhs and even a few amirs. Public-land distribution peaked at the start of the oil boom in 1974–5 when many beneficiaries were allotted more than one unit of land, averaging 30 hectares each, free of charge. Inefficiency, in terms of production costs exceeding the value of crops harvested, has been reported, especially in the case of wheat and fruits.[23] As they had little or no experience in farming, the land recipients became absentee rent-receivers, leaving unskilled migrant Yemeni and Egyptian workers to till the land as tenants. These arrangements, though considered illegal by the government, have prevailed, particularly in the large Tabuk scheme. Still, in an affluent society, greedy land recipients continue to press for the raising of farm size from 20 to 50 hectares and for farms to continue to be distributed free of charge, despite the King's earlier approval of doubling the limit from 10 to 20 hectares.

Available data suggest a prevailing high degree of land concentration. At the national level the results of the 1980 World Agriculture Census indicate that the distribution of landholdings, with its Gini index at 0.83, was the highest in the Middle East.[24]

Other countries

Several countries have actively pursued land-settlement policies for the spread of small-scale landownership into especially developed areas, complete with the necessary infrastructure. Perhaps the oldest schemes are those of Turkey, initiated between the 1930s and 1950s to resettle – free of charge – the Turkish families who had been forced to leave territories of the former Ottoman Empire, mainly Bulgaria, Romania and Greece. In terms of the scale of permanently irrigated land settled, Sudan is prominent, notably its giant Gezira, Managil and Khashm al-Girba schemes. Of those countries that redistributed privately owned land in radical reform programmes and, at the same time, distributed substantial areas of public land, Syria stands out with its 450,000 hectares of irrigated land benefiting some 40,000 families in the Sud el-Forat and el-Ghab schemes.[25]

Rich and poor countries, large and small schemes, all share the technical, social and economic problems of carving a technically modern farming community out of the wilderness of grazing area habitually used by nomadic people. Apart from satisfying an egocentric political leader's need to inaugurate a tangible success, it is often difficult to justify giving special privileges to a relatively tiny fraction of the total population, when millions of poor landless farmers are unable to rent or possess one acre of land. Economic viability and social justice do not usually (or necessarily) go hand in hand. From my experience in the study of several land settlement schemes, there are social organization problems that are common everywhere. Among them are the very wide gap between the levels of technical sophistication of government staff and of the settlers, and a prevailing mutual mistrust and lack of spontaneous participation by the settlers, reflected in the staff attitude of 'us versus them'. In addition, the schemes are highly capital-intensive and involve a large number of supervisors and bureaucrats.[26]

Income support

So far this chapter has discussed several countries' policies for the redistribution of property rights in tangible assets, that generate – together with education – primary, lifetime income. In this section, we focus on the policy of official income transfers that is followed in most countries, designed to provide secondary (unearned) income and to benefit mostly the poor, the disabled and the elderly. Income support to the disabled has risen in the Middle East as a consequence of frequent wars. With the rapid rise in the numbers and proportion of the population over the ages of 60 and 70, the demand for income support to the elderly is rising dramatically. For the purpose of illustration, I present the experiences of a large and a small economy in the region: Turkey and Jordan, respectively. Unofficial forms of income support by NGOs are discussed in the last section.

Turkey: an urban bias in social security

Despite frequent changes in power structure and in the form of government, the state has, since the mid-1940s, maintained its income support policy.[27] This policy consists of social insurance payments and a statutory minimum daily wage, but without unemployment compensation. Starting in 1946 and progressively regulated between 1957 and 1965, arrangements for social security have been expanded to cover old age, maternity, disability, occupational injury, permanent invalidity, illness and the dependants of pensioners. By 1993, nearly one-third of the total population had received benefits under this comprehensive programme, whose total expenditure represented nearly 5 per cent of national income (GDP), compared to only 1 per cent in Jordan and the high level of 12 per cent in Israel. However, there is an urban bias in the coverage. For example, in the large cities of Istanbul, Ankara and Izmir, the proportion of recipients was 70 per cent of total eligible people, in contrast to between 5 and 20 per cent in most of the rural areas, in which 42 per cent of the population live. Moreover, the beneficiaries are concentrated in construction, trade and industry and in public enterprises, where labour unions are much stronger and earnings higher than in the private sector and agriculture.[28]

The distributional effects of these social security arrangements are difficult to determine, because of several factors: variations in wage rates between unionized and non-unionized workers; the extent to which minimum-wage regulations are enforced; the fast-rising costs of living; the variations in Turkish workers' remittances and the extent of unemployment, against which no fully guaranteed compensation payments exist. First, with regard to the effect of unionization, available information on the labour market suggests that although Turkey has almost half its workforce in agriculture, they are not effectively unionized, being mostly self-employed, while statutory minimum wages are fully effective in the public sector, where the workforce is strongly unionized. Ozbudun and Ulusan (1980: 435) estimated that the wages of unionized workers were 30 per cent higher than those of comparable non-unionized workers. It seems that unionized urban workers have fully benefited from the social security programme, except during the three periods of military rule which restrained the unions' bargaining power (1961–2, 1971–3 and 1980–3).

Second, fast-rising consumer prices have rapidly eroded the real value of minimum-wage and social security payments.[29] In the 1980s, while minimum wages at current prices increased annually at an average of 45 per cent, they fell steadily in real terms owing to hyperinflation. Low-income groups have suffered further from rising unemployment. According to the Ministry of Labour and Social Security, the number of jobless adults during the period 1993–5 increased annually by an average of 65,000, mostly in the private sector and in the big urban centres (Adana, Ankara and Istanbul).[30] The unemployment situation has been worsened by the introduction of a structural adjustment programme in 1980 and by falling migration to Western industrial countries, particularly Germany, where unemployment is high.

In short, despite consistent government efforts to provide income support, a combination of inflation, unemployment and institutional forces has worsened inequality in the distribution of income. Whereas the already low share of the lowest quintile of income classes fell between 1973 and 1987 from 4 to only 2.5 per cent, the share of the richest 20 per cent increased, from 54 to 56 per cent during the same period. Also, the middle and upper-middle classes have gained substantially.[31] However, Turkish development analysts agree on equity data weaknesses which include under-reporting, exclusion of migrant workers' remittances and the extrapolation and blowing up to national totals of earlier survey results. While we cannot underrate these flaws, the design and implementation of social security arrangements are not solely to blame for the rising inequality. Apart from the combined influence of the factors outlined above, there are the distributional effects of economic reforms examined in Chapter 10.

Jordan: inequality in income support

This middle-income country with a small but fast-growing population of 4.1 million, mostly of Palestinian origin, achieved a remarkable prosperity in the 1970s, especially after the start of the civil war in Lebanon, when considerable trade and capital moved to Amman. However, the results of family-budget surveys indicate high inequality of income distribution: the share of the richest 20 per cent of total households was almost half the total income and over 7 times the share of the lowest 20 per cent.[32]

The government's concern over tackling inequalities and poverty problems had not been clearly expressed as an objective until the announcement of the 1980–5 development plan. Perhaps this is due to the fact that in conservative and tribally organized Jordanian society, income support has, for a long time, been informal, practised by families through the Islamic mandatory *Zakat* payments to the poor. It was only in 1980–1 that the social security scheme started, followed by the 'Aid Fund For The Needy' in 1986. An absolute poverty line for monitoring progress was only set in 1987, but the state has not set a legally binding minimum wage. The social security scheme has expanded since 1981 in two ways. First, its fund reached 45 million Jordanian dinars (JD) or 3 per cent of the national income in 1986 but fell to 1 per cent in 1993 as a result of budget cuts required by the 1989 economic reform. Second, mandatory and voluntary (affiliated) membership of the scheme together represent two-thirds of the total Jordanian workforce. Social security benefits are paid to old-age pensioners (at 60 years for men and 55 for women) and disabled persons. As the main employer, the government and its public enterprises contribute regularly to the social security fund, the ratio of which is half that of Turkey, or 8–9 per cent of the employees' wages. Private enterprises employing five or more employees are required by law to meet fully the payments for their own employees with regard to occupational accidents and injuries.

In spite of its expansion, the social security programme is inegalitarian. While nearly 63 per cent of the total beneficiaries earned an average monthly wage *below* the national average of JD 100 (US$280 in 1986), we find that more than one-third of the total beneficiaries are in the top wage-bracket of over JD 500 a month. The average wage-income of the latter, who are mostly the urban élite (business managers and senior professionals) is 10 times that of the lowest wage class, yet they receive full income support from the scheme.[33] Moreover, rising unemployment and persistent poverty have demonstrated the weakness of existing income support arrangements.[34] Estimates made in 1991 show widespread unemployment in urban centres: 41 per cent in the capital city Amman; 23 per cent in Zarka; and 20 per cent in Irbid, with much higher levels among the female than the male workforce (e.g. 23 per cent and 19.6 per cent respectively in Irbid). At the national level, whereas aggregate unemployment[35] has increased from 14.8 per cent in 1987 to 17.1 per cent in 1991, the country's social security programme still does not provide unemployment compensation payments.

Informal provision of social security

Social insecurity problems also concern religious institutions and other non-governmental organizations (NGOs). Depending on the nature of the political system, persistent poverty and deprivation should become a subject of public pressure, forcing governments to act. Historical experience tells us that people gain more benefits as groups than as individuals, and that government tends to respond more to group demands than to individuals.

Informal public action was widely recognized in such conspicuous miseries as famines in Sudan and earthquakes in Morocco, Algeria and Egypt. But what matters in the informal arena of social services and income support is regular and permanent action, and not temporary philanthropy and first aid during catastrophes. The informal action that satisfies these requirements is *zakat*, which has remained outside state control, and in some cases has been channelled through mosques and charitable organizations. The specified payment of *zakat* is so widely practised that in the conservative society of Yemen *zakat* payments represent nearly two-thirds of the total funds available for income support to the needy and for the provision of primary services in poor localities.[36] The payments collected by the community-based 5,000 *zakat* committees, and channelled regularly through Egypt's Bank Nasser al-Ijtima'i' for assisting poor families are another example of such informal social services.

In addition to *zakat*, in the Middle East the family remains a principal source of income support and security for childhood, youth, old age and disability (except among the very poor). There are also several forms of informal action taken by small groups of individuals. Low-income groups tend to organize themselves to pool their savings for the self-help activities that they need most. For example, one frequently finds small groups of between twenty and fifty persons who know each other, and contribute monthly equal shares of money to a fund kept by the group leader. At the end of the mutually agreed period, one member of the group receives, in rotation, the entire amount of money saved. Everything is conducted informally. Known in the Arab societies as *jam'iyas*, these self-help arrangements have proved successful and popular among low-income classes, especially women.

Whereas these income-support activities are provided by small and loosely established groups, large-scale public action on a wide range of welfare issues is the task of formally organized NGOs with national and international networks, operating within established rules (for example, the Red Cross, Red Crescent, trade unions, co-operatives, and women's organizations).[37] Many of these NGOs cannot function effectively and serve their constituents freely without their own governments' adherence to internationally established rules on minimum wages, equal opportunities for men and women, freedom of association and the protection of the right to organize. This government commitment is a prerequisite for a genuine participation of NGOs in the programming and realization of human development.

Table 9.2 List of international conventions relevant to socioeconomic security ratified by the Middle Eastern countries as of 31 December 1995

---

1 The 1949 ILO Convention No. 87 on freedom of association and protection of the right to organize

Algeria (1962)	Kuwait (1961)	Turkey (1993)
Egypt (1957)	Mauritania (1961)	Tunisia (1957)
Israel (1957)	Syria (1960)	Yemen (1976)
		Total: nine countries

2 The 1949 ILO Convention No. 95 concerning the protection of wages

Algeria (1962)	Lebanon (1977)	Tunisia (1958)
Egypt (1960)	Libya (1962)	Turkey (1961)
Iran (1972)	Mauritania (1961)	Yemen (1969)
Iraq (1960)	Sudan (1970)	*Total*: thirteen countries
Israel (1959)	Syria (1957)	

3 The 1970 ILO Convention No. 131 on minimum-wage fixing

Egypt (1976)	Lebanon (1977)	Syria (1972)
Iraq (1974)	Libya (1971)	Yemen (1976)
		Total: six countries

4 The 1973 ILO Convention No. 138 on minimum age for wage-work

Algeria (1984)	Libya (1975)	
Iraq (1985)	Tunisia (1995)	
Israel (1979)	*Total*: five countries	

5 The 1979 United Nations' Convention on the elimination of all forms of discrimination against women

Egypt (1981)	Jordan (1992)	Tunisia (1985)
Iraq (1986)	Libya (1989)	Turkey (1985)
Israel (1991)	Morocco (1993)	Yemen (1984)
		Total: nine countries

Sources: 1, 2, 3 and 4 are from ILO (1996). 5 is from *World Development Report* 1995, Appendix Table A-4. (World Bank, 1978–96).

Notes

Countries are listed in alphabetical order, with the year of ratification in brackets.

Compared to other regions, the Middle East is lagging behind as regards its governments' acceptance of principal UN conventions on these issues that are crucial to social security. The relevant international conventions and the state of their ratification in the region are presented in Table 9.2. For example, by the end of 1995, of the twenty-one countries of the region, only nine have, since 1949, signed and ratified the fundamental International Convention No. 87 on the freedom of association and the protection of the right of people to organize themselves, and only the same number of countries have signed and ratified the 1979 UN convention on the elimination of all forms of discrimination against women.

These simple statistics are telling. They indicate that most of the oil-rich countries of the Gulf are apathetic towards the right of their own workforces to organize and empower themselves in order to gain economic security and influence policy priorities. These populations are also denied the right to voice their grievances concerning gender inequality in employment, educational opportunities, and even in women's right to travel unaccompanied by an adult male relative. One example illustrates this inequality. While we recognize the underenumeration of women everywhere, in 1993, on average only 9 per cent of the total workforce in the rich countries of the Gulf were women, compared to 34 per cent in Turkey. There are also close links between the components of women's social insecurity: widespread illiteracy, high fertility among low-income women, very low legal age of marriage,[38] frequent pregnancies and births to women under 20, and undernourishment.

With this scale of women's deprivation in the 1990s, it is no longer convincing for some governments to say that such questions as the freedom of association and women's social security are matters for governments alone to decide. Actually, they are essential human rights for unstoppable social change, and are crucial for reducing social insecurity. Recent historical experience tells us that those countries where popular movements emancipated women at an early stage and those with liberal attitudes towards female education and women's employment (for example, Egypt, Lebanon, Tunisia and Turkey) have greater gender equality and social security for women at the end of the 1990s than those countries where women, representing almost half of society, are still suppressed.

Looking on the positive side, we also find that several women's organizations, working at country, regional and international levels, have succeeded in creating awareness about the negative effects of women's insecurity, and their exclusion from public life. Some women's NGOs have managed to change old legal provisions and customary practices that are diminishing women's earning power and their productive capacity at work.[39] A notable example of progress made in raising female capability is the promotion of family planning, especially in beginning to change attitudes towards contraceptive use.[40] Whereas the use of contraception remains strictly forbidden in many countries, it has been promoted by female NGOs and sponsored by governments free of charge in such Muslim societies as Egypt, Jordan, Morocco, Tunisia and Turkey. Hence the relationship between women's education, the extent of family planning use, the percentage of women in the total workforce, and gender equality in social security benefits.

Summary

This chapter began by identifying the determinant elements of redistributive policy, its losers and gainers. It then assessed four policy categories in selected countries: nationalization of foreign assets and major domestic enterprises; redistribution of private and public property rights in favour of low-income groups; a guaranteed minimum wage and social insurance; and the traditional, unofficial sources of social security. Since most of the Middle Eastern economies were agrarian at their initial stage of development, land reform was deemed necessary for providing direct and primary income and the removal of institutional barriers inhibiting social progress. We examined further the Saudi Arabian programme of public land distribution and its effects.

The discussion then turned to another set of policies designed to bring about secondary income for social security. These official money transfers can significantly benefit low-income groups and the poorest, provided that their design and implementation are not biased towards the non-poor and the formal labour market in urban areas. Financed mostly from public funds, many of these income transfers are susceptible to inflationary pressure and budgetary cuts.

Considering that tackling inequality and poverty is also of deep concern to informal groups and NGOs, I first stressed the important traditional role of the family and the widely practised informal but obligatory transfers of people's money to the poor. Next, I presented several forms of unofficial action for the provision of social security to disadvantaged sections of society. In discussing the role of NGOs, the chief barrier was identified as the large extent of anti-female bias, as well as the lack of political commitment to implement the relevant international conventions.

Suggested readings

Hasseeb *et al.* (1991) *The Future of the Arab Nations*, Part III, on policy options for the Arab states.

Todaro (1989) *Economic Development in the Third World*, Chapter 5, 'Growth, Poverty and Income Distribution'.

Waldron (1988) *The Right to Private Property.*

On land reform in general and the Middle East in particular:

M. R. El-Ghonemy (1990b) *The Political Economy of Rural Poverty: The Case for Land Reform*, especially Chapter 3, 'Accessible Opportunities: The Meaning of Land Reform', Chapter 7, 'The Pace of Poverty Reduction: Inter-Country Comparison'.

Warriner (1969) *Land Reform in Principle and Practice*, especially Chapter 4, 'Iraq', Chapter 5, 'Iran' and the Conclusion, 'The Relation to Development Reconsidered'.

On offical and informal actions for social security and income support:

Ahmad *et al.* (1991) *Social Security in Developing Countries.*

Drèze and Sen (1989) *Hunger and Public Action*, especially Chapter 4, 'Society, Class and Gender' and Chaper 12, on direct use of public support without waiting for the country in question to become rich.

Hijab (1988) *Woman Power: The Arab Debate on Women at Work.*

Stewart (1983) *Work, Income and Inequality*, especially her distinction between primary and secondary income, also explained in her *Adjustment and Poverty: Options and Choices* (1995: Chapter 1).

UNDP (1991–6) *Human Development Report* 1994, Chapter 2, 'New Dimensions of Human Security'.

The *World Labour Report* issued annually by the ILO provides reliable information on countries' social security, income support, minimum wages and unemployment.

Additional readings can be found in notes and in the Bibliography.

10

ECONOMIC POLICY
REFORMS
Distributional impact

Since 1980, most countries of the Middle East have introduced a mix of policies, termed simply 'economic reforms', in response to growing economic difficulties associated with serious foreign debt problems. Some initiated their own reform programmes without international support. But many who failed to get new loans from commercial creditors turned to the World Bank and the IMF for help, agreeing to take severe actions within a short period. Such conditionality requires not only the acceptance of a package of policies but also their sustained implementation. This contractual obligation, in effect, means that the World Bank and the IMF have become key policymakers in these countries, contradicting the aims of their establishment at Bretton Woods.[1]

This subject has preoccupied governments and has been widely debated. At the regional level (for instance the 1987 meeting of Arab states in Abu Dhabi), the debate has been not on whether to adjust or maintain the *status quo*, but on how to adjust with minimum social costs, and on whether domestic policies or external events in Western economies are largely to blame.[2] Moreover, the debate has been dominated by the aggregate level effects (economic growth, inflation and exports), giving little attention to distributional effects, that is, changes in personal income and consumption distribution and poverty levels, and the numbers of the poor both at the national and sectoral levels. Judging changes in these major areas of concern requires the identification of what has happened to employment and real wages, ownership of physical assets, costs of living, and the indicators of health, education and nutrition.

Based on a review of different countries' experiences, this chapter attempts to fill this gap. The first section deals with the controversy surrounding the distributional effects of the economic policy reforms. It discusses what adjustment is all about, and briefly examines the politics of these reforms. The second section reviews the experiences of each of eight countries that concluded agreements with the World Bank and

IMF. Such countries are henceforth referred to as 'adjusting countries'. The third section makes an inter-country comparison and explores how and why countries differ in growth and equity outcomes despite the adoption of almost identical adjustment policies. How have countries dealt with poverty and income distribution questions, while focusing on devaluation, price liberalization, budget cuts and export promotion, which form the pillars of the reform package?

I would like to make it clear at the outset that by undertaking a critical review of country experiences I do not underrate the importance of adjustment programmes or of the need for sustainable economic growth. My concern is the protection of the poor and equitable distribution of growth benefits. I believe that economic reforms are important, but should not be pursued principally for the purposes of debt recovery and export growth. I also do not dispute the importance of a dynamic private sector, but believe that the state has a central role in rapidly reducing income inequalities, unemployment and poverty.

Controversy

Most programmes of economic reform contain measures belonging to two main categories – short-term 'stabilization' and longer-term 'structural adjustment'. The former is the responsibility of the IMF, and entails the reform of fiscal and monetary policies (cuts in government expenditure, devaluation, reform of taxation and control of interest rates). This is intended to reduce public and personal consumption (demand-reducing policy), reduce inflation and budget deficits, and generate higher savings to be directed to investments. On the other hand, structural adjustment programmes lie in the domain of the World Bank. They entail the reform of policies and institutions designed to improve long-term efficiency in resource allocation (supply side in favour of tradable goods). Thus, the effects of the World Bank's programme on income distribution and poverty take much longer to appear than those of the IMF programme. However, the two programmes complement each other, and are overlapping in some elements. Moreover, the indebted countries' acceptance of the IMF terms is a pre-condition for the World Bank's financial support and debt relief.

Ambiguities

Although the World Bank and IMF speak with concern for poverty reduction, these institutions have not explicitly made it conditional for governments to protect the poor, to prevent worsening income distribution or to avoid the concentration of asset ownership resulting from the redistribution of public enterprises' assets via privatization. In fact, direct interventions by governments to reduce inequality in the distribution of assets are not on the agenda of economic reforms. Rather, it is implicitly believed that the alleviation of poverty and social injustice will probably be achieved in the long run through export-led economic growth. The hope on which the World Bank and IMF are riding is that all-round sustained economic growth brought about by the market mechanism will eventually benefit the poor and poorest groups. But how long this could take and whether the present generation of the poor would suffer are not of primary concern to the two institutions. Even with respect to reducing budget deficits, their directives, which are usually assertive, become rather timid with regard to cuts in military spending and the reallocation of resources to health, education and pro-poor social security.[3]

Confronted with empirical evidence of adverse effects of adjustment policies on the poor in the 1980s, the World Bank has admitted that 'little attention was paid to the effects on the poor . . . Evidence of decline in incomes and cutbacks in social services began to mount.'[4] Likewise, the IMF acknowledged that its programme can have adverse effects on income distribution, and that these should be examined, particularly with regard to 'the implications for the poorest members of society'.[5] Even with this admission, neither of these two most power-ful financial institutions has introduced fundamental changes in the design, speed and sequencing of their policies. The World Bank has, however, made a little effort to establish 'social funds' in a few coun-tries, which have had minimal effects, as we shall learn from the Egyptian experience.[6]

One additional issue needs some clarification. It concerns the question of who is to blame for most of the debt problems. There is a tendency among rich industrial countries, echoed by the World Bank and the IMF, to argue that indebted countries' own domestic policies should be entirely responsible. The reality, however, denies this assertion. Most – but not all – of the debt problems and their negative distributional effects originated largely from pricing and lending policies pursued in Western countries in 1979–82, when the economies of the Middle East were growing, on average, faster than in industrial countries.[7] I have elsewhere (M. R. El-Ghonemy, 1990b) argued that the post-1980 policy shifts in the World Bank and the IMF originated from the shift in the internal politics of the USA and Britain during the Reagan and Thatcher administra-tions. Specifically, I referred to the shift with regard to the roles of the private-property market and of the state in the distribution of income and wealth.[8] Collectively, the rich members of the widely known 'Paris Club' and their commercial banks, the 'London Club', influence economic reforms in the Middle East, as in many other developing countries, through their aid and lending programmes.

Empirical evidence and several development analysts agree that rich Western creditors were responsible for the sharp appreciation of the dollar and the falling world prices of primary commodities produced and exported by the countries of the Middle East. Together with the huge increase in the real value of interest rates (from -30 per cent in 1974 to a peak of $+20$ per cent in 1981), these factors had serious consequences for foreign-debt and balance-of-payments positions in debtor countries.[9]

Assumptions challenged

Among the controversial assumptions behind the remedies prescribed by the World Bank and the IMF is that income distribution remains unchanged during adjustment. This is unrealistic because changes in prices, wages, rent, profit and tax rates affect incomes, consumption and the accumulation of assets (from the privatization of public enterprises) differently across different income groups. Furthermore, prescribed policies are very likely to increase poverty and worsen the distribution of income, through rising unemployment, reduction of real wages, removal of food subsidies and overall deterioration in purchasing power as a result of severe devaluation.

There is also the assumption about existing uniformity in the labour market and within tradable and non-tradable sectors. While the exact distinction between tradable and non-tradable goods, and between the formal and the informal labour-market remains unclear, I consider this assumption an oversimplification of the real world of the Middle East in a number of ways. First, millions of small food producers (subsistence farmers in rainfed areas and sharecroppers), landless workers and petty traders form the bulk of the informal labour market (see Chapters 5 and 8), and are therefore likely to suffer from higher prices. Second, many employees in the formal sector, especially in the civil service, are increasingly engaged in subsidiary functions in the informal market to escape the hardships of economic reforms. This means that a decline in employment opportunities in the formal sector leads to increasing numbers in the informal sector. Third, the fall in demand for the poor unskilled labour is likely to increase inequality.

Perhaps the most controversial issue (which is fundamental in adjustment philosophy) is the pursuit of the single ideology of private property capitalism, with little or no government intervention, which is intended to be implemented across countries through the adoption of almost identical policy packages within a monolithic development path. The eight adjusting countries of the Middle East were told by rich Western countries, the World Bank and IMF that they must follow this path and assign an important role to interest rates and credit lending, despite the Islamic restrictions on *riba*, the changing of a predetermined rate of interest (see Chapter 3).

The economic reformers' assertion that maximum social welfare can accrue from complete mobility of resources (the factors of production) between tradable and non-tradable sectors, as well as from perfect knowledge of the market and competition under free market forces is faulty, because these conditions exist only in abstract theory and in textbook graphs. Also, the so-called miracles of the market economy – South Korea and Taiwan – reduced state management of the economy only after they had reached a high degree of equality in the distribution of wealth and income through radical land reforms (in 1945–55), lavish development assistance from the USA and heavy public investment in education and health. By following this path, these countries (which have strong planning capacity) established in the 1960s a solid foundation for a sustained and egalitarian pattern of growth.[10] At the same time, these countries still have selective state intervention in industry and technological change.

Lastly, there are ambiguities surrounding debt relief. When uncertainty increased about the economic capacity of the indebted countries to repay contractual debts and interest, rich creditor countries made arrangements with the World Bank and the IMF to act as a third party, rescheduling debts and granting new loans to enable indebted countries to repay their original creditors.[11] My review of countries' experiences will show whether or not these arrangements have actually reduced the total debt burden. Max Corden, an expert on the subject, rightly pointed out that when a third party intervenes 'the original creditors are clearly better off'.[12]

Before concluding this section, I wish to stress the controversy surrounding the politics of economic reforms. Like other policies, the reforms require social acceptability. The relationship between them and political liberalization is usually denied by many authoritarian Middle Eastern regimes. From the start, governments do not make public the content of, and the conditions attached to, adjustment programme lending. These governments secretly conduct negotiations with creditors, the World Bank and the IMF, hiding from their people and principal NGOs the expected painful effects on low-income groups and educated young people seeking jobs for the first time. Governments seem to fear that reforming the economy towards free trade and minimal government intervention may lead to public demands for reforming the political system towards parliamentary democracy. The impulse for political reform is likely to be strengthened by popular discontent with the pricing effects of devaluation, freezing wages, rising unemployment and the removal of subsidies, while affected groups have no say.

Moreover, there is an implicit assumption that the role of bureaucracy is neutral. Hence the failure to recognize that the reforms can harm bureaucrats through such measures as the freezing of salaries and the reduction of their opportunities for corruption (from licensing imports and exports, customs duties, and tax exemptions, for example) which invariably result in a slow-down in the implementation of the reforms. Otherwise, how can we explain why most Middle Eastern countries have delayed the introduction of economic reforms, or the very slow pace at which they have privatized public enterprises, despite recognizing these measures as necessary?

Countries' adjustment experiences

The discussion turns now to what has actually happened in the eight adjusting countries. In the order of presentation, they are Tunisia, Egypt, Morocco, Sudan, Turkey, Mauritania, Jordan and Algeria. Since 1980, these countries have received at least one contractual adjustment loan and accepted the standard policy package from the World Bank and the IMF. The presentation is uneven in detail. Turkey is presented briefly because there is a large amount of written material on its adjustment experience. By contrast, very little has so far been written on Algeria, Mauritania, Sudan, Tunisia and Egypt, which are therefore examined in more detail. Had space permitted, it would have been desirable to include other countries such as Israel, Iran, Syria and Saudi Arabia which have gradually adjusted their economies *without* lending support from the IMF and the World Bank. We start with the experiences of Tunisia and Egypt, which have had contrasting results. For the purpose of this study, adjustment experience is regarded as being 'successful' if it redresses most economic imbalances and, at the same time, reduces inequality of income distribution and absolute poverty.

Tunisia

In contrast to Egypt, Tunisia has a small population of 8.5 million (compared to 57 million in Egypt in 1993). Also, since independence from France in 1956, Tunisia's welfare-oriented strategy for national development has yielded valuable returns: steady economic growth, prosperous tourism and an efficient, qualified civil service combined with a reservoir of skilled labour. Importantly, it has attained a level of human development that places Tunisia higher than its economic rank among the countries of the Middle East, which is based solely on per capita income (see Table 6.4).

In order to understand the sequence and the distributional effects of economic reforms, two periods are used (1982–6 and 1987–90). During the first period, the government had to confront external shocks: the oil price crisis, the collapse of the world market for phosphates, the recurrence of short-term closure of the border with Libya and the severe drought of 1981–2. Foreign debt represented 40 per cent of Tunisia's total income in 1982, a ratio that is still moderate compared to that of Egypt (52 per cent) in the same year. The government responded to these difficulties with its own reform measures which were combined in the Sixth Development Plan (1982–6). The measures aimed to slow down public investment; tighten imports, especially luxury items; maintain priority for social welfare and reduce military spending. Public expenditure on education, health and social security was increased from 29.3 per cent in 1983 to 34.1 per cent in 1986, and food aid was directed to the needy and schoolchildren.

During this first period, cuts in public physical investment, not human capital investment, slowed down economic growth. In addition, the number of Tunisian migrant workers and their remittances began to diminish, owing to the economic recession everywhere. According to the Ministère des Affaires Sociales, the remittances of migrant workers, which were a significant source of the country's foreign exchange and family income support, fell from 219 million Tunisian dinars in 1982 to 190 million dinars in 1986. The hardships were compounded by the government's decision to devalue the dinar and reduce subsidies on essential goods. In response to the latter, popular anger burst out into violent street riots, in which 150 people were killed. This prompted the President to cancel the reforms on 7 January 1984.[13]

After adopting the standard adjustment programmes in 1987, Tunisia received generous financial support from the World Bank and IMF.[14] Nevertheless, throughout this second period (1987–90), the government did not compromise its commitment to social welfare and the protection of the poor. This determination was reflected in the establishment of a special programme targeting income support to the poor, and uniting the Islamic obligatory contribution (*zakat*) with food aid and with the government's allocations for social security. This programme, known as *Le Programme National d'Aide aux Familles Nécessiteuses*, and implemented under strict monitoring by the President of Tunisia himself, was a combination of governmental and NGO income support to the needy, and has, since 1987, targeted 101,000 destitute families.

The determination of the government has also been manifested in the introduction of class-based preferential tax rates. For example, high value added tax (VAT) and high customs duties were levied on luxury goods purchased by the rich, while, on the other hand, very low rates were levied on essential consumer goods. The government also avoided cutting salaries and wages. Instead, it froze them temporarily for two years, raising them gradually by 8 per cent in 1989, until a legally binding wage agreement was reached between the government and employers' association on the one hand, and the powerful labour unions (UGTT) on the other. Under this tripartite cooperation, short-term gains (1986–8) were forgone and there were no dismissals. Instead, the number of workers increased by 3 per cent and wages by 13–15 per cent annually in 1990, 1991 and 1992; higher than the rate of inflation (see Appendix Table 10.1). In addition to political stability, these cooperative relations between government and private business and between workers and employers appeared to have contributed to the success of economic reforms.

The government's commitment to welfare concerns was further demonstrated by its handling of the required budgetary cuts. Cuts in public works and in military spending were preferred to cuts in health, education and social security allocations, whose combined shares in total government expenditure were more or less maintained between 1987 and 1990, before being increased in 1992. Meanwhile, politically sensitive military spending was cut below its 1986 level and the budget deficit was reduced from −4.6 per cent of the national income in 1986 to −2.6 per cent in 1992. These favourable changes have been reinforced by political stability and prudent management of the economy, especially a controlled inflation of around 6 per cent, and a sustained rise in real wages. There was also a reduction in total consumption to raise savings and investment rates between 1986 and 1993, resulting in high rates of growth in total output, at an annual average of 5.4 per cent in 1990–3, despite the adverse effects of the 1991 Gulf War on financial aid from rich Arab states. However, the cuts in government spending on public works and infrastructure contributed to increasing unemployment, from 13.1 per cent of the total labour force in 1984 to nearly 16 per cent in 1992. The unemployed were mostly the young (18–29 years), who represented nearly 14 per cent of the total number of poor in 1990.[15]

Another adverse effect of economic reforms is the increase in inequality in the distribution of consumption expenditure in urban areas, where the income gap between the rich and the poor increased. From 1980 urban poverty began to exceed the level in the rural areas. Significantly, as noted in Chapter 8, the overall incidence of poverty fell between 1985 and 1990 and the growth of per person income was sustained, thanks to the substantial reduction in total fertility from 6.4 in 1970 to only 3.1 in 1993. All in all, despite its failure to combine its successful economic reforms with political liberalization, Tunisia provides a model of what has been described as 'adjustment with a human face'.

Egypt

Ranked higher than South Korea in economic terms until 1965, Egypt's income per person is now less than one-tenth that of South Korea and one-third of Tunisia's.[16] It is also among the world's low-income countries, and one of the four poor countries in the Middle East. Over one-third of its large population is crowded below the poverty line. In 1989, total foreign debt reached one and a half times the national income and the share of total government expenditure represented by annual interest payments exceeded the combined shares of health, education and social security. This is not the first time Egypt has faced severe debt problems. Almost a century earlier[17] the national debt was equal to the national income, which was one important factor leading to the British occupation of Egypt in 1882.

These dismaying statistics are manifestations of serious economic imbalances, the reform of which has been hesitant and piecemeal. However, before examining the phases of the reform, two distinct development characteristics of Egypt deserve some attention. First, from 1974 the government pursued a mixture of an 'open door' policy and the 'Arab socialism' inherited from President Nasser's regime. It was essentially egalitarian, provided heavy subsidies and generous social benefit payments, and it guaranteed jobs to all graduates, hence making labour a fixed factor of production. We should note that economic reforms had been recommended for nearly seventeen years[18] (1970–87), including the recommendations of the conference of economists held in February 1982 chaired by President Mubarak. Second, Egypt has been actively involved in the Middle East military conflict. The most conspicuous involvements were in the Yemeni civil war in 1963–6, the wars with Israel in 1956, 1967 and 1973, and more recently the alliance with the USA, Britain, France and Saudi Arabia during the Gulf War of 1991. These wars required heavy military spending, which absorbed 18–20 per cent of total government expenditure. The high expenditure continued even after Egypt had signed the peace treaty with Israel in 1979.

The attempts to reform the Egyptian economy are examined in three stages. The first was the government's own programme (1974–86), starting with the devaluation of the Egyptian pound (from US$1 worth E£0.39, to US$1 worth E£0.70 for private transactions) and limited reductions in subsidies, which were halted after violent street riots in January 1977. The riots were ruthlessly suppressed by the military. I witnessed these riots and saw that the targets for destruction were limited to signs of Egyptian affluence, government cars, police stations and nightclubs. In fact, the programme increased inequality, and created a class of 'new rich' in the construction and trade sectors. In order to enhance the inflow of foreign capital, a special exchange rate was set up for tourists and Egyptians working abroad, and Foreign Investment Law No. 43 provided generous incentives to investors. These actions, and the sharp rise in the oil price, enabled the economy to grow rapidly in 1975–82. Real income per person doubled, oil production increased at an average annual rate of 16 per cent and oil exports represented 70 per cent of total merchandise exports.

The boom was short lived, as the rate of economic (GDP) growth fell sharply from 9 per cent in 1975–82 to 2.6 per cent in 1986. Unbalanced development peaked, as resources were misallocated away from the main non-oil tradable sectors (agriculture and manufacturing) towards non-tradable sectors (construction, financial services, real-estate speculation). There was, in addition, a rapid expansion in both government expenditure and the over-staffed administration, as well as the military forces. The situation was made worse following the assassination of President Sadat by Muslim extremists (the Jama'a al-Jihad) on 6 October 1981. In addition to the collapse of oil prices, the uncertain political environment reduced earnings from tourism, and made private foreign investors reluctant to risk their capital.[19] There was also widespread corruption, as discussed in Chapter 7. In addition, the end of the oil boom in the Middle East resulted in a sharp fall in remittances from migrant workers. However, the expansionary government expenditure policy and heavy external borrowing continued, leading to a deterioration in the balance of payments and budget deficits to 15 and 17 per cent of national income respectively in 1986, the highest deficit during the last decade.

In May 1987, following long negotiations with the IMF and the World Bank, the government adopted an adjustment package contained in the Five-Year Plan of 1987–91. Accordingly, the Egyptian pound was devalued by 100 per cent, from US$1 worth E£0.7, to US$1 worth E£1.36 in 1987, and further to US$1 worth E£2.60 in fiscal year 1989/90. Steps were taken to abolish non-food subsidies (electricity, fuel and transport), and to reduce food subsidies from 11 per cent of the national income in 1981 to only 2.5 per cent in 1990. With worsening terms of trade and the rate of growth of national income falling below that of population, real per person income declined by 20 per cent, from US$750 in 1985/6 to US$600 in 1990. This deterioration took place in spite of massive economic assistance, grants and remittances. For example, official development assistance increased by 350 per cent (from US$1.6 billion in 1986 to US$5.6 billion in 1990), the highest figure in the world in 1990.[20] The big jump in aid represented a political reward to Egypt for its support to Saudi Arabia, Kuwait and the United States in the war against Iraq after its invasion of Kuwait in August 1990.

The poor economic performance during this first phase of the World Bank- and IMF-supported programme (1987–90) was partly due to the government mismanagement of the economy. In general, with the exceptions of the Suez Canal and Petroleum Authorities, most state-owned enterprises became major sources of indebtedness, unsound investment, low productivity and corruption that were drains on government finances.[21] There was also a severe deterioration in the trade balance, which reached a negative US$8.3 billion in 1989/90 or one-quarter of the national income (GDP).[22] It was, therefore, clear that the World Bank- and IMF-prescribed policy package of June 1987 was not working. Influenced by its close ties with the United States, Egypt agreed in 1991 to undertake for the second time a more comprehensive adjustment programme, officialy called the Economic Reform and Structured Adjustment Programmme (ERSAP).[23] The focus was on the completion of trade liberalization, further budget cuts and the privatization of 314 state-owned enterprises, whose total asset value was estimated by the Prime Minister, Dr El-Ganzoury, to be E£503 billion (*al-Ahram*, 12 March 1996: 14). The IMF insisted that the Egyptian pound be devalued further by 25–40 per cent and the remaining food subsidy removed, but these measures were rejected by the government.

There is evidence of the 1987 and 1991 adjustment programmes seriously hurting the existing poor, and creating a group of a 'new' poor (i.e. those living in poverty for the first time), especially in urban areas. As shown in Table 10.1, the increase in poverty is 'explained' by falling real wages, increasing unemployment, a sharp rise in the cost of living (CPI index), falling physical capital investment needed for job creation and greater inequality of income distribution. Thus the World Bank's promised economic requirements for poverty alleviation – sustained economic growth, greater investment and employment from the expansion of the private sector – have failed to materialize. The GDP average annual growth fell from 3.2 per cent before adjustment to about 0.3–0.5 per cent in 1992–3, while the population grew at an annual average of 2.4 per cent. Meanwhile, open unemployment increased from

5.7 per cent in 1982 to nearly 20 per cent in 1991–3, adding to a massive number of underemployed.

Of the total workforce of 15 million persons in 1992, an estimated 2.5 to 3 million were unemployed, nearly double the figure from the population census of 1986. For the first time in the country's recent history, about half a million university graduates were among the unemployed.[24] Since 1992 it has been estimated that nearly 400,000 adults per annum are looking for work. Moreover, in order to restructure public enterprises, the government pursued a policy of forced (officially termed 'encouraged') early retirement, with total compensation payments amounting to E£11 billion. Outright dismissal was almost impossible under the complex procedures of Law 137 of 1981. By the end of 1995, nearly one-quarter of the workforce of state-owned enterprises had been made redundant.[25] In the mean time, job-creating physical capital expenditure in the government budget was reduced over two years by almost half: from E£21 billion in the fiscal year 1990/1 to E£10.5 billion in 1992/3. With a rapid rise in living costs (CPI) of 15 per cent annually between 1989 and 1993, real wages of civil servants and low-salaried public employees fell sharply. The situation was more severe in urban areas, where two-thirds of personal income came from wages and salaries in 1991 (household survey of 1990/1). It will be recalled from the first section of this chapter that the reduction in real wages was an essential ingredient of the World Bank and IMF's demand-reducing policy, including reduction of labour costs, in order to stimulate private investment. Ironically, public and private investment and economic growth fell during this period (1987–94). The share of private investment in GDP fell from 11.2 per cent in 1987 to 9.4 per cent in 1994 (Eygpt, INP, 1995: Table 2.4).

Inequality of income distribution increased, as did the poverty level, especially in urban areas. According to the results of household income/consumption surveys of 1981/82 and 1990/91 (summarized in Table 10.1), the income share of the poorest class fell, while that of the richest increased; and the gap widened considerably in urban areas. A close examination of the items consumed by income class reveals two striking features. First, family expenditure on education and health, which are officially free, increased, owing to deterioration in the quality of public services and the government's encouragement of the private provision of these services. Second, on average, a rich family in 1991 spent on cosmetics, private transport and sports more than the entire yearly expenditure of the average poor family of six persons (less than E£1,000 a year).[26]

The numbers of people living in absolute poverty (as a percentage of

Table 10.1 Economic and social indicators related to economic reforms in Egypt, 1973–93

Indicators	1973–83	1985	1986	1987	1988	1989	1990	1991	1992	1993
A Economic Indicators										
1 GDP average annual growth	8.8	6.6	2.6	2.5	3.2	3.0	2.5	2.1	0.3	0.5
2 Gross domestic investment (% GDP)	28.0	26.7	23.7	18.0	24.2	23.3	21.5	20.4	18.0	17.0
3 Exchange rate (pounds per US$)	0.7	0.96	1.07	1.27	1.76	1.94	2.23	3.0	3.60	3.4
4 National account deficit (%GDP)	-2.5	-13.6	-15.2	-10.4	-7.7	-10	-4.2	-1.0	+4.5	+3.5
5 Budget deficit (% GDP)	-12.1	-22.8	-17.1	-14.1	-16.3	-13.8	-5.7	-1.0	-3.5	+1.6
6 Inflation rate (average annual rate)	13	12	24	20	18	21	17	20	14	12
7 Foreign debt (US$ billion)	14.0	42.1	28.6	51.0	48.9	49.0	39.9	41.6	40.5	40.6
8 Foreign debt (%GDP)	56.0	138.0	59.0	150.7	127.0	159.0	126.0	133.0	68.0	104.5
B Social Indicators										
9 Unemployed persons (% total labour force)	6	–	12	–	–	–	17.9	–	–	20
10 Real wages, government (1973 = 100)	85	71	60	55	45	38	35	33	34	33
11 Government expenditure										
a Share of education (%)	9.0	11.3	9.8	12.0	11.7	12.0	13.8	13.5	10.3	12.3
b Share of health (%)	2.5	2.5	2.3	2.5	2.4	2.7	2.8	2.7	2.1	2.4
c Share of social security (%)	12.0	11.6	10.8	11.1	12.0	11.9	12.9	11.2	9.0	10.9
d Sum (a+b+c) (%)	23.5	25.4	22.9	25.6	26.1	26.6	29.5	27.4	21.4	25.6
12 Total subsidies (% GDP)	8.0	6.0	5.0	2.0	2.5	2.5	2.7	2.4	2.1	1.8
13 Cost of living index (CPI) (annual growth)	13.6	17.0	23.0	21.0	19.6	22.7	16.8	17.7	12.3	12
14 Distribution of income consumption										
a Share of lowest 20%	7.7[(1982)]	–	–	–	–	–	–	–	–	7.3[(1991)]
b Share of highest 20%	41[(1982)]	–	–	–	–	–	–	–	–	44.0[(1991)]

15 Poverty estimates   1981/2
   a Approximate number in poverty (1,000s) 8,895–12,180
   b As % of population
     i Rural   24.2–29.7
     ii Urban   22.5–30.4
16 Poverty estimates 1990/1
   a Approximate number in poverty (1,000s) 21,930–24,500
   b As % of population
     i Rural   39.2–54.5
     ii Urban   35.9–43.5

Sources: Indicators 1–8: *World Tables* (World Bank, 1976–95), Central Bank of Egypt, *Annual Report* 1985/6–1991/2 and ESCWA (1995a: Appendix Table 1). Indicator 9: Handoussa and Potter (1991) and World Bank (1993a). Indicator 10 calculated from UN *Statistical Yearbook* 1991 and 1995: Tables 5–11 and 11–20 (United Nations, 1960–95), ILO (1995) and World Bank (1991: Table D5). Indicators 12 and 13: ESCWA, *ibid*. Indicators 11 and 14, see sources for social indicators in Appendix 10.1. Indicator 15, World Bank, *ibid*. and ESCWA, *ibid*. Different methodologies in estimates produced wide variations in both 1981/2 and 1990/1: see note 27.

the total population) increased considerably, but less in rural than in urban areas. The 1991 estimates by locality vary widely, from 36 to 54 per cent according to the criterion used in fixing the poverty line. Moreover, two studies suggest that the poor in 1991 were poorer than in 1982, especially in urban areas.[27] The increase in poverty was much higher in the southern provinces of Beni Suef, Menia, Assiut and Sohag, where poverty rose from 50 per cent in 1982 to more than 60 per cent in 1991. Not surprisingly, most of the recent violent confrontations between Muslim extremists and the government have taken place in these provinces. In contrast, in the affluent provinces of Ismailia and Damiett, where investment and commercialization have been extensive, poverty levels were much lower and the average income per household was 3–4 times higher than in the poor provinces.[28]

The design of the 1991 economic reform programme included two measures which had some potential to improve equity and protect vulnerable people: tax reform and the Social Fund for Development (SFD). Available information on the distribution of Egypt's tax burden before and after the reforms suggests a continuation of its regressive (i.e. pro-rich) nature, in which the burden of tax has been borne by low-income consumers, as is the case with the consumption tax (VAT). In 1994, taxes on commercial profits and private property remained a minute proportion of total tax revenue.[29] This is absurd, considering the magnitude of tax arrears, uncollected taxes and tax evasion by rich businessmen and wealthy professionals such as film actors, musicians, construction engineers and doctors. The revenue which has been lost is estimated at a staggering E£14 billion, or about 45 per cent of total tax revenue in 1994.[30]

The much publicized SFD of US$613 million (for 1993–7, to be raised later) is a joint fund consisting of a World Bank loan of $320 million and $293 million grants from the European Union and a few rich Arab states.[31] The amount is only 3.5 per cent of combined financial aid (US$4 billion) and debt relief (US$13.2 billion) to Egypt during the Gulf War. By disbursing an average of US$110 million a year, the SFD spends a mere 0.3 per cent of national income (GDP in 1994). This is an inadequate sum for an economy the size of Egypt's, with unemployment and poverty on such a large scale, and considering the number of intended beneficiaries. Moreover, the wide scope of the SFD blurs the problems of the truly needy. Target beneficiaries of the SFD include graduates from higher education, unemployed young people, displaced workers in the public sector, migrant workers who returned home because of the Gulf War, and NGOs assisting vulnerable groups. It therefore seems that the 'safety net' promised by the SFD has been spread wide: hence it is to be expected that the catch would be fewer of the poor but more of the miscellaneous categories. Many of the expected beneficiaries are not really poor. For example, returnees from the Gulf War are relatively affluent; displaced employees from the public sector receive compensatory payments; and many university graduates come from well-to-do families. On the other hand, the elderly and disabled who have been made poor as a result of adjustment-induced price increases have been excluded. This exclusion is tragic; and it incites enemies of reforms and plays into the hands of organized Islamic militants.

Some calculations will provide a realistic picture of the expected assistance from the fund. If we leave aside the 1.5 million workers who were already unemployed, and the 10 million living in absolute poverty when the adjustment programme was initiated in 1987, and assume that the SFD beneficiaries are limited only to the following categories: (a) those already displaced and (b) half the university and higher education graduates between 1987 and 1994 (excluding post-1994 graduates), we arrive at a rough estimate of 1.6 million candidates for SFD assistance. If we assume, further, that each of them will receive the modest amount of E£20,000 needed to create one and a half remunerative jobs, the total fund needed to assist these reduced categories of beneficiaries would amount to US$9.4 billion. It is clearly questionable how such a negligible amount of the SFD could 'remedy the adverse effects of the structural adjustment programme on low-income population groups, and strengthen Egypt's institutional capacity to develop new social pro-grammes, and upgrade existing ones', to quote the official objectives of the SFD.

Morocco

Until the 1983 economic reforms there was strong bias against agricul-ture, which employed over half the total workforce and contributed nearly one-fifth of total income, yet it received only 7 per cent of total public investment (M. R. El-Ghonemy, 1993: Tables 3.1 and 3.2). The result was a crippled agricultural sector, whose output in 1973–83 grew at the very low annual rate of 0.6 per cent, compared to 6 per cent in the non-agricultural sectors. There was also increasingly unbalanced devel-opment of human resources. Public expenditure on the military was nearly equal to the combined shares of health and education. By 1979, this imbalance led to a staggering 45 per cent of the population in rural areas and 29 per cent in urban areas living in poverty. By the early 1980s the Moroccan economy was in serious crisis.

The collapse of the world market for phosphates, prolonged drought in 1981–2 and the cessation of international lending resulted in worsening budget and balance of payments deficits. The foreign debt increased fivefold between 1976 and 1983, and the sharp rise in the international interest rate (by 50 per cent in real terms) raised debt-servicing to almost half the export earnings in 1983. The government introduced its own economic policy reform between 1978 and 1982: devaluing the dirham, freezing wages, cutting subsidies, and increasing taxes. The attempts to reform sparked social unrest in 1979 and 1981, forcing the government to abandon the austerity programme. With mounting foreign debt, an agreement with the IMF and the World Bank was concluded in 1983, consisting of the standard policy package.[32] In order to reduce the budget deficit, job-creating public investment was cut by two-thirds in just a short period (1983–5). Meanwhile, subsidies were slashed from 13 per cent of total public expenditure in 1983 to a mere 3 per cent in 1990. While military spending was increased, the combined expenditure share of health, education and social security was maintained at the pre-reform low level of 25 per cent, despite rising demand for services due to rapid population growth, from 20 million in 1983 to 25.1 million in 1990.

In order to redress the hitherto unbalanced development, the government assigned greater priority in investment and export to agriculture, and rapidly enhanced the role of the private sector in the economy. The exchange rate had been drastically reduced from 3.9 dirhams per US$1 in 1980 to 9.6 dirhams in 1985. The price of consumer goods and services rose sharply, provoking violent street riots in January 1984, threatening Morocco's political stability. Thanks to the good rainfalls in 1985, 1986 and 1988, both agricultural and total income grew during this period. We need to keep in mind the 28 per cent contribution of agricultural sector growth to national income.[33] Exports (including vegetables and citrus fruits) increased rapidly, from an annual rate of 0.1 per cent in 1980–4 to 4.9 per cent in 1985–9.

This improvement prompted the World Bank to classify Morocco as a successful case of adjustment, despite two failures. One was the inability of the economy to sustain growth of exports and the reduction in balance of payments during the period 1990–3. The other was the rise in unemployment, from 9 per cent in 1980 to 14 per cent in 1986 and 16.3 per cent in 1989. In that year 36 per cent of the total number of unemployed adults were educated young people.[34] Meanwhile, there was a downward trend in real wages, the largest fall being in manufacturing and government administration, which are concentrated in urban areas. The resulting deterioration in consumer purchasing power would have been greater had the government not raised the legal minimum wage and maintained the share of social security expenditure in the budget. As in Tunisia, basic food subsidies (flour, milk and fat, sugar and edible oil) were exempted from consumption tax (VAT). However, subsidies were not targeted; only 16 per cent of food subsidies went to the poorest 30 per cent of households, while nearly half went to the richest 30 per cent, thus 'making the programme an inefficient way of combating poverty'.[35]

Because budget cuts were conditional for disbursement of loans by the World Bank and IMF, the government found it politically easier to reduce public capital expenditure than to cut military spending, resulting in the fall in job-creating investment from 27.5 per cent of national income before adjustment to 23 per cent in 1989–93. The cuts have adversely affected physical capital expenditure on the construction of, and the provision of, equipment for schools, hospitals and the purification of drinking water in rural areas. The World Bank's own analysis found that both total and per person government spending on all social services have declined in real terms.[36] Alarmingly, public spending on primary education fell from 35.4 per cent in 1980 to 34 per cent in 1990, while it increased for secondary and higher education. In the mean time private primary education, which could not be afforded by poor parents, expanded.[37] Moreover, the number of hospital beds per 1,000 population fell in 1985–90.

What happened to income distribution and poverty? There is an information gap during 1980–3. The results of household expenditure surveys conducted by the Ministère du Plan in 1984/5 and 1990/1, together with that carried out in 1970, are summarized in Appendix 10.1, which reveals a slight worsening of income distribution and a substantial reduction in poverty.[38] With regard to the reduction in poverty, the estimates are controversial, which make any comparison difficult. For example when I examined rural poverty levels in Morocco (M. R. El-Ghonemy, 1993: 136–9) I found that the government used the average annual expenditure of the lowest 10 per cent as the poverty line, instead of the lowest 20 per cent as was recommended by the World Bank and used in the 1970s. For the year 1985, the published estimates are 17 per cent instead of 32 per cent, and between 40 and 45 per cent in the 1970s. This politicization of poverty gives the impression that poverty levels were substantially reduced. In 1992, according to the World Bank's estimate, absolute poverty at national level was 15.9 per cent in 1985 (using a monthly poverty level of 40 dollars at 1985 PPP). This rises to 27 per cent if 50 dollars is used. Using the same criteria in 1990, the World Bank's estimate of poverty fell to 7.12 and 14.8 per cent, respectively. Another source of controversy in making comparisons over time is the wide variation in sample size. The 1985 survey covered 14,500 families, compared to only 3,400 in the 1990/1 survey.

Irrespective of the disputed poverty estimates, all evidence points to a significant reduction in absolute poverty in rural areas. This cannot be attributed solely to the exceptionally good rainfall in 1985–9 and the maintenance of basic food subsidies during the adjustment period. One important reason is the redistribution of 327,000 hectares of fertile land with rich water resources lying near the Mediterranean and Atlantic coasts, to 23,600 poor peasants between 1974 and 1984. By a series of royal decrees (*al-dahir al-sharif*), a total of 0.7 million hectares recovered from former French settlers was redistributed into units, each yielding an annual income per family that was above the established poverty line.[39] This redistribution of assets in agriculture and the rise in producer price resulting from economic reforms have contributed to increasing peasants' productivity and reducing poverty in rural areas. However there is a large section of agricultural households (an estimated 33 per cent) who are still landless wage workers and constitute the rural poor.[40] Expansion in rural–urban migration and immigration for work abroad also partly explains the reduction in poverty in rural areas. The Ministry of Planning estimated that nearly 65 per cent of remittances of workers abroad went to rural families;[41] and total receipts doubled between 1981 and 1991.

Our review suggests that while Morocco has failed to realize the core macroeconomic objectives (GDP, investment and export growth) between 1983 and 1993 (Appendix Table 10.1), it has managed to reduce the social costs. The sacrifice in human welfare manifested in a widespread illiteracy of 56 per cent and under-5 mortality of 50 per 1,000 in 1993 could have been mitigated if the government had given priority to social services over non-essentials (military spending and the rapid repayment of foreign debt costs). Moreover, the hardship due to adjustment could have been reduced had the dirham not been abruptly and severely devalued when there was a wage freeze, rising unemployment and prolonged drought. Lastly, sudden and large profits (windfall profits) earned by entrepreneurs from trade liberalization have not been taxed for the benefit of the poor, which has contributed to greater inequality.[42]

Sudan

I earlier characterized the economy of Sudan as typically unbalanced, with inequalities resulting from government action (Chapter 5). With a per person income of US$600 in 1992, Sudan is the second-poorest country in the Middle East (after Mauritania). Unlike Morocco, Tunisia and Egypt, data on Sudan are patchy, largely because of the exclusion of the seven provinces in the southern region which have suffered from the long civil war. Furthermore, Sudan has experienced long political instability together with political and economic isolation, especially from Western governments, since the second half of the 1980s, probably because of the dominance of Islamic extremists and the present government's close ties with anti-American regimes in Libya, Iraq and Iran. Frequent and prolonged droughts have also severely affected living conditions and generated famine disasters in some parts of the country. These problems have been compounded by the sharp fall in migrant workers' remittances, from US$467 million in 1989 to only US$61.9 million in 1991 following the Gulf War.

However, in the 1970s and 1980s Sudan received generous financial support and cheap fuel from oil-rich Arab countries. Because of its high agricultural potential, Sudan was regarded the 'bread basket' of the Middle East. This led some Arab countries to support development of the country's agriculture in order to supply food to the region.[43] Economic policy reform has zigzagged in three phases between 1979 and 1988. The first was in 1979 when the government concluded an agreement with the IMF that was prompted by chronic balance of payments and budget deficits, mounting foreign debt, overvalued exchange rates and high inflation.[44] In the second phase (1980–3), Sudan received a World Bank loan of US$105 million to rehabilitate cotton, sesame and sorghum exports, in order to raise the foreign exchange earnings needed to service its debts and reduce balance of payments deficits. In line with the conditions attached to the agreements with the IMF and the World Bank, a series of devaluations were undertaken, which reduced the value of the Sudanese pound (S£) from US$1 to S£0.35, to US$1 to S£4.55. Subsidies on food and other commodities were gradually removed, and there were cutbacks in public expenditure. In 1983, President Numeiri made the application of Islamic Shari'ah law compulsory and extended it to the south of the country, which is predominantly non-Muslim, thus fuelling the civil war in the south. Meanwhile the austerity measures (especially the removal of subsidies on bread and sugar) that were instituted to revive links with the IMF caused social unrest in the capital, Khartoum, which culminated in the overthrow of Numeiri in April 1985.

By the time of the military takeover, the agreement with the IMF and Western donors had broken down; the military government was forced by difficult economic circumstances to negotiate a fresh agreement. In this final phase, which ended in 1988, the government agreed to undertake a number of reforms, including the regulation of lending by commercial banks, new austerity measures (petrol and food rationing), and further devaluation of the pound. But these measures did not satisfy the

IMF, which declared Sudan ineligible for further borrowing. After the elections which brought Sadiq al-Mahdi to power, several successive agreements with donors during his regime failed. His government's attempts in 1988 to remove subsidies on essential commodities, and to privatize major state enterprises, generated a series of workers' strikes which led to the reversal of these measures.[45] Al-Mahdi was subsequently removed from power in a *coup d'état*. A new exchange rate of US$1 to S£8.30 was introduced in 1990 for exporters of cotton.

The IMF- and World Bank-induced piecemeal reforms had an adverse impact on incomes, food security and social services. Devaluations, which were central to the reforms, resulted in astronomical increases in the prices of food and other basic goods and services. This led to a fall in real income per person of 22 per cent, from an average of US$410 in 1980 to US$320 in 1986, which severely affected wage-dependent families. Conditions were made worse by freezing salaries and wages, while the rapid rise in the cost of living eroded the purchasing power of all low-income groups and most civil servants. Indeed, the cost of the minimum diet per person rose nearly tenfold between 1977 and 1986.[46]

It is not possible to make an adequate assessment of the welfare consequences of Sudan's economic reforms because of limited data on health, education, income distribution and poverty, as can be seen from the information gaps in Appendix 10.1. This is compounded by both the patchy nature of the reforms and the already pervasive poverty before the introduction of economic reforms. However, some changes that are related to key components of the reforms are indicative. Cuts in public investment resulted in a sharp fall in the annual growth of gross domestic investment, from 8.2 per cent in 1970–80 to a negative 0.8 per cent in 1980–92. Also, there were delays in rehabilitating the export sector, especially irrigation projects in the cotton sector. Meanwhile, the massive cereal-producing rainfed sector (where poverty is concentrated) was neglected both by government development plans and by the World Bank's structural adjustment programme. As a result, food production per person fell by 2.2 per cent per annum in 1979–92,[47] cereal imports increased threefold between 1980 and 1992, and food aid doubled between 1979/80 and 1991/2 (from 212,000 to 481,000 tons). Thus, Sudan, which in the 1970s it was hoped would be the 'bread-basket' of the Arab world, was unable to feed its own people in the 1990s.

With high military spending being maintained, budget cuts resulted in the decline in the share of health expenditure in the national income in 1980–91 to a low of 0.5 per cent in 1991, while military expenditure rose from 2.8 to 4 per cent, almost equal to the combined share of health and education during the same period (see Table 6.2). Infant mortality per

1,000 continued to decline during the period of reforms, but the rate of decline lagged far behind the average for the Middle East.[48] Moreover, Sudan was the only country in the Middle East whose average daily calorie supply declined in 1984–9.

Turkey

This lower-middle-income country with a large population (60.8 million in 1994) pursued economic policy reforms from 1980, under the dynamic leadership of the late Turgut Ozal. Until the mid-1980s, the Turkish economy was characterized by extensive government control and a large public sector. By the late 1970s, the country was facing serious problems in its balance of payments, mounting foreign debt and very high annual inflation of 100 per cent.[49] The government was therefore forced to adopt reforms for which the World Bank provided structural adjustment loans of US$1.23 billion, in addition to IMF financing arrangements to improve the balance of payments during the structural adjutsment period (standby and extended facility) of SDR 1.7 billion. Turkey also received sizable financial assistance from the OECD and Saudi Arabia.

The reform has three distinctive features. First, Turkey was the first country in the Middle East to receive the World Bank's structural adjustment loans. Moreover, Turkey pursued trade reforms intended to harmonize its export and import regulations with those of other European countries, to fulfil its aspiration to become a member of the European Union. The initial own-programme of January 1980 included devaluation of the Turkish lira from 35 to 70 per US dollar. Later in 1980, other measures supported by the World Bank and the IMF included liberalization of foreign exchange regulations, abolition of many restrictions on imports, introduction of value added tax (VAT), the provision of incentives for exports and private investment, and the rescheduling of foreign debts.

Second, the economic reform has been piecemeal in nature, lasting nearly eleven years. This was most likely the outcome of a parliamentary democracy of fragile coalition governments whose attempts to appease all constituencies made it difficult to implement the necessary measures. The stop–go economic reforms created a vicious circle of imbalances and reforms – high inflation and large budgetary deficits requiring further reforms, which in turn generated inflation and deficits which were becoming endemic. For example, by 1993 foreign debt remained high at US$52 billion, inflation was around 60 per cent a year, and during the post-1990 recovery period the growth of both gross income and investment remained sluggish (Appendix Table 10.1).

The third feature is that economic-policy reform initiated by the military government in 1980–3 led to political liberalization. The resulting parliamentary democracy has increased the freedom of labour unionization and aroused interest in improving the long-standing class-biased education system that has been an important determinant of inequality of opportunities by favouring the high-income social classes.[50] The transition to democracy has led to the inability of coalition governments to make substantial cuts in government expenditure, because of the need to fulfil promises made to different constituencies during frequent elections. As a result, the budget deficit increased from 2.6 per cent of national income in 1983 to 6.2 per cent in 1992. In addition, interest payments on foreign debt, representing over 20 per cent of government expenditure, combined with a persistent rise in military spending, absorbed nearly double the resources allocated to health, housing and social security benefits during the period 1980–92.[51]

With fluctuating economic growth, rising inflation and a persistent budget deficit in 1990–3, it seems that the expected economic benefits of the adjustment programme have not fully materialized. There is evidence of success in sectoral components of the reforms, while the overall macroeconomic situation was less successful.[52] Other unfavourable social effects include increasing inequality of income distribution, rapid rises in the cost of living and falls in the real value of earnings and a sevenfold increase in open unemployment, mostly in urban areas (from 256,00 persons in 1980 to 1.8 million in 1990, increasing annually by 65,000 in 1991–4). There is also evidence of a falling share of health in total government expenditure and national income.[53]

Mauritania

Economic difficulties facing this very poor country peaked in 1984, one year before the initiation of economic reforms. In addition to severe drought that destroyed over three-quarters of agricultural products (1983–4), the balance of payments deficit reached US$200 million, and foreign debt US$1.5 billion, with annual payment of interest charges to creditors amounting to US$28 million, or more than double public expenditure on health. Relative to a population of 2 million in 1985, this was a heavy debt burden indeed. Total foreign debt represented almost 2.5 times the national income in that year. This economic catastrophe brought down the government of the independence hero, Mokhtar Ould Daddah. The new government prepared a three-year recovery programme supported by the IMF and the World Bank. The aims were to reduce the balance of payments and budget deficits, to restructure the public sector, to expand the private sector, and to rehabilitate the irrigation schemes. The total financial support from the World Bank was meagre, amounting to US$140 million between 1986 and 1995.

Based on the limited information available, very little has been achieved by the reform package of the IMF and the World Bank. Between 1985 and 1993, national economic growth fluctuated around the low annual average of 1.8 per cent, which was below the rate of population growth (2.5 per cent), meaning a fall in per capita income. Moreover, despite several steps to reschedule foreign debt, its total amount remained virtually unchanged at the high level of US$2.2 billion on average in 1990–3, twice Mauritania's national income in 1993. Also, total investment as a percentage of national income fell, and as in Sudan, the inflow of official aid declined due to Mauritania's support for Iraq during the Gulf War in 1990–1 and the country's role in sheltering the family of President Saddam Hussein.

The social impact has been adverse. Available information suggests a deterioration of living standards resulting from rising unemployment, high inflation and budgetary cuts, especially expenditure on health services, which fell from an already low average of 4.5 per cent of total expenditure in 1984–5 to 3.9 per cent in 1990–3. Expenditure on education also fell, from 5 to 4.7 per cent of total income (GNP) over the same period. These cruel effects of inflexible economic reforms are harmful to a country with high illiteracy (68 per cent, 80 per cent in rural areas) and a low ratio of enrolment in primary schools (only 48 per cent). Mauritania, moreover, was classified as one of the group of countries with the highest infant and under-5 mortality in the world in 1993. With this great magnitude of deprivation, absolute poverty in 1990 was high, at between 54 and 57 per cent (see Chapter 8, pp. 138–9). Inequality of household consumption was very high. The share of the poorest one-fifth was 3.6 per cent of total consumption of families surveyed, while the richest one-fifth consumed nearly 14 times more (46.5 per cent), the highest in North Africa.[54]

Jordan

Like Mauritania, Jordan has poor natural resource endowment. Only 5 per cent of the total land area is arable, and the contribution of phosphates and potash to the national income is only 3–4 per cent. The economy relies heavily on uncertain sources: a large service sector, remittances of earnings of a well-trained workforce and foreign aid and grants from oil-rich Arab states. Moreover, as Jordan is at the heart of regional hostilities, it requires high military spending. This vulner-ability to external shocks peaked in the second half of the 1980s, forcing the government to borrow heavily from the international market in order to finance the five-year development plans.[55] There was a rapid deter-ioration in the economic conditions during this period (1985–9); GDP annual rate of growth fell from 9.6 per cent in 1975–9 and 2.3 per cent in 1980–4 to a very low rate of 0.5 per cent in 1985–90; and total foreign debt rose to reach nearly double the country's national income in 1989. Furthermore, the government budget deficit was 17 per cent of national income (GDP) and the rate of inflation was 27 per cent in the same year (Jordan, Ministry of Planning, n.d.: Tables 6 and 7).

Confronted with these imbalances, the government was forced in 1989 to adopt the IMF recipe for economic reforms. This was incorporated into the development plan of 1989–93, but interrupted by the Gulf crisis of 1990–1. Because of Jordan's support for Iraq, on which Jordan depended for trade and oil assistance, the government and people (as in Sudan and Mauritania) were punished by severe cuts in aid and by the expulsion of nearly 300,000 Jordanians working in the Gulf countries. This resulted in the abrupt fall of remittances in 1991 to half their 1988 level. The recovery of agriculture, the IMF lending facilities and the World Bank's trade support loans contributed to a modest improvement in economic growth and gross investment, but total foreign debt and the balance of payments deficit deteriorated between 1989 and 1993.

The social impact was also very unfavourable, as the poor and low-income groups were hit hard in three ways. First, unemployment increased from 14.8 per cent of the total workforce in 1988 to 17.1 per cent in 1991; among the poor this was higher, at 27 per cent. Second, the purchasing power of low-income groups declined, due to the rise in prices after the devaluation of the dinar by 104 per cent in 1990. Combined with budgetary cuts affecting consumer subsidies and social services, income distribution worsened; the share of the poorest fifth of the population declined from 7.3 per cent of total income in 1987 to 5.9 per cent in 1991/2, while the share of the richest fifth increased rapidly from 43.9 per cent to 50.1 per cent over the same period (a rise in the Gini index of inequality from 0.361 in 1987 to 0.434 in 1992). Third, the net result of this deterioration has been the rise in levels of poverty, and in the number of people living in absolute poverty despite moderate inflation and a growing economy. One estimate suggests that poverty increased from 28.9 per cent of the total population in 1987 to 32.7 per cent in 1992, while another puts this at 18.7 and 21.3 per cent in 1987 and 1992, respectively.[56] Whichever level is accepted, the situation must have been aggravated by the removal of the bread subsidy in August 1996, as required by the IMF.

The removal of the bread subsidy is particularly insensitive because the expected fiscal benefit from its removal is disproportionately small. It represents only 3.7 per cent of total government expenditure, compared to 27 per cent spent on defence and 17 per cent on debt interest payments. Instead of its removal, it could have been targeted only to the poorest categories (the lowest 20 per cent of consumers), costing a mere 7–8 million Jordanian dinars or nearly 0.6 per cent of total government expenditure.[57] My fear is that both this action and increased poverty and unemployment are likely to threaten the survival of the successful Jordanian experiment with parliamentary democracy which began in 1994 after the 1989 economic reforms.

Algeria

Despite its mounting debt burden, socialist and petroleum-rich Algeria was reluctant to seek help from the World Bank and the IMF because of suspicion about their motives. However, in 1989 a bold step was taken to sign an agreement with the two institutions in order to ease Algeria's economic difficulties. President Benjadid's government's moderate trade liberalization and the devaluation of the dinar were not sufficient to redress the severe imbalances without serious restructuring of the huge state farms and gigantic public enterprises which were the main sources of foreign debt, low productivity and the trade deficit. Extensive trade liberalization and painful surgery on the public sector, demanded by the IMF, were rejected by the ruling regime, and the strong federation of labour unions (UGTT). They feared rising unemployment and the flooding of the country with expensive imports of luxury goods.

But these ideological concerns had to give way to pressing economic problems. In 1989, the foreign debt reached US$26 billion, which represented 66 per cent of the national income. In the mean time, foreign governments and commercial creditors refused to negotiate debt-relief arrangements on a bilateral basis with the Algerian government. The European Community and France also required Algeria to sign an agreement with the IMF before it could receive grants and financial aid. Algeria, therefore, had no choice but to accept these conditions in order to receive IMF loans totalling US$800 million (as standby and compensatory facilities) and the World Bank's structural adjustment lending, amounting to US$500 million, as well as the rescheduling of half of its total debt. To speed up the process of economic reform, and as in Egypt in 1996, the Prime Minister and the Ministers of

Economy and Finance were replaced by Algerian professionals friendly to the World Bank and the IMF.[58]

The devaluation undertaken in 1989 was so aggressive that it led to the value of the dinar relative to the US dollar falling from 3.9 in 1989 to 12.2 and 52.2 in 1990 and 1995, respectively. Consequently, prices rose sharply, to the benefit of producers and traders but not consumers, as the consumer price index (CPI 1985 = 100) rocketed to 530 by 1995. Inflation surged to 39.5 per cent a year in 1990–3, subsidies were cut by 80 per cent, real wages fell from 1985, and open unemployment rose from 17.0 per cent in 1989 to 23.8 per cent in 1992 (about 1.5 million persons).[59] Moreover, remittances of the 1 million migrant workers, mostly in France, dwindled, owing to growing unemployment in France itself and its hardline stance against Algerians suspected of being members of Islamic extremist groups.

In this situation, the favourable equity effects of the socialist policies pursued in 1962–80 and described in earlier chapters have been reversed, and the purchasing power of a large section of the population has plummeted. Not only did the gap between the rich and the poor widen, but there was also a downward trend in real income. In 1994, the average income per person was US$2,380 compared to US$2,410 in 1984. Meanwhile, the per person average annual consumption of cereals, the main staple of low-income Algerians, was lower after the reforms than before.[60] Moreover, there was no growth in private investment, contrary to what had been expected under the reforms, and despite numerous investment laws giving the private sector generous incentives since 1982.[61] These negative trends cannot be blamed wholly on the economic reforms, however. Increasing doubts about political stability and the absence of democracy have undoubtedly contributed to a situation in which high risks have discouraged private investment.[62]

Inter-country comparisons

This section presents a summary of the results of implemented economic reforms, for which a number of the key economic and social indicators presented in Appendix 10.1 are employed. Judgement is based on comparison of the averages over different periods. Admittedly, to compare averages for such a small sample of eight countries is a crude way to test the results of complex policy reforms. The main reason for using period averages is because they smoothen the year-to-year fluctuations due, for instance, to drought in Morocco, Mauritania and Sudan, or to the effect of the Gulf War on Egypt, Jordan and Sudan. No attempt was made to construct a single synthetic index from the two sets of indicators, because this is problematic. Combining all the indicators into a single index is

Table 10.2 Period of adjustment programme and World Bank financial commitment in eight countries as of August 1996

Countries in alphabetical order	Period of own reforms	Year of initiation of IMF/World Bank programmes	World Bank financial commitment (US$million)
Algeria	1982–8	1989	1,100
Egypt	1974–86	1987	300
Jordan	1984–8	1989	390
Mauritania	–	1986	246
Morocco	1978–82	1983	2,150
Sudan	–	1979/80	115
Tunisia	1983–6	1987	1,364
Turkey	1980	1980	3,294

Sources: World Bank database and 1992a: Table A1.5.

Note
– = period difficult to identify.

also controversial: it would involve the weighting of individual indicators; and it would conceal, rather than reveal, specific changes. For the convenience of the reader, the period of adjustment and the World Bank's financial commitment in the eight adjusting countries are presented in Table 10.2. Likewise, the economic indicators are summarized in Table 10.3, in which judgement on performances is expressed in symbols to

Table 10.3 Summary of economic performance in eight adjusting countries to 1993

Country	Growth of GDP	Growth of exports	Investment share in GDP	Balance of payments	Budget deficit	Total foreign debt	Inflation
Algeria	–	–	–	+	+	–	–
Egypt	–	–	–	+	+	+	–
Jordan	+	–	±	–	+	–	±
Mauritania	±	–	–	±	+	–	–
Morocco	–	–	–	–	+	–	±
Sudan	±	–	–	–	–	–	–
Tunisia	+	–	+	–	+	–	±
Turkey	+	+	+	–	–	–	–

Source: Appendix 10.1.

Notes
A plus (+) sign denotes an improvement, a minus (–) a deterioration, while ± signifies indeterminate. These are derived by comparing the performance in the period after adjustment with that before adjustment measures were introduced. It should be noted here that the duration varies from country to country, as shown in Table 10.2.

show improvement (+), stagnation (±), and deterioration (−). No summary is constructed for the social indicators. Aside from the cost of living index, the limited data available do not permit a complete and meaningful presentation in symbols.

It will be recalled from the case studies that economic reforms were initiated at different times in the eight adjusting countries. For each country, the 'before and after' comparison is based on the year the World Bank/IMF reform programmes were first adopted. The use of a uniform terminal year (1993) makes the duration of the outcomes longer in early reformers (Turkey, Mauritania, Sudan and Morocco) than in late reformers (Algeria, Egypt, Jordan and Tunisia).

An assessment of economic performance

Summary Table 10.3 suggests that only Jordan, Tunisia and Turkey improved economic growth (GDP) after the reforms, and only Turkey had combined economic growth and export growth, although the high rate in the initial period of reform (1980–4) could not be sustained. The link between GDP and export growth is much weaker in poorer countries (Egypt, Morocco, Mauritania, Sudan). Despite 'getting the prices right' as required by the adjustment programme, the economy failed to grow. On the IMF's central issue of deficits, the balance of payments improved in Algeria and Egypt (to some degree in Mauritania), but deteriorated in others. However, most of the countries improved their budget deficits through drastic cuts, with the exception of Turkey, whose government continued budget expansion to meet the demands of multiple constituencies in a parliamentary democracy. Contrary to expectations, total external debt worsened in all the countries except Egypt, because of the Gulf-War-related partial cancellation. Inflation continued to rise, particularly in Sudan and Turkey, but slowed down in Egypt, Morocco and Tunisia. Meanwhile, the share of investment in national income (GDP) fell, except in Tunisia and Turkey, where investment in both human capital and physical capital increased. Lastly, the decline in public investment in anticipation of a rise in the private sector's share had negative effects on GDP and export growth, as well as on employment. One possible link is that export growth requires public investment in such public works as roads, ports and telecommunications.

Social consequences of economic reforms

The economic effects summarized in the preceding section paint a disappointing picture, indeed. This is also the case with the social effects, especially in countries with poor economic growth. Devaluation and rising inflation have clearly raised the overall cost of living in all countries. This was made worse by rising unemployment as a result of: (a) budgetary cuts in job-creating public physical capital; (b) deliberate cuts in jobs in the public sector; and (c) a failure to create alternative jobs in the private sector. The reforms kindled high hopes that this would be the 'new engine' for employment expansion and prosperity, to use the World Bank's terminology. However, in Tunisia this unfavourable effect was reduced, by the country's unique promotion of tripartite cooperative relations between government, business and workers, leading to increasing real wages and political stability.

The provision of essential social services

The crucial question is, how have governments differed in adjusting public spending on health, education, food subsidies and social security? Taking 1975–9 as the base period, there has been an overall substantial decline in subsidy and a decline in public spending on health or education (or both) in six countries (Egypt, Jordan, Mauritania, Morocco, Sudan and Turkey). However, the outcomes vary owing to different health and education conditions at the time of adopting adjustment measures. Another important element is the extent to which NGOs and private agents provide private health and education services. With regard to health care, mortality of children under 5 (per 1,000 live births) shows a steady downward trend since 1975, but the proportionate decline was minimal in the poorest countries, Mauritania and Sudan. Another important indicator of post-adjustment changes in the health sector is the number of beds in hospitals and clinics per 1,000 population. The ratio fell in five of the eight countries, exhibiting the adverse effect of cuts in government capital expenditure (construction of hospitals, provision of equipment, etc).

Regarding education expenditure, the trend alone is misleading. For example, although Morocco slightly reduced public education spending while the share in Jordan increased, net enrolment in primary schools fell in both countries. Between 1980 and 1991 allocations within public spending on education were switched from primary to higher education (to secondary schools in Morocco and to university education in Jordan). The ugly result of this budgetary meddling during adjustment has been acute deterioration in the quality of primary schooling. This is well exhibited in crowded classrooms, the falling real value of teachers' salaries, rising levels of dropout rates among pupils, and increasing child labour among school-leavers to support their poor parents during the economic hardship.[63]

From a historical perspective, there was remarkable progress in health and education in 1960–79, prior to the introduction of economic reforms. The relapse has occurred since 1980, although up to then these countries had appeared to be well on their way to realizing good health targets and universal primary education by the end of the 1990s. With regard to the children of the poor, one explanation of the post-1980 relapse – other than the increase in child labour – is the policy shift to fostering the private sector, thus turning health and education from what is essentially a public service to a private commodity whose price, determined by the market, is unaffordable by the poor. Supported by the World Bank and the IMF, this policy shift meant that most of the burden of health and education spending was transferred onto families, irrespective of income class. Subsequently, poor families have been left at the mercy of such profit-making agents as private schools, tutors, book-shops, clinics, pharmacies, medical doctors and laboratories for medical analysis. The results of family expenditure surveys carried out between 1980 and 1992 and analysed in Chapter 8 show that family expenditure on health and education increased disproportionately among low-income groups. Using the same source, the World Bank estimates that the share of private sector expenditure on health in the national income has exceeded that of the public sector in Egypt, Jordan, Morocco and Turkey. We find the opposite situation in Algeria and Tunisia, which raised public expenditure to match rising population needs.[64]

What happened to poverty and income distribution

In this review, poverty is measured in terms of the proportion of the total population and the number of people below the poverty line, defined by each country and standardized, for comparative purposes, by the World Bank. These data are limited with regard to comparable estimates between two points in time, ideally before and after adjustment. As can be seen in Appendix 10.1, poverty and inequality in income dis-tribution increased in many countries, but declined in Tunisia. The review suggests that the important factors behind these differences are the initial distribution of wealth and standards of living prior to the adjustment programme, and the timing and scale of deliberate measures taken by governments to reduce its social costs in general, and to protect the poor in particular. Other important factors are land reforms under-taken before adjustment programmes; the extent to which fertility and female illiteracy have been reduced; the increase in real wages; and the promotion of labour-intensive manufacturing (e.g. textiles, carpets and leather products).

The inter-country comparisons presented here are, in a sense, an assessment of the prime belief of the World Bank and Western donors that the realization of export-led economic growth is a *necessary* condition for poverty alleviation in adjusting countries. They also assert that this necessary condition does not have a significant effect on income distribution, because economic growth benefits all income groups over time (trickle down). The evidence shows that sustained growth of income in 1980–93 has enabled poverty reduction in Tunisia, but not in Jordan or Morocco. It also demonstrates that inequality of income distribution has increased during periods both of high economic growth and of slow recovery. The increasing shares of education, health and social security payments in total government spending have also contributed to poverty reduction in Morocco, as has Morocco's continued access to generous financial support from the World Bank, the IMF and donor countries.

The evidence shows a change in the incidence of poverty. To the best of my knowledge, poverty has been predominantly rural throughout the recorded history of the eight countries studied. From around 1980, urban poverty and income inequality has exceeded that of rural areas. Of the countries for which estimates are available only Mauritania is an exception, owing to frequent droughts, very high illiteracy of 80 per cent and very low enrolment in primary schools (around 40 per cent in rural areas). Credit should be given to the World-Bank-supported sectoral reforms which gave priority to the hitherto neglected agricultural sector, and led to improvement in the terms of trade in favour of agriculture. The prevalence of small owner-operated landholdings (resulting from early land reforms) has enabled a large section of the farming population to benefit from higher market prices for tradable products.[65] There are, though, several disadvantaged groups in rural areas who have not benefited from rising producer prices. They include subsistence farmers in arid areas and wage-dependent landless workers. Together with the illiterate elderly and households with a female head and many children, these net food buyers were clearly harmed by economic reforms.

As documented by labour and household consumption surveys, the urban poor are mostly propertyless, unemployed, illiterate adults; the disabled; primary school leavers engaged in petty trade in city streets; unemployed university graduates from low-income and poor families; and 'honest' government clerks who support a large number of children. The results of the surveys also show that among the poorest categories affected by the economic reforms are single-person households of elderly widows, who live on casual earnings and are heavily dependent on an unindexed low pension, charity and payments from NGOs. More detailed information on the effects of particular elements of adjustment programmes is needed to enable a distinction to be made between the 'old' and 'new' poor in urban areas. On the other hand, the 'old' poor (those who were poor before economic reform), are seen by the World Bank to be the responsibility of governments and not the adjustment programme. Nevertheless, in the study of Egypt we have already seen that: (a) the intended beneficiaries of the World-Bank-supported Social Fund are not all poor; (b) the transition period of the Fund is limited; (c) its total amount is negligible; and (d) the future of its funding is uncertain.

My account of the effects on poverty and income distribution of economic reforms in the Middle East does not fundamentally differ from accounts of other developing regions. Of twenty-five adjusting countries whose experience was reviewed by development analysts, only six reduced poverty, twelve had negative economic growth, and thirteen countries – mostly in Latin America and Africa – experienced a rise in both poverty and inequality. The findings suggest that sharp devaluation and demand-reducing policies had overwhelmingly negative effects on poverty.[66]

The IMF and the World Bank should learn from past experience and review their standard programmes, eliminating those elements that clearly harm the poor. Adjusting countries' policymakers should also learn many lessons from their bitter experience during the difficult years of economic reforms, in order to reduce the likelihood of making mistakes in future.

Summary

This chapter began with a discussion on the principles upon which the World Bank- and IMF-supported policies package is based. Next, it reviewed what has actually happened in eight adjusting countries, many of which had implemented their own reforms before adopting those of the World Bank and the IMF. It is difficult to make generalizations about the effects of a *single* policy from the findings of this review, because of the interacting nexus created by economic reform policies. The ingredients seem to be more political, cultural and organizational than economic. Nevertheless, a few remarks could be made.

Using a number of key indicators, the review finds continuing problems of imbalances and generally disappointing results. In only one country (Tunisia) do the economic and social outcomes satisfy my criteria for a successful adjustment. By 1993, most countries were still experiencing a debt burden whose service payments were siphoning off domestic resources that were badly needed for financing human development, employment expansion and anti-poverty programmes. Evidence shows also that a principal objective of adjustment has not materialized, that is, promoting the private sector to offset the negative effects of cuts in public physical capital and privatization of public enterprises, and to serve as the new engine of investment and job creation. Moreover, fostering the role of the private sector in education and health care against fee payment has denied the children of the poor access to good-quality education.

Contrary to expectations raised at the time of the adoption of the World Bank and IMF adjustment package, country studies show no clear relationship between export-led economic growth and poverty reduction. Of the five countries for which data are available for two points in time between 1979 and 1993, only Tunisia combined economic growth with reduced income inequality and poverty, but not with export growth. And three countries (Egypt, Jordan and Mauritania) have neither promoted growth and exports simultaneously nor reduced poverty and inequality. Probably the period for comparison has not been long enough to show the poverty-reducing effect of sustained economic growth. A visible negative outcome shared by most countries is increased unemployment and inequality in the distribution of income in urban areas, with many people's average income falling below the poverty line for the first time. On the other hand, adjustment policies have, in general, contributed to poverty reduction in rural areas via the higher real value of workers' remittances from abroad and the rising prices of tradable crops produced by small farmers. The beneficial effect was greater in countries that implemented redistributive land reform *before* adjustment programmes, and which managed to sustain low inflation. Lastly, there is no evidence of adjustment programmes reversing existing regressive (pro-rich) taxation, while the new rich entrepreneurs' windfall profits (from private property expansion and trade liberalization) have not been taxed for the benefit of the poor.

In this review, I have been concerned with what actually happened rather than what would have happened in the absence of economic reforms. My interest is in the real world, not in speculative analysis.

Suggested readings

On the changing roles of the market, government and the World Bank and the IMF:
Singer (1992) 'Lessons of Post-War Development Experience', 1945–1988.
Stiglitz (1989) 'Markets, Market Failures, and Development'.

Toye (1987) *Dilemmas of Development.*
World Bank (1990a) *Making Adjustment Work for the Poor.*

On the theoretical arguments in the study of the effects of economic policy reform on income distribution and poverty:
Bourguignon *et al.* (1991) 'Poverty and Income Distribution during Adjustment: Issues and Evidence from the OECD Project'.
IMF (1988) *The Implications of the IMF-Supported Programs for Poverty.*
Stewart (1995) *Adjustment and Poverty: Options and Choices*, especially Chapter 2.

On economic reforms in the Arab states:
El-Naggar (1987) *Adjustment Policies and Development Strategies in the Arab World.*

Additional readings can be found in notes and the Bibliography.

APPENDIX 10.1 SELECTED ECONOMIC AND SOCIAL INDICATORS IN EIGHT ADJUSTING COUNTRIES, 1975–93

Unless otherwise indicated, the data are calculated averages for the periods shown. Where an alternaltive period or year is used, this is shown in parentheses or in the notes.

Economic indicators

Appendix Table 10.1 Economic indicators, 1975–93

	1975–79	1980–84	1985–89	1990–93
1 National income growth (GDP: average annual %)				
Algeria	7.1	4.3	1.8	−0.5
Egypt	10.8	7.9	3.8	1.3
Jordan	9.6[a]	2.3	0.5	5.1
Mauritania	0.9	1.0	3.4	2.0
Morocco	6.0	3.9	4.9	1.2
Sudan	6.9	2.6	0.6	3.5
Tunisia	6.4	4.5	2.6	5.4
Turkey	4.8	3.6	4.6	5.9
2 Merchandise export (average annual growth %)				
Algeria	2.8	−3.3	4.3	1.6
Egypt	−0.1	9.6	5.5	0.3
Jordan	26.6	13.1	7.6	−1.4
Mauritania	−21.9	17.5	6.6	−4.7
Morocco	4.6	0.1	4.2	11.6
Sudan	6.2	6.4	1.1	−19.1
Tunisia	6.3	−5.1	13.2	7.4
Turkey	4.2	31.1	4.6	6.0
3 Total investment (% GDP)				
Algeria	45.9	37.2	30.6	30.0
Egypt	31.1	28.7	23.2	19.3

3 Total investment (% GDP)

Jordan	n.a	31.9	23.9	28.8
Mauritania	34.5	33.6	27.0	21.2
Morocco	27.5	25.6	23.1	23.4
Sudan	17.1	16.4	12.4	13.5
Tunisia	29.9	31.0	22.8	28.0
Turkey	22.2	20.7	24.0	24.8

4 Balance of payments (US$m)

Algeria	−156	−4.2	−842	+1,298
Egypt	−1,704	−1,827	−2,186	+266
Jordan	−408	−1,362	−740	−941
Mauritania	−222	−281	−229	−160
Morocco	1,344	−1,517	−455	−666
Sudan	−430	−911	−881	−1,230
Tunisia	−436	−608	−326	−845
Turkey	−1,923	−2,034	−450	−3,667

5 Government budget deficit (excluding grants, as % GDP)

Algeria	n.a.	−8.5	−9.7	−0.4
Egypt	−18.8	−11.3	−10.0	−5
Jordan	n.a.	−5.2[b]	−15.9[b]	−5.4[b]
Mauritania	−22.4	−21.9	−14.5	−7.5
Morocco	−12.5	−9.3	−5.6	−2.4
Sudan	−5.2	−6.7	n.a.	n.a.
Tunisia	−4.5	−5.1	−5.4	−3.9
Turkey	n.a.	−4.5[b]	−3.2[b]	−5.3[b]

6 Total foreign debt (US$m)

Algeria	11,118	17,528	23,692	27,157
Egypt	11,224	28,543	49,015	40,655
Jordan	857	2,703	5,476	7,298
Mauritania	504	1,110	1,877	2,180
Morocco	4,861	12,112	19,579	21,987
Sudan	2,708	6,957	11,267	15,946
Tunisia	2,194	3,812	6,283	8,296
Turkey	10,659	19,996	36,350	55,654

7 Average annual rate of inflation (%)

Algeria	4.1	5.2	8.2	38.5
Egypt	2.3	6.2	16.5	27.9
Jordan	6.0	5.6	7.4	10.7
Mauritania	n.a.	n.a.	7.1	10.2
Morocco	3.7	5.5	4.5	7.5
Sudan	1.2	6.5	45.8	1,042.3
Tunisia	n.a	6.7	6.9	7.8
Turkey	0.8	6.4	69.3	461.9

Sources: Indicators 1, 2, 3, 4, 6 and 7: World Bank (1976–95). Indicator 1(a) is from Khader and Badfran (1987: Table 10.6) and applies to 1976–80. Indicator 5: UNDP and World Bank (1992). Indicator (b): *Government Finance Statistics Yearbook* 1994 (IMF, 1980–94).

Social indicators

Health

Appendix Table 10.2 Public expenditure on health (percentage of total expenditure), 1975–93

	1975–9	*1980–4*	*1985–9*	*1990–3*
Algeria	n.a.	n.a.	n.a.	n.a.
Egypt	3.0	2.5	2.5	2.6[b]
Jordan	n.a.	3.7[b]	4.7[b]	5.2[b]
Mauritania	3.2	n.a.	4.5[b]	3.9[b]
Morocco	3.3	3.0	2.8	3.0
Sudan	1.6	1.4	n.a.	n.a.
Tunisia	6.7	6.7	6.0	6.3
Turkey	n.a.	3.6[b]	2.3[b]	3.5.[b]

Sources: UNDP and World Bank *African Development Indicators* (1992). Indicator (b): *Government Finance Statistics Yearbook* 1994 (IMF, 1980–94).

Appendix Table 10.3 Hospital beds (per 1,000 population), 1975–90

	1975–7	*1985–90*
Algeria	2.7	2.6
Egypt	2.0	1.9
Jordan	1.2	1.9
Mauritania	0.4	n.a.
Morocco	1.3	1.2
Sudan	1.0	0.9
Tunisia	2.3	2.0
Turkey	2.1	2.1

Sources: 1975–7 computed from World Bank database and *World Tables* 1995 (World Bank (1976–95). 1985–93 from *World Development Report* 1993 (World Bank, 1978–96).

Appendix Table 10.4 Mortality of children under 5 and rate of change, 1975–95

| | Deaths per 1,000 live births | | | | Rate of change (%) | |
	1975–80	*1980–5*	*1985–90*	*1990–5*	*1975–85**	*1985–95**
Algeria	165	128	105	84	−22.4	−20.0
Egypt	186	148	124	100	−20.4	−19.4
Jordan	88	72	57	45	−18.2	−21.1
Mauritania	251	232	214	195	−7.6	−8.9
Morocco	165	142	118	96	−13.9	−18.6
Sudan	221	198	175	153	−10.4	−12.6
Tunisia	150	121	99	79	−19.3	−20.2
Turkey	159	115	92	75	−27.7	−18.5

Source: Ross *et al.* (1988).

Note
* Values for 1975–85 are a percentage change computed from the averages for 1975–80 and 1980–5; for 1985–95 they are derived from the periods 1985–90 and 1990–5.

Education

Appendix Table 10.5 Public expenditure on education (percentage of total expenditure), 1975–92

	1975–9	*1980–5*	*1986–9*	*1990–2*
Algeria	n.a.	n.a	n.a.	n.a.
Egypt	9.6	9.7	12.0	12.5
Jordan	n.a.	11.7[b]	14.1[b]	14.0[b]
Mauritania	10.9	n.a.	n.a.	22.0[c]
Morocco	15.0	17.4	17.3	18.2
Sudan	5.9	7.9	n.a.	n.a.
Tunisia	20.6	14.9	16.2	17.4
Turkey	n.a.	11.0[b]	13.2[b]	18.1[b]

Sources: World Bank (1976–95). Indicator (b): *Government Finance Statistics Yearbook* 1994 (IMF, 1980–94). Indicator (c) from *World Education Report* 19933 (UNESCO, 1991 and 1993).

Appendix Table 10.6 Net primary school enrolment: ratio and percentage change, 1980–92

| | Ratio | | | | Percentage change | |
	1980	1985	1990	1992	1980–5*	1990–2*
Algeria	81	86	93	94	5	1
Egypt	73	85	94	97[1989]	12	3
Jordan	93	n.a.	91	89	n.a.	−2
Mauritania	37	48	48	n.a	11	n.a.
Morocco	62	61	58	63	−1	5
Sudan	50	50	50	52[1991]	0	2
Tunisia	83	94	96	98[1993]	11	2
Turkey	n.a.	98	100	93[1993]	n.a.	−7

Source: *Statistical Yearbook* 1987, 1994 and 1995 (UNESCO, 1963–95).

Notes

Net primary school enrolment is defined as the number of pupils aged 6–11 years enrolled in primary education, as a percentage of the total number of pupils in the age group.
* For 1980–5, the values represent change in enrolment (percentage points) between 1980 and 1985; for 1990–2 this is the difference between 1990 and 1992.

Appendix Table 10.7 Adult illiteracy (15 years and over, as percentage of age group), 1975–95

	1975	1980	1985–90	1995
Algeria	n.a.	55.2[1982]	50.4[1986]	38.4
Egypt	61.8[1976]	n.a.	54.2[1986]	48.6
Jordan	n.a.	34.6[1979]	16.8[1991]	13.4
Mauritania	82.6[1976]	n.a.	64.9[1988]	62.3
Morocco	78.6[1971]	69.4[1992]	n.a.	56.3
Sudan	68.6[1973]	n.a.	67.6[1983]	53.9
Tunisia	62.0	53.5	49.3[1984]	33.3
Turkey	39.8	34.4	20.8[1990]	17.7

Source: *Statistical Yearbook* 1987, 1994 and 1995 (UNESCO, 1963–95).

Notes

Adult illiteracy is defined as the number of illiterate adults (aged 15 years and older) as a percentage of the total number of adults.

Appendix Table 10.8 Cost of living index (CPI) (1980 = 100), 1975–93

	1975–9	1980–4	1985–9	1990–3
Algeria	38.8	64.9	99.5	199.6
Egypt	23.8	45.9	102.3	211.7
Jordan	56.2	88.1	108.2	147.9
Mauritania	n.a.	n.a.	98.2	137.0
Morocco	42.4	69.1	99.0	124.8
Sudan	9.3	28.7	137.8	2029.5
Tunisia	n.a.	77.8	100.4	135.9
Turkey	2.7	21.2	232.3	1155.8

Source: World Bank (1993–5).

Appendix Table 10.9 Nutrition (calories per person/day) and percentage change, 1977–89

	Calories per person/day			Percentage change	
	1977–9	1980–4	1985–9	1977–84*	1984–9*
Algeria	2,317	2,682	2,944	15.8	9.8
Egypt	2,800	3,273	3,310	16.9	11.3
Jordan	2,447	2,646	2,711	8.1	2.5
Mauritania	1,992	2,216	2,447	11.4	10.4
Morocco	2,654	2,804	3,031	5.7	8.1
Sudan	2,267	2,049	2,043	−9.6	−0.3
Tunisia	2,653	2,829	3,002	6.6	6.1
Turkey	3,055	3,030	3,196	−0.8	5.5

Source: *The State of Food and Agriculture* 1992 (FAO 1992 and 1993).

Note

* For 1977–84, the values show percentage change in calories per person per day between the period averages for 1977–9. The 1984–9 values are computed from the average for 1980–4 and 1985–9.

Appendix Table 10.10 Unemployment (percentage of total workforce), 1977–93

	1977–9	1980–4	1985–9	1990–3
Algeria	n.a.	n.a.	17.0	23.8
Egypt	3.2[1977]	5.7[1982]	6.9	20.0[1991–3]
Jordan	n.a.	n.a.	14.8[1986]	17.1[1991]
Mauritania	n.a.	n.a.	16.2[1986]	20.4[u] 9[r]
Morocco	n.a.	9.0[1980]	14.0[1986]	16.0
Sudan	n.a.	11.7[1983]	n.a.	n.a.
Tunisia	n.a.	13.1[1984]	n.a.	16.0[1992–4]
Turkey	n.a.	n.a.	8.3[1988]	7.9[1993]

Source: *Yearbook of Labour Statistics* 1986 and 1995 (ILO 1983–95), except for Egypt, Jordan and Tunisia: see pp. 185, 196 and 179 respectively. Mauritania, McKay and Houeibib (1993: Table 4.1). r = rural and u = urban.

Appendix Table 10.11 Inequality (percentage share of income/consumption distribution), 1977–91

		Lowest 20 per cent	*Highest 20 per cent*
Algeria	1988	6.9	46.5
Egypt	$1982^{(1991)}$	$7.7^{(7.3)}$	$41.0^{(44.0)}$
Jordan	$1987^{(1991)}$	$7.3^{(6.5)}$	$43.9^{(50.1)}$
Mauritania	$1977/8^{(1990)}$	$3.5^{(3.6)}$	$46.3^{(46.5)}$
Morocco	$1985^{(1990-1)}$	$6.9^{(6.6)}$	$46.1^{(46.3)}$
Sudan	n.a.	n.a.	n.a.
Tunisia	$1985^{(1990)}$	$5.5^{(5.9)}$	$49.5^{(46.3)}$
Turkey	$1973^{(1987)}$	$2.5^{(4.0)}$	$54.0^{(56.5)}$

Source: *World Development Report* 1980, 1981, 1984, 1986, 1992, 1994 and 1996 (World Bank 1978–96).

Appendix Table 10.12 Poverty estimates (percentage of total population), 1977–93

	1977–9	*1980–4*	*1985–9*	*1990-3*
Algeria	20^{u}	n.a.	25^{r}	n.a.
Egypt	23^{n}	33.8^{n}	n.a.	39.2^{r} and $43.5^{u(1991)}$
Jordan	n.a.	n.a.	$28.9^{(1987)}$	$32.7^{(1992)}$
Mauritania	n.a.	n.a.	n.a.	$44–57\%^{(1990)}$
Morocco	37^{n}	n.a.	$15.9\ (27)^{(1985)}$	$7.12\ (14.8)^{(1990)}$
Sudan	n.a.	n.a.	75–80	$67^{r(1991)}$
Tunisia	n.a.	$13.0^{(1980)}$	$7.7^{(1985)}$	$6.7^{(1990)}$
Turkey	n.a	n.a.	14^{r}	n.a.

Source: See results of surveys quoted in Chapter 10. r = rural and u = urban.

11

PROSPECTS AND
CHALLENGES

Over the last four to five decades, the Middle East has not only witnessed the construction of new states but also the reconstruction of its existing economies and institutions. From the 1980s it has also given up part of its policy-making sovereignty with regard to tackling the debt crisis and domestic economic imbalances to rich Western creditors, the World Bank and IMF. This has set the countries of the Middle East on a monolithic path of 'free' market mechanisms and private entrepreneurship, irrespective of distributional consequences and variations in social organizations of their economies. This recent change is a new form of economic colonialism, and contrasts sharply with the political and economic powers that the region exercised freely before and during the world oil crisis (1973–9).

As we approach the new century, this change in government responsibilities is likely to have significant effects on prospects for the alleviation of poverty and for the already worsened inequalities of income distribution. These prospects depend largely on governmental and non-governmental responses to three challenges. The first is to cope with the outcomes of government and market failures in the implementation of economic reforms, that is, to compensate for the resulting rise in poverty, unemployment and inequalities. The second is to match the reduction already achieved in state control over the economy with the removal of state agents' monopoly over the political system. This is essential in order to bring about government accountability to the freely elected representatives of the people and popular participation in policy-making. The third challenge is the realization of peace dividends after the conclusion of the long-awaited peace accords between Israel and the Arab states, and among other adversaries in the region such as Kuwait and Iraq and the north and south both in Iraq and in Sudan.

From economic reforms to what?

The Middle East began the 1980s with an economic crisis and the 1990s with a human crisis, brought about by both the Gulf War and the unsuccessful implementation of some components of economic reforms. Empirical evidence indicates that – at the regional level – there are more people living in absolute poverty and more illiterate adults and under-nourished persons in the 1990s than in 1980. The distribution of wealth and income in relation to expenditure in most of the adjusting countries has also worsened, and the deliberate reduction in total demand has constrained economic growth, the pillar of economic reforms. Moreover, the rural–urban consumption gap has widened and over the last decade a class of new rich has emerged, whose images of affluent lifestyle are transmitted to poor people by modern mass media. Worse still are the threats to social stability from widespread discontent over corruption and rising unemployment, especially among the educated young in cities, supported by Muslim militants. Social disruptions not only increase the risks to private investment – on which the reformers' hopes for sustained development are pinned – but also tend to shorten a reforming government's term of office.

The greatest challenge

The extent of unemployment, poverty, illiteracy and undernourishment presents policymakers and donors with their greatest challenge in this last decade of the twentieth century and will do so into the next century. It was observed in Chapter 10 that the tendency has been for poor and low-income people in general, and their children and the young in particular, to have been left to bear the heaviest burden of economic reforms. By 1995, the scale of deprivation was staggering. Unlike illiteracy, the incidence of unemployment is difficult to aggregate because of variations in definition and in availability of reliable data. What is certain, however, is that declining public investment without compensation by the private sector, combined with deregulation of the public sector and rising costs of living, have contributed to substantial unemployment in urban areas, and to the erosion of the purchasing power of low-income groups. Hence the connection with increasing poverty and diminishing aggregate demand. Another source of rising unemployment is the entry ban by Gulf Arab states on workers from countries that admired the Iraqi invasion of Kuwait in 1990–1. Whatever the source of unemployment, policymakers and development analysts should keep in mind that the poor cannot afford to become unemployed.

215

Table 11.1 Estimates of the number of unemployed adults in eight Middle Eastern countries, 1990–3

Country and year of estimate	Number of workforce (millions)	Unemployed adults (% of workforce)	Number (millions)
Algeria (1993)	6.50	24.0	1.49
Egypt (1993)	17.30	20.0	3.40
Jordan (1991)	0.92	17.1	0.15
Israel (1992)	1.99	10.6	0.21
Mauritania (1990)	0.69	20.4[u]	0.41
Morocco (1991/2)	8.20	16.0	1.30
Tunisia (1992/3)	2.90	16.0	0.46
Turkey (1993)	25.30	7.9	2.40
Total			9.82

Sources: Appendix 10.1, except for Israel: ILO *Yearbook of Labour Statistics* 1995 (ILO 1983–95). The estimate includes East Jerusalem.

Notes
u = urban
The definition of the workforce and unemployed adults is that of ILO: the unemployed are 'jobseekers 15 years and older'.

Estimates of urban unemployment in developing countries reveal higher rates in many Middle Eastern countries than in other regions.[1] In eight countries of the Middle East for which comparable data are available and presented in Table 11.1, the total number of unemployed adults was nearly 10 million. The situation is likely to worsen by the year 2000 and in the first decade of the next century if the present high rates of population growth and entrance into the workforce continue and the expected substantial rise in the share of the private sector in total job-creating investment does not materialize. In addition, the speedy globalization of manufacturing and trade reducing labour intensive industry and the continuous rapid expansion in child labour (mostly in uneducated poor families) and the need for its ban present another challenge. Do policymakers and heads of state perceive rising unemployment and poverty, and their close connection with declining remittances and curtailed public investment, as a challenge that threatens political stability and increases the risk of social unrest that they wish to avoid? Unfortunately, judging from past experience, the answer is no. In their periodic summit meetings the heads of Arab states have invariably addressed political, and not social issues. Possibly, among the causes of this neglect is a combination of complacent irresponsibility and lack of parliamentary democracy.

For the convenience of the reader Table 11.2 combines aggregate estimates of poverty that were presented earlier, and adds other estimates

Table 11.2 Estimates of the numbers of the poor, adult illiterates and the undernourished in the Middle East, 1980–92 and 2000

	1980 (1)	1990–2 (2)	2000 (3)	% change (3 over 1)
People living in absolute poverty (millions)	80 (1985)	96[a]	118	+47
Adult illiterates, total (millions)	75.5	79.6	86	+14
male		32.1	44	
female		47.5	42	
Total undernourished (millions)	24	31		
Undernourished children under 5 (millions)	1.8 (1975)	3.8[b]	4	+122
Population without access to safe water (millions)[c]	97	90	99	+2

Sources: Poverty and undernourishment: Chapter 8 and 10 and *World Development Report* 1992: Table 1.1 (World Bank 1978–96). Illiteracy: Table 2.3 for 1990–2 and UNESCO (1993) for 1980.

Notes

For definitions, see Chapter 1, pp. 15–17, 23 and 202.

a   In addition to the World Bank estimate of 73 million plus my estimate of 20 million for Sudan, Mauritania and Israel, 3 million were added, corresponding to the increased number in Iraq after the 1991 Gulf War (the number in Iraq doubled between 1990 and 1994). The estimate for 2000 is based on an increase of 22 per cent over the 1990–2 estimate.

b   I added 1.1 million severely undernourished Iraqi children, between 1990 and 1993 (see Chapter 6). The number of undernourished children in the year 2000 is my estimate.

c   WHO data, and based on an estimate of 39 per cent in 1980, 25 per cent in 1992 and 23 per cent of a projected total population of 426 million in the year 2000.

of people deprived of access to safe drinking water, suggesting an overall deterioration by the year 2000. Given the data limitations indicated in the course of discussion, the worst retreat in progress is seen in the nutrition of children under the age of 5 and in the incidence of absolute poverty, though the expansion in illiteracy is also alarming. Despite technological breakthrough and unprecedented increase in the region's wealth, nearly 80 million adults, mostly women (59.7 per cent) still cannot read and write. According to UNESCO, women will represent nearly half (49.6 per cent) the total number of 86 million illiterates by the year 2000. This appalling scale of women's deprivation is connected with the expected loss of nearly 3.6 million children who are likely to die by the year 2000 before reaching the age of 5; an average of 725,000 a year according to UNICEF. This shattering of the hopes that have been pinned on health and education improvement since independence is due partly to past policy failure and partly to neglect during economic adjustment. Even under optimistic assumptions of economic recovery, the number of people living in absolute poverty in the Middle East at the turn of the century will be higher than in 1985, about 118 million; a projected rise of nearly 38 million persons. Among the factors contributing to increasing numbers is the continuing high rate of population growth between 1991 and 2000 (seven countries have annual rates over 3 per cent). This extensive deprivation is appalling. It will have terrible effects on human capabilities and in turn, on national economies. In the year 2000, the Middle East will be deprived of obtaining potential benefits, in terms of lost contribution to total productivity, from the region's population of nearly 426 million.[2]

Even with political will, making up for such large-scale deprivation would be difficult because of the limited accumulation of the necessary capital, especially from the private sector, in order to finance this scale of needs. By simply adopting a universal system modelled on a Western-style market mechanism for savings mobilization (banking transactions, insurance and stock market), economic reformers have neglected indigenous systems of mobilizing household savings for meeting the needs of the poor. These highly moral traditional systems based on trust and community cooperation have gained social legitimacy (see examples in Chapters 3 and 9). The adopted modern system is vulnerable to several moral hazards, and is backed by laws and cumbersome rules that are alien to the cultural tradition, such as borrowing money against mortgage and *riba* (interest payments). Examples of succesful efforts to meet primary education needs and use of scarce water are *qanats* in Iran and the *Hi'aat* organization in Yemen (see Chapter 9, note 36). Can Middle Eastern countries enhance households' savings for development by modernizing traditional systems?

Moreover, financing constraints created by the persisting debt burden have reduced government options for budgetary spending. Tackling the problems of unemployment and deteriorating health and education services requires budget restructuring. By this is meant the reallocation of resources according to a new order of priorities. Aside from the prospects for reduction in military spending, examined on pp. 224–6, my assessment of past experience (Chapter 6) suggests that the region's average spending on health is less than that of other developing regions. In six Middle Eastern countries for which data are available, spending on health is 50–70 per cent less than would have been expected from their economic and social characteristics. Chapters 2 and 10 also showed that privatization of health and education, as well as the introduction of user charges, are not affordable by the poor, who are also deprived of high-quality services, and bear transport costs.

After going through all the trouble of weakening their own powers by strengthening the private sector and coping with violent bread riots during economic reforms, most Middle Eastern governments had continuing foreign debts amounting to US$221.2 billion and annual average interest payments of US$6.7 billion by the end of 1993–4.[3] Debt servicing is in fact a chronic haemorrhage of indebted countries' limited resources and an obstacle to significant poverty reduction.

As the case studies in this book have revealed, government annual interest payments in some countries exceed the combined allocation for health, education and social security payments. Fundamental changes will take some time, but governments must make a start in reordering resource allocations to redress lopsided development. They must also negotiate the much-publicized debt-relief arrangements with foreign creditors, including debt swapping (for example, the conversion into purchase of goods abroad). They should make new arrangements for reducing interest payments that absorb nearly 3–5 times, on average, what many governments spent on health in 1992–4. I estimate that a tiny 6 per cent reduction in the interest charges actually paid on total foreign debts in a single year, 1992, could have created jobs for all unemployed persons in the four adjusting countries with the largest number of unemployed adults (see Table 11.1).[4] These issues have played into the hands of militant Muslims who equate interest payment with *riba* or usury, condemning it as a violation of Islamic principles (Chapter 3).

Monitoring what is happening

For policymakers and analysts to understand and monitor changes in the human dimension of economic development, a meaningful statistical information system needs to be instituted. Between 1980 and 1982, and as part of my work in the United Nations (FAO), I examined the adequacy of data in several Middle Eastern countries for measuring changes in poverty, nutrition and the distribution of wealth and income in rural areas. The findings were examined in a meeting of makers and users of statistics in national governments.[5] The main deficiencies identified were:

1 paucity of data on the distribution of income and living standards which contrasted with plentiful information on commodities and national income accounts;

2 shortage of data on special sections of the population (women, children, the rural landless, workers in the informal sector and the disabled);

3 inadequate disaggregation of statistics by sex, age, locality (urban, rural) and income/expenditure classes;

4   secrecy of data on government spending on defence and military establishments (to the extent that I looked foolish or at least naive when I asked senior officials for this information, which I later obtained from the IMF and SIPRI).

Thanks to a series of World Conferences on social issues and to the assistance from international organizations, statistical information on all identified areas, except (4), have improved.[6] Yet, in several countries (Algeria, Iraq, Lebanon, Libya, Saudi Arabia, Syria and Sudan) periodic information on the distribution of personal income and consumption is either decidedly lacking or patchy. To monitor welfare changes over time, policymakers and analysts need more than the standard data on national income accounts (trade, profits, total domestic expenditure and products from different activities). Monitoring private consumption and savings is also handicapped by a number of flaws in national income accounts. Examples include the omission of several components of affluent consumption and savings abroad, and the fact that the resources spent on education, health and supply of sanitation materials are misrecorded as consumption, instead of investment in people (human-capital formation).

What happens to 'people' and not solely to 'things' is the fundamental concern, and expresses the true meaning of 'development'. It is the sort of quantitative information presented throughout this book that is needed for the modification of existing policies and the design of new anti-poverty programmes. Moreover, because equity and poverty concerns are multi-sectoral, it is necessary to institutionalize the compilation of relevant data and the operational monitoring at multi-layered levels, preferably with the NGOs' participation. An accurate diagnosis of human welfare problems and assessment of programmes should be provided regularly to policymakers. The public must also be honestly informed.

The challenge of democracy for equitable development

In real democracy, issues of illegal enrichment in public office, extensive tax evasion by many rich people, pervasive illiteracy, widespread child labour, rising unemployment and government betrayal of declared obligations to eliminate deprivation are subjects of public debate. Likewise, misuse of public funds by heads of state and senior government officials should be accounted for to elected representatives of the people, and investigated freely by the media. In this democratic environment, heads of state and political parties compete to serve ordinary citizens, meet poor people's demands, and gain their support to be re-elected.

Can democracy with morality rapidly reduce inequalities and poverty?

One of the emerging issues in development thinking is the connection between democracy (or the lack of it) and the occurrence (or prevention) of famine.[7] Evidence has shown convincingly that famine is more likely to occur under authoritarian governments and in the absence of a free press (for example Sudan) than in parliamentary democracies with an educated public (for example, Lebanon, Israel or Turkey). Under an authoritarian regime, the outcomes of government failures, gross injustice and corruption are hidden by secretive and state-controlled media. My review of countries' development experiences reveals that, significantly, educational achievements have taken place in the three parliamentary democracies cited above. For example, Turkey has substantially increased education and public housing spending since the transformation of its political system from military rule to parliamentary democracy between 1983 and 1987, following the 1987 referendum (Chapters 6 and 10). Likewise, information on – and problems of – poverty, inequality and living costs are regularly monitored within Israel's democratic procedures, resulting in the lowest degree of income inequality among the countries of the Middle East for which comparable data are available (see Table 1.2).

Despite mounting internal and external pressures for combining liberalization of the market with liberalization of the political system, as we approach the twenty-first century only the three countries cited above have achieved this combination. Among the remaining eighteen states, Algeria, Egypt, Jordan, Kuwait, Morocco and Tunisia have introduced state-designed party systems with state-controlled media. Since the introduction of economic liberalization in these countries, some elements of democracy have emerged. First, a wide range of small political parties have been formed by centrally designed elections. This is a survival tactic by rulers who permit these parties to operate as long as they do not challenge their powers or the powers of those around them. Second, a combination of rapid urbanization, trade-unionization and riots that have erupted during economic reforms are likely to facilitate steps to political liberalization. Street riots have often succeeded in forcing heads of state to repeal the removal of food subsidies. Commonly, eoconomic-reform-related riots have taken place in the shanty towns and slums around capital cities, where poor workers, jobless young people and street children are concentrated and the Islamic extremists are influential. Third, a reconciliation between less extreme religious dogma and modern rules of government (a secular constitution and laws) has emerged in Turkey and to some extent in Jordan, while it has been submerged by force in Algeria and Egypt.[8] Will the Turkish model of reconciliation last and bring about alternative and morally defensible policies for equitable human development? More specifically, will these post-economic-reform elements enable expanding low-income groups and the lower middle class (who are the major losers from economic reforms, and tend to be supporters of Islamic militants) to demonstrate how moral principles of justice and equal opportunity can be practised in capitalism?

This will be the test of combining economic and political liberalization with morality in the management of the economy. It will also test my proposition that income inequality is likely to increase during the next two or so decades for a number of reasons. First, the state's redistributive role has been weakened by economic reforms, while the expansion of the private sector is likely to be dominated by an alliance between the new rich and the multinational corporations (MNCs) within a rapidly growing globalized system of production, advertising and trade. Second, this alliance is capable of shaping government policy towards a greater accumulation of wealth and concentration of income. Third, this tendency towards concentration of asset ownership is likely to be strengthened by the hurried privatization of government-owned firms. Such speedy privatization at give-away prices and under pressure from aid-giving Western countries, commercial creditors and the World Bank is expected to transfer state monopoly power to a small number of buyers, including the MNCs. Under this scenario, the interests of the buyers in profit maximization through cost reduction (primarily labour-saving and wage cuts) is likely to bring about social unrest, which discourages private investment and may lead to the revival of state command over economic activities. This command includes government intervention to reduce the resulting vast differences in wealth and opportunities.

In short, the challenge facing governments at the turn of the century is to regain the trust of social groups who have been hurt by the abrogation of social contracts that guaranteed protection to the poor and equal access to necessities. Governments must remember that it was not only over food prices that riots erupted and Muslim militants confronted them, but also over widespread corruption, social injustice and rising unemployment. Governments, aid-giving agencies and economic-policy reformers must also remember that it is not economic efficiency, the core of adjustment programmes, which is lobbied for by millions of ordinary citizens, but justice in the distribution of wealth and income. If the present inequality trend continues, trade unions, journalists, professional associations and the liberal intelligentsia are not likely to tolerate the ruling regimes' rhetoric of social justice and eliminating deprivation. Nor can non-governmental organizations tolerate for long educational bias towards the non-poor and gender discrimination in employment and political rights, especially in the rich Gulf states.[9]

The role of the state in reducing vast inequalities, especially with regard to the protection of the poor and elimination of deprivation has been a recurring theme. I have argued in Chapters 5, 8 and 9 that state intervention to reduce the pervasive social imbalance and the rising concentration of wealth and income should be a defensible policy. Is it the right time to defend government intervention, while the region is busy dismantling socialism and privatizing its economies? At the peak of the policy and ideological shift in the West and in powerful international agencies from the active role of the state towards a market-led economy, I made a strong case for land reform (M. R. El-Ghonemy, 1986 and 1990b). My arguments – that equity in the distribution of income is as important as efficiency in production, and that the orientation of the economy towards market mechanisms does not mean governments should be apathetic about worsening income distribution – remain as relevant today as ever. We have learnt from past development experience that greater equity in the distribution of income is conducive to social stability, investment expansion and economic growth. Of equal validity is the view that social disruption endangers economic growth. These connections have been argued by several development analysts in principle and in practice, stressing the fact that social loss from market failures is as dangerous to the economy as loss from government policy failures.[10]

Peace dividend: real expectation or elusive hope?

A reduction of military spending following the conclusion of peace accords acceptable to all adversaries is essential for sustainable, equitable human development. Otherwise, the expansion of investment in people and job creation and, in turn, poverty reduction, becomes unrealistic.

My review of country experiences has shown that excessive military spending, in the belief that the security of nations depends only on military force, has been proved by the Gulf War to be a narrow perception, championed by the vested interests of the military élite, arms manufacturers and dealers. The realities show that even such a narrow dimension of security could not provide the people of the wealthy, giant military spenders in the Gulf with their expected security. In the early 1990s, ordinary citizens of Kuwait and Saudi Arabia saw for themselves that their armed forces' arsenals of sophisticated missiles and aerial reconnaissance systems failed miserably to protect them from external threat, and that it was only foreign powers that saved them. The tens of billions of dollars spent on the armed forces were never matched by the funds needed to eliminate pervasive illiteracy and malnutrition among young children by the year 2000. We have also seen from the Iraqi case study how a combination of extensive militarization and an authoritarian regime has turned affluence into poverty and hunger.

Development and human costs

Region-wide high military spending has contributed to severe social imbalance, heavy foreign debts and budget deficits. Between 1980 and 1992, the Middle East spent approximately US$720 billion for military purposes, compared to roughly US$450 billion on health and education. The potential human development benefits from cuts in military spending (without reducing security) are enormous, provided that existing territorial conflicts are resolved and violent conflicts within countries end. This necessity is manifested in the high development and human

Table 11.3 Estimates of war- and conflict-related deaths in the Middle East, 1970–95

Country and conflict[a]	Year	Deaths (thousands)
Algeria: government vs. Islamic organizations[b]	1992–5	73
Egypt, Israel, Syria (Yom Kippur War)	October 1973	16
Iran–Iraq War	1980–8	610
Iraq vs. Kuwait (Gulf War)	1990–1	150
Iraq vs. Kurds[c]	1980–92	20
Lebanon: civil war	1975–89	100
Israeli invasion and attacks	1982–96	140
Sudan: north (government) vs. south[d]	1980–90	510
Turkey: government vs. Kurds[e]	1974–84 } 1984–92 }	10
Yemen: North vs. South	1986–94	11
Total		1,640

Sources: SIPRI (1996: Table 1A), Sivard (1993: 21), McNamara (1991: Appendix 1).

Notes
a Does not include Israeli and Palestinian deaths, for lack of data.
b These organizations are Jabhat al-Inqaz (ISF) and the Armed Islamic Group (GIA).
c Patriotic Union of Kurdistan and Democratic Party of Kurdistan.
d Sudanese People's Liberation Army (SPLA).
e Partiya Karkeren Kurdistan (PKK).

costs[11] incurred in the region, especially during the Iran–Iraq war (1980–8), the civil war in Lebanon (1975–90), the Gulf War (1990–1) and the ongoing civil war in Sudan. Estimates of related deaths are summarized in Table 11.3. My estimate of the direct development costs of the Iran–Iraq war given in Chaper 6 amounts to roughly US$400 billion. Informed analysts estimate the direct costs of the Gulf War at US$70 billion, in addition to nearly US$6 billion paid to Egypt, Turkey and Syria by the alliance of Western countries.[12] These colossal figures do not include the losses of non-military constructions and oil exports from Iraq, Iran and Kuwait, or workers' remittances and tourism revenues lost by labour-exporting countries.

Above all, the real catastrophe of armed conflicts within and between countries was the 1.64 million deaths, mostly of innocent civilians in Iraq, Iran, Lebanon, Algeria and in Sudan. Owing to the lack of reliable information, the table does not include the thousands of Palestinian and Israeli deaths. In addition there have been hundreds of thousands of physically handicapped people and the miseries of unpublicized child malnutrition, forced migration and deprivation caused by deteriorating basic social services and rising living costs. Moreover, we cannot underrate the lost potential productivity of some 4 million young people of the Middle East who were in the active armed forces in 1992–3.[13] By lost potential productivity is meant the loss of contributions to national income had at least half those at present in the armed forces remained in their productive civilian activities.

The true cost of *civil* war in the region is best illustrated by the case of Lebanon. Its sixteen-year-long intractable sectarian and class conflicts (between 1975 and 1990) combined with the Israeli invasion in 1982 have left massive destruction of its physical assets, estimated by the United Nations at US$25 billion. In addition, both the invasion and the civil strife caused immeasurable lifelong suffering to hundreds of thousands of disabled people and the loss of around 240,000 lives. This is a high proportion of Lebanon's small population (7–8 per cent of nearly 3.4 million in 1990 when the civil war ended). The war has also resulted in the Israeli occupation of one-tenth of the country in the south.

From my first-hand knowledge of pre-war living conditions in Lebanon (especially in Beirut) I recall the country as a good example of affluence and poverty co-existing within uncontrolled capitalism. Recent information suggests that inequality has worsened and income classes have become more polarized.[14] The US$600-million-project to rebuild Beirut city's commercial centre and its wealthy residential area has already evicted poor families. Lara Marlowe observed that 'No provision is made for urgently needed public schools, low-income housing and health programmes. Highly visible prestige construction projects fan the resentment of the have-nots' (1996: 8). In contrast to other countries, quality of life deteriorated, human longevity shortened and infant mortality increased from 39 per thousand in 1974 to 45 in 1990. The direct economic cost has been colossal. Total real income lost between 1975 and 1995 has been estimated by the IMF (1995a) and Nasser Saidi (1986) as between 98 billion Lebanese Lire (LL) and LL 203 billion, depending on the real income growth rate used in the calculation. It is estimated that the 1974 real income per person is unlikely to be attained until the year 2006, meaning the loss of three decades.[15]

New vision and hope

The massive development and human costs of all forms of militarization suggest that the region has reached the point at which a new vision that combines security with elimination of most poverty is needed. The elements of this vision are:

1 halving the 1995 figure for defence spending by the year 2005, and aiming at a ceiling of 1.5–2.0 per cent of national income;
2 reallocating the expected savings (the peace dividend) to social services, in a manner that removes institutional obstacles to equality of opportunity;
3 providing economic security for the Palestinians;
4 treating military spending (within the context of the economics of scarce-resource use and social-opportunity cost) as a national development issue. I shall briefly set out such a proposal, after mentioning a few encouraging points.

I am encouraged by three bridges of hope. One is the end of ideological conflict between the former Soviet Union and rich Western countries, with its race for regional power gains that pushed lethal arms into the region. The second is the reduced risks of military threats, as a result of the Israeli peace accords concluded with Egypt in 1979 and with Jordan in 1995, the unfinished peace agreement with the Palestinian Authority in 1995, and the expected accords with Lebanon and Syria in the near future. The third is the start of a downward trend in the region's total military spending as a necessary measure to reduce budgetary deficit in several countries. Starting in 1986, total spending (at a constant exchange rate) fell from an annual average of US$60 billion to US$51 billion in 1992, and further to US$50 billion in 1994.[16] Can these savings be used to meet urgently needed human-capital investment for enhancing equitable development?

My study of government spending between 1980 and 1994 in fifteen Middle Eastern countries suggests that where cuts in military budgets were made, not all savings were reallocated to health and education. Only five countries have combined a reduction in military spending with an increase in both health and education expenditure (Iran, Tunisia, Turkey, the United Arab Emirates and Yemen). Nevertheless, the hope is that once a genuine peace is established, policymakers in Middle Eastern countries must realize that the economics of military expenditure and its social-opportunity cost are development issues too important to be left to their military élites in coalition with arms traders. An important lesson they should learn from the Gulf War is the wisdom of collective security arrangements which pool resources, reduce the military burden on a single country, exchange information and monitor arms stockpiling.[17] They should learn also that what matters most in armed conflict is not the quantity of conventional arms possessed, but the high quality of armed forces' training and the level of popular support for entering into war.

If political commitment to greater justice and elimination of poverty exists, I venture to suggest a sustained, purposeful reduction in military spending, a subject that has been locally secret and sacrosanct, and decidedly excluded from development analysis. The 1995 level of defence expenditure could be halved by the year 2005 if the real value of expenditure were cut by a mere 5 per cent annually. The alternative proposal, for an established ceiling of 1.5–2.0 per cent on share of military expenditure in national income, is by no means a low level.[18] Tunisia and most African and Latin American countries have, since 1986, maintained this proportion, and it has proved adequate for satisfying defence needs as well as security. Importantly, the recent development record of Tunisia and many Latin American countries suggests that this level has permitted balanced development with social stability and a rapid reduction in poverty. Since 1990, Iran also has given the achievement of better human capabilities a higher priority over military considerations, as a peace dividend after its bitter experience in the eight-year war with Iraq.[19]

According to my proposal for halving the defence expenditure region-wide by the year 2005, nearly US$250 billion could be saved for an annual reallocation of US$25 billion to health and education on an equity basis, that is, provision to the poor and low-income sections of the population free of charge, while charging the better-off. This modest estimate of the defence dividend is in addition to regular budgetary allocations to education and health care that should be increased in real terms by 3–4 per cent annually to meet the rising demands of a rapidly growing population. This expansion in human-capital investment would be made possible by encouraging family planning and by the expected recovery of the region's economies. I realize, however, that any significant cut in military expenditure (despite being justified) is likely to be opposed by the strong lobby made up of national military élites and giant multinational corporations that monopolizes the manufacturing and sale of arms. [20] With such strong opposition expected, some may say that this discussion is a waste of time. The reply is, that in the absence of effective democratic accountability of the military élite, how else can we make any significant progress in eliminating poverty and hunger, the real enemies?

I realize also that there are implications for labour employment and transfer of resources from military to civilian activities, especially in the Middle Eastern countries that have developed the capacity to manufacture arms (Egypt, Israel, Iran and Morocco).[21] Countries' experiences show that the arms industry can be adjusted by way of conversion and diversification within the national economy. Undoubtedly, my proposal calls for collaboration with rich donors prepared to channel their aid towards poverty reduction efforts and away from military support.[22]

Perhaps the most likely beneficiaries of the peace dividend are the Palestinians. Since the end of the Second World War, they have suffered from injustice, humiliation, killings, forced displacement and economic insecurity. Without a durable resolution of these miseries, social deprivation and economic insecurity threaten the prospects of peace, the first steps towards which were taken in 1993–5. Yet the estimated 2 million residents of the West Bank and the Gaza Strip (excluding 300,000 residents of East Jerusalem) continued in 1996 to suffer from the twin problems of deprivation and unemployment.

The extent of insecurity is manifested in the Palestinians' high dependency on two external sources for survival. The first is the complete dependency of nearly half the workforce in the Gaza Strip and one-third in the West Bank on Israel's labour market, resulting in unemployment of approximately 40 per cent of the total workforce in 1993–6. The second is the dependency of nearly 1 million Palestinians living in refugeee camps on UNRWA for the provision of basic social services free of charge. Unfortunately, the financial resources of this UN agency are uncertain and depend upon the goodwill and political environment within donor countries and the United Nations administration. Thus, in the wake of reaching agreement on a complete peace, the challenge is to provide the 14–15,000 unemployed with full-time jobs, at an average cost of US$90,000 each. A World Bank study estimated that by 1998 the investment of a total of US$1.3 billion would be required for this purpose, and another US$1.6 billion by the year 2003. This amount is in addition to an estimated US$88 million per year for capital and recurrent expenditure on rehabilitation and the reconstruction of existing facilities for health, education, safe drinking water and necessary sanitation.[23] The desperately needed investment of nearly US$3.5 billion after over thirty years of deprivation represents 7 per cent of the total *annual* average military spending of the Middle East, based on 1993–4.

Channelling the peace dividend

A recurrent theme in this book has been the absolute importance of education for expanding job opportunities and alleviating income inequality and poverty. As discussed in Chapters 2, 6 and 8, because education is the root of lifetime income-yielding abilities, it leads to effective use of public health services. However, two momentous problems in education need to be resolved. One is the existence of nearly 14 million boys and girls of primary school age not enrolled in school, who are deprived of schooling. An estimated US$35 per child a year needs to be spent on primary education (US$210 for six years of primary schooling per child, a total US$2.9 billion for all 14 million). The second problem is that in 1992 there were nearly 80 million adult illiterates, including approximately 49 million female adults. My rough estimate of the sum needed for the eradication of illiteracy amounts to US$10 per person or a total of US$800 million. These millions of disadvantaged children and adults are mostly the poor living in rural areas, urban slums and nomadic communities. The large scale of the problem demonstrates the failure of past education policies and presents policymakers with a great challenge at the turn of the century. Recent studies show that educating boys and girls yields a higher return than any other investment, between 13 and 17 per cent annually, with about 15 per cent increase in earning for each additional year of schooling.[24]

Another feature of deprivation claiming priority in channelling the peace dividend is the provision of safe drinking water and elementary sanitation. As we approach the millennium there are about 85–90 million poor and low-income people, mostly living in rural areas and urban slums, with no access to these human necessities. Regionwide, some US$1.2 billion or a mere US$15 per person can avert death and health risks to these millions of people.[25] Adding this estimated figure to others for the provision of primary education for children and the eradication of illiteracy, we arrive at an approximate figure of US$4.5 billion, representing less than one-tenth of the Middle East average annual military spending of US$50 billion in 1993–4. This total estimate corresponds to a tiny fraction of the sale value of a few dozen jet fighters and submarines that can be destroyed in a few minutes, as witnessed during the Gulf War.[26]

Crude as they are, these estimates of the benefits of the peace dividend are indicative of the possible order of magnitude. The alternative is the continuation of the *status quo* with all its moral hazards as well as development and human costs.[27] There is little or no novelty in what I have presented about the peace dividend. In approaching some political issues from a common-sense perspective, my aim is twofold. First, I wish to show that it is possible to transform gains from military spending reduction into better living conditions, and that the eradication of illiteracy and the provision of basic sanitation to the present poor are affordable. As I stressed in the introduction, 'this book was written with a positive motivation; [it] may lead, not necessarily immediately, to some practical results enhancing human well-being'. My second aim is that we should remind ourselves during the closing years of this century of the great opportunities that exist for the eradication of most deprivation and injustice.

NOTES

INTRODUCTION

1 *Zakat*, meaning almsgiving to the poor and needy, is one of the five pillars of Islamic belief. It is a compulsory payment of a portion of earnings above a minimum level (*nisab*) specified in detail in Shari'ah, known in Western literature simply as 'Muslim law'. There is a rich literature on the meaning of *zakat* and its payment as well as its role in modern fiscal policy. See, for example, Ahmad (1981: 290–2) for a list of references compiled by the International Centre for Research in Islamic Economics, King Abdul Aziz University in Riyadh, Saudi Arabia.

2 Using a diversity of criteria in delineating social classes (including self-identification), anthropologists and sociologists have contributed to the understanding of the importance of class structure related to the distribution of wealth and income among the population. See, for example, an anthropological perspective on wealth accumulation and status among religious leaders in the Middle East in Gilsenan (1990).

1 BASIC CONCEPTS AND REALITIES

1 Economists with different ideologies have followed different analytical approaches to analyse inequality, and have reached different conclusions. It is beyond the scope of our study to review these conclusions. See for example Atkinson (1975: Introduction), Baranzini (1991), Sahota (1978) and Galbraith (1973). They agree that by neglecting conflicts of vested interests, economic power and the institutional determinants of wealth accumulation, income distribution and class structure many economists have placed more emphasis on resource use efficiency than on equity questions. See also the welfare-oriented institutional economics approach, for example, Commons (1934) and North (1990).

2 See a critical assessment of welfare measurement in Bigsten (1983: 41–50), Little (1965) and Sen (1982: Part IV).

3 In different integrated models for attaining economic growth, several economists have narrowed the long-established gap between efficiency in resource allocation and personal distribution of income. Examples are Atkinson (1975) and Baranzini (1991). In their theoretical analyses of wealth and income distribution, they attempted to combine institutional determinants of

ownership of the factors of production, output growth and personal income distribution, over a long time scale, in the study of wealth concentration. However, this plausible intellectual construction is still restricted by a number of assumptions.

4 The variation in earning abilities among classes in a society, as determined by inheriting biological bases of intelligence (IQ) through variation in genetic make-up, has been studied by geneticists and discussed in Jenks (1972) and Phelps Brown (1988: 473–8).

5 Ahmad *et al.* (1991).

6 The Human Development Index (HDI) is a composite and weighted index, comprising gross national product (GNP) per person, life expectancy at birth, and illiteracy rate. See technical note 1, *Human Development Report* 1991: 88–9 (UNDP, 1991–6) and the revision of the Index in the 1996 *Human Development Report:* 106 and Table 1 of Indicators.

7 These are composite indices for estimating food insecurity at the national level. Whereas IFAD's index is narrow and agricultural-production-oriented, FAO's is broader and it consists of many variables: the proportion of undernourished people in the total population, per person income (GDP), the proportion of the agricultural labour force to the total labour force, capacity to import food, land productivity and cropping intensity. See Gurkan (1995) and FAO (1992b).

8 *Capital: A Critique of Political Economy.* Translated form the third German edition by Samuel Moore and Edward Aveling. New York: The Modern Library. Part V, p. 558.

9 See Chapter 3.

10 On these moral aspects of the capitalist system, see Haslett (1994: Chapters 5 and 6).

11 See the list of these Arab countries in the notes to Figure 1.1. Israel belongs to this rich sub-group.

12 'Involuntary' hunger is distinguished here from 'voluntary' hunger, when people willingly fast for religious reasons or for political protest. These people do not lack the means for adequate nutrition but do not wish to eat. In the text, the term 'hunger' is used in a broad sense including: (a) starvation; (b) chronic undernourishment caused primarily by regular failure to meet the minimum dietary needs for an active, healthy life; and (c) deficiency of specific nutrients, such as certain elements of protein, vitamins, iodine and iron. Malnutrition is an ambiguous term that is often used to combine (b) and (c). Its extreme clinical form is expressed in loss of weight, especially among children, termed marasmus and kwashiokor. The form of malnutrition presented in the text is (b).

13 The results of the FAO/WHO study are presented in: WHO and FAO (1992), FAO (1992b) and 'Report of the Regional Meeting on Nutrition', Cairo, Egypt, 12-16 April 1992. The results do not include Israel and Mauritania.

14 Calorie supply per person is estimated by converting 100 grams of wheat into 315 calories.

15 Obesity is emphasized as being a high risk factor for coronary heart diseases and diabetes (mellitus). Obesity is measured by Body Mass Index, a test of body fat, height for age and weight for height, a sum of four skinfolds and arm-muscle circumference.

16 See note 7.

17 The inclusion of Oman in this group of countries with high food insecurity is due primarily to the strong influence of cereal production instability combined with a high proportion of food in total imports. These are important elements in the calculation of IFAD's Food Security Index. Oman's production instability alone is calculated at the very high 134 per cent, while that for Egypt is only 4 per cent because of the high proportion of irrigated areas. See IFAD (1992: Table 1 and technical notes). There are two other indices for food insecurity established by UNCTAD (1984: Table V-1) and FAO (1993).

18 See (a) the work of the Policy Research Department of the World Bank, covering eighty-six developing countries, whose results are published in *World Development Report* 1990 and 1992 (World Bank, 1978–96): the methodology used and lessons learnt are presented in Ravallion *et al.* (1991); and (b) the Luxembourg Income Study (LIS) which covers Israel together with six rich industrial countries, analysed by Smeeding *et al.* (1990).

19 Estimates for 1985 and 1990 are given in *World Development Report* 1992: Table 1.1 (World Bank, 1978–96). Using the data on comparable purchasing power expressed in international dollars, updated by Summers and Heston (1991), Chen, Datt and Ravallion published their revised estimates of poverty for 1985 and 1990 in Chen *et al.* (1994). The revised levels and intensity of poverty were lower than those published in 1992, but the upward poverty trend has not changed with respect to the Middle East. These are given in 'New Estimates of Aggregate Poverty in the Developing World, 1985–1990', Table 2, mimeographed and sent to me by courtesy of Martin Ravallion.

20 The World Bank's geographical classification includes Mauritania and Sudan in sub-Saharan Africa, not in the Middle East. Consumption per person is from Summers and Heston (1991).

2 HISTORICAL ORIGINS

1 Independence was gained in the following years: Egypt (partial) 1922 and (complete) 1954; Iraq, 1931; Lebanon and Syria, 1946; Israel, 1948; Libya, 1951; Morocco, 1955; Sudan, 1956; Tunisia, 1957; Mauritania, 1960; Algeria and Kuwait, 1962; South Yemen, 1968; Bahrain, Oman, Qatar and the United Arab Emirates, 1970; and Djibouti, 1977. For a detailed analysis of the making of the Middle Eastern states, see Owen (1992).

2 The State of Israel was founded in 1948 in line with earlier commitments by the British government and the League of Nations to establish a 'Jewish national home in Palestine'. The British position was set out in a letter dated 2 November 1917 from the Foreign Secretary, Arthur Balfour, to Lord Rothschild, the British Zionist leader, and later in a British White Paper (Cmd, 1700, pp. 17–21). The Council of the League of Nations, in its 'Mandate for Palestine', dated 24 July 1922, stated: 'In the event of the termination of the Mandate, hereby conferred upon the Mandatory. . . The Council agreed that the Mandatory (the British Government) should be responsible for putting into effect the Declaration originally made by the Government of His Britannic Majesty, and adopted by the Principal Allied Powers.'

3 For a detailed description of the minorities' social status and their role in the economies, see Issawi (1981: Chapter 13). On the dominance of European

culture in the conquered countries of the Middle East, see Hourani (1991: Chapters 17 and 18).

4 On the agrarian situation before 1940, see Haider (1944) and Warriner (1948). For the period 1940–65, see M. R. El-Ghonemy (1967: 220).

5 M. R. El-Ghonemy (1993: Chapter 4).

6 These quotations are taken from a letter from the British Governor to the District Commissioner in Torit, dated 2 November 1939 (Hodnebo, 1981: Appendix).

7 The Moroccan famine of 1945 is documented in Nouvele (1949) and cited in Swearingen (1988: 122). Data on cereal production are taken from FAO *Production Yearbook*, Vols 1, 4 and 5, Rome: FAO.

8 On Egypt, see Baer (1962), or Morocco, Lazarev (1977) and on Iraq, Alwan (1961). These writers give a detailed account of the process of property transfers to influential families and tribal sheikhs. They list the names of the recipients of large estates, many of whom are currently dominant in the countries' political and economic arenas. In her study of Lebanon, Warriner (1948: 86) lists existing estates belonging to the families of Arslan, Jumblat and Shehab that were granted to them during Ottoman rule and supported by the French Mandate.

9 See note 3.

10 See Todaro (1989: 349), and Knight and Sabot (1990: 20–1 and Chapter 3).

11 For an understanding of the principles of the economics of education, see Blaug (1970), Sahota (1978) and Schultz (1981). On the application of these principles to the situation in developing countries, see Todaro (1989: Chapter 11).

12 Illiteracy and schooling data in individual countries about 1960 are taken from *World Development Report* 1978 and 1980 (World Bank, 1978–96), UNESCO *Statistical Yearbook* 1964 and 1976 (UNESCO 1964–95), and Qubain (1966).

13 The data on Iraq in the preceding paragraph and on the Jewish and Arab students in this paragraph are calculated from Matthews and Akrawi (1949: Tables 21, 23, 36 and 43).

3 RELIGIOUS FOUNDATIONS OF JUSTICE AND INHERITANCE

1 Law is an important aspect of the Torah, which means 'teaching' or 'instruction' and the Talmud, the recorded interpretations of law. The content of the Torah is commonly referred to as 'Jewish law'. Two different versions of the Talmud exist, the Jerusalem and the Babylonian. There are also many codifications of law: Maimonides' *Mishneh Torah*, and Jacob ben Asher's *Arba'ah Turim* are among the most important of these. For a lucid presentation of these books, see de Lange (1986), especially Chapters 5 and 6.

2 Based on the results of social anthropological studies of Egypt, Lebanon and Morocco conducted by Eickelman (1976) and Gilsenan (1991).

3 Since the mid-1970s these principles have been applied to lending, savings and investment in a network of branches of the Faisal Islamic Bank established in several Arab countries. Some other commercial banks have also changed their operations to conform with these principles. The principle of *musharakah* or partnership requires that the bank and the client contribute to

an agreed investment operation and divide the net profit in a proportion agreed upon in advance. See Faisal Islamic Bank (1979; 1983) and a survey of literature on *riba*, interest-free banking, and profit sharing in Ahmad (1981: 287, 296, 306, 310). See also the careful survey made by the Mufti of Egypt, Tantawy (1992) of the issues related to interest charges, savings and lending. For an economic analysis of the replacement of interest-bearing credit by an Islamic credit system in Iran, see Yazdani and Hill (1993: 301–10) and a review of the experience of Iran and Pakistan in Iqbal and Mirakhor (1987).

4 Al-Azhar and the Egyptian Ministry of Waqfs compiled all fatwas related to birth control in *Islam's Attitude Towards Family Planning* (Egypt, Ministry of Waqfs and Ministry of Information, 1994).

5 For a discussion of the application of economic theory on consumer behaviour to Islamic practices, see Siddiqi and Monzer Kahf in Ahmad (1981).

6 The quotation is from Milton Friedman (1962: 161–2) and the American philosopher is David Haslett. The 'Proposal for Abolishing Inheritance' is presented in Haslett (1994: Chapter 6).

7 I have limited my presentation to principles of inheritance that were (and still are) practised by the Jewish community in the former Palestine Mandate, now the State of Israel. This information is taken from Scheftel (1947). My statement on Jewish inheritance law is based on personal communication with Rabbi Dr Julian Jacobs, the office of the Chief Rabbi, London (12 October 1993).

8 I am grateful to Dr Hussain Hamid, President of the International Islamic University, Islamabad, Pakistan for his clarification of this principle.

9 This field of economics was developed during the period 1960–80, primarily in Pakistan with contributions from Egyptian, Saudi and Turkish economists. It is concerned with the establishment of an Islamic framework of economics based on the value principles revealed in the Qur'an and the Hadith (the Prophet Mohammed's sayings). The first conference on this new approach was held in February 1976 in Mecca, organized by King Abdul Aziz University, Jeddah, Saudi Arabia. On the work of the conference, see Ahmad (1981).

10 The expressions of the Islamic militants' disapproval summarized in this paragraph are based on my talks with, and reading the published material of, some members of different groups over the past four decades. Examples of relevant publications of these groups, with country of issue shown in parentheses, are *al-Da'wa* (Egypt), *Majalat al-Ikhwan al-Muslimun* (Egypt), *Social Justice in Islam and Alamat ala al-Tareeq* (Egypt), *al-Jama'ah* (Morocco), *al-Monqiz* (Algeria), *al-Ma'refah* (Tunisia) and *al-Liwa' al-Islami* (Egypt).

11 Information about the situation during the period 1920–50 is taken from Hansen and Marzouk (1965: 2–5), Baer (1962: 139–46 and Tables 25, 27 and 28) and Cleland (1939: 465); rural poverty estimate is in M. R. El-Ghonemy (1990b: 247).

12 In a single year, 1994, the Egyptian journal *al-Mojtam'a al-Jadid* (1995: 15) reported that 84 were killed, including 24 policemen. See Saad-Eddin Ibrahim (1985). The Deputy Prime Minister for Economics compared tourism revenue in 1992 with that of 1993, when it fell from E£2.1 billion to E£900 million (*al-Ahram*, 24 February 1995).

13 For an understanding of the institutional characteristics of the Islamic state in Iran, see Akhaui (1980), Esposito (1987: 195–8) and Owen (1992: 171–7).

4 ECONOMIC FOUNDATIONS

1 Richards and Waterbury (1990: Table 3.3), based on data from *Oil and Gas Journal*, December 1987.
2 *Yearbook of World Energy Statistics* 1991 (United Nations, 1985 and 1991) and *Oil and Gas Journal*, December 1987.
3 *World Development Report* 1992, Table 2.1 (World Bank, 1978–96) and *From Scarcity to Security: Averting a Water Crisis in the Middle East and North Africa* (World Bank, 1995.)
4 See Dregne (1983: Tables 6.5 and 6.7 and Chapter 1) on desertification and food security respectively.
5 Source, Asfour (1972: 371). During my visit to Saudi Arabia in May 1994, I estimated total revenue from the pilgrimage at roughly US$3.1 billion, based on an estimation of earnings from the state-owned Saudi Airline, hotels, internal transport and the obligatory purchase of sheep for sacrifice in Mina (nearly 1.6 million head) during the Hajj (pilgrimage to Mecca), and excluding the value of consumer goods purchased by the estimated 1.5 million expatriate Muslims who perform the Hajj.
6 Based on data given by the Bank of Libya (1965) and the World Bank (1960: Statistical Appendix Tables 51 and 52). Foreign grants were shared among donors as follows: USA (50 per cent), UK (30 per cent) with 20 per cent shared by France, Egypt, Turkey and Pakistan. The percentage is an average for the period 1954–8. The grants were equivalent to US$60 million in 1958, one year before the discovery of oil.
7 Egypt: Anis (1950, Tables 1 and 3); Saudi Arabia: Asfour (1972); Libya: Higgins (1959: 3); Kuwait: World Bank (1965: 28). See also the United Nations (1951: 12).
8 *UN Statistical Yearbook* 1960 and 1970 (United Nations, 1960–95), Asfour (1972: Table 8.1) and the World Bank's *World Development Reports* 1981, 1982 and 1983 (World Bank, 1978–96). Iran started to produce and export oil in 1912.
9 This comparison is based on Ardriaansen and Waardenburgh (1992: Table 1.1). The countries are: Canada, USA, UK, Germany, France and Japan.
10 These new estimates for 1990 appear in *World Development Report* 1992: Table 30, Indicators (World Bank 1978–96). A substantial component of Jordan's GNP is foreign grants from the UK, USA and oil-rich Arab states, which amounted to one-quarter of total income in the 1980s.
11 For payment by oil companies to governments, see Issawi (1982: Table 10.3).
12 For an explanation of 'rentier state' in the Middle East context, see Beblawi and Luciani (1987). See the IMF (1991a) especially 'Saudi Arabia', pp. 11–13.
13 The superiority of income and reserves per person in Libya, United Arab Emirates, Qatar, and Kuwait over the corresponding data in the USA and UK is due chiefly to the small population in these Arab countries. The gold component is valued at year-end London prices an ounce in US$ as follows: average 1958–62 = $35, 1980 = $589.5 and 1985 = $327.36. The data are taken from *UN Statistical Yearbook*, 1965, 1970 and 1987 (United Nations, 1960–95).

14 Based on (a) IMF (1991a); (b) League of Arab States (1993); (c) Archilli and Khaldi (1984): and (d) OECD (1994: Report, Table 4.6). Aid is channelled directly through national funds and indirectly by established regional development funds.

15 In my capacity as the Deputy Regional Director of the UN/FAO office for the Near East at Cairo, Egypt (1975–80). When the amount of financial aid was decided in Riyadh and Kuwait, the authorities had no knowledge about the allocation of aid, and later they showed no interest.

16 This Saudi financial assistance to Iraq was reported in the *Middle East Economic Survey* 34, 16 (January 1991): B2 and B3. The IMF also reported that Kuwait had extended important sums to help Iraq in its long war with Iran (IMF, 1991a: 4).

17 *International Financial Statistics* (IMF, 1989 and 1992), and Choucri (1986: Tables 1 and 2).

18 On forecasting rainfall and drought in Sudan, see Abdulla (1986: 309 and Table 16.2). On the victims of the famine, see de Waal (1989: Table 7.1) and IFPRI (1991: 35).

19 The estimates of the World Resource Institute analysed by the World Bank are taken from *World Development Report* 1992: Tables 2.1a, A.3 and Table 33 of the Indicators and Technical Notes, p. 192 (World Bank, 1978–96). Availability of water per person is provided by the World Bank (1995: Table 3).

20 See Allan (1981: 201–7) and Gurney (1996: 208).

21 On these fears and potential danger of conflicts, see Kliot (1993).

22 For the methodology used in making a detailed assessment of land potential, see FAO (1993a: 119–38).

23 FAO (1986: 40–1), Carruthers and Clark (1981: Table 5.11) and *World Development Report* 1982: 61–4 (World Bank, 1978–96).

24 See a summary of the estimates in M. R. El-Ghonemy (1979: 43).

25 The data on the sale of government-owned newly irrigated lands between 1935 and 1949 are taken from Egypt, Ministry of Finance (1949: 37 and Table 3) (Arabic). The 1980 study is 'New Lands Productivity in Egypt', cited in 'Economic and Social Policy Aspects of Irrigated Agricultural Lands in the Near East', Near East Regional Economic Policy Commission, second session, Istanbul, 7–11 September 1987, p. 7. On the estimates of landless workers in agriculture, see M. R. El-Ghonemy (1990b: 159 and 181).

26 In addition to Egypt and Oman cited in the text, see examples from Libya in Allan (1981: 107–10 and 207–9); from Syria in *The State of Food and Agriculture* 1993: 164–7 (FAO, 1992 and 1993) and from Saudi Arabia in Akkad (1967: 296–305).

27 For example, some 30,000 hectares of the best fertile land, which includes 12,000 hectares of irrigated land, were lost in Algeria as a result of the construction of buildings and factories (Bounab, 1989: 97).

5 UNBALANCED DEVELOPMENT

1 The source on stagnated agriculture is IFAD (1988: Table 2.2). The grants were mostly of wheat and dairy products, reaching 910,000 tonnes in 1985 after a severe drought (FAO's *Food Aid in Figures*, 1983 and 1987 issues). The direct contribution of agricultural output is calculated by multiplying the rate of agricultural GDP growth by its percentage share in total GDP, then

dividing by the rate of growth of total GDP during the same period. For more details on the resulting economic crisis and social instability, see 'Sudan', pp. 190–2.

2 FAO's estimate of poverty incidence of 70 per cent at national level and 75 per cent in rural areas was made by a team of experts in 1983 and presented in FAO (1983). IFAD (1992: Appendix Table 2), the World Bank and UNDP use the estimate of 85 per cent of rural population. On the exclusion of the south and its conflict with the north, see Deng (1995).

3 See a detailed description of this inequality in Suliman (1974: 30–42) (Arabic).

4 Calculated from Table A.26, ILO and UNHCR (1984).

5 Lees and Brooks (1977: 49).

6 The IFAD mission found that fewer than 3 per cent of the small farmers in the traditional rainfed sector received credit from the Agricultural Credit Bank, while 75 per cent of the total lending was received by the large farmers of the mechanized rainfed sector (IFAD, 1988: 70).

7 The term 'Dutch disease' was first used by *The Economist* in the 26 November 1977 issue to refer to the adverse economic effects observed in the Netherlands – after the initial period of natural gas boom – on the exchange rate and the sectors producing tradable goods (manufacturing and agriculture) compared with the favoured sectors producing non-tradable goods (e.g. construction). See Ellman (1981).

8 According to Jazayeri (1988: Table 2.2) and the Libyan Ministry of Planning (1976 and 1981, in Arabic) the combined shares of agriculture and manufacturing were 38.3 per cent in Iran and 41.3 per cent in Libya, while the combined shares of construction and government services were 58.7 per cent and 59.0 per cent respectively. The definition of the components of government administration is not the same in both countries and, therefore, its share is not perfectly comparable between the two countries.

9 Food dependency ratio is the percentage of imported food to total domestic food supply for consumption. The source is *Human Development Report* 1994: Table 13 (UNDP, 1991–6). For data on food imports as an average percentage of total imports between 1979–81 and 1991, see *Country Tables: Basic Data on the Agricultural Sector* 1993 (FAO, 1985–93).

10 These growth rates are in real terms and, therefore, comparable. Despite Egypt's high average growth rates relative to other countries in 1980–8, annual rates fluctuated from the high 10 per cent in 1982 and 7.7 per cent in 1983 to the low 2.3 per cent in both 1986 and 1987. In 1989, the growth rate fell sharply to only 1 per cent. The deterioration was primarily due to the failure of production to expand in the manufacturing and agriculture sectors, combined with a rapid increase in foreign debts, which reached US$49 billion in 1989 (see p. 184).

11 See Bhalla (1992: 28–30) on the measurement of unbalanced growth between sectors of the economy. The measurement is in terms of the deviations of the sectoral GDP growth rates from the average national rate of growth of GDP over a given period of time, weighted by the relative share of each sector in total GDP. 'Fertility rate' represents an estimate of the number of children that would be born during a woman's childbearing years.

12 Information about the priority accorded to heavy industry and the falling

productivity of workers is based on data given in Bounab (1989: Tables 2.14, 2.16, 2.17 and 2.18).

13 Jazayeri (1988: 66, Table A.21 and Figure A.4).

14 In addition to Amin and Sayigh, other Middle Eastern scholars' writings include Katouzian (1978) and Amuzegar (1982) on Iran's experience and Atiqa (1967 and 1981) on Libya.

15 For rising real wages in Algeria, see Bounab (1989: Tables 3.15, 3.16 and 5.12). For Iran, see Jazayeri (1988: 63, 87 and Table A.11). For Libya, see Mabro (1970).

16 Bounab (1989: Tables 2.17, 2.18 and 2.25).

17 Based on data given in the Libyan Ministry of Agriculture's study which was prepared by Alwan for FAO in 1978 (Arabic).

18 Jazayeri (1988: 68–9 and Table A.21).

19 The three researchers are van Ginneken (1980: 639–76), Mohtadi (1986: 713–25) and Amid (1990: Table 6.4 and Figure 8.1).

20 El-Azzibi (1975) and Allan (1981: 62). The data on employment expansion in Libya are taken from UN *Statistical Yearbook* 1979/80 and 1980/81: Construction (United Nations, 1960–95).

6 SOCIAL IMBALANCE IN PUBLIC EXPENDITURE

1 Usually, programmes of action adopted by these world conferences are not binding on governments, and they contain provisions to suit all situations. For example, in the 1976 Employment Conference held in Bogota, Colombia, the adopted programme of action states 'to the extent that countries consider them to be desirable'. Also in the World Conference on Agrarian Reform and Rural Development, held in Rome (1979), governments committed themselves, 'to realize equitable distribution of land . . . and to quickly eliminate undernutrition before the year 2000'. Between 1980 and 1985, I was responsible for arrangements to monitor actions taken by governments, and I visited a number of Middle Eastern countries for this purpose. To my surprise, senior ministers who had attended the conference could not remember what it was all about. The World Social Summit in Copenhagen was no exception. It adopted a set of ten commitments, for example, 'to create an enabling economic, political, social, cultural and legal environment that will enable people to achieve social development'.

2 See Chapter 1 of this book for an explanation of the concepts used here, including HDI.

3 Although I have described military expenditure as non-productive and having adverse effects on public spending on education and health, there is also a debate on the military spending effects on investment and economic growth in rich industrialized countries which manufacture and export arms, in contrast to the findings on its negative effects in developing countries. See Deger (1986), Deger and Sen (1991) and the World Bank Discussion Paper No. 185 (1992b).

4 The IMF's *Government Finance Statistics Yearbook* 1989, 1993 and 1994 (IMF, 1980–94) and *International Comparisons of Government Expenditure Revisited* (IMF, 1990) were used.

5 *World Development Report* 1993: Development Indicators (World Bank, 1978–96).

6 *Human Development Report* 1993: Table 21 of indicators (UNDP, 1991–6).

7 Infant mortality is the number of deaths of infants under 1 year of age per 1,000 live births. The average cited here is weighted by population in 1990. The sums of government expenditure on defence, education and health are calculated from *World Military and Social Expenditure* 1993: Table II (Sivard, 1983, 1985, 1993) and SIPRI *Yearbook* (1996: Table 8A.2).

8 This estimate is based on data given in Table 2.2 in the text and population data given in *World Development Report* 1993: Indicators (World Bank, 1978–96) and UNESCO *Statistical Yearbook* 1992 (UNESCO, 1960–95). The estimate does not include Iraq, Lebanon, Qatar and the Palestinians in the Occupied Territories.

9 M. R. El-Ghonemy (1984: 41–8; 1986: 33–4), *The State of the World's Children* 1984: 57 and Figure 1.21 (UNICEF, 1984–96). The findings of four surveys conducted between 1970 and 1979 in Egypt show that illiterate wives, compared to others with at least a primary education certificate, have a lower marriage age, give birth to more children, and are much less likely to use contraceptives. See Kelley *et al.* (1982: Chapter 9).

10 Based on data given in *al-Tarbia al Jadida*: Table 11 (UNESCO, 1987).

11 *Ibid.* Table 13 and *World Education Report* 1991: World Education Indicators, Table 10 (UNESCO, 1991 and 1993). See also country studies in Chapter 10.

12 See the IMF's study *International Comparisons of Government Expenditure Revisited: The Developing Countries, 1975–86* (IMF, 1990: Tables 2 and 3).

13 See for example M. R. El-Ghonemy (1984 and 1991) *Development Strategies for the Rural Poor*. This study examines a proposed monitoring system for the implementation of anti-poverty programmes during the period 1979–83. There are also controversial techniques of social cost-benefit evaluation of projects and programmes. See a discussion of these techniques in Griffin and McKinley (1994). See also *Human Development Report* 1991: 39–45 (UNDP, 1991–6).

14 Using a regression analysis, the actual share of each of the main categories of expenditure in GDP is explained by the IMF's factors summarized on p. 103. The estimated coefficient by the regression is then used to predict the corresponding share, that is, what is expected. The index = actual − predicted shares × 100.

15 Owen (1992: 43) characterizes the authoritarian system by four features: (a) organized groups are not tolerated, (b) people are dealt with not as individuals but as members of some larger collectivity; (c) active class consciousness (free trade unions) for example is inhibited; and (d) economic policies are subordinated to political control.

16 In 1956 1ID equalled £1 sterling or US$2.8. Income is in 1956 prices. See Haseeb (1964: Table 15). Poverty conditions in 1950–8 are described in M. R. El-Ghonemy (1990b: 219–22 and Table 6.5).

17 For more details, see FAO's third and fourth World Food Surveys, 1963 and 1977 (FAO 1946–94) and my study on the land tenure system in M. R. El-Ghonemy (1990a: 210–11). See also Adams (1958) and Alwan (1961).

18 See Bakir (1979 and 1984) and M. R. El-Ghonemy (1990b: 222–4 and Figure 6.2).

19 Internally the National Action Charter concluded in November 1971 dealt with the question of the Kurds and externally three actions for peace were taken; the Algiers Agreement on the border dispute between Iran and Iraq in 1975, the settlement of outstanding territorial disputes with Kuwait in

1977 and the non-aggression pact with Saudi Arabia signed in 1988. Yet total military expenditure as a percentage of Iraqi national income was 7.3 in 1960 rising sharply to 29.7 in 1986 (*World Development Report* 1983 (World Bank, 1978–96) and *World Military and Social Expenditures* (Sivard, 1983, 1985, 1993)).

20 In 1980 the petroleum sector contributed 75 per cent of GDP and 99 per cent of total exports. Military expenditure and imports are taken from Sivard, *World Military and Social Expenditures* 1983, 1985 and 1993: Tables II and III.

21 *Iraq Statistical Abstract*, Government of Iraq, Baghdad, 1954. I knew the work of the Board from my study of the land tenure system in 1955 and my discussions with Darweesh al-Haidari and Hassan Thamer, senior economists in the Agriculture Division of the Board.

22 UNESOB, April 1971 in G. Amin (1974: Tables 7 and 9).

23 *World Military and Social Expenditures* 1985 (Sivard, 1983, 1985, 1993).

24 Mofid (1990: Tables 3.1, 3.2 and 7.2), and *Yearbook of World Energy Statistics* 1985 (United Nations, 1985 and 1991). On financial assistance from Saudi Arabia and Kuwait, see Chapter 4 of the present book and Mofid (1990: 134).

25 Data on falling industrial and agricultural production are from ESCWA (1994b: Tables III.I, IV.I and V.I) and on rising food imports are from FAO, *Country Tables* 1993 (FAO, 1985–93).

26 Mofid (1990: Table 10.4).

27 The following studies were conducted between August 1991 and June 1994: (1) Harvard Study (May 1991) 'Team Report on Public Health in Iraq after the Gulf War', mimeographed; (2) London Medical Education Trust (1991) 'Report of the International Study Team on Health and Welfare in Iraq after the Gulf War', mimeographed; (3) Dreze and Gazdar (1991) 'Hunger and Poverty in Iraq'. This was a contribution to the second report above; (4) report of the FAO/WFP mission (June 1993) 'Crop and Food Supply Assessment', mimeographed; (5) the study commissioned by the British government and carried out by Patrick Ward and Martin Rimmer during May and June 1994, *Targeting Basic Assistance in Northern Iraq: Findings from Household Expenditure Survey*; (6) report of the mission on 'Nutritional Status Assessment' (FAO, November 1993), mimeographed, Rome; (7) UN mission report to the Secretary General, 'Humanitarian Needs in Iraq', prepared by UN General Office. In addition, Save the Children Fund prepared two assessment reports in April and May 1991, and both UNICEF and WHO prepared several mimeographed reports on their staff visits to Iraq.

28 For details on 1972 and 1976 family surveys, see Bekir (1979; 1984), summarized in M. R. El-Ghonemy (1990b: 222–4). See also Alnasrawi (1994: Table 2) for data on 1980, 1985 and 1990. For data on 1990–1, see Drèze and Gazdar (1992: Table 1).

7   CORRUPTION

1 For a review of different definitions of corruption, see Van Roy (1970) and a study prepared by the UN Department of Technical Cooperation for Development (1989).

2 This example is based on Egypt's earthquake of 12 October 1992. Some 200 public schools collapsed and another 1,990 schools were badly

damaged. All were government-built, mostly less than ten years before the earthquake. The report of the National Committee on the follow-up to the effects of the earthquake was summarized by the Prime Minister, Dr Atef Sidky, in his statement to parliament on 28 December 1992.

3 The country's governance was absolutely personal during the rule of King Abdul Aziz ibn al-Saud and his elder son King Saud (reigned 1953–64). The first council of ministers established in 1954 comprised solely King Abdul Aziz ibn al-Saud's sons. Until now, the King has also been the Prime Minister, head of the al-Saud family, Commander-in-Chief of the armed forces, the Supreme Imam, custodian of the two holy mosques in Mecca and Medina and the supreme head of the judicial system. In the late 1950s, the King rejected the recommendations for separating his personal finances (private purse) from public finance that had been made by fiscal policy experts Dr Zaki Abdul Mit'al from Egypt, Dr Zaki Sa'd from the IMF and the Lebanese economist Mr Najeeb Salha.

4 This situation exists in other oil-rich sheikhdoms. Over the two years 1995–6 there was a highly publicized court case in London, in which the present Emir of Qatar, Sheikh Hamad bin Khalifa al-Thani, claimed that his deposed father, Sheikh Khalifa, had embezzled US$8 billion, transferring the money from public oil revenues to his American and European personal accounts. The father said that as Emir he was 'entitled to do what he wished with the state's money'. The dispute was settled by the Saudi rulers' intervention (*Financial Times*, 21 October 1996, p. 4).

5 Nelson (1978); see the chapter on Saudi Arabia.

6 The distribution of government civil expenditure, including allocations to royal households, is given in G. Amin (1974: Table 16) and EIU, *Saudi Arabia and Jordan*, Annual Supplement (1971: 4). See also Sayigh in Hopwood (1972: 289), Asfour (1972: 368–77) and Holden and Johns (1982: 163 and Chapters 12 and 13). The Fifth Development Plan (Saudi Arabia, Ministry of Planning, 1990: Table 5.6) shows a share of 17 per cent for unspecified general items, probably the privy purse.

7 This horrifying incident revealed the conflicting social values created by sudden affluence and modernity in a society which is fundamentally ultra-conservative (girls' schooling was not permitted until 1960). In July 1977, Princess Mishaal and Khaled Muhallal al-Sha'er, the young man she wanted to marry instead of her first cousin, were publicly executed in Jeddah. The only established evidence of her crime was her attempt to leave the country, accompanying her lover without the consent of her grandfather, Prince Mohammed al-Saud, the elder brother of the then King Khaled. The young couple were caught disguised at Jeddah airport. She was executed by a firing squad and her lover beheaded according to an order given by her grandfather to punish her for the dishonour that she had brought on the royal family. The story attracted wide attention both in the country and abroad. It was published in two British newspapers, the *Observer* on 22 January 1978 and the *Daily Express* on 28 January 1978. The episode was also dramatically presented in a film produced and broadcast by the British Independent Television Authority in March 1980, based on facts supplied by the German-born nanny of the Princess. Numerous copies of the film were sold on video cassette. The figure of US$500 million allegedly paid to prevent the film

being shown is estimated by Aburish (1994: 81), giving details of its components.

8 Based on Holden and Johns (1982: 412–14).

9 Data for military spending during the period 1990–4 are from SIPRI (1996: Table 8A.2). The values are in US dollars at fixed 1990 prices.

10 All published reports agree that the main intermediaries were Adnan Khashoggi and Ghaith Pharoun, the sons of the two private physicians of the late King Abdul Aziz ibn al-Saud. Both were always favoured over others in huge construction contracts and in strategic imports. Another prominent agent is Kamal Adham, the younger brother of the late King Faisal's third wife. Based on Aburish (1994: 179, 194, 200–7, 244, 264, 269 and 300) and Holden and Johns (1982: 358–66) for an account of deals with the companies cited in which these intermediaries were involved and commissions paid, as well as the sources of information, including some companies' own documents and the reports of the US Senate Foreign Relations Committee and its Sub-committee on Multinational Corporations. Commission payments cited by these three authors range from 10 to 25 per cent. In cases where the commissions demanded exceeded the limit permitted by US laws, the balance was termed 'consultancy fees'.

11 For a detailed account of these arms deals, see the results of investigations revealed in the *Sunday Times*, 9 October 1994 and Aburish (1994: 201–7). Aburish presents his own experience in witnessing these deals: 'I am in possession of copies of contracts which confirm its [British Aerospace's] willingness to pay huge commissions in connection with the selling of Jaguar fighter-bomber aircraft and the building of airbases. This programme has already produced US$300 million worth of direct commissions . . . *indirect* commissions are likely to be larger' (p. 203, emphasis is mine).

12 For an understanding of the relationships between power, politics and patronage in corruption, see Gellner and Waterbury (1977), Heidenheimer (1978) and Sadowski (1991).

13 See, for example Professor Saad el-Din Ibrahim, 'Tabaa'i al-Fasad' (The nature of corruption) in *al-Ahram al-Iqtisadi*, 5 December 1988, p. 10 and 12 December 1988, pp. 12–13; Salah el-Din Hafez, 'Kaifa tosbeh million-eran' (How to become a millionaire), *al-Ahram*, 26 February 1992, p. 9; Sadowski (1991: 118–38); and Hansen (1991: 116–18). The last, an authority on the Egyptian economy, views the widespread corruption as a form of a compact between ruler and élite, the élite sacrificing political freedom in the country for *la dolce vita*. See also G. Amin (1994: 50–2) on the effects of corruption on the government's budget deficits.

14 The results of the 1986 population census show the total workforce (15 years old and over) as 12.8 million persons, of whom 32.7 per cent were in government and public enterprises. CAPMAS *Statistical Yearbook*, 1994: Table II-21 shows that they increased to 39 per cent of total workforce (Egypt, CAPMAS, 1994). Percentage of wages in total government expenditure (current) is calculated from the IMF *Government Finance Statistics Yearbook* 1993 (IMF, 1980–94) and from the final accounts of the 1992/3 state budget summarized in *al-Ahram al-Iqtisadi*, 1 November 1992, p. 52.

15 In 1994, the Prime Minister's office reported that out of 314 – the total number of public enterprises – 90 were classified as high-loss companies (29 per cent). For the purpose of illustration, between 1982 and 1992 the

manager of the cement public company sucked the sum of E£70 million out of public funds for his own private wealth (report on illegal earnings prepared by Mr Mustafa Hassan, Assistant Minister of Justice, in *Akhbar al-Yaum*, 8 February 1992, p. 3).

16 It is believed that corrupt deals in this field, such as the scandals of Madinat Nasr in Cairo and al-Amereya in Alexandria, are widely practised by officials of local councils.

17 In the 1980s, the different rates of exchange per US$1 were: E£0.7 for the importation of essential consumer goods; E£0.83 for exchange on the official parallel market; E£1.12 for transfer of savings of Egyptians working abroad and E£1.27 for transactions on the open market.

18 These institutions are: (a) the central agency for public accountability (*al-jihaz al-markazi li'l muhasabat*); (b) the agency for judicial investigation by the Socialist Prosecutor (*jihaz al-mud'ai al-ishtiraki*); (c) the agency for the control of civil servants' use of public funds (*al-riqabah al-idariya*); (d) the Ministry of Justice's department for investigating illegal earnings and unlawful accumulation of public property (*jihaz al-kasb ghair al-mashrou'*); (e) the Ministry of Finance's department for monitoring illegal acquisition of state-owned real estate (*min ayna laka haza*); and (f) the Ministry of the Interior's department for investigation into the evasion of taxes (*mabahith al-dara'ib wal-rusoum*).

19 See note 13 and *Rose al-Yousef*, 19 August 1996. See also *al-Mujtama' al Madani* 1995, no. 43: 4–19 and no. 48: 4–15.

20 The sums of money are presented in Egyptian pounds because of the different rates of exchange in existence. Sources are Baker (1990: 25–45), Sadowski (1991: 123–30) and Abdul Qadir Shuhayb, *al-Sha'b*, 4 January and 1 February 1983. Othman's monopoly in the construction market is inseperable fom his political powers. As President of the Engineers' Syndicate and Chairman of the Arab Contractors' Company, which had nearly 65,000 employees, he was able to influence the entire construction market both in Egypt and in several oil-rich Arab countries. To the disadvantage of other firms, his company was favoured to construct such gigantic works as the High Dam, the Four Kilometre Flyover and October Bridge, the Myrtire tunnel beneath the Suez Canal, the Salheya Scheme and the King Faisal Bridge, as well as military installations.

21 See sources in notes 19 and 20. For a summary of Rashad Othman's case see *al-Ahali*, 28 December 1994, p. 3 and Baker (1990: 41). On Ismat Sadat's case, see Hopwood (1991: 189) and *Middle East Economic Digest* 32, 6: 12 February 1988).

22 The story of Alexandria's land for poor families housing scheme is taken from *al-Ahali*, 28 December 1994, p. 3.

23 This information is taken from the 1991 and 1992 annual reports of General Ahmad al-Adly, Assistant Minister of the Interior for the investigations into tax and customs duty evasions (*al-Ahram*, 16 February 1992, p. 3 and 30 January 1993, p. 7). These figures suggest a great loss to the Treasury, considering that Egypt's budget deficit was about E£8 billion. On examining this subject, Egypt's first Conference on Taxation (23–4 November 1991, Cairo) estimated that nearly two-thirds of potential taxpayers evaded payment.

24 On average, pilgrimage costs per individual in 1994 were E£6–8,000, reaching E£10,000 in the case of high-quality accommodation. The total

amount paid from public funds for members of parliament who performed the Hajj (pilgrimage) in 1994 was nearly E£2 million according to *al-Wafd*, 29 December 1994, p. 3.

25 For example, speculation in the foreign-exchange market with assistance from senior officials enabled Ahmad al-Rayan, who in the 1970s had been a street peddler selling eggs and plastic kitchenware, to make enormous profits at a time of foreign exchange control, and to facilitate the flight of US$500 million to private accounts in the Bahamas. In 1994, it was revealed that the value of al-Rayan's assets in Egypt was E£1,500 million. See the verdict and statement by Judge Hosny Abdel-Lateef on the scandal of Ahmad al-Rayan and his two brothers, *al-Ahram al-Dawli*, 29 April 1993, p. 3 and the report on Ashraf al-Sa'd's dealings from *al-Akhbar*, 2 February 1992. Both cases are summarized in *Rose al-Yousef*, 27 March 1995.

8 INEQUALITY IN PRIVATE CONSUMPTION

1 For a concise summary of these views on consumer behaviour, see James (1993), especially Chapters 1 and 10. The difference between the terms 'preference', 'attitude', and 'behaviour' of the consumer is explained on pp. 7–9 and pp. 199–204.

2 Examples of these limitations are: Iran's surveys exclude tribal and nomadic population; Israel's surveys usually cover urban areas only; Sudan's several national surveys exclude the southern provinces and the nomadic people of the north and some household surveys are even limited to greater Khartoum. The data on household expenditure described in the text are taken from *World Development Report* 1993: Table 10, Development Indicators (World Bank, 1978–96).

3 It seems that the region's food culture is strong enough to weaken widely known relationships, that is, the empirical observation or 'law' developed in 1864 by Ernst Engel and the general theory of Keynes (1936) with regard to the marginal propensity to consume (the ratio of change in consumption to change in income).

4 This astronomical rise in the number of private cars in Egypt took place at a time when importation was restricted and customs duty fixed at 300 per cent of the value of the car. My explanation of this contradiction is that instead of customs duty payment, arrangements are made for a temporary customs number plate for two years, costing E£20,000, before conversion to a permanent number plate, at a loss to government revenue of nearly E£10,000 per car. The data on cars by size of engine were provided to me by the computer centre of CAPMAS, Cairo, on 4 January 1995. From the same source, the number of registered private cars in 1993 (excluding those with diplomatic number plates) was 928,356 and of those with customs number plates was 114,307, making a total of 1,042,663, compared to only 10,342 public buses. Data on bicycles are from CAPMAS.

5 These estimates for 1989–90 were made by the US Carbon Dioxide Information Analysis Centre (CDIAC). They include carbon emissions from cement dust. They are calculated for developing regions by the World Bank and given in Appendix Table A.9, *World Development Report* 1992 (World Bank, 1978–96).

6 For example, in Egypt the traditional soap brands *Nabolsi Farouk* and *al-Mizan*

have disappeared. In fact, total domestic production of soap decreased by 5 per cent in 1987–93. *Nabolsi* soap was so sacrosanct that my mother gave me two pieces when I went to the USA on an Egyptian government scholarship in the early 1950s. Another traditional product is the poor people's brown sugar, molasses, whose production fell by 49 per cent in 1987–93 (*Statistical Yearbook*: June 1994 (Egypt, CAPMAS, 1981–95)).

7 For example, in Turkey manufacture of leather footwear fell by 26 per cent in 1990–4, and in Egypt the production of bicycles decreased by 45 per cent in 1987–93 (Turkey: *Monthly Bulletin of Statistics* 1995: May (Turkey, State Planning Organisation, 1985–95), and Egypt: *Statistical Yearbook* 1994: June (Egypt, CAPMAS, 1981–95)).

8 Nutritional values of traditional foods are described in FAO (1992a and 1993b). See also Musaiger (1987: Table VII).

9 See Mooij (1994: Tables 3.4, 3.6 and 3.7).

10 Data on Egypt are from *al-Kitab al-Sanawi* (Yearbook 1992–3: 185), Radio and Television Corporation, Cairo. For data on Turkey, see source in Table 8.2 in the text.

11 There are also regional Arabic-speaking satellite channels (MBC in London, Dubai Satellite, the Lebanese ART and the Egyptian ESC).

12 For example, despite a mounting concern over health risks, cigarette production in Israel increased by 49 per cent in 1970–92 and cigarette imports increased by 300 per cent in Kuwait and by 25 per cent in Egypt during 1988–93 (*Statistical Abstract of Israel*, 1993: Table 14.13 (Israel, Central Bureau of Statistics, 1993); *Annual Statistical Abstract of Kuwait*, 1993 (Kuwait, Ministry of Planning, 1990–3) and *Statistical Yearbook*: June 1994 (Egypt, CAPMAS, 1981–95)), respectively. Data on tobacco consumption are from FAO, presented in *World Development Report* 1993: Appendix Table A6 (World Bank, 1978–96). For details on cigarette advertising by Philip Morris of USA and by British Imperial Tobacco, see Taylor (1984).

13 The worldwide annual sales of baby foods manufactured by Nestlé Alementana of Vevey, Switzerland reached nearly US$11 billion in the late 1980s. UNICEF and WHO established a committee in 1984 to investigate the complaints about infant formulas and the content of advertisements. Few governments have yet ratified the recommended code.

14 These studies include: Musaiger (1987: 138–45, and Table XI); Musaiger and Lankarani (1986); Alothman (1994).

15 Income distribution for 1957 is taken from Paukert (1973: Table 6) and for 1993 from Table 8.4 of this chapter. For the growth and equity performance of the Israeli economy in the 1950s and 1960s, see Gaathon (1971: Table A-13).

16 See Achdut (1993, Table 1 and Figure 2a) on the sensitivity of different measurements of the degree of concentration to changes in inequality, with emphasis on what happens to the distribution of income among low-income families. This study also shows the importance of National Insurance benefits in reducing inequality and poverty. See Smeeding *et al.* (1990), Tables 3.4 and 3.5 on poverty estimates and Tables 4.5 and 4.6 on poverty and inequality estimates by age groups. The definition of poverty used in the study, and followed in Israel is on p. 93.

17 Sources of inequality among the elderly are analysed in Smeeding *et al.* (1990), especially Chapter 5, written by Lea Achdut and Yossi Tamin. See also Achdut and Bigman (1991).

18 I am grateful to Professor J. Yahav and Dr B. Bourstein of the Central
   Bureau of Statistics of the State of Israel for providing me with detailed
   information on the results of the Family Expenditure Survey 1986/7 and
   1992/3. The analysis and interpretation of changes are mine.
19 In 1992/3, the average person in the top 10 per cent of the expenditure
   scale spent NIS (New Israeli Shekels) 560 per month on sports and NIS 384
   on travel abroad, making a monthly total of NIS 944. The results of the
   1992/3 survey show also NIS (424 + 596) expenditure per month on food
   and housing respectively by a poor family in the lowest decile. During the
   survey, US$1 was equal to NIS 2.5. With regard to expenditure on alcohol
   and tobacco in proportionate terms, a rich person was found to spend 0.5
   per cent of total monthly expenditure, while the poor spent 1.7 per cent.
20 *Enquête Nationale sur le Budget et la Consommation des Ménages* (Tunisia, Ministry
   of Planning 1990: 35) shows an improvement at the national level in terms
   of the Gini index as follows:

1975	1980	1985	1990
0.440	0.430	0.434	0.401

21 The 1990 survey results show that in one year (1990) a rich person spent
   155 dinars on private cars, 48 dinars on foreign drinks and 164 dinars on
   leisure (sports and entertainment), making a total of 367 dinars. The poor
   person spent, in the same period, 68 dinars on food and 30 dinars on
   housing, making an annual total of 98 dinars.
22 The results of the surveys refer to the poor as a *population défavourisée*, or
   pauvres and poverty as *pauvreté*.
23 This work was carried out with the then director of the INS, Abdul-Salam
   Kamoun. The results are published in *al-Muashirat al-Ijtima'iya wal-Iqtisadiya*
   (Tunisia, Ministry of Planning, 1982).
24 See Radwan *et al.* (1990), especially Chapter 4, 'Income Distribution and
   Poverty' and Appendix C.
25 The methodology used and the estimates made are presented at regional level,
   as country-level estimates are not published. I obtained these estimates
   through a personal communication with Gauran Datt. See Chen *et al.* (1994).
26 1980 estimates are from the socio-economic indicators (Tunisia, Ministry of
   Planning (1982: 85) (Arabic) and 1990 data from *Resultats de l'Enquête Alimentaire et Nutritionnelle*, Vol. B: 46–8 (Tunisia, Ministry of Planning, 1993).
27 The 1990 nutrition survey Table N. 5: 128 (Tunisia, Ministry of Planning,
   1993).
28 M. R. El-Ghonemy (1993: 130 published in *Resultants de l'Enquête Alimentaire*).
   Productivity was measured by the FAO in terms of comparable international
   dollars. Based on 1970 = 100, Algeria was (215), Egypt (236), Morocco
   (250) and Tunisia (416).
29 'Carte des Priorités Régionales', Commissariat Général du Développement
   Régional, Ministry of Planning (Tunis, January 1983), mimeographed. The
   anti-poverty programme and the beneficiaries are defined in 'Le Programme
   National d'Aide aux Familles Nécessiteuses', a paper presented by Abdellatif
   ben-Kilani to the National Seminar on Planning Food and Nutrition Policies, February 1994, Tunis, in French.
30 These studies are as follows: (a) 1987/8 and 1989/90 household income/

NOTES

expenditure surveys conducted by Mauritania's Office National de la Statistique (ONS), published as *Enquête Permanent sur les Conditions de Vie des Ménages*, (*EPCV*), (b) USAID/University of Arizona's Consumption and Reconnaissance Survey of 1986 (both are analysed in McKay and Houeibib, 1992 and with Coulombe and McKay 1994); (c) food security study, Hunt (1992); (d) several studies conducted jointly by the Commission pour le Sécurité Alimentaire, UNICEF and the Ministry of Health, which are analysed in Mauritania's report to the FAO/WHO International Conference on Nutrition, Rome, 1992 (Mauritania, Ministère de la Santé (1992)).

31 Based on Tables 5A.2, 5A.6 and 5A.7 of McKay and Houeibib (1992).
32 Data on 1989/90 food consumption by class are from McKay and Houeibib (1992: Table 5E.4), and on food aid from *ibid.*: Table 5F.1 and Hunt (1992: 47).
33 Hunt (1992: Table 3.3).
34 See obesity measurement in Chapter 1, note 15.
35 Reports on children's undernourishment are presented in Musaiger (1987: Tables VIII, XIII and XVI), Amine (1980) and Eid *et al.* (1984).
36 ESCWA (1994b: 29, 39). The information on nutrition given in the text is taken from Amine (1980), Musaiger (1987: Tables XIII and XIV) and Musaiger (1990: 10–12).
37 See the results of the surveys in: (a) Bahrain Central Office for Statistics (1985); and (b) Abdel-Khaleq (1987: Table 10). Both references are in Arabic.
38 Musaiger and al-Ansari (1992: 133–5).
39 The main surveys are the household expenditure survey of 1982 and the nutrition surveys of 1982 and 1990, whose results were analysed by a team of Saudi professionals under the leadership of Dr Al-Shoshan, and presented in his (1991).
40 Al-Shoshan (1991: 41 and Table 16).
41 Al-Shoshan (1991: Tables 9 and 11). Anaemia is measured by haemoglobin level of below 12 grammes/100 millilitres.
42 UNICEF (1996: Table 1, Basic Indicators).

9 REDISTRIBUTION OF WEALTH AND INCOME

1 In Egypt, a fund amounting to E£40 million was established in 1956 to finance social services and income-generating activities in deprived localities. The fund was made up of the confiscated savings and money from the sale of jewellery belonging to members of ex-King Farouk's family.
2 It was estimated in 1993 that 130,000 Jewish settlers lived in 153 land settlements in the Occupied Territories. Apart from the loss of their land property, the Palestinian Arabs are not allowed to rent or repurchase these lands, which were bought with tax-free funds transferred from international Zionists, the United States' Jewish organizations and the reparations paid by Germans after the Second World War. Moreover, the Israeli government subsidizes the infrastructure in these Jewish settlements. On this subject, see Shalev (1992: 237–53 and 339–41).
3 'Agrarian Reform and Rural Development in Syria (Syria, Ministry of Agriculture and Agrarian Reform, 1990: Table 8). In the former People's Democratic Republic of Yemen (the southern provinces of the present Yemen) the expropriated area was managed in the form of twenty-two co-operatives and forty-six state farms until the start of privatization in 1990–4.

248

4 See M. R. El-Ghonemy (1993: 50–2).

5 Based on *Étude de Disparités des Revenues et Pouvoir d'Achat en Algérie*, 1968–79 (Algeria, INEAP, 1981), analysed in Bounab (1989: Tables 3.25 and 3.26).

6 Issawi (1982: 203).

7 This study was conducted for FAO, jointly with Professor Kenneth Parsons of the University of Wisconsin who was commissioned by USAID. The findings were presented at an FAO meeting on land policy held in Salahuddin, in northern Iraq, in October 1955.

8 On land tenure, see Lambton (1953) and its second edition, 1969. On the Iranian meaning of property in land, see Denman (1973: Chapter 2). Data on income distribution are taken from Issawi (1982: Table A.4).

9 Dr Arsanjani called for 'land to the tiller' and when he became Minister of Agriculture in 1961, he efficiently completed the first phase. After landlords and Muslim leaders mounted their attack, he was forced to resign in 1963. The US intervention, and successful experience in land reform programmes in Japan, Taiwan, South Korea and Italy, encouraged the American government to press for land reform in Iran, which had the then Soviet Union and its communist propaganda right at its northern borders. The late President Kennedy's Foreign Assistance Act of 1961 (Sections 102 and 103), stated that 'the establishment of more equitable and more secure land tenure arrangements is one means by which the productivity and income of the rural poor will be increased'.

10 During my 1961 and 1965 visits, I had discussions with, and collected information from, Dr Hoshang Ram, the Bank Omran of the Pahlavi Foundation, Dr Webster Johnson and Mr Kenneth Platt of USAID, Dr Price Gittinger, economist at the Plan Organization, Mr Khalkhali of the Public Domain Department and Mr Mosaed, Head of the Co-operatives Department. I interviewed farmers in the villages of Khaveh, Toghan, Dawood Abad and Khare Abad, which had Crown-land distribution programmes. I also visited Crown land villages in the northern region near the Caspian sea, where many former civil servants and army officers received 30–50 hectares each. Accompanied by Mr Mohammed Ja'far Behbahanian, the head of the Shah's estates, I attended the ceremony where the Shah himself presented property titles to the new owners at the Marble Palace on 8 April 1961. By that date, I was told that 266 villages of the Shah's private estate, amounting to 154,111 hectares had been distributed to 32,874 new owners. For the complete story of the programme, see Farhang Rad's account in M. R. El-Ghonemy (1967: 273–91).

11 See Amid (1990: 103) for the quality of land retained by landlords.

12 I was assisted in this village study by Mr Ahmed Behpour of the research centre of the Land Reform agency. Useful information was gained from my interview with Mr. Ahmed Jalali, Director of the Agricultural Economics Department, Dr Ferhad Ghareman of the Plan Organization and his advisor, Dr Price Gittinger of the Harvard Advisory Group.

13 Public investment favoured the corporations to the disadvantage of the peasant sector, comprising the beneficiaries of land reform who were new owners and many small tenants who gained rent reductions. Their area represented 85–90 per cent of total landholdings' area in 1978, compared to only 3 per cent of the corporations. See Moghadam's study (1978: Tables 1 and 16) cited in Katouzian (1983: Tables 8.13, 8.14 and 8.15).

NOTES

14 The farm corporations visited were Aria Mehr (1,500 hectares near Shiraz), Saheb Granich (20,000 hectares managed by the army for the production of meat and caviar near Rasht on the Caspian coast) and Roke Beesh (710 hectares in Gilan province). The assessment in the text was based on my interviews with farmers and the Director General of the Ministry of Rural Affairs, Mr Hassan Askaripour. Field research conducted by Najafi (1970) in three farm corporations showed that 44 per cent of the farmers did not agree to surrender their individual rights to farm corporations. See also Katouzian (1983: 316–19) and Amid (1990: 141).

15 Shirazi (1993: 194 and Table 8.2).

16 The call for land reform in Egypt was made in the 1940s by three NGOs. The first to do so was *Jam'iya al-Nahda al-Qaumia* in 1948. They demanded the fixing of a ceiling on private landownership of 100 feddans (40 hectares) The second was the Association of Agricultural Colleges Graduates' conference in 1949. The third urge for reform was made by the *Fellah* society in May 1952, two months before Nasser's *coup d'état* that declared Land Reform Law in September 1952.

17 For information on rent control, see M. R. El-Ghonemy (1992) 'The Egyptian State and Agricultural Land Market 1810–1986', *Journal of Agricultural Economics*, 43, 2: 175–90

18 The results of this field study are analysed in M. R. El-Ghonemy (1990b: 234–6).

19 *Ibid.*, Table 6, except for 1991 which is taken from Korayem (1994: Table 4).

20 A. Ibrahim (1982: Tables 2 and 3).

21 One donum equals one-tenth of a hectare. On this scheme, see M. R. El-Ghonemy, (1967: 296–305).

22 In his assessment of this programme, Hajrah (1982) says (the settlers) 'have a mind saturated with bedouin traditions and cannot be convinced of modern farming methods in a short period . . . many of these settled bedouins have little or no experience of cultivation' (p. 142).

23 Data on land recipients are from the Ministry of Agriculture, cited in Hajrah (1982: Tables 7.1, 7.2 and 7.8). See also his Table 7.7 on efficiency criteria.

24 *The Impact of Development Strategies on the Rural Poor, 1979–89* (FAO, 1988: 47 and Table 3).

25 Data on Syria are from Syria, Ministry of Agriculture (1990: Table 8). Some countries' experiences in land settlement schemes are studied in M. R. El-Ghonemy (1967) and (1993). The Jewish settlements in Israel are not included because of the obvious religious and military motives for their establishment in the highly unequal political environment of the militarily occupied or semi-occupied Palestinian lands.

26 There is approximately one technical supervisor to 200 settlers, compared to one extension service agent (technical assistant) to 1500–2000 farmers in the 'old' lands.

27 Changes in the form of government refer to shifts in political power when the Kemalist Republican People's Party (i.e. the followers of Kemal Ataturk's ideology) was defeated in 1950 by the Democrat Party of Adnan Mendres. The latter was succeeded by Kemalist-oriented military government in 1960–1, the Justice Party of Demirel, the new Republican People's Party of Ecevit and the return of military rule, twice, in 1971–3 and 1980–3.

250

28 Based on data given in *Statistical Yearbook* 1993 (Turkey, Social Insurance Institute, 1993: Tables 4 and 5.1).

29 At 1987 = 100, the Consumer Price Index was: 1988 = 173; 1990 = 545; 1992 = 1283; 1993 = 2131. According to IMF, *World Financial Survey* (IMF, 1995d), the rate of exchange (Turkish lira to US$1) was:

1958	1960	1975	1980	1985	1990	1993
3	9	15	90	577	2,930	144,000

Real minimum wage rates are from the State Planning Organization, Ankara. Additional information is given in Chapter 10 and Appendix Table 10.1.

30 Personal communication (in August and November 1995) from Mr Banu Akkuzu, and Mr Gulay Aslantepe, Turkish Ministry of Labour and Social Security and based on 1993 *Statistical Yearbook* Part VI (Turkey, Turkish Employment Organization, 1993).

31 This statement on increasing inequality and the upper classes' gains is based on data given in: (a) Ozbudun and Ulusan (1980); (b) Turkey's *Country Report* (1990: Tables 1.1 and 1.4) prepared by the Turkish government for FAO on progress made in the implementation of the World Conference on Agrarian Reform and Rural Developments programme of action; (c) the results of the 1973 and 1987 *Surveys of Household Income and Expenditure* conducted by the Institute of Statistics (Turkey, Institute of Statistics, 1973 and 1987); (d) Hansen (1991: Tables 6.6, 6.7 and 6.8) whose critical review of the surveys appears on pp. 275–80; and (e) The World Bank's *Trends in Developing Economies* (1993b: 492).

32 See Shaban (1990: Tables 2.5 and 2.6).

33 Many of the high-wage earners benefiting from the Social Security Scheme live in the two biggest cities, Amman and Irbid. Information on the occupational distribution of the beneficiaries by monthly earnings is from the Computer Section of the Social Security Organization, Amman.

34 See Abu Jaber *et al.* (1990: Table 8.4). People living in poverty were estimated at 18.7 per cent of total households in 1987. In the preface to the Arabic version of the 1993–7 development plan, the King states: 'This plan concentrates on tackling poverty and unemployment problems, and it reflects the priority Jordanian people give to securing a fair distribution of the benefits from economic growth' (the translation from Arabic is mine).

35 Source: *al-Khita al-Iqtisadiya wal-Ijtima'iya, 1993–1997* (The 1993–7 economic and social plan) (Jordan, Ministry of Planning, n. d.: Tables 14 and 15 (Arabic).

36 Based on a field study conducted in October 1985 in Gisha, al-Rayasha and Sabah, accompanied by Dr Godfrey Tyler of Oxford University and Mr Amin al-Sayed Abu Ras, the then Secretary-General of the Confederation of Local Cooperation and Development (*Hi'aat*). See M. R. El-Ghonemy, Tyler and Azam (1986).

37 Starting around 1985, rich Western governments have shifted their aid procedure away from government-to-government aid towards channelling aid through their own NGOs. Given the weak financial capacity of the NGOs in most countries of the Middle East, there is a real risk of change in priorities imposed by donor NGOs on local NGOs. In a personal communication with Jon Bennett, author of *Meeting Needs* (1995) I learned that the total amount of money for NGOs provided during the last few years by

the USA, Norway and the EC in Brussels has exceeded the amount of United Nations total assistance to certain countries in the region.

38 The legal age of marriage for girls is 13–15 years in Iran and the Gulf countries, and mostly 16–18 years in the rest. However, the actual age is below this legal age, especially among the bedouin and in rural communities.

39 Examples of these successful efforts are raising the minimum legal age for girls' marriage and making progress towards abolishing the cruel practice of female circumcision among illiterate, unskilled women. See the work of women's NGOs in Sudan and Yemen in Thijssen (ed.) (1994). This study and many others cited show how circumcision-related health risks inhibit the earning capacity of women because primitive methods of removing the clitoris and labia cause later miscarriages and permanent encapsulating cysts in adult women, and inhibit their ability to engage in productive activities. For other factors, see Hijab (1988) and Moghadam (1995).

40 Among Muslim countries, the three early adopters of family planning in the Middle East were Egypt (1953), Tunisia (1963) and Turkey (1965). Married women using contraceptives, as a percentage of all married women in those countries with contraceptive usage are as follows for 1988–93: Turkey (63 per cent), Tunisia (50 per cent), Egypt (47 per cent), Morocco (42 per cent) and Jordan (40 per cent), source *World Development Report 1995*, Indicators: Table 26.

10 ECONOMIC POLICY REFORMS

1 This refers to Bretton Woods, New Hampshire, USA, where in 1944 an international conference established a world system of financial rules and regulation of exchange rates. At that conference the World Bank and the IMF were set up. For a review of the shifts in their roles and the effects on current economic problems, see the account given by Hans Singer, a leading authority: 'Lessons of Post-War Development Experience 1945–1988', in W. Andriaansen et al. (1992). In his review, Sir Hans Singer says 'At just the time when these institutions were needed, they surrendered to an ideology which made them agents of retrenchment rather than development' (p. 101).

2 All Arab states, except Qatar and Libya, participated in this meeting organized by the IMF and the Arab Monetary Fund at Abu-Dhabi, UAE, 1987. See El-Naggar (1987).

3 See conditionality and directives concerning cuts in spending in World Bank (1992a: Table A2.1 and p. 6 of the Executive Summary).

4 See *World Development Report* 1988: 65 and 1990: 103 (World Bank, 1978–96). A clear admission of the adverse distributional effects of economic reforms is made by three senior economists of the World Bank, Bruno, Ravallion and Squire (1995: 11–16).

5 Statements by Mr Camdessus, Managing Director of the IMF in his foreword to El-Naggar (1987) and at the United Nations Economic and Social Council (ECOSOC), Geneva, 11 July 1990. After her appraisal of the World Bank's approach, Frances Stewart (1991: 1860–1) says 'the review has suggested some serious deficiencies from the perspective of poverty reduction . . . . The adjustment package is not systematically designed to bring about equitable patterns of . . . primary income distribution'.

6 See the case study of Egypt, pp. 186–7. The issues of the social effects of

post-1980 economic reforms are analysed in UNICEF's pioneer study *Adjustment with Human Face* (Cornia *et al.* 1987), Van der Hoevan (1981) and Stewart (1995).

7 GDP average annual growth in the Middle East was 4.7 per cent in 1980 and 2.7 per cent in 1982, compared to 1.3 per cent and -0.2 per cent respectively in the industrialized countries.

8 On the influence of ideological and internal political change in the rich industrial countries, see Toye (1987) and M. R. El-Ghonemy (1990b: 54–63). For the domestic policy effects on the US foreign assistance, see Ruttan (1996: Part II).

9 See *World Development Report* 1983: Figure 2.3 (World Bank, 1978–96).

10 For a careful review of various schools of economic thought on economic policy reform prescribed by the World Bank and the IMF, see Sinha (1995). On the experience of South Korea and Taiwan, see Wade (1990).

11 See, among others: J. Sachs (ed.) (1989) *New Approaches to the Latin American Debt Crisis: Essays in International Finance*. Princeton, NJ: Princeton University Press.

12 For an analysis of debt relief and the American Brady Plan, see Corden (1991), especially pp. 141–2.

13 Known as the 'Bread Riots'. Three political scientists (Tessler, Entelis and White) argue that 'the scope and intensity of the rioting showed that public anger appeared to be directed not only at the government, but also at the consumption-oriented middle and upper classes, . . . perceived to be prospering from the government's economic policies at the time when the economic situation of the poor was steadily deteriorating and the government was asking the poor to tighten their belts even more'. In Long and Reich (1995: 431–2).

14 The World Bank loans were US$254 million for agriculture, US$150 million for industry and trade, US$250 million for economic and finance reforms and US$150 million for private enterprise. By 1996 total World Bank lending to Tunisia had reached US$1,364 million.

15 From the results of Tunisia's Population Census of 1994: Table 10, Chomeurs par age et sexe and Table 11a.

16 According to the World Bank's *Trends in Developing Countries* (1973: Table 2.6); and *World Development Report* 1979 and 1995 (World Bank 1978–96), Egypt had higher GNP per person in 1950 and 1965 (US$180 and 230) than South Korea (US$100 and 160). But by 1993, South Korea surpassed Egypt, with $7,660 and $660 respectively. Also, the share of industry in GDP in Egypt declined from a higher proportion of 24 per cent to 22 per cent, while that of South Korea rose from 19 per cent to 43 per cent in 1965 and 1993, respectively. Similarly, the share of exports in GDP declined in Egypt from 20 per cent to 6 per cent while it rose in South Korea from 3 per cent to 25 per cent over the same period.

17 According to Crabitès (1933: 238–43) and Crouchley (1938: 18–24), Egypt's total external debt in 1880 ranged between E£72 million and E£91 million, with an average of E£83 million, equivalent to US$406.7 million. At that time national income was approximately $680–700 million (E£1 = US$4.9).

18 See for example El-Gritley (1977), Zaki in Abdel-Khaleq and Tignor (1982); G. Amin (1988) and El-Naggar 1991, all in Arabic.

19 Fluctuating oil prices played an important role in the instability of the Egyptian economy. Its share in total exports being 65–70 per cent, oil-export

NOTES

revenue in real terms fell by 20 per cent in 1981–4 and fell further by 50–60 per cent between 1985 and 1989. As a result, the balance of trade deficit increased fivefold between 1980 and 1984. Sources: *Statistical Yearbook* 1986 and 1995 (Egypt, CAPMAS, 1981–95) and *Economic Review*, 30; 32 (Egypt, Central Bank of Egypt, 1989/90; 1991/2).

20 My calculated averages for 1986–90 in billion dollars are: aid US$2.4; Egyptian remittances US$3; grants and loans US$2; private foreign capital US$0.1. Sources: World Bank data and *Statistical Abstracts of the ESCWA Region, 1983–1992* (ESCWA, 1994b).

21 For detailed information on the state of the public sector, see Handoussa and Potter (1991) and *World Development Report* 1988: Chapter 8 (World Bank, 1978–96); Egypt and Turkey were included in the Bank's study of public economic enterprises.

22 Egypt, Central Bank of Egypt (1991/92: 113).

23 The dependence of Egypt on US assistance and its close international ties were the subject of a popular comedy performed in a Cairo theatre under the title *Mama America*. Alan Richards (1991: 1728), commenting on the lengthy negotiations with the IMF, writes, 'The GOE [Government of Egypt] seemed to base its strategy on a syllogism: (a) the IMF is a US institution; (b) US strategic interests are paramount (or, the US government is a single, rational actor); (c) US strategic interests require Egyptian stability; (d) therefore, the US will force the IMF to accede to GOE's views.' See *Middle East Economic Digest* 31, nos 13 and 21, and 32 (28 March and 10 November 1987; 7 May 1988).

24 Handoussa and Potter (1991: 6–10), and the World Bank's study of Egypt (1991: 43–54). The main problem in unemployment measurement is the different working ages used. The workforce of 15 million are in the age group 15–63.

25 Information obtained from the Public Enterprise Office, Cairo, in January 1996.

26 Calculated from Tables 2–1 and 2–2 of *Bahth al-Dakhl wal-Infaq wal-Istihlak fi Jumhuriya Misral-Arabiya, 1990/91* (Survey of income and consumption in Egypt, 1990/91) (Egypt, CAPMAS, 1993: Vol. 2). The difference in expenditure on luxury items is from CAPMAS, August 1992 (Arabic) in FAO 1995b: Table 37).

27 The two studies are Korayem (1994) and ESCWA (1995a: Table 6). The increased poverty among the poor is measured by the proportionate increase in the distance between the average income/expenditure of the poor and the estimated poverty line. Korayem also shows that between 1982 and 1991 inequality in the distribution of income increased more in urban areas than in rural areas. In terms of the Gini index, it increased from 0.32 to 0.38 in the former and from 0.29 to 0.32 in rural areas (Korayem, 1994: Table 4).

28 ESCWA (1995a: Table 5), World Bank's study of Egypt (1991: Tables 2.1 and 2.10), and Korayem (1994: Tables 20A and 20B), and FAO (1995a).

29 My judgement is based on the results of (a) the Central Bank of Egypt's study 'The Taxation System in Egypt', *Economic Bulletin* 37 (Egypt, Central Bank, 1984), and (b) the World Bank's study of the distribution of the tax burden among income classes presented in World Bank (1991: Tables 3.11, 3.12 and 3.13). Both studies conclude that the Egyptian tax burden fell heavily on low-income groups because of its reliance on indirect taxation.

The results also show how the corporate income tax levied on public enterprises is shifted to consumers. The data on taxes in 1994 are from Egypt's *Statistical Yearbook*, June 1995: Table 11–10 (Egypt, CAPMAS, 1981–95).

30 The figure of E£7 billion arrears is from a statement given by the Minister of Finance in *al-Wafd*, 12 February 1996, p. 3. A figure of E£7.2 billion for tax evasion at December 1995 was reported by the Tax Evasion Control Unit of the Ministry of Interior (*al-Ahali*, 31 January 1996, p. 1). For earlier years see Chapter 7. The *Statistical Yearbook* 1995 gives the figure of E£31.2 billion for total tax revenue in 1994 (Egypt, CAPMAS, 1981–95).

31 Source: *Social Fund for Development* (Egypt, Prime Minister's Office, 1994). Loans are allocated on formal application in amounts varying from E£10,000 to E£50,000, in some cases reaching E£200,000, against 10 per cent interest. My estimate of beneficiaries and the amount of loan required is based on data on graduates (1987–94) given in *Statistical Yearbook* 1995 (Egypt, CAPMAS, 1981–95). The fund is also insufficient even if we focus only on the 400,000 new entrants a year into the labour force, plus about 350,000 public-sector workers expected to be laid off in the next 3–4 years and assume the lower average loan of E£15,000 per applicant. As a rough estimate, the present amount of $613 million would create only some 140,000 jobs by the end of 1997. The cost of creating one job is based on estimates made by the Ministries of Planning and Economic Cooperation, ranging from E£5,000 to E£50,000.

32 For detailed information on the adjustment programme, see World Bank's *Morocco: Analysis and Reform of Economic Policy* (1990b). See also Hamdouch, in El-Naggar (1987). IMF loan support consisted of a compensatory financing facility, a standby facility and extended funds totalling US$1 billion in 1986. World Bank financial support comprised a structural adjustment loan (US$500 million), industry and trade policy adjustment (US$350 million), agriculture (US$300 million), education (US$150 million) and the restructuring of public enterprises (US$240 million), totalling US$1.34 billion in June 1988.

33 The direct contribution of agricultural growth is calculated by multiplying the rate of agricultural GDP growth by its percentage share in total GDP, then dividing by the rate of GDP growth.

34 *Annuaire Statistique du Maroc* (Morocco, Ministry of Planning, 1990, 1991 and 1994: Chapter 12); *Yearbook of Labour Statistics* 1983, 1987 and 1993 (ILO, 1983–95) and IMF (1995c: Table 5). The percentages for unemployment in 1989 are calculated from *Annuaire Statistique* 1990: Tables 12.3 and 12.5. In his study, Morrisson (1991: 1638) says that unemployment was higher in urban areas (15.6 per cent compared to a national figure of 14 per cent in 1986). However, there are sectoral differences: employment increased in rural areas as a result of high producer prices that stimulated crop production and in export-oriented industries and tourism services.

35 Morrisson (1991: 1638). See also Laraki (1989).

36 *Structural Adjustment and Living Conditions in Developing Countries* (World Bank, 1990c: Tables 6 and 7).

37 See the UNESCO regional office's study of primary education in the Arab states, in *al-Tarbiya al-Jadida* 40, 41 (UNESCO, 1987: 34–45). The results are tabulated in *World Education Report*, 1993: Tables 10 and 11 (Arabic) (UNESCO, 1991 and 1993).

38 Morrisson (1991: 1636–7) identifies the gainers and losers by occupation (entrepreneurs, large and small farmers, and employees in the public sector). He concludes that inequality has increased in urban areas and decreased in rural areas.

39 Morocco, Ministry of Agriculture, 1989 and 1990. The land redistributed was in units ranging from 5 hectares in irrigated areas to 16–20 hectares of rainfed lands per household beneficiary. The land was sold to the beneficiaries at half its market value, payable over thirty years.

40 M. R. El-Ghonemy (1993: Tables 3.2 and 5.3). The estimate of landlessness is by Ennaji and Pascon in FAO (1988: Table 5).

41 *Consommation et Depenses des Ménages* 1984–85: Vol. 1, pp. 13–14 (Morocco, Ministry of Planning, 1987).

42 Despite the emphasis on structural tax reform and 'ensuring social justice', tax on income and profit as a percentage of national income (GDP) remains almost unchanged from 4.8 per cent in 1981 to 4.6 per cent in 1985 and 5.3 per cent in 1990. Source: IMF (1995c: Table 4).

43 According to UN data, commitments from OPEC members and Arab institutions to Sudan amounted to $585.2 million in 1983. In 1975, the Arab Fund for Economic and Social Development announced a ten-year plan centred on a massive US$6,000 million investment programme – the so-called 'bread-basket' policy – to expand agricultural and agro-industrial production sufficiently to meet a significant percentage of Arab food needs. The plan was never fully implemented.

44 *World Tables* 1995 shows that the current account balance deteriorated from a surplus of US$29 million in 1973 to US$−493.8 million by 1978 and the budget deficit widened from S£16.2 million in 1973 to S£151.7 million in 1978 (World Bank, 1976–95).

45 The civilian government of al-Mahdi entered negotiations with the IMF for an interim recovery programme and a medium-term programme which were approved by the World Bank and the IMF in March 1988. They provided for a further devaluation of the pound, liberalization of exchange rates and of trade, budgetary controls and measures to generate revenue.

46 Hussain (1991).

47 FAO *Production Yearbook* 1986 and 1993 reveals that the index of food production (1979–81 = 100) declined from 100.34 in 1978 to 75.76 in 1993.

48 Average infant mortality for Sudan and for Middle Eastern countries in 1982 was 118 and 98 per 1,000 live births respectively, compared with 1987 (108 and 76), and 1992 (99 and 56). The mortality rate of children under 5 (per 1,000 live births) in Sudan in 1992 was 162 compared with 79 for the Middle East.

49 See Krueger (1995). For detailed information on the economic conditions leading to the acceptance of the World Bank and IMF lending facilities, see Kirkpatrick and Onis (1991).

50 The share of education in total government expenditure has increased during the period of parliamentary democracy from 9.9 per cent in 1985 to 19.1 per cent in 1990, and further to 20.0 per cent in 1992. For an understanding of the effects of frequent elections on budget deficit and inflation during the parliamentary democracy period (post-1983), see Krueger (1995).

51 According to *Government Finance Statistics Yearbook* 1993 (IMF, 1980–94), while expenditure on defence increased between 1985 and 1992, the shares of

health and social security declined as a percentage of total government spending. In 1992, the shares were 3.5 per cent and 3.9 per cent respectively, while that of defence was 11.3 per cent.

52 Krueger (1995: 358–63) and Table 10.3 in the present chapter.

53 Chapter 6, Table 6.2; *Trends in Developing Countries* (World Bank, 1993: 493); *Statistical Yearbook* 1991 and 1996: Tables 157 and 166 for unemployment 1992–5 (Turkey, State Institute of Statistics, 1991 and 1996); and Hansen, (1991 Table 12–16). See also Chapter 9, pp. 164–5 in the present book, on unemployment in Turkey.

54 See sources in Chapter 8, notes 30–3; estimates for poverty and unemployment were taken from Coulombe and McKay (1994) and McKay and Houebib (1993: Table 4.3) for unemployment in 1990.

55 The Fifth Development Plan 1981–5 was examined during my visit to Jordan in 1981 for the assessment of Jordan's rural development policy and programmes. Most of the information in the following paragraphs is taken from Jawad Anani in El-Naggar (1987) and from *al Khita al-Iqtisadiya wal-Ijtima'iya* 1993–7 (National economic and social development plan *1993–7*) (Jordan, Ministry of Planning, n.d.)

56 Data on income distribution are from ESCWA (1995a: Table 13). The two estimates of poverty incidence were made by the Ministry of Social Affairs of Jordan and by the World Bank, and both are cited in the ESCWA study, Table 7.

57 On 16 August 1996 riots started in the south (in Karak, where poverty is very high) and spread to other cities in the following days. Dressed in military uniform, the King addressed the nation on television, supporting the government's action and blaming foreign elements for instigating the riots. He ordered his army and police to 'strike with iron fist'. On falling nutritional levels, see ESCWA (1995a: Table 18) and FAO (1995b: Table 19). The cost of bread subsidy is calculated from IMF (1991b: Table 2). In 1991 total bread subsidy was 40 million Jordanian dinars. It is estimated that 7–8 million of that accrued to the lowest two deciles of consumers, compared with 283 million dinars for defence and 180 million dinars for debt interest payment in 1991 (*Government Finance Statistics Yearbook* 1993 (IMF, 1980–94)). See my article 'Economic solution to Jordan unrest', *The Times* (London), 23 August 1996, p. 21.

58 Information on the World Bank and IMF loans is taken from World Bank (1992a), and from *The Middle East and North Africa* (1996: *Algeria, The Economy*). In 1993, the Prime Minister Abdul Salam, who opposed change from a socialist to a private-market economy, was replaced by the pro-privatization Reda Malek and his Minister of Economy Ben Ashenou, who was closely associated with the World Bank. A similar situation occurred in Egypt in January 1996.

59 *Yearbook of Labour Statistics* 1995 (ILO, 1983–95). Other estimates of unemployment are from a study by Francis Ghiles in the *Financial Times Survey*, 28 January 1991.

60 Cases of illegal enrichment have been reported by Ghiles *ibid.*, and by Long and Reich (1995: 399–407). Growth of the GDP in 1990–4 was negative (−0.4 per cent). The data on consumption per person are from FAO (1994: Table 4), showing average growth rates falling from 2.8 per cent in 1970–80 to 0.1 per cent in 1980–90. Poverty and income distribution in 1980 are

from the Ministry of Planning (MPAT) and INEAP's purchasing-power survey (Algeria, INEAP, 1981).

61 World Bank data show that the annual rate of growth of private investment fell from 5 per cent in 1970–80 to 1.9 per cent in 1980–82, while total investment declined by 6.8 per cent in 1989–94. Net foreign direct investment was also negative or zero between 1988 and 1992.

62 Essentially, since independence in 1962, the country has been ruled by the military. The attempts made in 1990 and 1991 to reform the political system were crushed by the military for fear of the parliamentary democracy bringing the Islamic Salvation Front (FIS) into power. President Benjadid, the architect of economic and political reforms, was forced to resign by the military, who continued to have the upper hand after they appointed the former Defence Minister, General Lamine Zerwal, to the presidency of the country. Zerwal was re-elected in 1996.

63 *World Education Report* 1993: Tables 2 and 11 (UNESCO, 1991 and 1993). See Chapters 2 and 5 on school-leaving before completion of primary education.

64 Public expenditure on health in 1990 was 5.4 per cent of GNP for Algeria and 4.3 per cent for Tunisia, compared to the private-sector share of 1.6 per cent in both countries.

65 See M. R. El-Ghonemy (1993: 129–31 and Tables 7.3 and 7.5).

66 I refer here to Bourguignon *et al.* (1991) and Stewart (1995: Chapter 2, Table 2.1 and Diagram 2.3).

11 PROSPECTS AND CHALLENGES

1 For a comparison between unemployment rates in the Middle East and other developing regions, see Turnham (1993: Tables 2.1 and 2.2) and Shaban *et al.* (1995: 74).

2 Based on country estimates in *World Development Report* 1994: Table 25 of development indicators (World Bank, 1978–96), to which I added 37 million for Bahrain, Iraq, Kuwait, Lebanon, Libya, Qatar and the Palestinians living in the Gaza Strip and West Bank.

3 *Ibid.* (Tables 20 and 23) and my Appendix Table 10.1. In 1992, total external debt of the eight adjusting countries was US$181.1 billion in addition to US$40.1 billion for Yemen, Iran, Syria and Oman.

4 Based on estimates given in the countries' development plans, I calculated a rough average of US$30,000 for creating one job. The four adjusting countries and the interest charges actually paid in 1992 in US million dollars are: Algeria ($2,001), Egypt ($198.3), Morocco ($449.4), Turkey ($1,957.1).

5 I studied Egypt, Jordan, Oman, Tunisia and Yemen. The meeting was organized in collaboration with the INS and FAO statistician Dr Clifford Morojela, and held in Tunis in June 1982. The findings and the developed socioeconomic indicators are contained in M. R. El-Ghonemy (1984 and 1991) and (1986).

6 Since 1976, World Conferences on health for all, employment, agrarian reform, population, food, nutrition, human rights, children, women, and on social development have issued plans of action and set quantifiable targets, including the development of socioeconomic indicators for which international financial and technical assistance was provided. The World Bank has

also assisted countries in conducting household surveys on living conditions and poverty.

7 See Sen (1981) and Drèze and Sen (1989) for the relationship between democracy with a free press and famine.

8 For a country-by-country review of political systems, see Owen (1992) and Deegan (1993). In 1996, as a result of the election in Turkey, the Islamic activists' welfare party (Rafat) under its leader Najm el-Din Arbakan formed a coalition government with The True Path, the secular party holding pro-Western ideologies of the former Prime Minister Mrs Tansu Ciller (1993–5).

9 See *Human Development Report* 1995: Figures 2.1–2.6 and Appendix Tables 2.1 and 2.4 (UNDP, 1991–6) for a striking difference between women's literacy, employment and political rights in the Arab states and other developing regions.

10 For example Krueger (1974), Stiglitz (1989) and *Human Development Report* 1996 (UNDP, 1991–6).

11 See a framework for analysis of war-related costs in Stewart (1993).

12 In Chapter 10, I described this payment as a reward for supporting the USA-led coalition of Western powers against Iraq after its invasion of Kuwait in 1990. For more details on these payments and the total costs to Saudi Arabia, see *Middle East Economic Digest*, May 3, 1991 and Sadowski (1993: 20).

13 The size of the armed forces is taken from *The Military Balance* (IISS, 1992–3: 59 and 104–26). In 1992, the largest numbers of armed forces, *excluding* reserves, were (in thousands): Turkey (560), Iran (524), Egypt (410), Syria (408), Iraq (385), Morocco (195), Saudi Arabia (175), and Israel (175).

14 The share of the poorest fifth of households in total personal income was only 4 per cent while the richest fifth held 55 per cent. See Issawi (1982: Table A.4) and IMF (1995a: Table A.1). Lara Marlow says, 'an estimated one-third of the Lebanese live in absolute poverty' (1996: 18).

15 IMF (1995a: Tables 1 and 2 and pp. 3–6) and Saidi (1986). After the Israeli invasion in 1982, real income per person dropped to 39 per cent of its 1974 value. It then started recovering slowly, but still only reached (in 1993) 48 per cent of the 1974 level.

16 Calculated from SIPRI (1996: Table 8 A.2).

17 After the Gulf War, the Saudi, Kuwaiti, Omani and UAE heads of state agreed in 1991 to form a military security pact, together with Egypt and Syria. One year later, the Saudi and Kuwaiti governments preferred concluding formal military accords with the USA and UK for long-term security arrangements. In the mean time, Egypt considers that any collective security scheme is ineffective as long as Israel possesses nuclear weapons, and refuses to sign the UN Treaty on the non-proliferation of nuclear weapons. Such refusal – it is claimed – presents an enormous potential threat.

18 The average share in national income (GDP) during the period 1990–4 was very high in Oman and Saudi Arabia (15 per cent), and Israel and Syria (11 per cent), compared to Jordan (8 per cent), Egypt, Morocco, Turkey (4 per cent) and Tunisia (1.8 per cent). In absolute terms, these shares are enormous (for example, US$15 billion in Saudi Arabia and US$6.4 billion in Israel). The figures are in constant 1990 US dollars taken from SIPRI (1996: Tables 8 A.2 and 8 A.3).

19 After the end of the war with Iraq in 1988, President Ali Akbar Rafsanjani of

Iran gradually reduced military spending. In 1990–1 it reached less than half its 1980–1 level. He also replaced the revolutionary Islamic faction in the government with liberal economists.

20 According to the SIPRI *Yearbook* (1996: Tables 10.1 and 10.2) the USA and the Western European countries have a monopoly over the production and sale of arms with a total sale value of US$148 billion in 1994. Seven multinationals dominate the Middle East arms market: Lockheed, Raytheon, Northrop Grumman in the USA and British Aerospace, the French DCN and the German Daimler-Benz.

21 See lists of countries and types of arms manufactured in World Bank (1992b).

22 In addition to the sale of arms, the major suppliers listed in note 20 above provide the Middle Eastern countries with bilateral economic cooperation. This cooperation includes military assistance and lending for the purchase of arms which, in turn, influence individual countries' military spending. The US government has adopted the inexorable logic of the 'balance-of-power' by which Israel maintains an absolute superiority over all Arab states. For details, see McNamara (1991: 104).

23 Based on estimates given in the World Bank (1993a: Vol. 1, Tables 5.1 and 5.2).

24 Summers (1994: 7–8) and Noor (1981: Appendix 1) present estimates of unit costs.

25 This estimate is based on average cost given in *World Development Report* 1993: Box 4.5 and 1994: Table A.2 (World Bank, 1978–96).

26 Citing the sources, Sadowski (1993: 65–8) gives the unit price of arms as follows: a jet fighter US$20–$25 million, an F-15 fighter plane US$57 million and a submarine US$250 million.

27 Another form of peace dividend that has not been examined in this study is the involvement of Israel, countries outside the region and the UN agencies in regional economic activities designed to promote private-sector cooperation in investment and trade. Some Arab states are reluctant to participate in this project prior to a genuine peace. Progress has taken two parallel forms: the European Union's meeting in Barcelona (November 1995); and a series of regional conferences for promoting cooperation in inter-country economic collaboration (Casablanca in October 1994, Amman in October 1995 and Cairo in November 1996). The EU meeting in Barcelona called for regular debate on cooperation for alleviating instability and poverty. On the Arab states' prospects for economic and political cooperation, and even unity, see Hasseeb *et al.* (1991).

BIBLIOGRAPHY

Abdel-Kader, A. (1959) 'Land Property and Land Tenure in Islam', *The Islamic Quarterly* 5: 4–11.

Abdel-Karim, A. (1988) 'Some Aspects of Commoditisation and Transformation in Rural Sudan', in T. Barnett and A. Abdel Karim (eds), *Sudan: State Capital and Transformation*. London: Croom Helm.

Abdel-Khaleq, G. (1987) 'Taqdeer Khat al-Faqr Lil-Osar al-Bahraniya' (Poverty-line for Bahrain households). Report prepared for ESCWA. Amman: ESCWA. Mimeographed.

Abdel-Khaleq, G. and Tignor, R. (eds) (1982) *The Political Economy of Income Distribution in Egypt*. New York: Holmes and Meier.

Abdulla, A. (1986) 'Water Supply Factor in Sudan', in A. Zahlan and W. Magar (eds), *The Agricultural Sector of Sudan*. London: Ithaca Press.

Abdul-Malek, A. (1953) *al-Tafawut fi al-Dukhoul* (Inequality of income distribution). Cairo: Dar el-Fikr al-Arabi.

Abu-Alsorour, G. (1994) *Ra'i al-Azhar fi Mashrou' Barnamaj A'mal al-Mu'tamar al-Dawli lil Sukan wa al-Tanmiya* (Al-Azhar's opinion of the programme of work of the International Conference on Population and Development). Cairo: al-Azhar.

Abu-Jaber, K., Buhbe, M. and Smadi M. (eds) (1990) *Income Distribution in Jordan*. Boulder, Colo: Westview Press.

Abun-Nasr, J. M. (1971) *A History of the Maghreb*. Cambridge, Mass.: Cambridge University Press.

Aburish, S. K. (1994) *The Rise, Corruption and Coming Fall of the House of Saud*. London: Bloomsbury Publishing.

Abu-Zahra, M. (1963) *Ahkam al-Tarika wal Mawareeth* (Laws of legacies and inheritance). Cairo: Dar al-Fikr al-Arabi.

Achdut, L. (1993) *Income Inequality and Income Composition in Israel 1979–1991*. Discussion Paper 50. Jerusalem: National Insurance Institute.

Achdut, L. and Bigman, D. (1991) 'The Anatomy of Changes in Poverty and Income Inequality under Rapid Inflation: Israel 1979–1984', *Structural Change and Economic Dynamics* 2, 1: 229–43.

Achdut, L. and Tamir, Y. (1990) 'Retirement and Well-Being among the Elderly', in T. Smeeding *et al.* (eds) *Poverty, Inequality and Income Distribution in Comparative Perspective. The Luxembourg Income Study.* Hemel Hempstead: Harvester Wheatsheaf.

Adams, D. (1958) *Iraq's People and Resources.* Berkeley: University of California Press.

Ades, A. and di Tella, R. (1995) 'Competition and Corruption'. Applied Economics Discussion Paper 169. Oxford: Institute of Economics and Research.

Adriaansen, W. and Waardenburgh, J. (eds) (1992) *A Dual World Economy.* Bombay: Oxford University Press.

Ahmad, E., Drèze, J. Hills, J. and Sen, A. (eds) (1991) *Social Security in Developing Countries.* Oxford: Clarendon Press.

Ahmad, K. (ed.) (1981) *Studies in Islamic Economics.* 1st edn. 1980. Leicester (UK): The Islamic Foundation.

Akhaui, S. (1980) *Religion and Politics in Contemporary Iran.* Albany, NY: State University of New York Press.

Akkad, H. (1967) 'The Nomads' Problem and the Implementation of a Settlement Scheme', in M. R. El-Ghonemy (ed.) *Land Policy in the Near East.* Rome: FAO.

Alexandratos, N. (ed.) (1995) *World Agriculture Towards 2010.* An FAO study. London: John Wiley.

Algeria
Commission Nationale de la Révolution Agraire (1975) *Révolution Agraire: Textes Fondamentaux.* Algiers: Commission Nationale de la Révolution Agraire.

INEAP (1981) *Étude de Disparites des Revenues et Pouvoir d'Achat en Algerie 1968–1979.* Algiers: INEAP.

Ministry of Planning (1985) *Deuxieme Plan Quinquennal, 1985–1989, Rapport General.* Algiers: Ministry of Planning.

Ali, A. (1986) 'Finance and Credit', in A. Zahlan and W. Magar, (eds) *The Agricultural Sector of Sudan.* London: Ithaca Press.

Allan, J. A. (1981) *Libya: The Experience of Oil.* London: Croom Helm.

Almazrou, Y. (1990) *Levels, Trends and Differentials of Infant and Child Mortality in Saudi Arabia,* Riyadh: UNICEF.

Alnasrawi, A. (1994) 'Economic Devastation, Underdevelopment and Outlook', in F. Hazelton (ed.) *Iraq Since the Gulf War.* London: Zed Books.

Alothman, A. M. (1994) 'Nutritional Evaluation of Some Commercial Baby Food Consumed in Saudi Arabia'. Unpublished M.Sc. thesis, King Saud University, Riyadh.

Al-Qaddafi, M. (1976 and 1979) *al-Kitab al-Akhdar* (The green book). Tripoli: Ministry of Information. (Arabic and English).

Al-Shoshan, A. (1991) 'Saudi Arabia: The Country Nutrition Profile'. A study prepared for the FAO/WHO International Conference on Nutrition. Rome: FAO Mimeographed.

Alwan, A. (1961) *Diraasat fi al-Islah al-Zira'i* (Studies in agrarian reform). Baghdad: al-Tijariya Press.

Amid, M. J. (1990) *Agriculture, Poverty and Reform in Iran.* London: Routledge.

Amin, G. (1974) *The Modernization of Poverty: A Study of the Political Economy of Growth in Nine Arab Countries 1945–1970* Leiden: E. J. Brill.

—— (1988) *Qissat Duyoun Misr al-Kharijïya min 'Asr Mohammed Ali ila al-Yaum.* (The story of Egypt's foreign debts since Mohammed Ali). Cairo: Dar Aly Nokhta lil- Nashr.

—— (1994) *Mu'delat al-lqtisad al-Misri* (The predicament of the Egyptian economy). Cairo: Misr al-Arabia lil Nashr wal Tawzee'.

Amin, S. (1966) *L'Economie du Maghreb.* Paris: Presse de Minuit.

Amine, K. (1980) *Some Results of the Nutrition Status Surveys in Oman and Bahrain.* Abu-Dhabi: UNICEF.

Amuzegar, J. (1982) 'Oil Wealth: A Very Mixed Blessing', *Foreign Affairs* 60: 814–34.

Anani, J. (1987) 'Adjustment and Development: The Case of Jordan', in S. El-Naggar (ed.) *Adjustment Policies and Development Strategies in the Arab World.* Washington, DC: IMF.

Anis, M. (1950) 'A Study of the National Income of Egypt', *L'Egypte Contemporaine* November/December: 663–924.

Archilli, M. and Khaldi, M. (eds) (1984) *The Role of the Arab Development Funds in the World Economy.* London: Croom Helm.

Asfour, E. (1972) 'Prospects and Problems of Economic Development of Saudi Arabia, Kuwait and the Gulf Principalities', in C. Cooper and S. Alexander (eds) *Economic Development and Population Growth in the Middle East.* New York: Elsevier.

Assaf, G. (1979) *The Size Distribution of Income in Jordan.* Amman: The Royal Scientific Society.

Atiqa, A. (1967) 'How Oil, Industrialization and Urbanization Adversely Affect Agriculture' in M. R. El-Ghonemy (ed.) *Land Policy in the Near East.* Rome: FAO

—— (1981) 'How Oil Revenues can Destroy a Country', *Petroleum Intelligence Weekly* special supplement, October.

Atkinson, A. B. (1975) *The Economics of Inequality.* Oxford: Clarendon Press.

Awad, M. H. (1983) *Socio-Economic Change in the Sudan.* Selected Essays, Monograph 6. Khartoum: University of Khartoum.

Ayoob, M. (ed.) (1981) *The Politics of Islamic Reassertion.* London: Croom Helm.

Baer, G. (1962) *A History of Landowners in Modern Egypt, 1800–1950.* Oxford: Oxford University Press.

Bahrain

    Central Office for Statistics (1985) *Household and Income Survey 1983/4.* Manama: The Prime Minister's Office. (Arabic).

Baker, R. (1990) *Sadat and After: Struggles for Egypt's Political Soul.* London: I. B. Tauris & Co.

Bangura, A. (1995) *The Effects of American Foreign Aid to Egypt, 1957–1987.* Lampeter, Dyfed (UK): The Edwin Mellen Press.

Baranzini, M. (1991) *A Theory of Wealth Distribution and Accumulation.* Oxford: Clarendon Press.

Barnett, T. and Abdel-Karim, A., (eds) (1988) *Sudan: State, Capital and Transformation*. London: Croom Helm.

Bauer, P. (1982) *Equality: The Third World and Economic Delusion*. London: Methuen.

Beblawi, H. and Luciani, G. (eds) (1987) *The Rentier State*. London: Croom Helm.

Bekir, M. (1979) 'The Development of Level of Living in Iraq'. Unpublished Ph.D. thesis, University of Leeds, UK.

—— (1984) 'Distribution of Income in Iraq during the 1970s', in *Proceedings of UN/ECWA Expert Group Meeting on Income Distribution Statistics*. Baghdad: ECWA.

Beshai, A. (1993) 'Interpretations and Misinterpretations of the Egyptian Economy', in C. Tripp (ed.) *Contemporary Egypt through Egyptian Eyes*. London: Routledge.

Bhagwati, J. (1973) 'Education, Class Structure and Income Equality', *World Development* 1, 5: 21–36.

Bhalla, A. (1992) *Uneven Development in the Third World: A Study of China and India*. London: Macmillan.

Bigsten, A. (1983) *Income Distribution and Development*. London: Heinemann Educational Books.

Biswas, A. (1991). 'Land and Water Management for Sustainable Agricultural Development in Egypt: Opportunities and Constraints: a study prepared for FAO'. Project TCP/EGY/0052. Rome: FAO and Egyptian Ministry of Agriculture. Mimeographed.

—— (1994) *International Waters of the Middle East: From Euphrates–Tigris to the Nile*. Bombay: Oxford University Press.

Blaug, M. (ed.) (1968) *Economics of Education*. Harmondsworth (UK): Penguin Books.

Bounab, A. (1989) 'The Algerian Development Strategy, Income Distribution and Poverty'. Unpublished Ph.D. thesis, University of Glasgow, UK.

Bourguignon, F., de Melo, J. and Morrison, C. (1991). 'Poverty and Income Distribution during Adjustment', *World Development* 19, 11: 1485–508.

Bruno, M., Ravallion, M. and Squire, L. (1995) 'Equity and Growth in Developing Countries: Old and New Perspectives on the Policy Issues'. Paper presented at the IMF Conference on Income Distribution and Sustainable Growth, Washington, DC, August 1995. Mimeographed.

Carruthers, I. and Clark, C. (1981) *The Economics of Irrigation*. Liverpool: Liverpool University Press.

Chen, S., Datt, G. and Ravallion, M. (1994) 'Is Poverty Increasing in the Developing World?' *Review of Income and Wealth* 40, 4: 359–76.

Chenery, H. (1979) *Structural Change and Development Policy*. Oxford: Oxford University Press.

Chenery, H. and Syrquin, M. (1975) *Patterns of Development*. London: Oxford University Press.

Choucri, N. (1986) 'The Hidden Economy: A New View of Remittances in the Arab World', *World Development* 14, 6: 697–712.

CIMMYT (International Maize and Wheat Improvement Centre) (1991) *World Wheat Facts and Figures, 1990–91.* Mexico City: CIMMYT.

Clayton, A. (ed.) (1994) *Governance, Democracy and Conditionality: What Role for NGOs?*, Oxford: Intrac.

Cleland, W. (1939) 'Population Plan for Egypt', *L'Egypt Contemporaine* 185, May: 461–84.

Commons, J. (1934) *Institutional Economics: Its Place in Political Economy.* New York: Macmillan.

Cooper, C. and Alexander, S. (eds) (1972) *The Economic Development and Population Growth in the Middle East.* New York: Elsevier.

Corden, W. (1984) 'Booming Sector and Dutch Disease Economics: Survey and Consolidation', *Oxford Economic Papers* 36: 359–80.

—— (1991) 'The Theory of Debt Relief: Sorting out some Issues' *The Journal of Development Studies* 27: 135–45.

Cornia, G, Jolly, R. and Stewart, F. (eds) (1987) *Adjustment with a Human Face: Protecting the Vulnerable and Protecting the Poor. A UNICEF Study.* Oxford: Clarendon Press.

Coulombe, H. and McKay, A. (1994) 'The Causes of Poverty: A Study Based on the Mauritania Living Standards Survey, 1989–90', in T. Lloyd and O. Morrissey (eds) *Poverty, Inequality and Rural Development.* Case Studies. London: Macmillan.

Crabitès, P. (1993) *Ismail: The Maligned Kedive.* London: George Routledge and Sons.

Crouchley, A. (1938) *Economic Development of Modern Egypt.* London: Longmans, Green.

Daden, M. (1978) *La Subvention dans le Cadre du Code des Investissements Agricoles et la Conception Dualiste de la Modernisation de Gharb.* Rabat: Institut Hassan II.

Dasgupta, B. K. (1973) 'Investment in Libyan Agriculture', in J. Allan *et al.* (eds) *Libya: Agriculture and Economic Development.* London: Frank Cass.

Dasgupta, P. (1995) *An Inquiry into Well-Being and Destitution.* Oxford: Clarendon Press (paperback edition).

Deegan, H. (1993) *The Middle East and Problems of Democracy.* Buckingham (UK): Open University Press.

Degar, S. (1986) *Military Expenditures in Third World Countries: The Economic Effects.* London: Routledge and Kegan Paul

Degar, S. and Sen, S. (1991) 'Military Expenditure, Aid and Economic Development', in *Proceedings of The World Bank Annual Conference on Development Economics.* Washington, DC: The World Bank.

de Lange, N. (1986) *Judaism.* Oxford: Oxford University Press.

de Mooij, M. K. (1994) *Advertising Worldwide.* New York: Prentice Hall.

Deng, F. (1995) *War of Visions: Conflict of Identities in the Sudan.* Washington, DC: The Brookings Institution.

Denman, D. (1973) *The King's Vista: A Land Reform which has Changed the Face of Persia*. London: Geographical Publications Limited.

de Waal, A. (1989) *Famine That Kills: Darfur, Sudan, 1984–1985*. Oxford: Clarendon Press.

Diab, M. and David, E. (1991) 'Food Security, Income Distribution and Growth in Sudan', in S. Maxwell (ed.) *To Cure All Hunger: Food Policy and Food Security in Sudan*. London: IT Publications.

Doig, A. (1995) 'Good Government and Sustainable Anti-Corruption Strategies', *Public Administration and Development* 15: 151–65.

Dregne, H. E. (1983) *Desertification of Arid Lands*. Chur (Switzerland): Harwood Academic Publishers.

Drèze, J. and Gazdar, H. (1992) 'Hunger and Poverty in Iraq, 1991', *World Development* 24, 7: 921–45.

Drèze, J. and Sen, A. (1989) *Hunger and Public Action*. Oxford: Clarendon Press.

Edward, M. and Hulme, D. (eds) (1995) *Non-Governmental Organisations: Performance and Accountability*: London: Earthscan Publications.

Egypt
  CAPMAS (Central Agency for Public Mobilization and Statistics) (1981–95) *Statistical Yearbook*. Cairo: CAPMAS.
  —— (1987) *Census of Population, Housing and Establishments*. Cairo: CAPMAS.
  —— (1993) *Bahth al-Dakhl wal-Infaq wal-Istihlak fi Jumhuriyan Misr al-Arabiya 1990/91* (Income, expenditure and consumption survey of Egypt, 1990/91). 5 vols. Cairo: CAPMAS.
  Central Bank of Egypt (1984) *Economic Bulletin*, Number 37. (Arabic and English).
  —— (1989/90) *Economic Review*. Volume 30. (Arabic and English).
  —— (1991/2) *Economic Review*. Volume 32. (Arabic and English).
  INP (Institute of National Planning) (1995) *Egypt: Human Development Report*. Cairo: INP. (Arabic and English).
  Ministry of Finance (1946) *Taqdeer Dara'ib al-Arady al-Zirai'iya* (Law no. 53 and its regulations (Assessment of agricultural land-tax procedures)) Cairo: Ministry of Finance.
  —— (1949) 'Maslahat al-Amlak al-Ameriya Insha'uha wa A'amaluha' (Public domain department: its establishment and works.) Cairo Ministry of Finance. Mimeographed.
  Ministry of Waqfs and Ministry of Information (1994) *Mawqif al-Islam min Tanzeem al-Osrah* (Islam's attitude towards family planning). Cairo: Ministry of Waqwfs and Ministry of Information.
  Prime Minister's Office (1994) *Social Fund for Development*. 4 vols: *Mission and Objectives*; *Public Works Programme*; *Enterprise Development Programme*; *Community Development Programme*. Cairo: Prime Minister's Office.
Eid, N., Alhouti, S., Allam, M. and Bourisly, N. (1981) *Household Food Wastage in Kuwait*. Annual Research Report. Kuwait: Institute for Scientific Research.
  —— (1984) *Nutritional Status of Schoolchildren in Kuwait*. Annual Research Reports. Kuwait: Institute for Scientific Research.

EIU (Economist Intelligence Unit) (1991) *Libya: Country Profile*. London: Business International.

EIU and UNIDO (United Nations Industrial Development Organization) (1996) *Iran: Industrial Development Review*. London EIU and UNIDO.

El-Azzabi, A. (1975) 'Road Transport Development and Economic Change in Libya'. Unpublished Ph.D. thesis, University of London.

El-Ghonemy, H. (1992) 'Well Permit Regulations as a Means of Protecting the Groundwater Resources of the Nejd Region of Oman and the Western Desert of Egypt', *Geology of the Arab World*: 135–46.

El-Ghonemy, M. R. (1965) 'The Development of Tribal Lands and Settlements in Libya', *Land Reform*: 5–16.

—— (ed.) (1967) *Land Policy in the Near East*. Rome: FAO.

—— (1968) 'Land Reform and Economic Development in the Near East', *Land Economics* 44, 1: 36–49.

—— (1979) *Agrarian Reform and Rural Development in the Near East*. Cairo: FAO Regional Office.

—— (1984 and 1991) *Development Strategies for the Rural Poor*. Economic and Social Development Paper 44. Rome: FAO.

—— (1984) *Economic Growth, Income Distribution and Rural Poverty in the Near East*. Rome: FAO.

—— (ed.) (1986) *The Dynamics of Rural Poverty*. Rome: FAO.

—— (1990a) 'Land Tenure Systems and Rural Poverty in the Near East and North Africa', a study prepared for IFAD. Mimeographed. Summarized in IFAD (1992) *The State of World Rural Poverty*. London: IT Publications.

—— (1990b) *The Political Economy of Rural Poverty: The Case for Land Reform*, London: Routledge.

—— (1993) *Land, Food and Rural Development in North Africa*, Boulder, Colo.: Westview Press and London: IT Publications.

—— (1995) 'Food Security Equals Social Security', *Ceres* April/May: 17–22.

El-Ghonemy, M. R., Tyler, G. and Azam, K. (1986) *Yemen Arab Republic Rural Development Strategy and Implementation*. An assessment report of the ESCWA. Amman: ESCWA.

El-Gritley, A. (1977). *Khamsa wa Ishrouna Aman: dirasa tahliliya Lil Siyasat al-Iqtisadiya fi Misr 1952–1977* (Twenty-five years: an analytical study of economic policies in Egypt 1952–1977). Cairo: al-Hai'a al-Ama lil-Kitab.

El-Hassan, A. (1988) 'The Encroachment of Large Scale Mechanised Agriculture: Elements of Differentiation among the Peasantry', in T. Barnett and A. Abdel Karim (eds) *Sudan: State, Capital and Transformation*. London: Croom Helm.

El-Naggar, S. (ed.) (1987) *Adjustment Policies and Development Strategies in the Arab World*. Papers presented at a meeting organised by the IMF in Abu-Dhabi, UAE Washington, DC: IMF.

—— (1991) *Nahwa Istratijiyah Qawmiyah Lil-Islah al-Iqtisadi* (Towards a new strategy for economic reform). Cairo: Dar al-Shurous.

Ellman, M. (1981) 'Natural Gas, Restructuring and Re-industrialization: The

Dutch Experience of Industrial Policy', in T. Barker and V. Brailovsky (eds), *Oil or Industry?* London: Academic Press.

El-Wifati, B. (1978) 'Evaluation of Land Settlement Programme in Libya'. A study prepared for the FAO Regional Office for the Near East, Cairo. Mimeographed.

Emmanuel, S. and Friedman, M. (1990) *Religious Radicalism and Politics in the Middle East.* Albany, NY: State University of New York Press.

ESCWA (United Nations Economic and Social Commission for Western Asia).

—— (1994a) *Agriculture and Development: A Special Issue on the Agricultural Sector in the Occupied Palestinian Territories.* Amman: ESCWA.

—— (1994b) *Statistical Abstract of the ESCWA Region, 1983–1992.* Fourteenth Issue. Amman: ESCWA.

—— (1995a) *Impact of Selected Macroeconomic and Social Policies on Poverty: The Case of Egypt, Jordan and Yemen.* New York: United Nations.

—— (1995b) *Review of Development and Trends in the Monetary and Financial Sectors of the ESCWA Region, 1994*, New York: United Nations.

Esposito, J. (1987) *Islam and Politics.* Syracuse, NY: Syracuse University Press, 1987 (2nd edn).

Faisal Islamic Bank (1979) *Faisal Islamic Bank: Its Objectives and Operational Methods.* Khartoum: Faisal Islamic Bank. (Arabic and English).

—— (1983) 'Report of the Board of Directors'. Khartoum: Faisal Islamic Bank. Mimeographed (Arabic).

FAO (Food and Agriculture Organization of the UN)

—— (1946–94) *World Food Survey.* Rome: FAO.

—— (1983) 'Towards the Alleviation of Rural Poverty in Sudan'. Poverty Studies Series 1, prepared by A. Abu-Sheikha. Rome: FAO. Mimeographed.

—— (1985–93) *Country Tables: Basic Data on the Agricultural Sector.* Rome: FAO.

—— (1985, 1986, 1993) *Production Yearbook.* Vols. 39, 40, 47. Rome: FAO.

—— (1986) *Irrigation in Africa.* Investment Centre Technical paper 5. Rome: FAO.

—— (1987) *Economic and Social Policy Aspects of Irrigated Agriculture in the Near East.* Project ESPC/NE/87/3. Rome: FAO.

—— (1988) *The Impact of Development Strategies on the Rural Poor 1979–89.* Rome: FAO.

—— (1989) *The Implications of Changing Food Consumption for Food Production and Trade in the Near East*, ESPC/NE/89/3 Cairo: RNEA.

—— (1990) *Street Foods.* Food and Nutrition Paper 46. Rome: FAO.

—— (1992a) *Traditional Foods in the Near East.* Cairo: RNEA.

—— (1992b) *World Food Supplies and Prevalence of Chronic Undernutrition in Developing Regions as Assessed in 1992.* Rome: FAO Statistics Division.

—— (1992 and 1993) *The State of Food and Agriculture.* Rome: FAO.

—— (1993a) *Agriculture Towards 2010.* Document C93.24. Rome: FAO. Later published as Alexandratos, N. (1995), London: John Wiley.

—— (1993b) *Traditional Foods in the Arabian Gulf Countries.* Cairo: RNEA.

—— (1994) Changes in Food Consumption Patterns in the Arab Middle Eastern Countries. Cairo: RNEA.

—— (1995a) *The Impact of Population Growth and Urbanization on Food Consumption Patterns in Egypt*, Cairo: RNEA.

—— (1995b) *The Impact of the Structural Adjustment Programme on Food Consumption in Jordan*, Cairo: RNEA.

FAO and WFP (1993) 'Crop and Food Supply Assessment'. Report of FAO mission to Iraq. Mimeographed.

FAO and WHO (1992) *Nutrition and Development: A Global Assessment*. International Conference on Nutrition. 5–11 December, Rome. Rome: FAO.

Fields, G. (1980) *Poverty, Inequality and Development*. Cambridge: Cambridge University Press.

Friedman, M. (1962) *Capitalism and Freedom*. Chicago: University of Chicago Press.

Gaathon, A. (1971) *Economic Productivity in Israel*. Jerusalem: Bank of Israel and Praeger.

Galbraith, J. (1973) *The Affluent Society*. Harmondsworth, (UK). Pelican Heathcote, (Third Edition).

Gelb, A. and associates (1988) *Oil Windfalls: Blessing or Curse*. A World Bank Research Publication New York: Oxford University Press.

Gellner, E. and Waterbury, J. (eds) (1977) *Patrons and Clients in Mediterranean Societies*. London: Buckworth.

Gerteiny, A. (1981) *Historical Dictionary of Mauritania*. London: The Scarecrow Press.

Gibb, H. and Bowen, H. (1950) *Islamic Society and the West*. London: Oxford University Press.

Gilsenan, M. (1990) *Recognising Islam*. London: I. B. Tauris & Co.

Gould, D. and Amaro-Reyes, J. (1983) *The Effects of Corruption on Administrative Performance: Illustrations from Developing Countries*. World Bank staff working paper 580. Washington, DC: The World Bank.

Griffin, K. (1976) *Land Concentration and Rural Poverty*. London: Macmillan.

Griffin, K. and McKinley, T. (1994) *Implementing a Human Development Strategy*. London: Macmillan.

Gurkan, A. (1995) 'The Mathematics of Hunger', *Ceres*. April/May: 31–3.

Gurney, J. (1996) *Libya: The Political Economy of Oil*. Oxford: Oxford University Press.

Haggard, S. and Webb, S. (1993) 'What do we Know about the Political Economy of Economic Policy Reform?' *The World Bank Research Observer* 8, 2: 143–67.

Haider, S. (1944) 'The Problem of the Land in Iraq'. Unpublished Ph.D. thesis, University of London.

Hajrah, H. (1982) *Public Land Distribution in Saudi Arabia*. London: Longman Group.

Hamdouch, B. (1987) 'Adjustment and Development: The Case of Morocco', in S. El-Naggar (ed.) *Adjustment Policies and Development Strategies in the Arab World*. Washington, DC: IMF.

Handoussa, H. and Potter, G. (eds) (1991) *Employment and Structural Adjustment: Egypt in the 1990s*. Cairo: The American University in Cairo Press.

Hansen, B. (1991) *The Political Economy of Poverty, Equity and Growth: Egypt and Turkey*. A World Bank Comparative Study. Oxford: Oxford University Press.

Hansen, B. and Marzouk, G. (1965) *Development and Economic Policy in the UAR (Egypt)*. Amsterdam: North-Holland Publishing Company.

Hansen, B. and Radwan, S. (1982) *Employment Opportunities and Equity in Egypt*. Geneva: ILO.

Hashim, H. (1994) *Suwar min al-Fassad al-Jami'yi* (Features of corruption in universities). Cairo: Dar al-Shorouk.

Haslett, D. (1994) *Capitalism with Morality*. Oxford: Clarendon Paperbacks.

Hasseeb, K. (1964) *The National Income of Iraq, 1953–61*. Oxford: Oxford University Press.

Hasseeb, K., Ibrahim, S., Nasser, A., Saad el-Din, I. and Hilal, A. (1991). *The Future of the Arab Nations: Challenges and Options*. London: Routledge and the Centre for Arab Unity Studies.

Hayek, F. (1978) *The Mirage of Social Justice*. London: Routledge and Kegan Paul.

Hazelton, F. (ed.) (1994) *Iraq since the Gulf War: Prospects for Democracy*. London: Zed Books.

Heidenheimer, A. (ed.) (1978) *Political Corruption: Readings in Comparative Analysis*. New Brunswick, NJ: Transaction Books.

Higgins, B. (1959) *Economic Development: Principles, Problems and Policies*. London: Constable Press.

Hijab, N. (1988) *Woman Power: The Arab Debate on Women at Work*. Cambridge: Cambridge University Press.

Hodnebo, J. (1981) *Cotton, Cattle and Crisis: Production in East Equatoria Province, 1920–50*. Fantoft (Norway): Chr Michelsen Institute, Bergen.

Hoevan, van der R. (1987) 'External Shocks and Stabilisation Policies: Spreading the Load', *International Labour Review* 126, 2: 133–50.

Holden, D. and Johns, D. (1982) *The House of Saud*. London: Pan Books.

Hopwood, E. (ed.) (1992) *The Arabian Peninsula*. London: Allen & Unwin.

—— (1991) *Egypt: Politics and Society 1945–1990*. 3rd edn. Worcester (UK): HarperCollins Academic.

Horawitz, D. (1985) *The Morality of Spending*. Baltimore: The Johns Hopkins University Press.

Hourani, A. (1991) *A History of the Arab Peoples*. London: Faber and Faber.

Hunt, S. (1992) *Mauritania: Towards a Food Security Strategy*. Oxford: Food Studies Group, University of Oxford.

Hussain, M. (1991) 'Food Security and Adjustment Programmes: The Conflict', in Simon Maxwell (ed.) *To Cure All Hunger: Food Policy and Food Security in Sudan*. London: IT Publications.

Ibrahim, A. (1982) 'Impact of Agricultural Policies on Income Distribution', in G. Abdel-Khalek and R. Tignor (eds) *The Political Economy of Income Distribution in Egypt*. New York: Holmes & Meier.

Ibrahim, S. (1985) 'Peripheral Urbanism and the Sudan'. Unpublished Ph.D. thesis, University of Hull, UK.

Ibrahim, Saad-Eddin (1985) 'Islamic Militancy as a Social Movement: The Case of Two Groups in Egypt', in Dessouki, A. (ed.) *Islamic Resurgence in the Arab World*. New York: Praeger.

IFAD (International Fund for Agricultural Development) (1988) *Report of the Special Programming Mission in Sudan*. Rome: IFAD.

—— (1990) *Report of the Rural Development Mission to the Sultanate of Oman*. Rome: IFAD.

—— (1992) *The State of the World Rural Poverty*. Prepared by Idriss Jazairi, Mohiuddin Alamgir and Theresa Panuccio. London: IT Publications.

IFPRI (International Food Policy Research Institute) (1991) *Draught and Famine Relationships in Sudan: Policy Implications*, a study prepared by Testaye Teklu et al. Research Report 88, Washington, DC: IFPRI.

IISS (International Institute for Strategic Studies) (1991–2) *The Military Balance*. London: Brassey's.

ILO (International Labour Organization) (1976) *Employment, Growth and Basic Needs: A One World Problem*. Geneva: ILO.

—— (1983–95). *Yearbook of Labour Statistics*. Geneva: ILO.

—— (1987 and 1995) *World Labour Report*. Oxford: Oxford University Press.

—— (1996) *Lists of Ratification by Convention and Country*. Report of ILO Conferencem, Report 3, Part 5. Geneva: ILO.

—— (1984) *Labour Markets in the Sudan*. Geneva: ILO.

IMF (International Monetary Fund) (1980–94) *Government Finance Statistics Yearbook*. Washington, DC: IMF.

—— (1988) *The Implications of the IMF-Supported Programs for Poverty*. Occasional paper 58, prepared by P. Heller, A. Borember, T. Catsambeg, K. Chu and P. Shome. Washington, DC: IMF.

—— (1989 and 1992) *International Financial Statistics*. Washington, DC: IMF.

—— (1990) *International Comparisons of Government Expenditure Revisited: The Developing Countries 1975–86*. Occasional paper 69, prepared by P. Heller and J. Diamond. Washington, DC: IMF.

—— (1991a) *Financial Assistance from Arab Countries and Arab Regional Institutions*. Occasional paper 87. Washington, DC: IMF.

—— (1991b) 'Jordan: Restructuring Public Expenditures and Protecting the Poor'. Working paper 91/82. Washington, DC: IMF.

—— (1993a) 'Arab Republic of Egypt: Staff Report for the 1993 Article IV Consultation and Request for Extended Arrangement'. August. Washington, DC: IMF.

-(1993b) *The Path to Convertibility and Growth: The Tunisian Experience*. Occasional paper 109, Washington, DC: IMF.

—— (1995a) *Economic Dislocation and Recovery in Lebanon*. Occasional paper 120. Washington DC: IMF.

—— (1995b) *IMF Conditionality: Experience under stand-by and extended arrangements*. Part I: *Key Issues and Findings*. Washington, DC: IMF.

—— (1995c) *Resilience and Growth Through Sustained Growth: The Moroccan Experience*. Occasional paper 117, Washington, DC: IMF.

—— (1995d) *World Financial Survey*. Washington, DC: IMF.

Inalcik, H. (1977) *The Ottoman Empire: Conquest, Organization and Economy*. London: Weidenfeld.

Iqbal, Z. and Mirakhor, A. (1987) *Islamic Banking.* Occasional paper 49. Washington, DC: IMF.

Iran

Akhbar Ruz Institute, Tehran (1990) 'Text of the First Economic, Social and Cultural Development Plan of the Islamic Republic of Iran, 1989–1994'. A translation from Farsi. Mimeographed.

Bank Markazi (Central Bank of Iran) *Annual Report* (1971–80) Tehran: Central Bank of Iran. Farsi and English.

Issawi, C. (1981) *The Arab World's Legacy.* Princeton: Darwin Press.

—— (1982) *An Economic History of the Middle East and North Africa.* London: Methuen.

Issawi, C. and Yeganeh, M. (1962) *The Economics of Middle Eastern Oil.* New York: Praeger.

Israel

Central Bureau of Statistics (1970–93) *Statistical Abstract of Israel.* Jerusalem: Central Bureau of Statistics.

—— (1986/7) *Family Expenditure Survey.* Jerusalem: Central Bureau of Statistics.

—— (1992/3) *Family Expenditure Survey.* Jerusalem: Central Bureau of Statistics.

National Insurance Institute (1994) *National Insurance Programs.* Jerusalem: National Insurance Institute.

Jalal, F. (1972) *The Role of Government in the Industrialization of Iraq, 1950–1965.* London: Frank Cass.

James, J. (1993) *Consumption and Development.* London: Macmillan.

Jazayeri, A. (1988) *Economic Adjustment in Oil-Based Economies.* London: Avebury.

Jenks, C. (1972) *Inequality: A Reassessment of the Effect of Family and Schooling.* New York: Basic Books.

Jordan

Government of Jordan Department of Statistics (1980, 1986/7, 1992) *Family Expenditure Survey.* Amman: Department of Statistics. (Arabic and English).

Ministry of Planning (n.d.) *al-Khita al-Iqtisadiya wal Ijtima'iya 1993–7* (National economic and social development plan) 1993. Amman: Ministry of Planning.

The Royal Scientific Society (1979) *The Size Distribution of Income.* Amman: Royal Scientific Society.

Kahf, M. (1981) 'A Contribution to the Theory of Consumer Behaviour in an Islamic Society', in K. Ahmad (ed.) *Studies in Islamic Economics.* Jeddah: King Abdul Aziz University and Leicester: The Islamic Foundation.

Karatas, C. (1995) 'Has Privatisation Improved Profitability and Performance of the Public Enterprises in Turkey?', in P. Cook and C. Kirkpatrick (eds) *Privatisation Policy and Performance,* London: Prentice Hall.

Katouzian, M. (1978) 'Oil versus Agriculture: A Case of Dual Resource Depletion', *Journal of Peasant Studies* 5, 2 (April): 347–69.

—— (1983) 'The Agrarian Question in Iran', in A. K. Ghose (ed.) *Agrarian Reform in Contemporary Developing Countries.* London: Croom Helm.

Keen, D. (1994) *The Benefits of Famine: A Political Economy of Famine and Relief in Southwestern Sudan, 1983–1989.* Princeton, NJ: Princeton University Press.

Kelley, A. Khalifa, A. and El-Khorasaty, M. (1982) *Population and Development in Rural Egypt.* Durham, NC: Duke University Press.

Keyder, C. (1987) *State and Class in Turkey: A Study in Capitalist Development.* London: Verso.

Keynes, J. (1936) *The General Theory of Employment, Interest and Money.* New York: Harcourt Brace & Co.

Khader, B. and Badran, A. (1987) *The Economic Development of Jordan.* London: Croom Helm.

Kirkpatrick, C. and Onis, Z. (1991) 'Turkey', in P. Mosley, J. Harrigan, and J. Toye (eds) *Aid and Power.* Vol. 2: *Case Studies.* London: Routledge.

Kliot, N. (1993) *Water Resources and Conflicts in the Middle East.* London: Routledge.

Knight, J. and Sabot, R. (1990) *Education, Productivity and Inequality.* Oxford: Oxford University Press.

Korayem, K. (1993) 'Structure and Reform Policies in Egypt: Economic and Social Implications'. Amman: ESCWA. Mimeographed.

—— (1994) *al-Faqr wa-Tauzi' al-Dakhl fi Misr* (Poverty and income distribution in Egypt), Cairo: The Third World Forum, Middle East Centre.

—— (1996) 'Egypt: Comparing Poverty Measures', in E. Oyen, S. Miller and S. Samad (eds) *Poverty: A Global Review.* Oslo: Scandinavian University Press.

Krueger, A. (1974) 'The Political Economy of a Rent-Seeking Society'. *American Economic Review* 64, 3: 291–303.

—— (1995) 'Partial Adjustment and Growth in the 1980s in Turkey', in R. Dornbusch and S. Edwards (eds) *Reform, Recovery and Growth: Latin America and the Middle East.* Chicago: University of Chicago Press.

Kuwait
  Ministry of Planning (1990–3) *Annual Statistical Abstract.* Kuwait: Central Statistical Office.

Kuznets, S. (1995) 'Economic Growth and Income Inequality'. *American Economic Review* 65, 1: 1–28.

—— (1966) *Modern Economic Growth.* New Haven, Conn.: Yale University Press.

Lambton, A. K. (1953) *Landlord and Peasant in Persia.* Oxford: Oxford University Press. 2nd edn. 1969.

Laraki, K. (1989) *Les Programmes de Subventions Alimentaires; Etude de Cas de la Reforme des prix du Maroc.* Living Standards Measurement Study. Washington, DC: World Bank.

Lazarev, G. (1977) 'Aspects du Capitalisme Agraire au Maroc Avant le Protectorat', in B. Etienne (ed.) *Les Problems Agraires au Maghreb.* Paris: Centre National de la Recherche.

League of Arab States (1993) *al-Taqreer al-Iqtisadi al-Arabi al-Muwahad* (The unified report on the Arab economy). Cairo: Economic Department of the League.

Lees, F. and Brooks, H. C. (1997) *The Economic and Political Development of the Sudan.* London: Macmillan Press.

Le Grand, J. (1991) *Equity and Choice.* London: HarperCollins Academic.

Libya
  Bank of Libya (1965) The Development of Public Finance in Libya (1944–64).

Ministry of Agriculture (1978) 'Dirasa an Siyasat wa Baramej al-Islah al-Zira'i wal Tanmiya al-Rifiya' (A study on agrarian reform and rural development in Libya). Prepared by FAO consultant A. Alwan. Mimeographed. Tripoli: Ministry of Agriculture.

Ministry of Planning (1976) *Khitat al-Tahawul al-Ishtiraki wal-Ijtima'i 1976–80* (Socialist transformation plan) Tripoli: Ministry of Planning.

—— (1981) *Socio-Economic Transformation Plan 1981–85*, Summary Tripoli: Ministry of Planning.

Lipton, M. (1977) *Why Poor People Stay Poor: Urban Bias in World Development*. London: Temple Smith.

—— (1983a) *Demography and Poverty*, World Bank Staff Working Paper 6 23. Washington, DC: World Bank.

Lipton, M. (1983b) *Poverty, Undernutrition and Hunger*, World Bank Staff Working Paper 597. Washington, DC: World Bank.

—— (1988) *The Poor and The Poorest*, Discussion Paper 25. Washington, DC: World Bank.

Lipton, M. and Ravallion, M. (1995) 'Poverty and Policy', Chapter 41 in J. Behram and T. Srinivasan (eds) *Handbook of Development Economics*, volume 3. Amsterdam: Elsevier Science.

Little, I. (1965) *A Critique of Welfare Economics*. Oxford: Oxford University Press.

Livingstone, I. (1984) *Pastoralism*. Rome: FAO.

Long, D. and Reich, B. (eds) (1995) *The Government and Politics of the Middle East and North Africa*. Boulder, Colo.: Westview Press.

Mabro, R. (1970) 'Labour Supplies and Labour Stability: A Case Study of the Oil Industry in Libya', *Bulletin of the Oxford Institute of Economics and Statistics* 32, 4: 319–38.

—— (1985) *The Economic Consequences of the Fall in Future Energy Demand in the Arab World*. Oxford: Oxford Institute for Energy Studies.

Mangane, A. (1984) 'Major Changes in Agrarian Structure and Land Tenure in Mauritania, During the Last Ten Years'. A study prepared for FAO. Mimeographed.

Marlowe, L. (1996) 'Up From Despair', *Times International*, January 15, p. 18.

Matthews, R. D. and Akrawi, M. (1949) *Education in Arab Countries of the Near East*. Menasha, Wis.: George Banta Publishing Co.

McKay, A. and Houeibib, A. (1992) 'Project Dimensions Sociales: Profil de Pauvreté en Mauritanie. Volume 1, Parti Descriptive'. Nouakchott: Ministère du Plan. Mimeographed.

—— (1993) 'Project Dimensions Sociales: Profil de Pauvreté en Mauritanie'. Volume 2. Nouakchott: Ministère du Plan. Mimeographed.

McNamara, R. (1991) 'The Post-Cold War World: Implications for Military Expenditure in the Developing Countries', *Proceedings of the World Bank Annual Conference on Development Economics*, pp. 95–156. Washington, DC: The World Bank.

Meade, J. (1964) *Efficiency, Equality and the Ownership of Property*. London: Allen & Unwin.

Middle East Economic Survey (1991) 24, 16.

Mofid, K. (1990) *The Economic Consequences of the Gulf War.* London: Routledge.

Moghadam, E. (1978) 'The Effect of Farm Size and Management System on Agricultural Production'. Unpublished D.Phil thesis, University of Oxford.

Moghadam, V. (1995) 'Economic Reforms and Women's Employment in Egypt', in V. Moghadam (ed.) *Economic Reforms, Women's Employment and Social Policies.* Helsinki: UNU/WIDER.

Mohtadi, H. (1986) 'Rural Stratification, Rural to Urban Migration, and Urban Inequality: Evidence from Iran', *World Development* 14, 6: 713–25.

Mooij, de M. (1994) *Advertising Worldwide*, second edition. London: Prentice Hall International.

Morocco

　Direction de la Statistique (1987) *Consummation et Dépenses des Ménages 1984– 1985*, Premiers Resultats. Volume 1: *Rapport de Synthèse.* Rabat: Ministry of Planning.

　—— *Morocco in 1991: Thirty Years of Social and Economic Development.* Rabat: Ministry of Planning.

　—— (1990, 1991 and 1994) *Annuaire Statistique du Maroc.* Rabat: Ministry of Planning.

　Ministry of Agriculture (1989) 'al-Felahan fi Tanmiya Mustamira' (Agriculture in continued development). Rabat: Ministry of Agriculture. Mimeographed.

　—— (1990) 'Rapport sur l'Avancement du Dévelopment Rural'. Rabat: Ministry of Agriculture. Mimeographed.

　Ministère de la Santé etr des Affaires Sociales (1992) 'Situation Alimentaire et Nutritionelle en Mauritanie'. Nouakchott: Ministère de la Santé. Mimeographed.

Morrison, C. (1991) 'Adjustment, Incomes and Poverty in Morocco', *World Development*, 19, 11: 1633–51.

Morrissey, O. and Stewart, F. (eds) *Economic and Political Reform in Developing Countries.* London: Macmillan, for the Development Studies Association.

Mosley, P., Harrigan, J. and Toye, J. (1991) *Aid and Power: The World Bank and Policy-based Lending* Two vols. London: Routledge.

Myrdal, G. (1968) *Asian Drama.* London: The Penguin Press.

Musaiger, A. O. (1987) 'The State of Food and Nutrition in the Arabian Gulf Countries', *World Review of Nutrition and Dietetics* 54: 105.

—— (1990) 'Nutritional Disorders Associated with Affluence in Bahrain'. *Family Practice* 7, 1: 1–13.

Musaiger, A. O. and Alansari, M. (1992) 'Factors Associated with Obesity Among Women in Bahrain', *International Quarterly of Community Health Education* 12, 2: 129–38.

Musaiger, A. O. and Lankarani, S. (1986) *A Study on Baby Foods in Bahrain.* Manama: Nutrition Unit, Ministry of Health.

Najafi, B. (1970) 'The Effectiveness of Farm Corporations in Iran'. Unpublished M.Sc. thesis, American University, Beirut.

Nelson, R. (ed.) (1978) *Corporate Development in the Middle East*. London: Oyez Publishing.

Niblock, T. and Murphy, E. (eds) (1993) *Economic and Political Liberalization in the Middle East*, London: British Academic Press.

North, D. (1990) *Institutions, Institutional Change and Economic Performance*. Cambridge: Cambridge University Press.

Noor, A. (1981) *Education and Human Basic Needs*. World Bank Staff Working Paper 450. Washington, DC: World Bank.

Nouvelle, J. (1949) 'La Crise agricole de 1943–1946 au Maroc et ses conséquences économiques et sociales', *Revue de Géographie Humaine* 1: 87–9.

Nozick, R. (1974) *Anarchy, State and Utopia*. Oxford: Basil Blackwell.

OECD (Organization for Economic Cooperation and Development) (1994) *Development Cooperation*. Paris: Development Assistance Committee.

Oman
  Ministry of Information (1993) *Oman in 1993*. Muscat: Ministry of Information.
  Central Bank (1992) *al-Markazi*. Bi-monthly report January–October. Muscat: Central Bank.

Osman, O. (1987) 'Some Economic Aspects of Private Pump Schemes', in E. Shaaeldin (ed.) *The Evolution of Agrarian Relations in the Sudan*. The Hague: Institute of Social Studies.

Owen, R. (1992) *State, Power and Politics in the Making of the Modern Middle East*. London: Routledge.

Ozbudun, E and Ulisan, A., (eds) (1980) *The Political Economy of Income Distribution in Turkey*. New York: Holmes and Meier.

Paukert, F. C. (1973) 'Income Distribution at Different Levels of Development: A Survey of Evidence', *International Labour Review*: 97–125.

Phelps-Brown, H. (1988) *Egalitarianism and the Generation of Inequality*. Oxford: Clarendon Press.

Philby, H. St. John (1954) 'The New Reign in Saudi Arabia', *Foreign Affairs*, 1 April: 446–50.

Platt, K. (1970) *Land Reform in Iran*. Washington, DC: Agency for International Development.

Pool, D. (1993) 'The Links between Economic and Political Liberalization', in T. Niblock and E. Murphy (eds) *Economic and Political Liberalization in the Middle East*. London: British Academic Press.

Qubain, F. (1966) *Education and Science in the Arab World*. Baltimore: The Johns Hopkins University Press.

Radwan, S., Jamal, V. and Ghose, A. (1990) *Tunisia: Rural Labour and Structural Transformation*. London: Routledge.

Ravallion, M. (1987) *Markets and Famine*. Oxford: Clarendon Press.

Ravallion, M., Datt, G., and Walle, D. van de (1991). 'Quantifying Absolute Poverty in the Developing World', *Review of Income and Wealth* 37, 4: 345–61.

—— (1994) 'Is Poverty Increasing in the Developing World?', *Review of Income and Wealth* 40, 4: 359–76.

Rawls, J. (1972) *A Theory of Justice*. Oxford: Oxford University Press.

Richards, A. (1991) 'The Political Economy of Dilatory Reform: Egypt in the 1980s', *World Development* 19, 12: 1721–30.

Richards, A. and Waterbury, J. (1990) *The Political Economy of the Middle East: State, Class and Economic Development*. Boulder, Colo.: Westview Press.

Robinson, J. (1979) *Aspects of Development and Underdevelopment*. Cambridge: Cambridge University Press.

Roemer, J. (1982) *A General Theory of Exploitation and Class*. Cambridge, Mass.: Harvard University Press.

Ross, J., Rich, M., Molzan, J. and Panzak, M. (1988) *Family Planning and Child Survival: 100 Developing Countries*. New York: Columbia University Press.

Ruedy, J. (1992) *Modern Algeria: The Origins and Development of a Nation*. Bloomington and Indianapolis: Indiana University Press.

Ruttan, V. (1996) *United States Development Assistance Policy: The Domestic Politics of Foreign Economic Aid*. Baltimore: The Johns Hopkins University Press.

Saidi, N. (1986) 'Economic Consequences of the War in Lebanon', *Bulletin Trimestriel* 28–30. Beirut: Banque du Liban.

Sadowski, Y. (1991) *Political Vegetables? Businessman and Bureaucracy in the Development of Egyptian Agriculture*, Washington, DC: The Brookings Institution.

—— (1993) *Scuds or Butter? The Political Economy of Arms Control in the Middle East*, Washington, DC: The Brookings Institution.

Sahota, G. S. (1978) 'Theories of Personal Income Distribution: A Survey', *Journal of Economic Literature* 16, 1: 1–55.

Saudi Arabia, Kingdom of
Ministry of Planning (1990) *Fifth Development Plan 1990–5 (1410–15 Hijriya)*. Riyadh: Ministry of Planning Press. Arabic and English.

Sayari, S. (1996) 'Party Systems and Economic Reforms: The Turkish Case', *Studies in Comparative International Development* 31, 4: 29–45.

Sayigh, Y. (1990) *Elusive Development: From Dependence to Self-Reliance in the Arab Region*, London: Routledge.

Scheftel, E. (1947) *The Jewish Law of Family and Inheritance*. Tel Aviv: Martin Feuchtwagner.

Schultz, T. (1981) *Investing in People: The Economics of Population Quality*. Berkeley: University of California Press.

Seba'i, A. (1984) *The Health of the Family in a Changing Arabia*, fourth edition. Jeddah: Tohama Publications.

—— (1987) 'Nutritional Disorders in Saudi Arabia', *Family Practice* 5, 1: 56–61.

Seddon, D. (1993) 'Austerity Protests in Response to Economic Liberalization, in the Middle East', in Niblock, T. and Murphy, M. (eds) *Economic and Political Liberalization in the Middle East*. London: British Academic Press.

Sen, A. (1981) *Poverty and Famine: An Essay on Entitlement and Deprivation*. Oxford: Clarendon Press.

—— (1982) *Choice, Welfare and Measurement*. Oxford: Basil Blackwell.

Shaban, R. (1990) *Economic Inequality in Jordan 1973–86*, in K. Abu-Jaber *et al.* (eds) *Income Distribution in Jordan*, Boulder, Colo.: Westview Press.

—— (1993) 'Palestinian Labour Mobility', *International Labour Review* 134, 5 and 6: 655–72

Shaban, R., Assaad, R. and al-Qudsi, S. (1995) 'The Challenge of Unemployment in the Arab Region', *International Labour Review* 134, 1: 65–81.

Shalev, M. (1992) *Labour and the Political Economy of Israel*, Oxford: Oxford University Press.

Shirazi, A. (1993) *Islamic Development Policy: The Agrarian Question in Iran*. Boulder, Colo.: Lynne Rienner Publishers.

Siddiqi, M. (1981) 'Muslem Economic Thinking: A Survey of Contemporary Literature', in K. Ahmad (ed.) *Studies in Islam Economics*, Leicester (UK): The Islamic Foundation.

Simpson, M. (1987) 'Large-Scale Mechanized Rainfed Development in The Sudan', in E. Shaaeldin (ed.) *The Evolution of Agrarian Relations in The Sudan: A Reader*. The Hague: The Institute of Social Studies and the University of Khartoum.

Singer, H. (1992) 'Lessons of Post-War Development Experience, 1945–1988', in W. Andriaansen and J. Waardenburg (eds) *A Dual World Economy: Forty Years of Development Experience*. Bombay: Oxford University Press.

Sinha, R. (1995) 'Economic Reforms in Developing Countries: Some Conceptual Issues', *World Development* 23, 4: 557–75.

SIPRI (Stockholm International Peace Research Institute) (1996) *Yearbook: Armaments, Disarmament and International Security*. Oxford: Oxford University Press.

Sivan, E. and Friedman, M. (eds) (1990) *Religious Radicalism and Politics in the Middle East*. Albany, NY: State University of New York Press.

Sivard, R. C. (1983, 1985, 1993) *World Military and Social Expenditure*. Washington, DC: World Priorities.

Smeeding, T., O'Higgins, M. and Rainwater, L. (eds) (1990) *Poverty, Inequality and Income Distribution in Comparative Perspective*. The Luxembourg Income Study. Hemel Hempstead (UK): Harvester Wheatsheaf.

Springborg, R. (1979) 'Patrimonialism and Policy Making in Egypt', *Middle Eastern Studies* 15, 1: 49–69.

Stauffer, T. (1987) 'Income Measurement in Arab States', in H. Beblawi and G. Luciani (eds) *The Rentier State*. London: Croom Helm.

Stewart, F. (ed.) (1983) *Work, Income and Inequality: Payments Systems in the Third World*. London: Macmillan.

—— (1991) 'The Many Faces of Adjustment', *World Development* 19, 12: 1847–64.

—— (1993) 'War and Underdevelopment: Can Economic Analysis help Reduce the Costs?' *Journal of International Development* 5, 4: 357–80.

—— (1995) *Adjustment and Poverty: Options and Choices*, London: Routledge.

Stiglitz, J. (1989) 'Markets, Market Failures, and Development', *American Economic Review* 79, May: 197–203.

Streeten, P. (1959) 'Unbalanced Growth', *Oxford Economic Papers* 2, June: 167–90.

—— (1981) *Development Perspectives*. London: The Macmillan Press.

—— (1983) 'Development Dichotomies', *World Development* 11, 10: 873–89.

Steeten, P., Burki, S., Ilaq, M., Hicks, N. and Stewart, F. (1981) *First Things First: Meeting Basic Needs in Developing Countries.* Oxford: Oxford University Press.

Sudan

Bank of the Sudan (1969, 1985, 1989) *Annual Report* Khartoum: Khartoum University Press.

Ministry of Finance and National Planning (1977a) *The Perspective Plan 1977/78–1994/95.* Khartoum; Ministry of Finance and National Planning.

—— *Six-Year Plan of Economic and Social Development 1977/78–1982/83.* Khartoum: Ministry of Finance and National Planning.

—— (1992) 'Ten-Year National Strategy of Sudan'. Mimeographed.

Suliman, A. (1974) *al-Ujur wa Mashakil al-'amaal fi al-Sudan* (Wages and labour problems in Sudan). Khartoum: Khartoum University Press.

Summers, L. (1994) *Investing in All People.* Economic Development Institute Paper 45. Washington, DC: The World Bank.

Summers, R. and Heston, A. (1991) 'The Penn World Table (Mark 5): An Extended Set of International Comparisons, 1950–1988', *Quarterly Journal of Economics* 106: 327–68.

Swearingen, W. (1988) *Moroccan Mirages: Agrarian Dreams and Deceptions 1912–1986.* London: I. B. Tauris & Co.

Syria

(1990) Ministry of Agriculture and Agrarian Reform 'Agrarian Reform and Rural Development in Syria', A report to FAO. Damascus: Ministry of Agriculture and Agrarian Reform. (Arabic). Mimeographed.

Tantawy, M. (1992) *al-Halal wal-Haram fi Mu'amalat al-Bunouk* (Permitted and prohibited banking transactions). Cairo: al-Ahram al-Iqtisadi.

Taylor, P. (1984) *Smoke King: The Politics of Tobacco.* London: The Bodley Head.

The Middle East and North Africa (1995) Rochester (UK): Europa Publications.

The Middle East and North Africa: Algeria (1996) Rochester (UK): Europa Publications.

Theobald, R. (1990) *Corruption, Development and Underdevelopment,* London: Macmillan.

Thijssen, H. (ed.) (1994) *Women and Islam in Muslim Societies.* Volume 7 of *Poverty and Development,* ed. J. Saffe. The Hague: Ministry of Foreign Affairs.

Thomas, D. and Middleton, N. J. (1994) *Desertification: Exploding the Myth.* Chichester, UK: John Wiley.

Tilak, J. B. (1989) *Education and its Relation to Economic Growth, Poverty and Income Distribution: Past Evidence and Further Analysis.* World Bank Discussion Paper 46. Washington, DC: The World Bank.

Todaro, M. (1989) *Economic Develoment in the Third World.* New York: Longman. 4th edn.

Toye, J. (1987) *Dilemmas of Development,* Oxford: Basil Blackwell.

Tunisia

Ministry of Planning and Regional Development (1982) *al-Mu'ashirat al Ijtima'iya wal-Iqtisadiya* (Socio-economic indicators) Tunis: Ministry of Planning.

—— (1992) *Vlle Plan du Dévelopment Economique et Social, 1992–1996.* Tunis: Institut National de la Statistique.

—— (1993) *Resultats de l'Enquête Nationale sur le Budget et la Consummation des Ménages, 1990*. Volumes A and B. Tunis: Institut National de la Statistique.

Ministry of Public Health (1994) 'La Situation Nutritionelle de la Population Tunisienne'. Tunis: Institut Nationale de la Nutrition. Mimeographed.

Turkey

Social Insurance Institute (1993) *Statistical Yearbook*, Ankara: Social Insurance Institute.

State Institute of Statistics (1973 and 1987) *Household Income and Expenditure* Ankara: State Institute of Statistics.

—— (1991–6) *Statistical Yearbook*. Ankara: State Institute of Statistics.

State Planning Organization *Monthly Bulletin of Statistics* (1985–95). Ankara: State Institute of Statistics.

—— (1990) *Sixth Five-Year Plan, (1990–1994)* Ankara: State Planning Organization.

Turkish Employment Organization (1993) *Statistical Yearbook*. Ankara: Turkish Employment Organization.

Turnham, D. (1993) *Employment and Development: A Review of Evidence*. Paris: OECD.

UNCTAD (United Nations Conference on Trade and Development) (1984) *Food Insecurity in Developing Countries: Causes, Trends and Policy Options*. A study prepared by Peter Svedberg. Geneva: UNCTAD.

UNDP (United Nations Development Programme) (1991–6) *Human Development Report*, New York: Oxford University Press.

UNDP and World Bank (1992) *African Development Indicators*. Washington, DC: UNDP and the World Bank.

UNESCO (United National Educational, Scientific and Cultural Organization)

—— (1963–95) *Statistical Yearbook*. Paris: UNESCO.

—— (1987) *al-Tarbiya al-Jadida*. Journal of the UNESCO regional office for the Arab states, 40, 41. Amman, Jordan: UNESCO.

—— (1991 and 1993) *World Education Report*. Paris: UNESCO.

UNESOB (United Nations Economic and Social Bureau) (1971) *La Croissance Économique et la Niveau de la Population Active au Moyen Orient*. Beirut: UNESOB.

UNICEF (United Nations Children's Fund) *The State of the World's Children*, 1984–96, Oxford: Oxford University Press.

—— (1991 and 1993) Reports on the nutritional status of Iraqi children. Geneva, New York and Cairo: UNICEF. Mimeographed.

United Nations (1951) *Review of Economic Conditions in the Middle East*. New York: United Nations.

—— (1960–95) *Statistical Yearbook*. New York: United Nations.

—— (1985 and 1991) *Yearbook of World Energy Statistics* New York: Department of Economic Information, United Nations.

—— (1991) *Assistance for The Reconstruction and Development of Lebanon*. New York: United Nations.

United Nations Centre on Transnational Corporations (1979) *Transnational Corporations in Advertising*. New York: United Nations.

United Nations Department of Technical Cooperation for Development (1989)

Corruption in Government, report of an inter-regional seminar. New York: United Nations.

Van der Hoeven, R. (1981) 'External Shocks and Stabilisation Policies: Spreading the Load', *International Labour Review* 126, 2: 133–50.

van Ginneken, W. (1980) 'Some Methods of Poverty Analysis: An Application to Iranian Data, 1975–1976', *World Development* 8, 9: 639–46.

van Ginneken, W. and Park, J. (eds) (1984) *Generating Internationally Comparable Income Distribution Estimates*. A World Employment Programme study, Geneva: ILO.

Van Roy, E. (1970) 'On the Theory of Corruption', *Economic Development and Cultural Change* 19, October: 86–110.

Wade, R. (1990) *Governing the Market*. Princeton, NJ: Princeton University Press.

Waldron, J. (1988) *The Right to Private Property*. Oxford: Clarendon Paperbacks.

Ward, F. and Rimmer, M. (1994) *Targeting Basic Assistance in Iraq: Findings from Household Expenditure Survey*. Oxford: Food Studies Group, University of Oxford for ODA.

Warriner, D. (1948) *Land and Poverty in the Middle East*. London: Royal Institute of International Affairs.

—— (1969) *Land Reform in Principle and Practice*. Oxford: Clarendon Press.

Watt, W. M. (1988) *Islamic Fundamentalism and Modernity*. London: Routledge.

Wilson, R. (1979) *The Economics of the Middle East*. London: Macmillan.

—— (1995) *Economic Development in the Middle East*. London: Routledge.

Woodward, D. (1992) *Debt Adjustment and Poverty in Developing Countries*. Volume 1: *National and International Dimensions of Debt and Adjustment in Developing Countries*. A 'Save the Children' Study. London: Pinter Publications.

World Bank/The International Bank for Reconstruction and Development (IBRD) (1960) *The Economic Development of Libya*. Baltimore: The Johns Hopkins University Press.

—— (1965) *The Economic Development of Kuwait*. Baltimore: The Johns Hopkins University Press.

—— (1973) *Trends in Developing Countries*. Baltimore: The Johns Hopkins University Press.

—— (1978–96) *World Development Report*. Oxford: Oxford University Press.

—— (1985 and 1993) *Annual Report*. Washington, DC: The World Bank.

—— (1988) 'Social Indicators Data Sheet', June. Washington, DC: the World Bank. Mimeographed.

—— (1990a) *Making Adjustment Work for the Poor: A Framework for Policy in Africa*. Washington, DC: The World Bank.

—— (1990b) *Morocco: Analysis and Reform of Economic Policy*. Economic Development Institute, Analytical Case Study 4. Prepared by Brendon Horton. Washington, DC: The World Bank.

—— (1990c) *Structural Adjustment and Living Conditions in Developing Countries*. Prepared by N. Kakwani *et al.*, Working Paper 467. Washington, DC: The World Bank.

—— (1991) *Egypt: Alleviating Poverty During Structural Adjustment*. Washington, DC: The World Bank.

—— (1992a) *Adjustment Lending and Mobilization of Private and Public Resources for Growth*. Policy and Research Series 22. Washington, DC: The World Bank.

—— (1992b) *Military Expenditure and Economic Development*. Discussion Paper 185. Washington, DC: The World Bank.

—— (1993a) *Developing the Occupied Territories: An Investment in Peace*. Six volumes. Washington, DC: The World Bank.

—— (1993b) *Trends in Developing Economics*. Washington, DC: The World Bank.

—— (1993–5) *African Development Indicators*. Washington, DC: The World Bank.

—— (1995) *From Scarcity to Security: Averting a Water Crisis in the Middle East and North Africa*. Washington, DC: The World Bank.

WHO (World Health Organization) (1992) *Our Planet, Our Health*. Geneva: WHO Commission on Health and the Environment.

WHO and FAO (1992) 'Nutrition and Development – A Global Assessment' and 'Improving Household Food Security', in *Major Issues for Nutrition Strategies*, International Conference on Nutrition. Project ICN/92. Rome: FAO and WHO.

Wright, R. (1992) 'Islamic Democracy and the West', *Foreign Affairs* summer issue: 131–45.

Wulf, H. (1991) *Disarmament as a Chance for Human Development: Is there a Peace Dividend?* Human Development Report Office Occasional Paper 5 New York: UNDP.

Yazdani, S. and Hill, G. (1993) 'Islamic Credit: The Iranian Experience', *Journal of Agricultural Economics* 44, 2: 301–10.

Zahlan, A. (ed.) (1978) *Technology Transfer and Change in the Arab Countries*. Oxford: Pergamon Press.

Zahlan, A. and Magar, W. (eds) (1986) *The Agricultural Sector of Sudan*. London: Ithaca Press.

Zaki, R. (1985) *Diraasat fi Duyoun Misr al-Kharijiya* (A study of Egypt's foreign debts) Cairo: Maktabet Madbouly.

Zaytoun, M. (1991) 'Earnings and the Cost of Living: an Analysis of Recent Developments in the Egyptian Economy', in H. Handoussa and G. Potter (eds), *Employment and Structural Adjustment: Egypt in the 1990s*. Cairo: The American University Press in Cairo.

Zenith Media Worldwide (1990) *Advertising Expenditure Forecast*, London: Zenith Media Worldwide.

NAME INDEX

SUBJECT INDEX

Abu Dhabi (UAE) 172, 252

abundance: of labour 77; of land 54, 105; of oil windfalls 55–7; of water 54, 105; of wealth 14

access, inequality/equality of: to education 36–8, 42, 98, 138, 205; to health 98; to jobs 20, 205; to land 33

accountability of governments 17, 63, 112, 114

accumulation: of capital 84; of land 32, 155; of wealth 4, 12, 14, 35, 44, 46, 113, 115, 151

Aden (Yemen) 30

adjustment, structural: meaning of 172–5; adjusting countries 172, 175, 177, 198–9, 204, 219; criteria of success 77, 198, 204; *see also* economic policy reforms; stabilization programme

advertising 13, 124–5, 127, 129–31, 144–5, 246

affluence: coexisting with anaemia 140–2, 145, 248; coexisting with illiteracy 100, 143; coexisting with malnutrition 124, 141, 144, 248; definition of 14; level of 14–56, 58–60, 89, 92; oil-based 21, 24, 51, 82, 85–6, 100, 111, 141; pace of 56–7; related consumption pattern 23, 124, 125–8, 133, 141, 144, 181, 248; related health risks 23, 127, 140, 142; *see also* opulence

Africa 204, 227; North 30, 33–5

agrarian: structure 77, 87; reform 154–6; *see also* land reform

agriculture: contribution to total economic growth 75, 187–8, 225, 237; during colonial rule 32–5; economic capacity to invest in land development 54, 65–138; effects of economic reform on 190–2, 203, 205; irrigation costs 67, 69–70, 161; irrigation expansion 77, 138, 158; neglect of 75, 81–4, 87, 156, 187, 191, 203; potential agricultural land 64–5, 68, 138; rain-fed 175, 192, 194

aid: from Arab states 62–4, 70, 179, 191, 193, 196, 237; from OECD 175–6, 193, 228; from former Soviet Union 68; total 138, 236, 251, 256

al-Ahram 120, 182, 243

Alexandria (Egypt) 120, 244

Algeria 30, 34, 37, 49, 55, 60, 62, 66, 81–3, 87, 93–4, 99, 101, 151–3, 167; education 37–9, 258; employment policy 85–6; foreign debt 197–8, 208; historical origin of inequality 33–4, 38; income distribution 34, 157; Islamic militants 198; land reform 155–7, 161; oil boom and unbalanced development 81–4; poverty estimates 34, 213, 257; remittances 198; structural adjustment experience 177,